EAST ASIA INTEGRATES

A Trade Policy Agenda for Shared Growth

EAST ASIA INTEGRATES

A Trade Policy Agenda for Shared Growth

Kathie Krumm and Homi Kharas, Editors

A copublication of the World Bank and Oxford University Press

1 2 3 4 06 05 04

A co-publication of the World Bank and Oxford University Press.

ISBN 0-8213-5514-7

Cover photo: World Bank

Library of Congress Cataloguing-in-Publication data has been applied for.

Contents

FIGURES

TABLES

BOXES

FOREWORD

This collection of studies focuses on one of the most important economic issues facing East Asian and Pacific nations today. We have titled this collection *East Asia Integrates: A Trade Policy Agenda for Shared Growth* to capture three forces operating in the region.

- First, a strong force for policy integration is sweeping through the region, and it has gathered strength since the 1997–98 Asian financial crisis. This new regionalism in East Asia is based on a strategic re-rethinking of what needs to be done to bolster growth and stability across the region.
- Second, trade policy has gained prominence as a central force, in part because trade within the region has been one of the dynamos of growth in recent years, accounting for almost 90 percent of East Asian export growth in 2002, and in part because of the historic accession of China to the World Trade Organization in November 2001. Other countries in the region will have to adapt their own national development strategies as China adjusts to its new commitments.

- The third force is the determination that East Asia should develop strategies to narrow the gap between richer and poorer countries and between urban and rural households to promote regional stability and reduce poverty.

This is a very broad agenda, and, of course, no single volume can tackle all the problems in depth. But in launching this work we felt it was important to broaden the approach beyond the technical perspective of trade policy to emphasize development outcomes and the links to social stability. Increasingly, the development agenda in the region—with its focus on growth, jobs, and social stability—and the trade policy agenda—with its focus on market access and competitiveness—have become intertwined. Economic integration is a growing force, and we want to ensure it is managed carefully so that its benefits can be shared broadly by poorer countries and the poor within countries.

To be sure, East Asia is a very diverse region, and our analysis shows that there is no one-size-fits-all approach. Yet the studies included here suggest several policy priorities for East Asia as well as directions for further empirical analysis that would carry policymaking to a conclusive stage. It is imperative that all countries have the capacity to undertake detailed analysis on these priority issues, because today there is an urgency to the policymaking process. Negotiating positions are now being developed for an array of regional and bilateral agreements and for the Doha Development Agenda after Cancun. The stakes are high, so we must move from debate and academic discussions to the real world of negotiations and concrete policies.

The World Bank has a long and proud tradition of supporting the expansion of trade in East Asia and around the world as a crucial tool in promoting growth and development. But this support does not mean a blind adherence to lower tariffs and reduced nontariff barriers. It does mean supporting measures to ensure that the opportunities afforded by trade are available to everyone and benefit everyone. Thus this volume contains studies on agriculture, market access for the goods produced by the poor, logistics to connect far-flung producers with markets, environmental and labor standards, income and employment vulnerability, and the effects on households of opening trade. A comprehensive approach is needed to link trade to development and poverty reduction, and we urge policymakers to develop such a comprehensive approach in their national development strategies, in their regional and bilateral agreements, and in their global negotiating positions.

We hope you, the reader, will find the studies in this volume interesting and that in turn you will contribute your voice to this critical debate.

Jemal-ed-din Kassum
Vice President
East Asia and Pacific Region
World Bank

ACKNOWLEDGMENTS

We have benefited from the input and guidance of numerous colleagues and officials who have supported the analysis underpinning this volume. We would like to express our particular appreciation to the authors of the chapters and the background papers. Earlier drafts of the chapters and the main findings were presented at seminars and workshops throughout East Asia, including Bangkok, Beijing, Hanoi, Jakarta, Phnom Penh, Seoul, Singapore, Tokyo, Ulaanbaatar, and Vientiane. We would like to thank the organizers, including the Institute for Southeast Asian Studies at the National University of Singapore, the Development Research Center and Tsinghua University in China, the Thailand Development and Research Institute, and the World Bank Institute, as well as the staff of the country offices of the World Bank. We also benefited from interaction with scholars and policymakers at the Fourth Asia Development Forum on Trade and Poverty held in Seoul and organized jointly with the Korean Institute for International Economic Policy, the Korea Development Institute, and the Asia Development Bank. Valuable comments and contributions were provided, and we would like to thank all of those who participated in these seminars as moderators, discussants, and presenters. Special thanks go to Narongchai Akrasanee, Ataman Aksoy, Myrna Austria, Choong Yong Ahn, Florian Alburo, Kanemi Ban, Douglas Brooks, Siow Yue Chia, Lu Ding, Carsten Fink, Yujiro Hajami, Masahiro Kawai, Jeffrey Lewis, Mai Lu, Aaditya Matoo, Deunden Nikomborirak, Hadi Soesastro, Jomo Sundaram, Somkiat Tangkitvanich, Jose Tongzan, Shujiro Urata, Dominique Van der Mensbrugghe, Sangui Wang, John Wilson, Lan Xue, and Ippei Yamazawa.

The views expressed in this book are those of the authors and should not be attributed to any particular institution, including institutions with which individual authors may be associated, including the World Bank and the World Trade Organization.

OVERVIEW

Kathie Krumm
Homi Kharas

Emerging East Asian economies[1] have seen their share of world exports more than triple during the past quarter-century, from 5.4 percent in 1975 to 19.8 percent in 2002. Their trade with one another has grown faster than their trade with any other market and now makes up 7.2 percent of global trade.[2] Broad measures of development in East Asia have improved at the same headlong pace; since 1990 more than 300 million people have seen their incomes rise above a poverty threshold of US$2.00 a day.[3]

But performance has varied sharply over time and across the region. Most recent trends show mildly rising inequality within countries, including China, Vietnam, and the Philippines, and a widening income gap between richer economies such as Singapore and Hong Kong (China) and the poorest, Lao People's Democratic Republic (Lao PDR) and Cambodia.[4] Both trends are of concern to policymakers interested in a stable, prosperous region, and both trends have been linked with economic liberalization.

Against this background, some analysts estimate that East Asia would still benefit more than any other region from global liberalization (World Bank 2002c)—because of the potential shown by its dynamic exporters—and that it could achieve much of the benefits of liberalization through regional integration—because of the wide scope of intraregional trade among what are very diverse economies. The potential gains to the region from global liberalization are estimated at hundreds of billions of U.S. dollars by 2015. Increasingly, the development agenda in the region, with its focus on growth, jobs, and social stability, and the trade policy agenda, with its focus on market access and competitiveness, have become intertwined.

Pursuit of a "trade for development" strategy in East Asia will not be easy. It involves economic change at a time when policymakers are trying to manage major financial and corporate restructuring, repair overstretched social safety nets, respond to the challenges posed by China, listen to the greater plurality of voices and interest groups competing for political power, and adapt to sometimes vicious global economic cycles. Given that stability is seen as a key to investor confidence and a return to high growth, it is not surprising that there is resistance to still further change.

Why Push Integration Now?

Two economic events of historic proportions provide the context for East Asian development today.

The first event, the currency and financial crisis of 1997–98, still affects every aspect of economic policymaking. The crisis shattered a deeply held and broadly shared view of the policy keys to development success, and called for a review of what now needs to be done to build on the basic tenets of macroeconomic stability, high savings and investment, rapid expansion of education, and a strong export orientation.[5] Many in the region consider the crisis to have been a "defining moment" (World Bank 2002b).

The second major event was China's accession to the World Trade Organization (WTO) in November 2001—the culmination of a 15-year-long bid for membership. China's economy is already one of the largest in the world, and China's prominence as an economic force in the region has clearly risen since the crisis.[6] China's strong currency and strong growth, set against the weakening currencies and weak growth of other developing countries in the region, have meant that China's gross domestic product (GDP) now surpasses that of the rest of emerging East Asia combined.[7] China was the world's largest recipient of foreign direct investment in 2002. Moreover, with its trade growing rapidly, China has become an important destination for exports from the rest of the region, and it is a fierce competitor in third-country markets.[8] Because of its size and diversity, China resists easy definitions of its comparative advantage in terms of high-tech or low-wage manufacturing, and now that it has acceded to the WTO its comparative advantage may change appreciably. Thus it is no surprise that many policymakers in the region feel the need to understand the trends at work in China before they can formulate their own development strategies (World Bank 2002b). Typically, too, they recognize that overcoming the formidable challenges of implementing China's WTO commitments will be as important for the rest of East Asia as it is for China itself.

The region is now shaping its responses to these two events. The financial crisis has forced policymakers to rethink the financial, trade, and investment linkages that connect regional economies. At the same time, it has given new impetus to ideas for regional institutions to help shape common responses. East Asian countries had historically pursued unilateral and nonpreferential approaches to liberalization, sealed through commitments made under WTO agreements. Indeed, through the crisis market access was largely preserved. But equally, significant gaps in the international architecture were exposed, in finance, investment flows, and macroeconomic (especially exchange rate) coordination.

On the financial front of this new regionalism, the Chiang Mai initiative has created a web of swap agreements between regional central banks to be deployed in case of future liquidity problems. The Asian Bond Fund concept has been endorsed by several countries. Informal economic cooperation forums have discussed regional currency cooperation and a host of other economic and noneconomic issues.

In this context, the trade policy agenda for integration—the subject of this volume—is only one element of a broader set of policy and institutional changes taking place in the region. Although regional trade negotiations have not advanced as far as those governing financial arrangements, many analysts consider them to be more fundamental and the foundation for regional economic cooperation. Success will ultimately depend on the consistency of approaches among all elements of integration. To achieve such consistency, the scope of discussion must be broadened. To this end, the integration agenda discussed in this volume covers three areas:

1. Widening opportunities, globally and regionally, in trade arrangements
2. A behind-the-border agenda to maximize the development impact of international commitments
3. Broad sharing of benefits to reinforce social stability and a long-term political commitment to further reforms.

These areas are discussed in sections of this overview, and the concluding section outlines priority areas for action.

Context: Recent Trends in Trade

Rapid and sustained growth in international trade has long been a hallmark of successful growth and development strategies in East Asia. Some success stories are well known: those of the newly industrializing economies (NIEs) such as the Republic of Korea, as well as middle-income economies such as Malaysia and the transition economy of China. More recent entrants to world markets that have seen rapid export growth include low-income economies such as Cambodia and Vietnam. Trade has been an important factor in growth in the region, enabling progress in poverty reduction. Although the 1997–98 financial crisis interrupted this progress, recovery since then has brought poverty rates in every emerging economy in the region to record lows, and in economies like that of Vietnam, trade growth has brought with it a rapid reduction in poverty.

Intraregional trade in East Asia has grown faster than trade with any other market, and while the largest economies account for the bulk of this trade, the regional trade of most smaller economies has also grown. Trade integration has been market-led, stemming from a combination of unilateral reforms, fulfillment of multilateral commitments, and a pattern of relocation of production processes (see Kawai and Urata 2002). Intraregional trade has been driven not only by growing demand but increasingly by improved competitiveness in regional markets, as reflected in increased market shares (Figure 1). China has been particularly dynamic, but almost all countries increased their competitiveness in regional markets during 1995–2001.[9] This increase was accomplished without loss of competitiveness in other markets; East Asia continued to expand its market shares in the European Union (EU) and North American Free Trade Agreement (NAFTA) markets in the same period.

The product composition of intraregional trade has become highly concentrated. The top 30 exports now account for more than half of total trade, with 38 percent in just four subsectors: office machinery, telecommunications equipment, electronics, and textiles and clothing (Figure 2).

One of the major factors in the concentration of intraregional trade has been the remarkable increase in international production networks, as reflected in the growth of trade in components or partly assembled goods. China is increasingly a central player in such production networks, both as a final assembler of products and as an efficient provider of components. Although Japan remains an important center of production-sharing operations in East Asia and is the origin of about one-third of all regional exports of components for assembly, China is finding niches; its exports of parts and components grew by almost $20 billion during 1996–2001. At the same time, other East Asian economies have been finding their own niches within China's markets and increasing their shares of China's imports.

Meanwhile, East Asian trade profiles have become more mutually complementary, and the degree of complementarity for emerging East Asia is now comparable to that of the EU and NAFTA.[10]

The exceptions are low-income countries such as Cambodia, Lao PDR, and, to a lesser extent, Vietnam. This finding is perhaps not surprising, given that a country's trade structure becomes more like the world's trade structure as the country's income rises. The wide gap between rich and poor countries in East Asia is also largely responsible for a rise in regional income inequality (see Milanovic 2003 and the discussion later in this chapter). Policies and institutions that contribute to fuller integration of the low-income countries and regions of East Asia will be critical to addressing income inequality in East Asia and contributing to a stable region.

Widening Opportunities in Trade Arrangements

Today, the region's policymakers see trade and investment integration as key elements of strategy. Although a few trade barriers were erected in response to the Asian economic crisis, they were minor and temporary.[11] Indeed, instead of more protection, the crisis produced a new impetus for openness. A multitrack approach is being followed, with support for a new global round of trade negotiations as well as for regional and bilateral arrangements.

Liberalization of trade and investment policies is recognized as a way to spur gains in efficiency. As such, it fits well with the new emphasis in Asia on innovation in firms and on economy-wide produc-

FIGURE 1   Trends in Regional Trade

Emerging East Asia economies' share of world exports grew...and trade among these economies grew even faster.

Intraregional trade is driven increasingly by competitiveness and growing market share.

Emerging East Asia: share of world trade

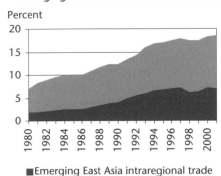

■Emerging East Asia intraregional trade

Intraregional trade: share of export change accounted for by competitiveness and demand changes

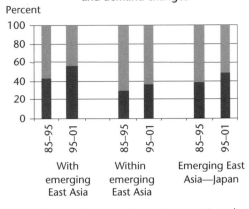

■ Competitive factor[a]   ▨Demand factor[b]

Note: Emerging East Asia is ASEAN plus other newly industrializing economies plus China plus Mongolia.
Source: IMF, *Direction of Trade Statistics* (various years); data reported from exporter country accounts.

Note: Diversification, or change in exports due to new products, accounts for a small share.
a. Competitive factor = change in market share.
b. Demand factor = change in market size.
Source: Ng and Yeats (2003: Table 9.1).

Exports to China are particularly dynamic, with East Asia finding niches in China's markets.

East Asia NIEs: export markets (as % of total exports)

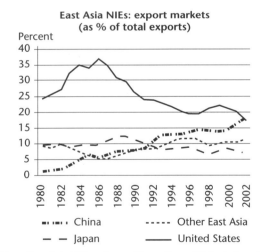

■·■·· China   ----- Other East Asia
— — Japan   —— United States

Developing East Asia: export markets (as % of total exports)

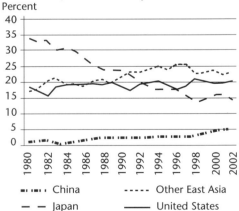

■·■·· China   ----- Other East Asia
— — Japan   —— United States

Note: East Asia NIEs refers to Hong Kong (China), Republic of Korea, Singapore, Taiwan (China).
Sources: IMF, *Direction of Trade Statistics* (various years); data reported from exporter country accounts.

Note: Developing East Asia refers to Indonesia, Malaysia, Philippines, Thailand, Cambodia, Lao PDR, Mongolia, Myanmar, Vietnam.
Sources: IMF, *Direction of Trade Statistics* (various years); data reported from exporter country accounts.

tivity growth to replace the old model of growth through physical and human capital accumulation (Yusuf and others 2003). There is ample evidence that export-oriented firms and those with foreign equity participation are far more productive than

domestic-oriented firms, with productivity differentials of 40 percent in Indonesia and the Philippines and 15–20 percent in Thailand and Korea (Hallward-Driemeier, Iarossi, and Sokoloff 2002). Moreover, China's restructuring provides an impe-

FIGURE 2   Intraregional Trade

Intraregional trade is increasingly concentrated...and production sharing is a major determinant.

Share of 2001 intraregional trade accounted for by 30 largest four-digit SITC exports

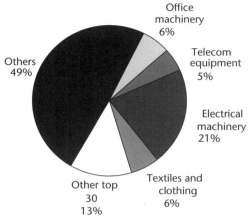

Share of 2001 five-digit SITC parts and components in top 30 exports

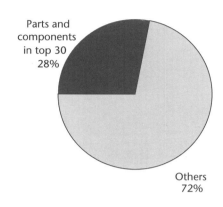

Note: SITC = Standard International Trade Classification.
Source: Ng and Yeats (2003: Table 12.1).

Note: In addition, parts and components in the non–top 30 exports account for an additional US$8.3 billion or 4 percent of total non–top 30 exports.
Source: Ng and Yeats (2003: Table 17.1).

China is an increasingly central player in production networks.

Share of components in China's imports relative to share of components in world trade

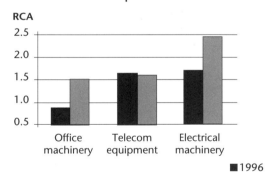

Share of components in China's exports relative to share of components in world trade

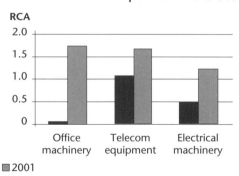

Note: Revealed comparative advantage (RCA) measures a country's relative export performance in a good j. It is defined as the country's share of world exports of good j (x_{ij}/x_{wj}) divided by its share of total world exports (X_i/X_w), where x_{ij} and x_{wj} represent the value of good j exported by country i and the world, respectively, and X_i and X_w are country i's and the world's total exports, respectively. If the value of the index exceeds unity, the country is said to have a comparative advantage in the production of good j.
Source: Ng and Yeats (2003).

tus for establishing new regional production networks, initially in electronics, that would promote highly productive firms. For now, these production networks are oriented toward exports to developed countries, but the growing markets within East Asia provide a potential complementary source of demand.[12]

Policies can support these natural economic forces, and the drive to liberalize is shaping new institutional arrangements. The willingness of the world's richer countries to target the needs of developing countries in the context of the Doha Development Agenda is helpful, but the outcome of these negotiations is still uncertain. And regional and bilateral agreements fit in well with other political aims of East Asian countries, giving these agreements a momentum that the global discussions have yet to achieve. ASEAN has moved to a

FIGURE 3   China's Trade in Third-Country Markets

This trade is expanding...but not at East Asia's expense.

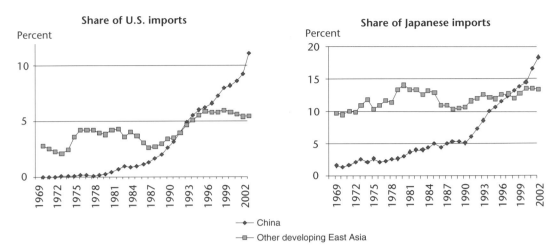

Source: IMF, *Direction of Trade Statistics* (various years.)

two-tier system to permit its more advanced members to accelerate trade reform, while launching new initiatives to integrate its less-developed members—Cambodia, Lao PDR, Myanmar, and Vietnam. At the same time, the speed with which the ASEAN-China Framework Agreement has been launched and the ideas for a new ASEAN-Japan are creating new alliances in favor of liberalization within the region. As Philippines president Gloria Arroyo noted in a speech of May 2002, combining the Association of Southeast Asian Nations (ASEAN) and Chinese economies "would give birth to a market of 1.8 billion consumers or almost one third of humanity."

China's Role in the Region

In line with its own reforms, China has been a growing economic force in East Asia. Exports to China have been dynamic over the last decade, particularly for the newly industrializing economies but also for the rest of developing East Asia (Figure 1), while shares to the United States and Japan have been flat or declining. China's trade with major markets also has been expanding, but not at the expense of developing East Asia (Figure 3).

Membership in the WTO and the reforms associated with membership give China an opportunity to play an even larger and growing role in the world economy, and in the regional economy, amplifying preexisting trends.

What WTO Accession Means for China: Sectoral Shifts. As explained in Chapter 1, assessing the implications of major economy-wide reform such as that involved in China's WTO accession is inherently difficult. Much of the impact will consist of reinforcing the structural changes already under way. The experience with other trade events such as the formation of NAFTA suggests that the actual overall impact will be much greater than suggested by ex ante modeling, largely as a result of productivity and other changes that are hard for models to capture.

In *agriculture*, the initial levels of effective protection are in fact likely to be far lower than others have estimated, implying that sectoral shifts are likely to be less dramatic than others are predicting.[13] Nonetheless, China's agricultural trade liberalization plan is the expected source of about half of the efficiency gains from the WTO accession package. Reduced protection and greater scope for imports are likely in a range of products, including oilseeds, sugar, and dairy products (where the principal form of protection has been tariffs, which are being reduced substantially) and cotton (where export subsidies are now ruled out) (Figure 4). And demand will sharply increase for other raw materials and natural resources such as wood and energy products.

China's decision to contain agricultural protection has more far-reaching implications.[14] This use of WTO rules as a commitment device will focus

FIGURE 4   Reduced Agricultural Protection in China

China is following a strategy of reducing agricultural protection...albeit from a lower starting point than commonly measured.

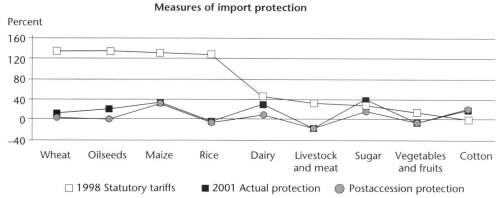

Sources: Chapter 1. Average statutory rates taken from Schmidhuber (2001) and www.chinavista.com. See Huang and Rozelle (2002) for estimates of protection.

policymakers on other types of policies that are needed to deal with the very real problems of rural poverty—such as improving rural education and reducing barriers to labor mobility. At both the regional and global levels, China's commitment to a low-protection agricultural regime sets the stage for its interests to coincide with those of countries that are calling for opening the large and currently highly protected markets for labor-intensive agricultural exports.

In *industrial products,* the accession agreement builds on the substantial liberalization already undertaken. The 6 percentage point reduction in average tariffs that remains to be implemented is small relative to the 33 percentage points achieved over the last decade; the number of products subject to import licenses has already fallen from about two-thirds of tariff lines to less than one-twentieth (see Ianchovichina and Martin 2002 and Lardy 2002, respectively.)

In the case of automobiles, a massive sectoral rationalization is expected to lead to scale economies that could more than offset the impact of the reduction in protection, making China's automobile industry internationally competitive.[15]

Another major impact of accession will be a strong expansion in China's textile and clothing sectors. Importing countries have committed to abolishing, by 2005, the quotas on textiles and clothing originally imposed under the Multi-fiber Arrangement (MFA), and the United States and other countries have agreed to impose most-

favored-nation (MFN) tariffs on China. Analysis indicates that China's clothing production could more than double and its textile production could expand by nearly 50 percent as a result of WTO accession combined with the proposed phase-out of quotas as part of the Agreement on Textiles and Clothing (ATC).[16]

These estimates, however, omit some important potential elements of trade policy—namely, the application of antidumping and safeguards measures against China and the possibility that China itself will increasingly apply such measures. One feature of the accession agreement is the product-specific transitional safeguard provisions, lasting over a 12-year period, which may be applied to China by any WTO Member and may then trigger actions against the diversion of Chinese exports to other markets, with special textile safeguards for three years. These provisions are particularly troublesome: no such measure targeted specifically at China existed before China's accession.[17] Similarly, in the area of antidumping provisions China could remain vulnerable for up to 15 years to nonmarket economy provisions that dramatically increase the probability of dumping being found and the relevant antidumping duties being applied. China's own increased use of antidumping and safeguard measures would be legal and consistent with the rules-focused approach to WTO implementation. But one hopes such scenarios can be avoided because the scenarios would be inconsistent with the emphasis on development that has characterized China's trade reform agenda since the beginning of the reform era.

China's trade in *services* was the subject of one of the most radical services reforms ever negotiated in the WTO. The potential for rapidly increasing trade in services is significant. The important feature of China's commitments is that they focus on market access and do not discriminate between domestic and foreign suppliers. With China expected to be the largest market for telecommunications in the world by 2010, its commitments in that sector are profound in that they allow foreign entry for a wide range of activities. One area of services with an important bearing on trade is the activities that make up the logistical chain. China's WTO commitments promise increased competition and reduced costs in several areas, including through the development of third-party logistical firms. Yet restrictions remain in place on the form of establishments, such as requirements for joint ventures, and on geographic scope.[18]

What WTO Accession Means for China: Ways of Doing Business. The implications for China of accession to the WTO go beyond the specific commitments in its accession package. Changes in the ways of doing business—elimination of dual pricing, phasing out of restrictions on trading, more uniform administrative arrangements, and judicial review—are likely to result in dynamic gains that will outweigh those based on comparative-static estimates of efficiency gains. Every 1 percent gain in

productivity in the services sector from expanded competition and foreign entry, for example, implies welfare gains of $10 billion and a real GDP increase of 2.2 percent, equivalent to the total estimated static gain from China's accession to the WTO (Ianchovichina and Walmsley 2002).

What WTO Accession Means for the Rest of East Asia: On Balance, More Opportunity. The foremost opportunity for the rest of East Asia arising from China's WTO accession lies in expanding exports to China's growing and more open markets; China's imports are expected to grow from 3 percent of global GDP in 2000 to more than 6 percent by 2005 across an array of commodities (Figure 5). China receives 55 percent of its imports from East Asia and 37 percent from emerging East Asia. All groups of countries in East Asia will benefit from China's more open markets, but evidence suggests the scope is especially large for China's major trading partners of Japan and the newly industrializing economies, but will still be significant for the middle-income countries and the lowest-income countries, as explained in Chapter 2.

Indeed, the sectoral landscape just described suggests significant export opportunities for developing East Asian economies. For countries such as Indonesia and Thailand, the weighted average tariff on their top 100 export products falls by a half as the result of China's accession, and some of their top agricultural and raw material exports—rubber, sugar, urea, and to a lesser extent rice—will benefit

FIGURE 5   Chinese Imports, 1995 and 2005

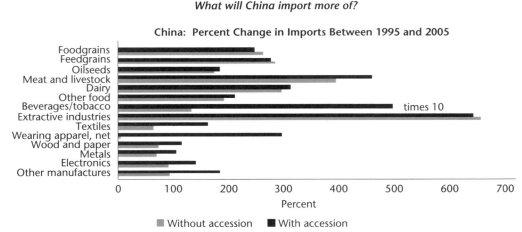

What will China import more of?

Source: Ianchovichina and Martin (2001).

from a reduction in nontariff barriers. These countries also may see increased interindustry trade and production sharing as China's electronics and other manufacturing industries, for example, grow.

For the lowest-income countries such as Cambodia and Lao PDR, there also will be opportunities. The decline in these countries' weighted average tariff for the top 100 exports to China is quite small (from 4.3 to 2.6 percent for Cambodia and from 7.3 to 6.0 percent for Lao PDR), and only about 10 percent of Cambodia's exports and less than 1 percent of Lao PDR's exports, including wood and rubber, will face fewer quantitative restrictions. However, given the trade intensity with China, they will benefit from China as a powerful source of external demand.[19]

China's accession also offers the rest of the region the opportunity to import cheaper produced goods. Most obviously, consumers of Chinese finished good imports will benefit. But many producers will also gain by access to cheaper intermediate inputs into production processes. For example, chemicals already represent nearly 10 percent of imports from China in Indonesia and Thailand. By 2001 China was exporting more than $20 billion in parts and components to other parts of emerging East Asia, representing up to 20 percent of those countries' parts and components trade. Continued growth in imports of parts and components from China will represent an opportunity for the rest of emerging East Asia to develop competitive firms.

To benefit from these opportunities, it will be important that East Asian countries resist the growing protectionist pressures for imposition of excessive safeguard measures in a futile effort to protect all domestic producers. In Thailand, local manufacturers are complaining about low-cost imports of electrical appliances and motorbikes from China. In 2002 Indonesia imposed temporary safeguard measures for garment imports, and Vietnam did so for motorbikes. Such decisions can only prolong the shifts in production that are necessary to realize regional comparative advantages, and distract policymakers from facilitating the adjustment of workers through appropriate labor market and safety net policies and programs.

China's WTO entry also implies increased competition in third-country markets. If recent Chinese export performance (Figure 3) is an indicator,

the expansion of China's presence in major markets will not necessarily crowd out other developing East Asian exports, although it may constrain their growth prospects to levels below those of the late 1980s.

Nonetheless, certain exports appear at risk. Clearly, the apparel and textile sectors in other East Asian countries will face additional competition in markets that are currently constrained by quota restrictions. The market-by-market and product-by-product analysis in Chapter 2 indicates that for Thailand, for example, only about 15 percent of exports to the United States are at risk from increased competition from China, but that 25 percent of exports to Japan are at risk. For Indonesia, the second and third most important exports to the United States—footwear and video-recording and -reproducing apparatuses—face direct competition with China, as do about a quarter of exports to Japan.

Among lower-income countries, Cambodia is particularly vulnerable because its exports are highly concentrated in apparel. Roughly 30 percent of Cambodia's exports to the United States have unit values similar to those of Chinese exports, indicating direct competition, or are in categories in which China is currently quota-constrained, indicating that competition from China is likely to increase. This prospect highlights the need for urgency; such countries must speed up their governance and other reforms to ensure the development of alternative products.

Nonetheless, on balance, China represents more of an opportunity than a threat to the rest of East Asia. Certain challenges will need to be met, and adjustments made. However, the scope for gains from a dynamic China is large across the range of countries in East Asia.

Regional Interdependence

Recent trends in the magnitude and composition of intra–East Asian trade bode well for further integration (also see Ng and Yeats 2003). Comparisons show that conditions within East Asia are now very similar to those in countries that were previously able to implement such successful regional arrangements as the European Union and NAFTA.

East Asia has achieved a high degree of market-driven regional integration, but regionalism—more formal economic cooperation and economic integration arrangements and agreements between countries—has traditionally been quite limited, as explained in Chapter 3.[20] The major exceptions have been the ASEAN Free Trade Area (AFTA), established in 1993, and dialogue under the Asia-Pacific Economic Cooperation (APEC) forum. However, the past several years have seen a plethora of proposals for new bilateral and regional trade arrangements: the Framework Agreement on ASEAN-China Comprehensive Economic Cooperation, signed in November 2002; an East Asia–wide free trade agreement; a more recent proposal by Japan for an ASEAN-plus-Japan free trade agreement; and bilateral agreements under negotiation, in particular by Japan, Singapore, Korea, and Thailand.

Scope for Gains from Regionalism. Addressing intraregional barriers can ensure continued dynamism in regional trade and investment flows—including in response to China's growing role. The stated motivation of several initiatives, including the ASEAN-China Framework Agreement, is to take advantage of complementarities and build on existing strengths in order to make the region collectively more efficient and competitive and thereby attract investment. The regional agreements under consideration are increasingly comprehensive in scope, going beyond the removal of tariffs and nontariff barriers on trade in goods to include trade facilitation measures, such as conformity of standards and procedures across national boundaries, and trade in services. The New-Age Partnership between Singapore and Japan announced in January 2002 is notable in this regard.

The countries in the region could reap worthwhile economic benefits from increased regionalism aimed at removing border barriers, according to analysis using the standard models for evaluating benefits from regional trading arrangements (Table 1). As is typical in these models, the gains are shown to be greater the wider the country coverage and the wider the sectoral coverage of the regional arrangements. Notably, the gains for ASEAN countries are shown to be greater than those for the other countries in the region. Given that the lower- and middle-income countries of ASEAN are likely to benefit less from China's WTO accession than the newly industrializing economies, greater regionalism in East Asia can help spread the gains across a wider set of economies.[21]

One danger with the current regional arrangements is that they have extensive provisions for excluding sensitive sectors. Such exclusions could substantially reduce the potential for welfare gains from an agreement. Within AFTA, for example, the lack of progress in agriculture and other sensitive sectors has been disappointing. To give some indi-

TABLE 1 Effects on Economic Welfare of Various Regional Trade Proposals

Proposal	% of GDP (% of GDP excluding agricultural liberalization)				
	ASEAN	China	Korea, Rep. of	Japan	USA
China + Korea + Japan	−0.26 (−0.16)	+0.1 (−0.2)	+1.0 (+0.6)	+0.1 (+0.2)	+0.0 (+0.0)
ASEAN – China	+0.9 (+0.5)	+0.0 (+0.1)	−0.1 (−0.1)	+0.0 (+0.0)	+0.0 (+0.0)
ASEAN – Japan	+1.1 (+0.2)	−0.1 (−0.1)	−0.2 (−0.1)	+0.0 (+0.1)	+0.0 (+0.0)
ASEAN + 3	+1.5 (+0.6)	+0.1 (−0.2)	+1.1 (+0.8)	+0.2 (+0.2)	−0.1 (+0.0)
ASEAN + 3 + CER	+1.3 (+0.6)	+0.0 (−0.1)	+1.1 (+0.9)	+0.2 (+0.2)	−0.1 (+0.0)
APEC liberalization (MFN)	+0.7	+0.5	+0.7	+0.4	−0.0
APEC preferential liberalization	+0.8	+0.6	+0.9	+0.4	+0.0

Note: Calculations for ASEAN include only Indonesia, Malaysia, the Philippines, Singapore, Thailand, and Vietnam. CER (Australia–New Zealand Closer Economics Relations Trade Agreement) includes Australia and New Zealand. Figures in parentheses refer to net welfare effects when agriculture is excluded.
Sources: Scollay and Gilbert (2003) for free trade agreement proposals and Scollay and Gilbert (2001) for APEC liberalization proposals.

cation of the importance of this point, some economic models suggest that if agriculture is included in the ASEAN-China or ASEAN + 3 proposals, the estimated welfare gains for ASEAN countries roughly doubles (Table 1).

The greatest welfare gains, however, are likely to come from addressing the deeper integration agenda being proposed here. In particular, the benefits from integrating trade in services and overcoming technical barriers to trade are likely to be many times those from reducing border barriers alone.[22] Gains from liberalizing services trade are felt not only within the services sector itself, but also within other sectors because services are vital inputs in their production processes. As manufacturing in East Asia moves into a phase where participating in global markets will become more dependent on services, it increasingly will be held back by poor efficiency in the services sector, which has been protected from competition. Services liberalization in East Asia lags relative to that of other regions, and action to integrate trade in services could help restore its global competitiveness. Simulation results from China, consistent with findings from other parts of the world, indicate that even small productivity gains of 1 percent in services outweigh those based on static border trade efficiency gains alone.[23]

The policy scope for enhancing efficiency in services, as well as in other sensitive sectors such as agriculture, may well be wider initially in a regional context than in a global one. In fact, expanding integration into these sectors is one of the main potential advantages of regional, as opposed to global, liberalization. Most regional partnerships already in place or under discussion include the services and agriculture sectors, whereas these sectors have proven much harder to tackle in global talks. Because the liberalization of services may be necessary for industries to benefit fully from the removal of regional barriers to goods trade, it may be preferable to give the services sector a high priority from the start of any negotiations.

Making East Asian Arrangements a Stepping-stone to Global Integration. Liberalization goals can be well served by moving on multiple fronts. In the East Asian goods trade, traditional concerns that a regional arrangement will merely divert, rather than create, trade are less worrisome because a rela-

tively low-tariff bloc already exists, and because many of the region's economies, especially the more developed, are moving toward lower average tariffs. To generate momentum, measures can be taken before the parties agree on formal arrangements. The "Early Harvest" aspect of the ASEAN-China Framework Agreement exemplifies this approach. As part of the Early Harvest, the agreement provides accelerated access for key products to China and ASEAN markets (ahead of the MFN schedule that is part of the WTO accession agreement). Also, China has extended most-favored-nation status to the low-income non–WTO Member countries Lao PDR and Cambodia.

The challenge in pursuing regional integration arrangements will be to avoid the "spaghetti bowl" effect of different rules and regulations associated with different agreements, which can add unnecessary administrative costs to firms doing business across the region and result in a bloc-ed up world (Figure 6). Such costs can be especially high when a host of bilateral agreements are put in place, with large numbers of side agreements that each permit some discriminatory treatment. Inconsistencies between agreements with overlapping membership also can become a problem. The exchange of ideas on a regional basis can help avoid such difficulties. While, in theory, there are some reasons to expect that uncoordinated bilateral and regional agreements build in incentives toward global free trade, this outcome depends crucially on maintaining a common set of principles for each agreement— that is, focusing on trade facilitation measures; allowing the most liberal rules of origin; and generally contributing positively to multilateral trade liberalization. For example, allowing for accumulation under rules of origin will be important to the facilitation of production networks in the region, and allowing for multiple rules for conferring origin would make it easier for more firms to participate in regional trade (see Brenton 2003b).

Unless countries tackle the sensitive sectors in regional trade arrangements—and ultimately at the global level—many of the potential economic benefits alluded to earlier will not be realized. China's binding to low tariff levels as part of its agricultural policy therefore offers scope for the liberalization of agriculture in a regional setting, which could set in place a favorable political dynamic for more open agricultural sectors throughout East Asia.

FIGURE 6   Regional Trade Arrangements

Low-tariff bloc reduces trade diversion.

Average tariff rates: comparison
of MFN with preferential rates

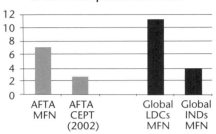

Note: AFTA = ASEAN Free Trade Area; MFN = most-favored nation; CEPT = common effective preferential tariff; LDCs = less developed countries; INDs = industrial countries.
Source: World Bank (2001a) and www. aseansec.org.

Multidimensional nature of agreements compounds "spaghetti bowl" and impedes merging.

Number of articles of agreement:
recent East Asia initiatives

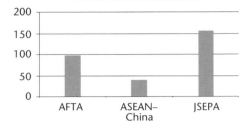

Note: JSEPA = Japan-Singapore Economic Partnership Agreement.
Source: www. aseansec.org and www.mofa.go.jp.

Another way to proceed would be to unbundle proposed agreements into components for deeper integration that could realistically be agreed on and would yield immediate results in terms of increased efficiency and development of intraindustry trade and production networks. In the case of China and ASEAN, for example, two-way business transactions are already proliferating, and—long before government policymakers began to act—businesses had recognized and responded to the China challenge. Such transactions could be facilitated and enhanced by an agreement that focuses on trade and investment facilitation, such as customs.

It also would be preferable to focus attention and the resources of policymakers on as few regional arrangements as possible but to make them broad in scope and country coverage, especially for small economies that have limited capacity to evaluate the development implications of these arrangements.

Finally, a further benefit from stronger regional cooperation could be to link issues of common interest to an effective multilateral stance, whether in services liberalization or discipline on antidumping measures.

Expanding Market Access Globally

One of the motivating factors behind the move to regional integration in East Asia is disappointment with the pace of multilateral trade liberalization in products of most interest to developing countries.

As discussed in Chapter 4, a consensus appears to be growing about the negative impact on developing countries of trade barriers on products that are exported by the poor—particularly agricultural products and labor-intensive manufactures such as textiles and clothing, which are the sectors that confront the greatest entry barriers in high-income countries. One of the disappointments of the Uruguay Round was its failure to achieve greater market access in these products. The Doha Development Agenda launched in November 2001 has the potential to make the world trading system more conducive to development. It includes a large number of policy reforms that can and should be undertaken by high-income countries and that will generate significant benefits for ordinary people in developing East Asia.

Trade in Textiles and Clothing. As noted earlier, the textiles and clothing sector poses a special challenge for East Asia. Many countries of the region have large garment export businesses employing sizable numbers of low-skilled workers, many of whom are female. These businesses will be threatened by competition from China in the form of both a macroeconomic threat to the balance of payments (from lost exports) and a social threat of lost jobs and lower wage incomes for many poor households.

Implementation of agreements for further trade liberalization in textiles and garments is critical to social stability in East Asia. Under the Agreement on Textiles and Clothing as part of the Uruguay Round, quota restrictions were to be gradually abolished over a 10-year period (that is, no later that January 2005) in three stages, and the remaining quotas were to be subject to a progressive increase in their rates of expansion. However, implementation to date has been disappointing. Acceleration of the quota phase-out under the ATC would have a significant impact on poverty by sustaining or increasing employment in these industries. It would help maintain export growth in low-income East Asia, for example, permitting 20 percent more exports from Vietnam. It also would help protect workers in middle-income economies such as Thailand, where it would affect an estimated 50,000 jobs for garment workers and 10,000 jobs for textile workers, about 20,000 of whom are from poor households. Finally, acceleration would benefit workers in the textile and clothing sector in China—workers who are mainly women drawn from poor, remote regions—and could result in 5 million fewer poor Chinese overall.[24]

At the same time, some economies in East Asia will lose. Garment industries in several countries have depended on quotas, benefiting from some of the rents accruing from preferential access to EU and U.S. markets. Garment exports from higher-income economies such as Korea are likely to decline. And in Cambodia, in particular, ATC implementation is likely to put pressure on employment and wages in the garment sector. Cambodia will have to pursue a broader agenda to open up other trade opportunities.

Agricultural and Rural-Based Trade. Reduction of trade barriers in agriculture is particularly important for poverty reduction. Agriculture is the main livelihood for poor households: for more than 90 percent in Cambodia and Vietnam, more than 75 percent in Indonesia, and roughly 70 percent in Thailand and the Philippines (World Bank 2002a).

Gains from agricultural liberalization by higher-income countries are estimated at more than $10 billion for developing East Asia, and that figure triples once dynamic productivity gains are taken into account.[25] In contrast to the move toward increased transparency in trade policy for manufacturers, agriculture remains protected in myriad ways, as laid out in Chapter 4. However, the direct impact of agricultural subsidies and domestic sup-

port programs in Europe and the United States on farmers in East Asia is limited; such domestic programs are heavily concentrated on meat, dairy products, and cereals.[26] Thus with the notable exception of rice, East Asian farmers are not directly engaged in these distorted world markets. But other barriers in international agricultural markets are important for East Asia, and four practices of the developed countries are especially harmful. First, their use of specific rather than ad valorem tariffs often leads to very high effective protection, particularly on low-quality goods produced by the poorest countries. Products such as palm oil, rice, and sugar, as well as fish, crustaceans, and fruits and vegetables are the ones most affected. Second, developed countries use tariffs that cascade upward on goods such as coffee and vegetables as protective devices for their agroprocessing industries. Third, complex rules of origin make it hard for countries to avail themselves of all the incentives theoretically made available to them. Fourth, conformance with health and safety regulations, notably maximum pesticide residue levels, and difficulties with understanding and administering standards are costly for many exporting countries.

Agricultural trade barriers are not just an issue for developed countries; the emerging economies of East Asia also maintain high barriers. Regional agricultural markets already are large. China's commitment to a regime of low protection in agriculture is fortunate for other countries that are well placed to supply it with imports, providing a direct boost to their foreign exchange earnings and to the incomes of poor households. The ASEAN-China trade agreement, with its "Early Harvest" provisions, provides another avenue to ensure that poor agricultural households have every opportunity to benefit from trade opportunities in the region. There may be further scope to address the sensitive food security and safety issues initially within the context of East Asian arrangements.

Development Orientation for a Behind-the-Border Agenda

As WTO director general Supachai Panitchpakdi eloquently stated in November 2002, "Trade policies do not stand alone. Mutually supportive companion policies are also necessary." Many of the mechanisms required to maximize the developmental benefits of trade and investment liberalization are "behind-the-border" institutional and regulatory reforms. Each of the new regional and bilateral partnerships reflects this business reality. Technical barriers and product standards, logistics, services sectors, intellectual property rights, competition policy, and environmental and labor standards have become as important a part of the private sector environment as trade policy itself. These "behind-the-border" issues also are featured prominently on the Doha Development Agenda. The thrust is to place trade policy within a broader framework of development and poverty reduction.

Technical Barriers and Standards: Balancing Trade with Consumer Interests

As the traditional barriers to market access decline, measures aimed at trade facilitation become more critical. Conformity with health and safety standards can be one of the most decisive determinants of access.[27] Many of the standards in use represent legitimate consumer interests, but the use of technical regulations, such as standards, has risen to further commercial policy in multilateral, regional, and global trade. An important problem for exporters is that different national governments often apply different technical specifications to meet the same goal.

For East Asian developing countries, importing countries' sanitary and phytosanitary (SPS) standards can impose significant additional costs that impede exports. For example, it has been estimated that application of the strictest EU standard rather than the international Codex Alimentarius standard for aflatoxin has cost Thailand $350 million in export losses in cereals and dried fruit, China $380 million, and Vietnam $15 million. The adoption of a Codex standard on tetracycline could double Thailand and China's beef exports (Otsuki and Wilson 2001, 2002). Exporting countries also have to contend with importers' use of precautionary measures, such as the EU import ban on genetically modified organisms (GMOs), which hurts Thailand's tuna exports as well as exports from China, which is the third largest GMO producer in the world. Only some of these standards may be justified on grounds of consumer safety and preferences; others may simply be protectionism in disguise.

The WTO rules in this area aim at ensuring that technical regulations, voluntary standards, and testing and certification of products do not constitute unnecessary barriers to trade. Under the Sanitary and Phytosanitary Standards (SPS) Agreement, WTO Members are encouraged to adopt internationally recognized standards, but also are free to apply stricter ones. Although the agreement recognizes importing countries' right to implement SPS measures that diverge from international norms, it does require them to provide scientific justification for such measures and applies risk assessment mechanisms.

In many cases, East Asian economies will want to adopt unilaterally the international standards being set.[28] China is further strengthening its food safety regulations and capacity to implement these regulations as part of its WTO accession and is adopting various authentications and labeling systems. Compliance with SPS in export markets can induce changes in production systems and supply channels, but it is likely to require modernization of standards infrastructure as well as information and training. Countries may need to seek technical assistance and support for additional projects in this area. A Standards and Trade Development Facility to address this need is being established, to be administered by WTO in collaboration with the World Bank, the World Health Organization (WHO), the UN Food and Agriculture Organization (FAO), Codex Alimentarius, and others.

At the same time, East Asian countries can benefit from rationalizing standards in a regional and global context. Cooperation on standards is one of the important issues generally encompassed in regional arrangements. Recognizing that foreign standards can achieve the same level of social or consumer protection as domestic standards, mutual recognition agreements (MRAs) are one option. Such agreements have mainly been used between developed countries, but ASEAN currently has signed two MRAs, with plans for an additional 20 products, thus avoiding duplication of testing and conformity assessment.

Transport and Logistics

The commodity mix in East Asia is changing rapidly from resource-based commodities to low- and medium-technology goods to high-technology goods (Table 2). Logistics improvements, essential for moving up the value chain, have very high payoffs in East Asia, as discussed in Chapter 5. High-value agriculture (flowers, fruits, seafood) and manufacturing (electronics) demand sophistication not only in production but also in logistics handling. Timeliness matters, and a fast, reliable supply chain is essential.

In East Asia, the key logistical bottlenecks seem to be high internal land transport costs and port logistics. This situation is in sharp contrast to external transport costs: with the sharp decline in trans-Pacific shipping costs over the last decade, produc-ers in many parts of East Asia can reach the U.S. market more cheaply than inland areas or neighboring countries. For example, the inland transport costs of moving goods from some remote regions of China to external markets are roughly 10 times the inland transport costs at the other end (Figure 7). Port logistics have been identified as a high priority (Figure 8). Considerable scope exists for reduction of transport cost margins (Figure 9). Modest improvements could lead to more than $50 billion in additional exports from emerging East Asia to the rest of APEC, with an even larger impact on efficiency of imports (Wilson and others 2002).

TABLE 2   Structure of Manufactured Exports by Country, 1985 and 1996 (% by value)

	Resource-based		Low-/medium-technology		High-technology		
	1985	1996	1985	1996	1985	1996	
Hong Kong (China)	2.1	4.4	78.5	66.7	19.4	28.9	
Singapore	42.3	12.7	25.4	21.9	32.3	65.4	
Korea, Rep. of	7.8	9.4	72.1	55.0	20.1	35.6	
Taiwan (China)	8.7	5.1	70.6	54.1	20.7	40.8	
Indonesia	72.2	34.9	25.1	50.4	2.7	14.7	
Malaysia	53.7	17.8	15.2	21.8	31.1	60.4	
Thailand	42.1	14.5	44.8	49.1	13.1	36.4	
China	11.7	9.8	78.9	69.7	9.4	20.5	

Source: Lall (1998).

FIGURE 7   Inland Transport Costs for Remote Regions

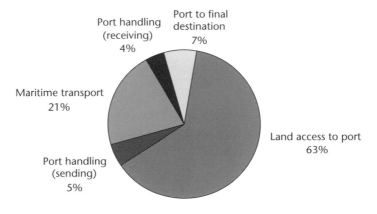

Logistics costs of container transport from Chongqing, China to the U.S. West Coast: breakdown of total cost of US$3,650 per 20-foot equivalent unit (TEU)

Port handling (receiving) 4%

Port to final destination 7%

Maritime transport 21%

Port handling (sending) 5%

Land access to port 63%

Source: Carruthers and Bajpai (2002).

FIGURE 8   Expanded Exports to APEC from Improvements in Trade Facilitation

Better logistics and harmonized standards are central to expanding trade.

Expansion in exports to APEC from improvements in trade facilitation
(% change in manufactured, agriculture and raw material exports from base)

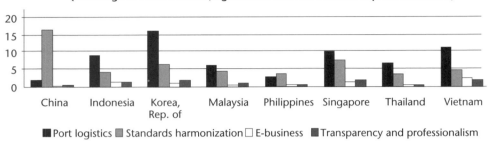

■ Port logistics ■ Standards harmonization □ E-business ■ Transparency and professionalism

Source: Wilson and others (2002).

FIGURE 9   Costs of Producer Services

Significant scope exists for reduction of transport costs...

and telecommunication costs.

Estimated transport cost margins for exports of textiles to United States, using Singapore as a benchmark, 2000

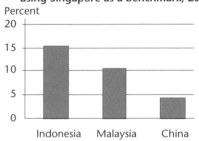

International calling price comparison for selected Asian countries (US$ per three minutes), 2002

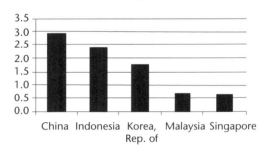

Source: Bureau of Economic Statistics, U.S. Department of Commerce.

Sources: International Telecommunications Union and operative Web sites.

High inland transport and logistics costs are a particular impediment for the poor in remote areas or landlocked countries. In Lao PDR, poor inland transport contributes to a 25 percent differential in paddy prices for farmers. On the island of Mindanao in the Philippines, agricultural producers are plagued by poor access roads, lack of storage facilities, and inadequate trading areas, leading to small volumes and high costs, compounded by interisland shipping fraught with high tariffs, product deterioration, and cargo losses. In Mongolia, poor transport between Ulaanbaatar and the central regions contributes to a 40–85 percent price difference for the flour staple. Constraints on internal logistics also impede the shipment of food commodities from surplus to deficit areas, worsening food security.

Logistics requirements become more onerous for trade in differentiated products than for trade in homogenous products. Manufacturing firms, especially those integrated into global production chains, seek not only low transport costs but also a host of sophisticated logistical needs: short transit times, reliable delivery schedules, careful handling of goods in cold storage chains, certification of product quality, and security from theft. This situation suggests that, by strengthening infrastructure services, East Asian economies can influence their comparative advantage and, particularly, their prospects for expanding production of more sophisticated products (see Chapter 5 and Fink, Mattoo, and Neagu forthcoming).

Improving logistics involves investing in transport infrastructure, but also introducing complementary policies outside the transport sector. Transport regulatory agencies can improve logistics performance by allowing paperwork clearance for inland travel of containers and removing distortionary queuing pricing for commodities accessing the transport system. Multimodal coordination is essential to promote seamless freight movement. In Korea, for example, inland container terminals and the development of intermodal exchanges have made it easy for containers to reach cities far from the ports. Coordination is also critical for urban land use, standards, licensing, and security. Examples of helpful urban land use policies include diverting traffic around congested areas and providing space for landside container storage.

Better cross-border trade facilitation—customs, e-commerce, paperless clearance, electronic processing, and safety measures—can stimulate trade throughout the region. Some studies show that for emerging East Asia, modest improvements in trade facilitation could expand trade by more than $200 billion (Wilson and others 2002; also see Figure 8). Customs is the most obvious example. In some East Asian countries such as Singapore, trade documentation takes only 15 minutes to clear; two to three days is required for customs documentation and clearance of sea cargo. By contrast, customs clearance takes a minimum of five days in Manila and seven days in Jakarta. In China, trade documentation clearance takes a day, whereas sea containers can take 30–35 days to clear (Janet Tay Consultants 2002). Several countries, including Cambodia and Vietnam, are addressing corruption in customs as critical to private sector trade (World Bank 2001b, 2003a).

Certain logistics needs are best served by the private sector, particularly in ports, freight forwarding, third-party logistics, warehousing, trucking, and the bus industry. Foreign entry may play an important role in increasing competition and the quality of logistics.

Services Sector Liberalization

East Asia has lagged behind other developing regions in liberalizing trade in services.[29] Evidence suggests that the productivity gains associated with more efficient services are particularly high, and that competitiveness in high-value, differentiated agriculture and in manufacturing depends on efficient business services. Static gains for developing East Asia and Korea from services liberalization throughout the developing world are estimated at about $270 billion, or 10 percent higher income, by 2015 (World Bank 2002c).

To realize gains, reforms in the services sector need to be designed with broader development objectives in mind and with an eye toward introducing competition, ensuring effective regulation to remedy market failure, and providing essential services to the poor. Pro-competitive regulation is particularly important in network-based services such as transport, telecommunications, and energy services. In East Asia, the importance of regulatory and pro-competitive reforms to complement privatization has not always been fully appreciated (Figure 10).

In this context, international trade agreements in services offer East Asia three main benefits: improved access to markets abroad and greater openness at home through reciprocal liberalization; credibility of reforms as the result of binding international commitments; and regulatory cooperation. In some services in which East Asian countries have a stake in cross-border trade—for example, in data processing and other information technology-enabled services—they could secure access to other countries' markets through legally binding commitments from their trading partners. Some countries in East Asia have the potential to export significant transport and logistics, tourism, and business services to China. East Asia also has a stake in temporary labor mobility, as, for example, when its construction workers or accountants work abroad.

A nonpreferential approach to market opening, negotiated within a multilateral context, may be important for overall efficiency. It ensures that access is provided by the most competitive providers and avoids conferring a first-mover advantage on inferior regional suppliers.

Nonetheless, regional arrangements may provide the advantages of greater policy space for regulatory cooperation and learning-by-doing. East Asia is actively pursuing services liberalization in the context of the regional arrangements just outlined. Even preferential liberalization can improve the status quo, given that many existing barriers are

FIGURE 10   Regulatory and Competitive Reforms, Selected Countries

Many regulatory and competitive reforms have not kept pace with privatization.

Sequence of fixed line telecom reform in selected Asian countries

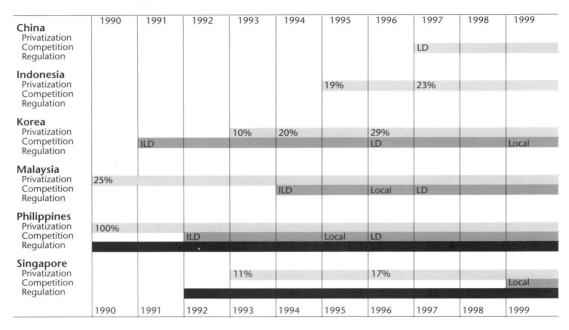

Note: The percentage figures indicate the share of private equity ownership in the incumbent operator. Local, LD, and ILD refer to the local long-distance and international fixed-line segments, respectively. Regulation only captures the existence of a separate regulatory authority.
Source: Fink, Mattoo, and Rathindran (2002).

frictional (such as unnecessary qualification requirements for foreign professionals and border hurdles for foreign transporters). Initial opening among regional partners may provide opportunities for learning-by-doing and lessen concerns that foreign competition would prematurely drive out potentially competitive domestic providers. Regulatory cooperation, such as the harmonization and mutual recognition of domestic regulations in financial, professional, and a range of other services, may be more feasible in a regional context.

Investment and Competition Policies

Raising the productivity of investment in East Asia requires harnessing the full force of competition inherent in global markets.[30] Lower barriers to international trade and investment can be a powerful pro-competitive force, like in the services sector where investment is one of the major modes for trade in services. The greatest potential for making investment more productive lies in unilateral domestic reforms to remove policy barriers to competition. International agreements on investment and competition can provide benefits through reciprocity. However, most of the remaining restrictions on reciprocal market liberalization and nondiscrimination are in the services sector. Vehicles already exist at both the regional and multilateral (General Agreement on Trade in Services, or GATS) levels for realizing gains potentially arising from service investment commitments.

International agreements that focus on protecting investors cannot be expected to expand markedly the flow of investment to new signatory countries. The bilateral investment treaties of East Asian countries (Figure 11) already contain many protections, and, even though they are relatively strong, these protections do not seem to have increased investment flows to their signatories.

Policy barriers to trade, such as high tariffs or quotas, are the most important restraints on competition. Another restraint on competition is frequent recourse to antidumping and other types of

FIGURE 11   Geographic Distribution of Bilateral Trade Treaties

Many protections for investors are already contained.

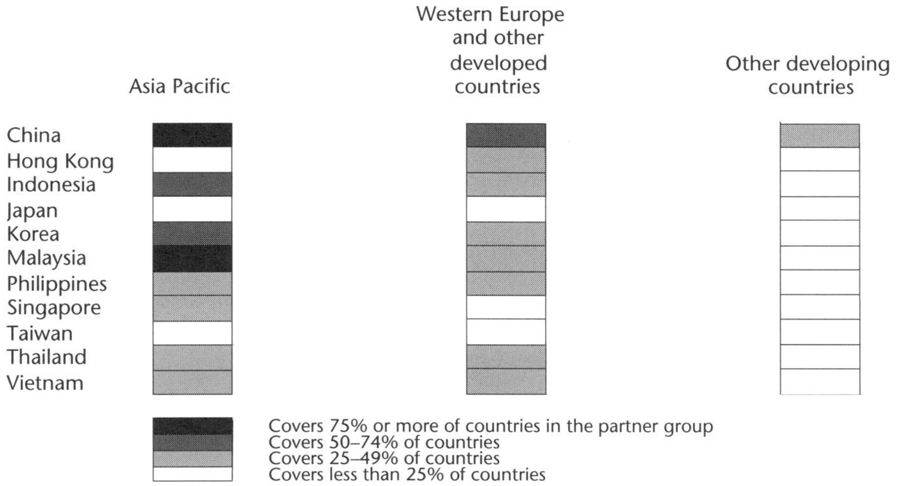

Covers 75% or more of countries in the partner group
Covers 50–74% of countries
Covers 25–49% of countries
Covers less than 25% of countries

Source: Bora (2001).

contingent protection. Antidumping laws were originally created to counteract the predatory practices of foreign sellers into a home market. In practice, more than 90 percent of the antidumping cases investigated would never have been launched if a competition standard—potential threat of injury to competition—had been used as a criterion (Messerlin 2000). Since 1995, more than 1,800 antidumping investigations have been initiated, many of them against East Asian exporters. In 2001 the countries most often subject to investigations included China (53), Korea (19), and Indonesia and Thailand (16 each).

Large international companies with market power can form cartels that fix prices, allocate markets, and restrain competition. The uncovering of several international cartels in the late 1990s has encouraged prosecutions, including by Korea. And there may be further scope for initiatives to discipline international cartels, ranging from extending the reach of industrial nations' anticartel laws to notification and information exchanges by national enforcement authorities to a multilateral agreement.

Intellectual Property Rights: Nurturing Domestic Innovation

Given the recent surge in knowledge-intensive trade and investment flows, intellectual property

rights (IPRs) have become a mainstream topic in global trade discussions. As the subject of the 1995 Trade-Related Aspects of Intellectual Property Rights (TRIPS) agreement, IPRs have in fact become a contentious issue in the WTO, with developing countries concerned that across-the-board upgrading is premature, given their positions as users rather than producers of technological innovations. Much of the debate has focused on the impact of more stringent rights on East Asia as a user of technology created elsewhere, but strengthened IPR regimes also play a role in local technology generation by compensating inventors and creators.

Within the more advanced emerging economies and parts of China, stronger IPR regimes, successfully enforced, could stimulate innovation in technology, as outlined in Chapter 6, provided other conditions are favorable. Korea's dramatic success in patenting may be particularly relevant: The number of Korean patents registered in the United States grew quickly in the late 1990s, propelling Korea to sixth in the U.S. patent ranking, overtaking India, Brazil, and Singapore. Korea's strengthened IPR regime played a role, but so did industrial upgrading, a big push in research and development from the *chaebols* (big company groups), and the government's selective targeting of the semiconductor/electronics industry, where Korea has emerged as a leading innovator worldwide. Given that impending TRIPS-related obligations mandate stronger patent protection, it will be worthwhile for countries to identify complementary policies to boost innovative activity among private firms in their economies.

For a broader range of middle- to low-income East Asian economies, copyrights might offer more scope for gains, given the considerable talents of software developers, musicians, artists, and authors. Indonesia is one example of a country in which there is potential for expansion in copyright-sensitive industries as rights are improved and successfully enforced, particularly for the software industry, small film industry, and investment in artist development by music recording companies.

Traditional knowledge happens to be concentrated in lower-income nations, and its protection is generally expected to have direct benefits for reducing poverty. Often overlooked is the fact that protecting traditional knowledge and genetic resources also promotes efficient innovation in agriculture and biosciences. Yet traditional knowledge needs to be combined with research and development (R&D) activity, which is heavily concentrated in industrial countries, for mutual benefits from derived products. Chapter 6 identifies

some difficult conceptual and practical obstacles that will need to be overcome before substantive progress can be made in protecting or compensating the ownership of traditional knowledge. In East Asia, the Philippines is experimenting in this field with existing and pending legislation.

Environment and Labor Standards

In general, environmental standards and workers' rights are weaker in East Asia than in other parts of the world with similar income levels; indices of environmental sustainability and regulation place East Asia near the bottom, as do indices of labor standards (Figure 12). Many observers have assumed that the region's weak standards play a role in its strong export competitiveness and ability to attract foreign investment. And within the region there is great suspicion that efforts to introduce higher standards in global trade talks are backdoor ways for rich countries to deny new export opportunities to developing countries.

But, in fact, the available evidence does not suggest that stricter environmental and core labor standards would hurt trade. As documented in Chapter 7, econometric evidence contradicts the "pollution haven hypothesis," showing no significant relationship between environmental regula-

FIGURE 12   Environmental and Labor Standards, East Asia

These standards are generally lower in East Asia than predicted by level of income.

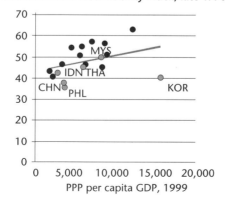

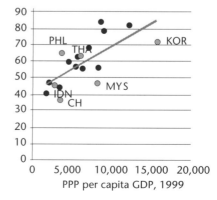

Note: PPP = purchasing power parity.
Source: Esty and Cornelius (2002) and World Bank (2001a).

Sources: Verite (2002) and World Bank (2001a).

tion and exports of pollution-intensive manufactures for East Asia (see Table 7.5 in Chapter 7). Analysis shows that exports and investments in East Asia in the most sensitive sectors (pollution-intensive industries and labor-intensive industries) appear to benefit when standards are raised. The argument is that standards help set transparent "rules of the game," which then promote technological upgrading and skills development from which all parties benefit. Thus the evidence suggests that East Asian countries can raise their environmental standards without adversely affecting their exports and investment inflows.

As for the impact of trade on the environment, evidence suggests that, while trade-induced growth adds to pollution and the output of dirty industries, this effect is outweighed by the demand for a cleaner environment as a country raises its income and acquires better technologies. For example, an analysis of the effects of trade liberalization on water pollution in Chinese provinces during 1987–95—a period in which there was both an extensive pollution levy system and significant opening to trade—illustrates that trade opening was beneficial to the environment overall (Dean 2002).

The links between trade competitiveness and core labor standards are equally complex. As with trade and the environment, causality operates in both directions: Weak labor standards and poor working conditions may influence trade flows and patterns, but labor standards themselves are policies determined by many factors, including openness to trade. Within East Asia, labor standards appear to be strengthening. The number of International Labour Organization (ILO) fundamental ratifications has been increasing, and there is no evidence of backsliding on regulations or legislation. While better labor standards and improved working conditions could raise the costs of labor, workers who are treated better may also respond with more effort and invest in more skills, which could lower costs overall.

Econometric evidence suggests that stronger labor rights are empirically associated with higher export performance in East Asia (see Table 7.3 in Chapter 7). This association is particularly the case for core labor standards, including rights of free association and a ban on child labor. It is therefore likely that East Asian countries could introduce core labor standards, based on social concerns, without undue concern that their export competitiveness will suffer.

Reinforcing Social Stability through Broad Sharing of Benefits

To pursue these trade arrangements and behind-the-border agendas, East Asian policymakers will need a supportive authorizing environment. To be effective, trade policy must be widely perceived as reinforcing social stability and not contributing to further inequalities. Since the economic crisis of 1997–98, many Asian countries have become more democratic and their authorities more broadly accountable for economic policy decisions. Important constituencies question the distribution of benefits that are produced by complex trade negotiations. Evidence on how trade policies affect different groups in society and different countries in the region must be brought into the policy debate more squarely in East Asia. Here it is important not simply to generalize from other countries' experiences; East Asia has specific characteristics that determine the distribution of benefits from trade. This understanding is critical for designing a set of measures that enable the poor and the population more broadly to take fuller advantage of the growth opportunities from trade. As Oxfam noted, "[W]hen trade is harnessed to effective economic policies and positive poverty reduction strategies, it can act as a powerful force for change" (Oxfam 2002).

While progress in poverty reduction has been significant in the region, more needs to be done. Well ahead of schedule, the region has attained the Millennium Development Goal of reducing extreme poverty incidence by half.[31] Even so, roughly 13 percent of the people of emerging East Asia were living on less than $1 a day in 2001. Intercountry differences are wide, with the proportion ranging from virtually zero in Korea and Malaysia to more than 30 percent in Cambodia and Lao PDR. Using the $2.00 a day poverty line, estimates for 2001 range from virtually zero in Korea to more than 75 percent of the population in Cambodia and Lao PDR (World Bank 2003c).

The wide gap between rich and poor countries in East Asia has been responsible for a rise in regional income inequality.[32] The most recent estimate of the Gini coefficient for interpersonal inequality within emerging East Asia is 46, higher than that in high-income countries (40), though lower than that in Latin America (58). Part of the increase has been driven by mildly rising inequality within countries, including China, Vietnam, and the Philippines. But the bulk of the interpersonal inequality within emerging East Asia—70 percent—is driven by inequality across location and across countries (Figure 13).[33] Policies and institutions that contribute to trade and the fuller integration of the low-income countries and regions of East Asia will be critical to addressing income inequality in East Asia and contributing to a stable region.

Impact of Trade Reforms on Households

At the household level, the impacts of the changes induced by specific trade policy reforms are complex. Policymakers need tools to better understand how households will be affected in order to guide their policy sequencing and to help them identify concrete risk-mitigation measures where needed.

One of the more promising approaches is a micro simulation–cum–computable general equilibrium modeling approach that draws on the richness of detail available from a modern integrated household survey to provide a reasonably detailed "map" of predicted welfare impacts by location and socioeconomic characteristics. The authors of Chapter 8 apply this approach to assess who within China will gain from accession to the WTO. They find that, overall, the reduction in tariffs, quantitative restrictions, and export subsidies associated with accession will have only a small immediate impact on mean household income, inequality, and the incidence of poverty. These findings are perhaps not surprising in the case of China, given that the changes in agricultural effective protection are likely to be far lower than others have estimated and that significant changes already have been taking place in the manufacturing sector. Nonetheless, the approach allows policymakers to go beyond averages and aggregates that may hide offsetting impacts across various households and to identify those segments of the population for which the impact may well be more significant. For China,

FIGURE 13 Poverty and Inequality

Although poverty has declined steadily...

...inequality, driven by gaps between countries and locations, is cause for concern.

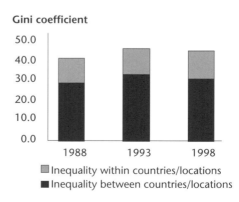

Source: World Bank (2003a).

Note: "Country" is defined such that both China and Indonesia are divided into rural and urban parts.
Source: Milanovic (2003). Based on household survey data.

importantly, all gains accrue to urban households. Meanwhile, rural families in some provinces will suffer income losses (Figure 14). The severest impacts will be felt in the northeast region covering Heilongjiang, Jilin, Liaoning, and Inner Mongolia—a region in which rural households depend more heavily on feed grain production (for which falling prices are expected from WTO accession) than those elsewhere in China. The most vulnerable households are those dependent on agriculture, with relatively fewer workers and weak economic links to the outside economy through migration.[34]

These impact analyses suggest that efforts to encourage labor flexibility are central to protecting households adversely affected by reforms. Workers need skills to be flexible, and they must be allowed to move occupationally and geographically. In some cases, labor market reforms must be carried out in parallel with trade reforms. In China, for example, while there is a considerable degree of labor mobility (as evidenced by the large migrant population), restrictions and impediments remain. With increased labor flexibility, all households—not only urban—can potentially benefit from WTO accession. In Vietnam, expanding the labor market options for vulnerable rural households and urban workers affected by enterprise restructuring will be critical. Impact "mapping" can also be used to guide targeted safety net programs.

Sectors Important to Social Stability: Specific Micro Interventions

In any economy, a handful of sectors tend to be critically important to social stability and the poor. The extent to which poor people, especially poor producers, benefit from expanded trade opportunities depends not only on trade policy but also on complementary measures designed to tackle behind-the-border constraints to efficient production and exports. These measures, among other things, foster the development of competitive markets and public action to provide information, reduce transaction costs (often linked to corruption), call for delivery of public services, and address market and collective action failures. Poor producers are not only economically disadvantaged but often politically powerless, and when their interests are pitted against those of more powerful actors, they frequently lose. It is crucial that anyone designing a set of measures that enables the poor to take fuller advantage of greater access to markets understand the institutional and political economy underpinnings of the organizational structure of a particular commodity or sector.

Chapter 9 applies this approach to rice in Cambodia and Vietnam and cashmere in Mongolia. In Cambodia and Vietnam, as in much of East Asia, most of the poor earn a living by growing rice. In

FIGURE 14   Effects of China's Accession to WTO on Household Incomes

All gains from China WTO accession accrue to urban households.

Some regions suffer rural income losses.

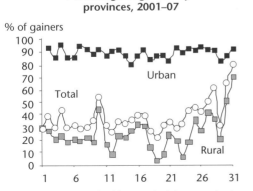

Percentage of gainers by provinces, 2001–07

Net gain or loss as a percentage of income by provinces, 2001–07

Provinces ranked by provincial per capita income

Provinces ranked by provincial per capita income

Source: Chapter 8.

Mongolia, the livestock herding tradition, which is centuries old, provides a livelihood to the bulk of the rural population. Domestic resource cost estimates confirm that these two commodities offer scope for efficient and expanding international trade opportunities. In these economies, the external trade policies for rice and cashmere, by and large, no longer represent important impediments. This situation suggests that policymakers look more deeply into domestic institutions and the value chain domestically to identify the sectoral institutional and policy constraints between the two ends of the supply chains for rice and cashmere that reduce the ability of poor producers to benefit from these expanding trade opportunities.

As presented in Chapter 9, analysis of institutional arrangements along the value chain for these two sectors highlights the considerable impediments that exist both to upgrading the value of rice and cashmere production and to increasing the share of poor producers in the value chains. In all three countries, powerful constituents appropriate rents through explicit preferences (credit for state-owned enterprises in Vietnam, export tax in Mongolia), industrial structure (near monopsony for a few millers in Cambodia), and corrupt practices (illegal fees) that are tolerated while poor producers remain trapped in low-productivity states in the absence of improvements in public service delivery (poor road network, inadequate research and extension, and so forth). Similar forces may be present in many economies, but they are compounded in these three transition economies by the absence of strong market institutions—institutions that are still developing as part of the transition from planned to market economies. According to the analysis, the poor can benefit from expanded opportunities presented by global integration, provided that these constraints are addressed. Giving voice to poor producers' interests by placing these issues on the policy agenda is crucial to fostering reforms that unleash the productivity potential of poor people and increase their bargaining power.

The trading arrangements and behind-the-border agendas just discussed are also critical to ensuring a broad sharing of the benefits from trade in key commodities. Reducing market access barriers in agriculture in developed countries is critical for sectors that are central to social stability, including

agricultural staple crops such as rice. Efforts to relieve transport and logistics constraints in remote areas are an important component of realizing efficiencies along the value chain. Many of the people who have yet to benefit from East Asia's successful trade strategies are located in these more remote areas. As illustrated by the research findings on the effects of China's WTO accession, changes in trade policy alone may have a relatively small impact. Other complementary policies will be essential for benefits to reach the poor more broadly.

Trade and Stability

Employment and earnings stability is another important element in efforts to ensure a supportive authorizing environment for trade. In most of the region's economies, labor is flexible; the adjustment to demand shocks takes place through wages, protecting employment, and spreading the gains or losses over the broad labor force.[35] The East Asia financial crisis and more recent global slowdown have brought concerns about volatility to the forefront. Trade liberalization, it is argued, may have increased the exposure of the economy to more and larger shocks in the tradable goods sectors. If a sector faces larger or more frequent shocks, workers in that sector may experience greater fluctuation in employment or earnings and therefore greater job and earnings insecurity. Adjustment can be costly, with loss in efficiency and displacement of workers. There is particular concern that volatility transmitted via trade liberalization may make workers more vulnerable and that poorer workers might be hurt disproportionately.

The analysis presented here for East Asia suggests that trade liberalization has *not* resulted in increased volatility or vulnerability for wage workers. As outlined in Chapter 10, research in three countries (Korea, Thailand, and Indonesia) examined the relationship among trade, idiosyncratic shocks, and fluctuations in workers' earnings and employment. The first comparison is between periods of different degrees of openness to trade; the second is among industries characterized by different degrees of trade exposure (see Korea in Figure 15). Although the analysis is constrained by data availability, it finds no correlation between greater exposure to trade and greater variability in earnings or employment. Indeed, worker cohorts experienced lower year-to-year fluctuations in their earnings during the 1990s—characterized by fewer trade barriers—than in the previous decade. There is some evidence that employment is more volatile in trade-intensive industries; at the onset of the East Asia financial crisis, employment fluctuated more widely in the more trade-intensive industries than in the less trade-intensive industries. However, employment in these industries recovered rapidly, with few long-term adverse impacts.

The analysis does find a clear relationship between vulnerability and workers' educational level and gender. Workers who have little education and those who are female are much more likely to fall into poverty. In Indonesia, for example, the pro-

portion of unskilled workers falling from high-paying jobs into low-paying jobs was two to three times that of skilled workers. Thus, while trade openness makes an important contribution to growth and does not worsen vulnerability, policies to reduce the vulnerability of workers must also focus on broadening education and developing skills.

Conclusions

East Asia is emerging from the financial and currency crises of 1997–98 with a new perspective on development. East Asian policymakers are turning to the region as well as to the rest of the world to develop a coherent set of economic policies that

FIGURE 15 Trade and Stability in Labor Markets, Republic of Korea

No higher earnings volatility is evident in periods of greater openness.

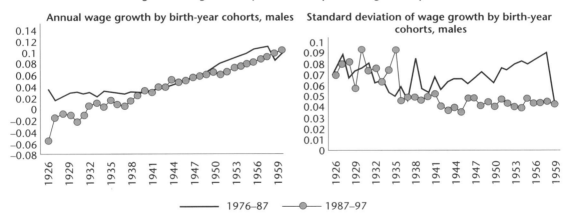

Nor is higher earning volatility evident in sectors more exposed to trade.

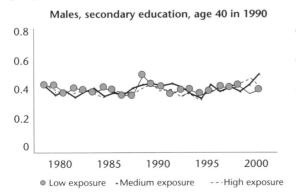

Source: Kim (2002).

can deliver stability, growth, and regional integration. This volume does not try to be comprehensive, but focuses on fundamental strategies that promote cross-border flows of trade, along with domestic policies to maximize the impact of these flows on development and distribute the gains from trade widely.

Several bilateral, regional, and multilateral initiatives have been advanced to pursue this strategic agenda. But to succeed, these initiatives must have two features. First, they must provide a compelling vision of how integration can deliver broadly shared growth and prosperity. There are concerns in Asia that a narrowly focused approach to globalization, like that found in the 1980s and early 1990s, has worsened the income distribution within countries and widened the gap between the richer and poorer countries of the region. Even though the evidence may not support such concerns, the new initiatives must move beyond the perspective of trade policy to broader approaches that emphasize the links between trade and social stability and the coherence with overall development, stability, and growth. For this reason, the chapters in this volume contain several studies of the impacts of integration on poorer countries and on vulnerable groups within countries.

Second, as initiatives for integration move beyond the narrow confines of trade policy, they must deal increasingly with second-best issues and trade-offs, including in areas once treated as sensitive. For example, policymakers must balance user rights and incentives for innovation in deciding on an intellectual property rights regime; decide where to allocate scarce resources to reduce logistics costs and improve competitiveness; introduce appropriate environmental and labor standards; and expand liberalization into services and agriculture.

An empirical approach is required to guide countries on the priorities in these areas; after all, East Asian countries are diverse and each has a different set of priorities. The empirical estimates of the potential gains are often substantial, amounting to hundreds of billions of dollars for the priority areas identified in the rest of this section. It is clearly worthwhile for policymakers to devote major effort to get the reforms right. The chapters in this volume suggest some broadly applicable priority areas for action, as described in the following list.

- *Broadening agreements to include agriculture and services.* China's approach to agricultural trade liberalization offers scope for the region, especially Southeast Asia, to benefit significantly.[36] China will emerge as a major importer of agricultural and natural resource–intensive commodities. If agriculture can be liberalized in a regional setting, as in the proposed ASEAN-China free trade agreement, then a favorable political dynamic can be set in place that will lead to more open agricultural sectors overall. As for the region's agricultural exports to the developed world, all countries need to improve their ability to meet sanitary and phytosanitary standards through better laboratories, standards, and negotiation of mutual recognition agreements, and rich countries need to reduce the degree of cascading tariffs in agricultural processing and move toward the imposition of transparent ad valorem tariffs. For ASEAN countries in particular, the inclusion of agriculture in global and regional trade agreements is important—potential welfare gains can be roughly doubled.

Several international studies[37] suggest that the gains from liberalizing services could be very substantial—the same order of magnitude as that for liberalizing trade in manufactured goods and agriculture. This is an area in which East Asia has lagged behind other developing regions. The imperative for moving ahead with services liberalization is stronger because of the emergence of China as a low-wage, efficient manufacturer. Other countries in the region will find it very difficult to compete in international markets on the basis of wages alone. Instead, they must rely on better producer services to enhance their competitiveness. Improved services will permit them to participate in regional production networks that offer prospects for maximum efficiency.

- *Improving logistics and trade facilitation.* East Asia's progress on logistics has failed to keep pace with its growth in trade. Logistics costs in many parts of East Asia are high, and logistics industries are underdeveloped. Logistics plays a critical role both in determining aggregate levels of trade and in ensuring that development benefits spread beyond coastal regions. For East Asia's less open and accessible countries and regions, the development of more tightly integrated domestic markets and logistics systems is a high priority. Complementary institutional actions are needed not only ·to promote an appropriate mix of transport modes, but also to extend better transport services to remote areas and establish better conditions for market development. Beyond strengthening physical infrastructure, governments also need to undertake improvements in the regulatory environment and in the conditions for cross-border facilitation. Customs clearances deserve special attention; addressing corruption has been highlighted as an issue in several countries.

- *Institutional strengthening to safeguard and benefit the poor.* The fear that globalization has increased volatility seems to be misplaced. Available evidence for East Asia suggests that greater openness to trade does not make workers more vulnerable; indeed, greater openness has in fact stabilized wage incomes and employment across all skill categories. That said, women workers and workers with little education are noticeably more vulnerable than others to falling into poverty, emphasizing the need for policies to broaden education and develop skills. To ensure that the poor within countries benefit from openness, policies are also needed to support workers' geographic and occupational mobility, as are specific actions to reduce transport and marketing costs in order to improve farm gate prices for the products on which the poor rely.

Beyond these immediate priorities, several other findings are highlighted in this volume:

- *Easing adjustment in labor-intensive industries.* Certain sectors in East Asia, especially the garment sector, are likely to be seriously affected by expanded output and exports from China. The region's more developed economies will be able to shift out of garment-making into higher value added industries, and today's presence of current account surpluses implies that the external adjustment will be manageable. For other countries, supply chain analysis suggests that there is scope for greatly improving competitiveness in the garment and other manufacturing industries by improving logistics and reducing the costs of corruption.

- *Framing policies on intellectual property rights.* Intellectual property rights are a part of the multilateral framework for trade. Strong protection of intellectual property rights encourages innovation, but it is not a magic bullet; other conditions, including investments in skills and provision of a competitive business environment, are also needed. Several of the region's more advanced countries, and parts of China, can hope to stimulate technological advances if they better protect intellectual property and pay more attention to competition policy (Yusuf and others 2003). Stronger copyright laws, provided they can be enforced, may yield some significant gains for domestic software industries as well as the arts and music sectors. As for traditional knowledge, some important conceptual and practical problems need to be sorted out before progress can be made in protecting its ownership and linking traditional knowledge issues to WTO agreements or other mechanisms for managing research and development.

- *Reconsidering environmental and labor standards.* There is no evidence from East Asia to support the argument that improved environmental and core labor standards would unfairly affect manufacturing competitiveness. Indeed, the evidence suggests that East Asian countries can raise their environmental and core labor standards without adversely affecting their exports and investment inflows. The fierce resistance of many in the region to considering these issues in line with broader development strategies may be misplaced.

This rich agenda suggests scope for East Asian countries to build on the international commitment to a new development round of trade negotiations based on the Doha Development Agenda, and on their own commitment to deepening regional economic ties. Countries must operate on three levels. Internationally, they can influence the negotiations, and, in doing so, they should pay particular attention to standards and to liberalization in agroindustries and services. Regionally and bilaterally, they can achieve deeper integration, which offers prospects for gains in sensitive sectors (although with due care to use these agreements to further multilateral liberalization). Nationally, countries need to take a more comprehensive approach to policy than before, moving beyond narrow trade and industry interests focused on protecting specific manufacturing subsectors to adopt a strategy with sectoral components that are aligned to encourage integration and competition as means of delivering growth, stability, and poverty reduction.

Endnotes

1. Emerging East Asia is defined here as the Association of Southeast Asian Nations (ASEAN), plus other newly industrializing economies, China, and Mongolia. ASEAN members are Brunei Darussalam, Cambodia, Indonesia, Lao People's Democratic Republic, Malaysia, Myanmar, the Philippines, Singapore, Thailand, and Vietnam.
2. This figure is not much less than the 7.7 percent share of global trade among the North American economies when the North American Free Trade Agreement went into force in 1994.
3. $2.15 per day in 1993 PPP$. See World Bank (2003c). All other dollar amounts are current U.S. dollars.
4. East Asia is perhaps the most diverse region in the world. The income per capita, in purchasing power terms, of Singapore, for example, is 25 times that of Lao PDR, and the gap between the two in institutional capacity to manage development may be even greater.
5. See World Bank (2000) for a first assessment of the new policy and institutional agenda.
6. China is widely seen as having contributed to stability in 1997–98 by maintaining a stable exchange rate in the face of major devaluations of other currencies. Few scholars give credence to the notion that competition from China was the cause of the Asian crisis.
7. The ratio of China's GDP to that of the rest of emerging East Asia was 1:2 in 1996 and 1:1 in 2002.
8. China's share of East Asian exports has grown significantly over the last decade—from 10 to 20 percent for Singapore, Korea, and Taiwan (China), and from 2 to 5 percent for ASEAN countries.
9. Exceptions were Singapore, Cambodia, and Brunei.
10. The trade complementarity index measures how well the export profile of one country matches the import profile of another. The index is zero when no good exported by one country is imported by the other, and 100 when the export-import profiles exactly match. Higher index values indicate more favorable prospects for a successful trade arrangement between countries. The index stands at more than 60 for emerging East Asia. By contrast, indices for previous failed trade arrangements ranged from values of 7 to 22. See Ng and Yeats (2003).
11. During the crisis, real exchange rate depreciation also played a role in reducing protectionist tensions. Nonetheless, the dangers of protectionism and of vested interests capturing political support in specific cases should not be underestimated.
12. China's domestic market is the largest of these, but recent trends show Korea, Thailand, and other economies growing on the strength of domestic consumption demand.
13. Assessments of the impact of WTO accession on China's agricultural sector based on limited comparisons of statutory tariffs and the rates agreed on in the accession process would be

misleading. Recent research reveals that overall protection for crops such as rice, wheat, and maize is far less than indicated by statutory tariff rates (Huang and Rozelle 2002).
14. The decision contrasts with the costly and wasteful path to ever higher protection followed by previous high-growth East Asian economies.
15. The positive impact on the automobile sector is a relatively new finding from François and Spinanger (2002), as discussed in Chapters 1 and 2.
16. See François and Spinanger (2002). The agreement requires the elimination of quotas by January 2005.
17. The situation also highlights the importance of improving this area of WTO rules.
18. The number of sectors with guaranteed unrestricted access is still lower in China than in most other countries for cross-border trade and consumption abroad (modes 1 and 2) and essentially zero for establishment trade (mode 3).
19. Trade intensity is the degree to which the value of trade between two countries conforms to expectations that are based on the partners' relative importance in world trade. It is computed as the ratio of the share of country i's exports going to country j (x_{ij}/X_{it}, where x_{ij} and X_{it} are the values of i's exports to j's and i's total exports) relative to the share of world trade destined for country j (x_{wj}/X_{wt}, where x_{wj} and X_w are the values of the world's exports to j and the world's total exports). An index of more than unity indicates that bilateral trade is larger than expected given the partner country's importance in world trade.
20. See Schiff and Winters (2003) for a discussion of regionalism from the perspective of developing countries more broadly.
21. Nonmembers may be net losers, though Table 1 suggests these losses may be minimal. Nonetheless, consistency with the WTO could be questioned, and such arrangements could be subject to challenge in the WTO.
22. See results in Hoekman and Konan (1999) for the European Union and Egypt and in Brenton and Manchin (2002) for the European Union and Russia.
23. See Ianchovichina and Walmsley (2002) for China.
24. See Kalima and Krumm (2002), which draws on a combination of labor market surveys, World Bank income distribution data, and computable general equilibrium (CGE) modeling results.
25. World Bank (2002c). Real income gains for Korea and developing East Asia are estimated for 2015 at $11 billion, assuming fixed productivity, and $32 billion with endogenous productivity, excluding production subsidies, compared with baseline income. Static gains are slightly less, including production subsidies, but dynamic gains would increase to $76 billion. China would capture one-third of static gains and two-thirds of dynamic gains.
26. The direct impact of domestic support programs is of less relevance to East Asia because this support is concentrated in products that are not of crucial importance to East Asia developing countries, with the exception of rice. Products such as fruits, vegetables, and spices together account for only 7 percent of the developed countries' total domestic support payments.
27. Many nonreciprocal preference schemes have had a low rate of uptake by developing countries, including those in East Asia, in large part because of stringent rules of origin. For example, Cambodia made use of only 36 percent of its entitlement under the EU's Everything but Arms initiative in 2001 (Brenton 2003a).

28. For example, by Codex Alimentarius, the Organization for Animal Health, the International Organization for Epizootics, or the Hazard Analysis Critical Control Point (HACCP). In Malaysia, the Ministry of Health operates a voluntary certification program for private firms in the food processing sector. This program was introduced in 1996–97 in response to EU requirements for HACCP in fish processing plants.

29. See Mattoo, Rathindran, and Subramanian (2001).

30. The discussion in this section is based on World Bank (2003b).

31. On the basis of a higher poverty line of $2.00 per day, two-thirds of the population was poor in 1990; this has declined to about two-fifths today (Figure 14).

32. The Gini coefficient for interpersonal inequality in emerging East Asia was estimated at 42.0 in 1988 and 46.8 in 1993.

33. The Gini coefficient of income inequality (G) can be decomposed into a within-country inequality component and a between-country inequality component ($G = S\, G_i\, p_i\, p_i + S\, S\, [(y_j - y_i\,)/\, y_i]\, p_i\, p_j +$ residual). The within-country component refers to the weighted sum of within-country inequalities, where each country's (i-th) inequality is represented by its own Gini coefficient (G_i), and the weight is given by the product of the country's share in the world's population (p_i) and the country's share in world income (p_i). The between-country component is derived such that all countries are ranked by their mean income (from poorest to the richest) and the relative distance between countries' mean incomes $[(y_j - y_i\,)/\, y_i]$ is weighted by the product of the poorer country's share in world population (p_j) and the richer country's share in world income (p_i).

    This situation contrasts with the one in Latin America, where the bulk of inequality reflects differences within countries, and only 19 Gini points are attributable to between-country differences. For East Asia, the definition of country is such that both China and Indonesia are divided into rural and urban areas.

34. A similar approach assessed the impact of the ASEAN Free Trade Area and the U.S. bilateral agreement on aggregative Vietnam household groupings—see Centre for International Economics (2002). That analysis suggests that the benefits are spread across the income deciles and across rural and urban areas. However, the poorest rural deciles benefit the least, and individual households could experience vulnerabilities.

35. The most severe test of this occurred during the Asian economic crisis. Except in Korea, unemployment in the crisis countries was kept to manageable levels; most of the adjustment fell on wages.

36. As noted earlier, the adjustments in China's agricultural sector resulting from WTO accession may be smaller than some other analysts suggest, because China's current practices are already more liberal than implied by statutory rates.

37. See Yusuf and others (2003) on producer services.

References

The word *processed* describes informally reproduced works that may not be commonly available through libraries.

Bora, Bijit. 2001. "Prospects for Harmonizing Investment Policies in the East Asian Region." Draft prepared for the World Bank. UNCTAD, Geneva.

Brenton, Paul. 2003a. "Integrating the Least Developed Countries into the World Trading System: The Current Impact of EU Preferences under Everything But Arms." Policy Research Working Paper. World Bank, Washington, D.C. Forthcoming, *Journal of World Trade*.

———. 2003b. "Notes on Rules of Origin with Implications for Regional Integration in South East Asia." World Bank, Washington, D.C. Processed.

Brenton, P., and M. Manchin. 2002. "Trade in Services, Foreign Direct Investment and Technology Transfer: Implications of an EU-Russia Free Trade Agreement for Economic Efficiency and Growth." Report prepared for the European Commission. Processed.

Carruthers, Robin, and Jitendra N. Bajpai. 2002. "Trends in Trade and Logistics: An East Asian Perspective." Working Paper No. 2. World Bank, Transport Sector Unit, Washington, D.C.

Centre for International Economics. 2002. "Integration and Poverty: An Economy-Wide Analysis." Draft prepared for the World Bank. Canberra and Sydney, November.

Dean, Judith M. 2002. "Does Trade Liberalization Harm the Environment? A New Test." *Canadian Journal of Economics* 35 (4): 819–42.

Esty, Daniel C., and Peter K. Cornelius. 2002. *Environmental Performance Measurement: The Global Report 2001–2002*. Oxford: Oxford University Press.

Fink, Carsten, Aaditya Mattoo, and Ileana Cristina Neagu. Forthcoming. "Assessing the Impact of Communication on Trade." Policy Research Working Paper. World Bank, Washington, D.C.

Fink, Carsten, Aaditya Mattoo, and Randeep Rathindran. 2002. "Liberalizing Basic Telecommunications: The Asian Experience." HWWA-Institut fur Wirtschaftsforschung Discussion Paper 63.

François, Joseph F., and Den Spinanger. 2002. "Market Access in Textiles and Clothing." Prepared for Conference on Informing the Doha Process: New Trade Research for Developing Countries, Cairo, May.

Hallward-Driemeier, Mary, Giuseppe Iarossi, and Kenneth L. Sokoloff. 2002. "Export and Manufacturing Productivity in East Asia: A Comparative Analysis with Firm-Level Data." NBER Working Paper No. W8894. National Bureau of Economic Research, Cambridge, Mass.

Hoekman, Bernard, and Denise Eby Konan. 1999. "Deep Integration, Nondiscrimination, and Euro-Mediterranean Free Trade CEPR." Policy Research Working Paper 2130. World Bank, Washington, D.C.

Huang, J., and S. Rozelle. 2002. "The Nature of Distortions to Agricultural Incentives in China and Implications of WTO Accession." Paper presented at Seminar on WTO Accession, Policy Reform and Poverty Reduction in China, World Bank, Beijing, June 28–29.

Ianchovichina, Elena, and William Martin. 2001. "Trade Liberalization in China's Accession to the World Trade Organization." *Journal of Economic Integrations* 16 (4): 421–45.

———. 2002. "Economic Impacts of China's Accession to the WTO." Paper presented at Seminar on WTO Accession, Policy Reform and Poverty Reduction in China, World Bank, Beijing, June 28–29.

Ianchovichina, Elena, and Terrie Walmsley. 2002. "Regional Impact of China's Accession." World Bank, Washington, D.C. Processed.

IMF (International Monetary Fund). Various years. *Direction of Trade Statistics*. Washington, D.C.

Janet Tay Consultants. 2002. "Facilitating Trade: The East Asian Experience in a Comparative Context." World Bank, Washington, D.C., May. Processed.

Kalima, Blandina, and Kathie Krumm. 2002. "Delays in Implementation of Agreement on Textiles and Clothing: Poverty Impact in East Asia." World Bank, Washington, D.C., August. Processed.

Kawai, Masahiro, and Shujiro Urata. 2002. "Trade and Foreign Direct Investment in East Asia." Paper presented to Conference on Linkages in East Asia: Implications for Currency Regimes and Policy Dialogue, Seoul, September.

Kim, Dae Il. 2002. "Openness and Worker Vulnerability in Korea: A Descriptive Study." World Bank, Washington, D.C. Processed.

Lall, Sanjaya. 1998. "Exports of Manufactures by Developing Countries: Emerging Patterns of Trade and Location." *Oxford Review of Economic Policy* 14: 54–74.

Lardy, Nicholas. 2002. *Integrating China into Global Economy.* Washington, D.C.: Brookings Institution Press.

Mattoo, Aaditya, Randeep Rathindran, and Arvind Subramanian. 2001. "Measuring Trade Liberalization and Its Impact on Economic Growth: An Illustration." World Bank, Washington, D.C. Processed.

Messerlin, Patrick. 2000. *Measuring the Costs of Protection in Europe.* Washington, D.C.: Institute for International Economics.

Milanovic, Branko. 2003. "Worlds Apart: International and World Inequality, 1950–2000." World Bank, Washington, D.C. Processed.

Ng, F., and A. Yeats. 2003. "Major Trade Trends in East Asia: What Are Their Implications for Regional Cooperation and Growth?" Policy Research Working Paper 3084. World Bank, Washington, D.C.

Otsuki, Tsunehiro, and John S. Wilson. 2001. "Global Trade and Food Safety: Winners and Losers in a Fragmented System." Working Paper 2689. World Bank, Washington, D.C.

———. 2002. "Beef Trade and Veterinary Drug Standards." World Bank, Washington, D.C. Processed.

Oxfam. 2002. *Rigged Rules and Double Standards: Trade, Globalization, and the Fight against Poverty.* Oxford: Oxfam.

Schiff, Maurice, and L. Alan Winters. 2003. *Regional Integration and Development.* Oxford: Oxford University Press.

Schmidhuber, J. 2001. "Changes in China's Agricultural Trade Policy Regime: Impacts on Agricultural Production, Con-

sumption, Prices, and Trade." In *OECD, China's Agriculture in the International Trading System, OECD Proceedings.* April.

Scollay, Robert, and John Gilbert. 2001. *New Subregional Trading Arrangements in the Asia-Pacific.* Washington, D.C.: Institute for International Economics.

———. 2003. "Impact of East Asian Regional or Subregional FTAs." Report for Australian Department of Foreign Affairs and Trade. May.

Verite. 2002. "Report to California Public Employees' Retirement System (CalPERS): Emerging Markets Research Project." Available at verite@verite.org.

Wilson, John, Catherine Mann, Yuen Pau Woo, Nizar Assanie, and Inbom Choi. 2002. "Trade Facilitation: A Development Perspective in the Asia Pacific Region." World Bank working paper presented to APEC. World Bank, Washington, D.C. Processed.

World Bank. 2000. *East Asia Regional Overview: Recovery and Beyond.* Washington, D.C.

———. 2001a. *Indonesia: "Environment and Natural Resource Management in a Time of Transition."* Washington, D.C.

———. 2001b. *Cambodia Integrated Framework.* Washington, D.C.

———. 2002a. *East Asia Regional Overview: Making Progress in Uncertain Times.* Washington, D.C. November.

———. 2002b: "Trends, Issues and a Glimpse of the Future." East Asia Regional Office Mimeo. Washington, D.C.

———. 2002c. *Global Economic Prospects, and Developing Countries: Making Trade Work for the Poor.* Washington, D.C.

———. 2003a. *Vietnam's Exports: Challenges and Opportunities.* Washington, D.C.

———. 2003b. *Global Economic Prospects and Developing Countries: Investing to Unlock Global Opportunities.* Washington, D.C.

———. 2003c. *East Asia Regional Overview. East Asia Navigates Short-Term Shocks for a Stronger Future.* Washington, D.C. Available at: www.worldbank.org/eap/eapnsf.

Yusuf, Shahid, with M. Anjum Altaf, Barry Eichengreen, Sudarshan Gooptu, Kaoru Nabeshima, Charles Kenny, Dwight H. Perkins, and Marc Shotten. 2003. *Innovative East Asia: The Future of Growth.* Washington, D.C: World Bank and Oxford University Press.

PART I

WIDENING
OPPORTUNITIES
IN TRADE
ARRANGEMENTS

1

CHINA'S ACCESSION TO THE WTO: IMPACTS ON CHINA

William J. Martin
Deepak Bhattasali
Shantong Li

One of the great milestones for economic reform in China, and for the world trading system, was the accession of China to the World Trade Organization (WTO) in December 2001. China's accession will have an enormous impact on both China and the world trading system (Martin and Ianchovichina 2001).

Other developing countries will feel the impact of China's WTO accession through four main channels:

1. Expansion of markets in China for exports
2. Increases in the supply of exports into others' markets
3. Competition in third-country markets
4. Expansion of investment in China and, potentially, outward foreign investment from China.

Understanding how these linkages will play out requires a good understanding of how WTO accession will affect China itself and, particularly, of how policy might develop in the many areas of reform that go beyond the specific commitments in China's WTO accession package. Many excellent studies have been conducted of aspects of the impact of WTO accession on China, including symposia in the *China Quarterly* (see Fewsmith 2001) and *China Economic Review* (see Chun, Fleisher, and Parker 2001); surveys of the estimated impacts of trade liberalization (see McKibbin and Tang 2000; Gilbert and Wahl 2002); and studies of the impact of WTO on China and vice versa (Martin and Ianchovichina 2001). This chapter builds on a large integrated study—undertaken by China's Development Research Centre of the State Council and the World Bank—that examines the legal aspects of accession; estimates the impacts of the resulting policy changes on the overall economy; and then assesses impacts on poverty and policy options for dealing with these problems.[1]

There are many perspectives on China's accession to the WTO. According to one view, which focuses on legal rights and responsibilities, China's key challenges are to meet its legal commitments to implement particular policies and to ensure that its rights are maintained through WTO mechanisms such as its dispute settlement mechanism. Another, purely economic, view is that accession involves a

This chapter draws on a program of research presented in further detail in Bhattasali, Li, and Martin (forthcoming). The research benefited from the support of UK Department for International Development. Particular thanks are due to Ippei Yamazawa and Shujiro Urata for their comments at a seminar held at the World Bank office in Tokyo.

set of economic policy changes that will open up China's economy and make it much more engaged in the global economy. The most compelling perspective is the one that sees WTO accession as a component of the broader set of reforms that China has undertaken since 1978—that is, as a set of policies that can contribute to development and poverty reduction.

WTO rules are important ingredients in formulating good policies for development, but they do not constitute a complete recipe. Like most other laws, their intent is to reduce the adverse impacts of the actions of one individual or group on another rather than to guide a country on the best way to achieve its goals. Many WTO agreements allow a great deal of choice within the range of legally permissible policy options. Within the framework of its WTO commitments, China may choose to pursue its development goals either aggressively or quite tentatively.[2]

In seeking to understand the implications of China's accession to the WTO, we examine the nature of the policy changes associated with accession; the implications of these policy changes for the Chinese economy at large and for individual households; and the complementary policies needed to take advantage of the opportunities created by accession and to minimize the adjustment costs.

Policy Reforms Associated with Accession

The five basic principles of the General Agreement on Tariffs and Trade (GATT) and the WTO provide a useful framework for analyzing the implications of China's accession. These principles are: (1) nondiscrimination (the most-favored-nation [MFN] principle, under which the best market access given to any one Member is extended to all other Members); (2) market opening; (3) transparency and predictability; (4) undistorted trade; and (5) preferential treatment for developing countries.[3]

Nondiscrimination

The general principle of nondiscrimination requires WTO Members to give equal treatment to competing suppliers and not to discriminate between domestically produced and imported goods or services in their internal markets. In

China's case, the application of this general principle has involved some additional commitments, including eliminating dual pricing systems, phasing out restrictions on trading, and introducing more uniform administrative arrangements and judicial review. These agreements are of crucial importance not just for the central authorities but also for the lower tiers of government, which are often involved in internal trade and regulation.

Market Opening

The market opening principle is reflected in commitments by China to abolish nontariff barriers, reduce tariffs, and open its service sectors; in commitments by countries importing from China to abolish the quotas on textiles and clothing that were originally imposed under the Multi-fiber Arrangement (MFA); and in commitments by the United States and other countries to impose MFN tariffs on China.

The cuts in import tariffs that China has offered are very substantial, and will result in a reduction in the weighted average tariff from 12 percent in 2001 to 6.8 percent at the end of China's WTO implementation period.[4] But these reductions are small compared with the reduction of 29 percentage points that China achieved between 1992 and 2001. China's commitments to liberalize trade in services are extremely large relative to those of almost all other countries, although they are more often subject to qualifications or reservations than those of other countries.

China's trading partners, for their part, have made an important "concession" in abolishing the quotas that were imposed under the MFA. The abolishment of these quotas is likely to provide significant opportunities for China to increase its exports of textiles and clothing, given its strong comparative advantage in these goods, although the effects will be tempered if the importers exercise their right to impose special textile and clothing safeguards for a year at a time during a transition period up to 2007.

Another important "concession" by almost all existing members of the WTO is to refrain from invoking nonapplication provisions of the type that were widely invoked against Japan when it joined the GATT. Even though this concession does not involve much actual market opening, it means that

China now receives permanent MFN status in virtually all markets. Having this status frees China from onerous one-sided review procedures, such as the former annual review of China's MFN status in the United States, and it assures investors in China's export industries that foreign markets will be available to them on a continuing basis.

Transparency and Predictability

The transparency and predictability of trade policy are enhanced both through general WTO policy rules, such as the need to publish trade rules and regulations, and through specific commitments China has made, including provisions for uniform application of the trade regime and for independent judicial review. China has also put in place a mechanism whereby concerned parties can bring problems of local protectionism to the attention of the central government. Another important contributing factor is China's binding of its entire tariff schedule for goods, almost always at tariff levels below previous applied rates. This binding not only reduces tariffs and their variance, but also increases predictability by ruling out tariff increases in the future. The annual transitional reviews to be held for eight years after China's accession will provide additional information about China's regime and its reforms during that period. Also important for increasing transparency are China's commitments to phase out restrictions on trading rights for all products, except for a short list of commodities that may remain subject to state trading, and to allow the entry of foreign, and frequently domestic, suppliers into distribution and wholesale services.

The emphasis on transparency, and the specific requirements to this effect, may help to avoid costly and acrimonious disputes of the kind that marred trade relations between Japan and (in particular) the United States during Japan's era of high export growth.

Undistorted Trade

The WTO principle of undistorted trade involves general disciplines in areas such as subsidies and countervailing measures, antidumping, and safeguards. China has made more stringent commitments than those normally required, including one not to subsidize its agricultural exports, and, for industrial goods, disciplines on some forms of export subsidies generally allowed in developing countries.

The existing regime of antidumping and safeguard measures has troubling implications for China's access to export markets. The WTO rules against dumping are biased toward finding dumping even where no economically meaningful dumping exists (Messerlin 2002). The situation is worse for China than for other WTO Members, because 70 percent of China's exports are in products that are most vulnerable to antidumping measures. Furthermore, China could remain vulnerable, for up to 15 years, to highly discriminatory provisions that are applied to nonmarket economies and dramatically increase the probability of dumping being found. When antidumping duties are applied under these provisions, they are generally much higher than the duties applied to market economies. For example, the average 40 percent duty applied by the United States against nonmarket economies was more than 10 times higher than that applied where the margin was calculated based on actual costs.

A particularly worrying feature of China's accession agreement is the product-specific transitional safeguard provisions. These provisions may be applied by any WTO Member, and may then trigger actions against the diversion of Chinese exports to other markets (Panitchpakdi and Clifford 2002). They are, in a sense, worse than the provisions on nonmarket economy treatment in that they introduce an entirely new form of protection, targeted specifically against China; they are more readily triggered than regular safeguards; and they are available to China's trading partners for up to 12 years from the date of China's accession (Anderson and Lau 2001). The trade diversion measures allowed under these provisions are particularly troubling, because they provide even less procedural protection than is available under regular safeguards.

Proposals to use the product-specific safeguards against China's exports of textiles and clothing have already surfaced in the United States, despite the continuing presence of quotas originally imposed under the Multi-fiber Arrangement. If the product-specific safeguards are invoked and other countries do not resist the temptation to use the trade diversion measures, there is a risk of a domino effect: China's exports would be diverted to fewer and fewer markets, and China would increasingly be tempted to retaliate against what it would almost certainly see as unfair barriers against its exports. For example, China might increase its use of antidumping actions and contest the safeguard actions through the WTO's dispute settlement mechanism, or it might mount a concerted campaign for reform of the rules in the Doha negotiations, particularly in the area of antidumping (Messerlin 2002). Whatever the case, the result could be serious damage to both China and the trading system.

Clearly, China will need to contest unjustified actions and seek settlement of disputes. But retaliation that involves launching antidumping actions is likely to be extremely costly to its economy, both by reversing the liberalization process and by increasing the uncertainty about trade policy. Even though retaliation is likely to be politically attractive (as confirmed by the recent upsurge in antidumping actions in China—and the dramatic upsurge in these actions by developing countries such as Argentina, India, Mexico, and South Africa), the economic costs to China in particular suggest that it should be avoided as much as possible.

If China chooses instead to lead a push for reform of the antidumping and safeguard rules to reduce the abuses of these protectionist measures, it could greatly improve the performance of its own economy in the short run and that of the global trading system in the longer run. Messerlin (2002) suggests two courses of action. First, related to its treatment as a nonmarket economy, China could press for new rules on the automatic granting of market economy status in a particular commodity, applicable as long as a country meets basic conditions such as low rates of protection, an absence of serious nontariff barriers, and an absence of state monopoly in the distribution of that commodity. Second, as for antidumping measures more generally, China could put forward, or strongly support, proposals to narrow the use of antidumping measures and to reduce their severity. China might also seek similar relief on the product-specific safeguards. The abuse of antidumping policies by the major trading countries and by a growing number of developing countries is a problem for most of the other economies of East Asia, and China could surely strengthen the coalitions formed at the WTO to push for stronger rules against this abuse.

Preferential Treatment for Developing Countries

Preferential treatment was a particularly vexing issue throughout the negotiations. Although China has a much lower per capita income than many economies in the WTO that are classified as developing, its size and growth performance made existing WTO Members reluctant to accord it full developing country treatment. In many areas of the agreement, China is likely to have full access to the developing country provisions, but in particular cases it faces tighter restrictions than other developing countries.[5] At the same time, China has obtained specific transitional arrangements in areas such as the phasing out of quotas and licenses and phased entry of foreign enterprises—areas that are not generally available to developing country members. Because special treatment in the form of preferential access to industrial country markets is not important for China, it has a strong interest in reducing the trade barriers in industrial countries in the only way it is able—through multilateral trade reform that lowers protection in the industrial countries, particularly on labor-intensive products such as textiles, clothing, and footwear in which China has a strong comparative advantage.

Intellectual Property Rights

The Agreement on Trade-Related Aspects of Intellectual Property Rights, or TRIPS, which is an integral part of the WTO, involves a number of GATT principles such as nondiscrimination and seeks to achieve a balance between offering incentives for innovation and allowing broad access to information. An intellectual property regime appropriate to a developed country may be much too rigorous for a developing country; such a regime may inhibit growth by limiting innovation and diffusion and result in excessive transfers to foreign producers of intellectual property. But all countries require regulations to ensure that markets remain competitive without excessively reducing the incentive to innovate. The TRIPS agreement is generally seen as providing the flexibility needed to design such a regime, but implementation will not be easy.

For China, the TRIPS agreement is a key aspect of WTO accession. Recognizing the need to stimulate innovation domestically and gain access to foreign technology and responding to pressure from its trading partners, China has strengthened its intellectual property rights (IPR) regime. Since 1990, China has updated its laws on copyrights, trademarks, patents, and trade secrets and adopted protection for new plant varieties and integrated circuits. These changes are particularly important for China's East Asian neighbors, many of whom are engaged in intellectual property–intensive activities in China.

China's intellectual property rights regime is broadly appropriate to China's situation.[6] In particular, Maskus (2002) believes that China's policy of public procurement of pharmaceuticals at negotiated prices is appropriate for providing public health services. He also concludes that, with current reforms, the regime will be fully consistent with the TRIPS requirements.

However, Maskus raises some important issues about TRIPS policies and their implementation in China. One concerns proposals to extend patent protection to computer software, giving a level of protection currently provided only in the United States, Japan, and Australia that is perhaps excessive for a young industry such as China's. Serious problems in enforcing trademarks, patents, and trade secrets in particular could inhibit the transfer of technology in China and the development of innovative domestic businesses. For China, with its current low allocation of resources to research and development, laws protecting domestic innovations are of limited benefit. Key issues for the future include enhancing pricing regulations on pharmaceuticals as patent protection becomes stronger and developing a broader competition policy regime to deal with abuses of IPRs such as monopoly pricing and restrictive licensing arrangements.

Sectoral Impacts of Accession

To evaluate the impacts of changes in China's trade policy arising from WTO accession, we first assessed the policy stance prior to accession and then traced the implications of the policy measures being introduced. This section describes the evidence on agriculture, manufacturing, and services in turn.

Agriculture

Many authors have raised concerns about the impact of WTO accession on China's agriculture and the many poor people engaged in this sector. Much of the concern has arisen from comparisons of China's statutory tariffs on agriculture in the 1990s with the rates agreed on in the accession process (see, for example, Schmidhuber 2001). But other authors have pointed out that the statutory tariff rates bore little relationship to the actual protection (or taxation) that China's agricultural sector experienced (see, for example, Johnson 2000 and Lin 2000).

The evidence on the actual rates of protection applying to agriculture is still extremely limited and often contradictory. Agricultural trade in China has been influenced by a bewildering array of policies on imports and exports, including state trading, designated trading, quotas, licenses, tariffs, and tariff-rate quotas. Many studies have tried to deal with this problem by summarizing the protective impact of agricultural trade policies in terms of the price distortions created by these measures. The more restrictive the trade measure, in general, the larger will be the distortion—that is, the gap between the domestic price and the international price.

Several studies have estimated the size of the agricultural distortions using the available series on domestic and international prices. Unfortunately, the results obtained have varied widely.[7] And while Carter (2000) and Martin (2001) felt that WTO accession would require relatively little liberalization in China, Schmidhuber (2001) and many others believed that dramatic changes would be needed. Clearly, a new approach was required, especially because the policy consequences are so large.

Huang and Rozelle (2002) adopted a new approach by basing their analysis of policy impacts on detailed interviews with participants in China's agricultural markets rather than on available price series. Their approach provides a much clearer indication of the implications of agricultural trade policies for product prices and of the real-world impacts of policies. They show, for example, that a major source of the discrepancies in earlier research is differences in quality between domestic products and those traded internationally. They also identify features of the trade regime, such as export subsidies on maize and cotton, that have important impacts on product markets.

What then do China's accession commitments imply for agricultural markets? For those products protected by ad valorem tariffs, the implications are straightforward. A reduction in the tariff indicates directly the reduction in the domestic price of the good, and this change, together with information on the slope of the import demand curve, can be used to estimate the cost of protection. For those products protected by both a tariff and an export subsidy, it may be necessary to consider changes in both variables. For products that are being protected, or are to be protected, using tariff-rate quotas, the analysis becomes much more complex. For them, the impact of a tariff reduction depends greatly on whether it is the within-quota or the out-of-quota tariff that determines the price of the good. And where the quota will be filled in some years but not in others, the average rate of protection may be a combination of the two tariff rates.

Table 1.1 shows some key assessments of the implications of the level of protection and the changes associated with WTO accession. The statutory tariff rates for 1998 used by Schmidhuber (2001) and others are given in the first column; the estimates by Huang and Rozelle (2002) of protection in 2001 are given in the second. The third column shows the anticipated average rates of protection after accession, taking into account the reforms required by accession and likely market outcomes.

For rice, wheat, and maize, the adjustments required by WTO accession will be much smaller than those suggested by analyses based on the statutory rates of protection. For rice, Huang and Rozelle (2002) estimate that the average rate of protection was slightly negative before accession, implying that China's system of state trading for rice operated in a

way in which rice exports were taxed slightly in 2001. After accession, the rate of protection is expected to remain the same, because accession to WTO does not require reductions in negative protection that is administered by state trading or an export tax. For wheat, protection averaged an estimated 12 percent before accession—much lower than would be suggested by simple price comparisons. After accession, this rate of protection need not be greatly reduced on average, because it seems likely that wheat imports will exceed the tariff-rate quota reasonably often (Martin 2001), allowing the imposition of a tariff of up to 65 percent. For maize, the rate of protection before accession was higher, at 32 percent, because of an export subsidy. After accession, the level of import protection need not change greatly on average, because there is a significant probability that the tariff-rate quota will bind by the end of the decade (Martin 2001). But the maize export subsidy must be abolished, implying a potentially substantial reduction in the price support given to maize.

Oilseeds present a different case. Here, the principal form of protection has been a tariff, and the tariff is being reduced substantially. For sugar, the protection provided must be halved to meet China's commitments to a bound tariff of 20 percent. On cotton, import protection will not change greatly, but export subsidies such as the 10 percent export subsidy observed in 2001 are ruled out in the future. For livestock and meat, protection could remain negative as a consequence of export restrictions to markets such as Hong Kong (China). Protection of dairy products can be expected to decline

TABLE 1.1   Some Measures of Import Protection in China's Agriculture (percent)

	1998 statutory tariffs	2001 actual protection	Postaccession protection
Rice	127	−3.3	−3.3
Wheat	133	12.0	12.0
Maize	130	32.0	32.0
Vegetables and fruits	15	−4.0	−4.0
Oilseeds	132	20.0	3.0
Sugar	30	40.0	20.0
Cotton	3	17.0	20.0
Livestock and meat	35	−15.0	−15.0
Dairy	46	30.0	11.0

Source: Average statutory rates taken from Schmidhuber (2001) and www.chinavista.com. See Huang and Rozelle (2002) for estimates of protection.

to meet China's tariff-binding commitments.

The reductions in protection shown in Table 1.1 (also Figure 4 of the Overview) are just one set of possible outcomes in a situation in which rates of agricultural protection can vary substantially, particularly if import levels exceed the tariff-rate quotas. However, the reductions show that China's policymakers will still be able to exercise significant discretion after accession.

Removing the negative protection from labor-intensive products would be consistent with WTO rules and is likely to be particularly beneficial for employment in rural areas, as well as for economic efficiency. By taking part in the WTO agricultural negotiations being conducted under the Doha Development Agenda, China could potentially reinforce these benefits by opening large, and currently highly protected, markets for its labor-intensive agricultural exports. Unfortunately, the high rates of agricultural protection that arose when GATT rules on agriculture were extremely weak mean that China faces barriers to its agricultural exports that are four times as high as those it faces on its other merchandise exports (Martin 2001).

China's accession to the WTO with relatively low tariff bindings on agricultural products prevents it from following the path of ever-increasing agricultural protection that other high-growth East Asian economies have followed (Anderson and others 1986). Even China's highest tariff bindings, of 65 percent, provide only one-tenth of the protection currently observed for wheat and rice in Japan (Martin 2002). Given China's size, this situation is extremely important for world agricultural markets; had China gone down the road of Japan, the world market for rice and other agricultural commodities would be permanently depressed.

China's commitment to a low-protection agricultural regime will greatly reduce the costs of achieving successful economic development. Moreover, it will force future policymakers to focus on policies such as improvements in rural education and reductions in barriers to labor mobility that will deal effectively with the problems of rural poverty in China—rather than resort to commodity price distortions, which serve, at best, as a short-term, palliative measure.

China's agricultural trade commitments throw into stark contrast the costly and inefficient regimes in neighboring economies (OECD 2002a) and

increase the pressure for their reform. Looking ahead, China is unlikely to be satisfied if traders such as Japan and the Republic of Korea are allowed to maintain agricultural protection rates much higher than its own. The increasing openness of China's market for agricultural products will create much bigger markets for land-intensive products such as rice from some East Asian countries, and for specialty, high-quality products from almost all countries. But strong policy efforts by China and other agricultural exporters in the current WTO negotiations will be required to expand market access in the current highly protected agricultural markets.

China will clearly have a strong interest in expanding its access to export markets for its labor-intensive agricultural products. Particularly for perishable products such as fruits and vegetables, many of the logical markets are in East Asia. It is vitally important that China's trading partners provide opportunities for China to expand its exports of these products, which are so important for creating employment for relatively poor rural people. Analysis by Yu and Frandsen (2002) suggests that agricultural liberalization by member countries of the Organisation for Economic Co-operation and Development (OECD) would benefit China and improve its agricultural trade balance. China's rights as a WTO Member at least give it an opportunity to insist that adequate procedures be followed and to limit the duration of measures such as safeguards. It would be particularly unfortunate if China's trading partners resorted to the use of standards as a means of restricting access. Such measures are not transparent and are divisive in nature.

If China elects to remove its negative protection from key commodities such as rice, vegetables, and meats, Anderson, Huang, and Ianchovichina (2002) estimate that the returns to unskilled rural labor and to farmland would rise slightly, so that the overall impact of the accession on rural wages would be –0.5 percent instead of –0.7 percent. If, on the other hand, the in-quota tariff rates were uniformly applied, then the returns to farm factors would deteriorate by about the same amount.

Industrial Products

Most of the adjustment needed in industrial tariffs has already occurred, and what remains are an expansion in both imports and exports and a likely painful restructuring of some key industries.

China substantially reduced its tariffs on manufactures during the 1990s: weighted average tariffs on manufactures fell from 46.5 percent in 1992 to 25 percent in 1995 and to around 13 percent by the time of accession in 2001. With full implementation of China's accession commitments, these tariffs will fall to 6.9 percent. The 6 percent reduction in average tariffs that remains to be implemented is important, but small relative to the 33 percent reduction since 1992 or the 12 percent reduction since 1995 (Ianchovichina and Martin 2002).

The largest reductions in industrial tariffs are now required in beverages and tobacco (a 28 percent reduction from 2001 levels) and in automobiles (a 15 percent reduction from 2001 levels)—see Table 1.2. While large, these reductions are much smaller than those already undertaken since 1995. The reduction in protection to the automobile sector is particularly important given the high profile of this industry and its linkages throughout the economy (see the next section on motor vehicles).

Other industries in which substantial reductions in tariffs will be needed include textiles, clothing, electronics, and light manufactures. Many of these industries are relatively labor-intensive ones in which China has a comparative advantage and in which liberalization will help to maintain efficiency and competitiveness.

The new tariff concessions in manufacturing will provide enormous opportunities for expanding trade in both final goods and production inputs between China and its regional neighbors. China's imports will grow because of the reductions in protection, and exports will expand because of induced drops in production costs in China.

Industry in China will face substantial adjustment pressures in key products such as automobiles, beverages, and tobacco, where external protection is being substantially reduced. Restructuring of scale-intensive industries such as the motor vehicle will be essential and can generate substantial productivity gains.

Ianchovichina and Martin (2002) estimate that China's imports of merchandise will rise by 17 percent on average as a result of the WTO-induced tariff reductions after 2001, with particularly large increases in products such as beverages and tobacco (112 percent). Much of the benefit is likely to accrue to China's neighbors in East Asia.

Motor Vehicles. In the absence of reform and restructuring, China's output of motor vehicles would likely drop sharply in the postaccession years, notwithstanding strong increases in domestic demand and the shift in China's comparative advantage to more capital- and skill-intensive products such as motor vehicles (Francois 2002). China's auto industry has been shaped by protective policies that have encouraged inefficient production and allowed for market segmentation; indeed, most plants are operating well below global standards for efficient production. Development of a healthy and internationally competitive industry will require consider-

TABLE 1.2 Protection of Industrial Sectors in China (percent)

	1995	2001	Postaccession
Processed food	20.1	26.2	9.9
Beverages and tobacco	137.2	43.2	15.6
Extractive industries	3.4	1.0	0.6
Textiles	56.0	21.6	8.9
Apparel	76.1	23.7	14.9
Light manufactures	32.3	12.3	8.4
Petrochemicals	20.2	12.8	7.1
Metals	17.4	8.9	5.7
Automobiles	123.1	28.9	13.8
Electronics	24.4	10.3	2.3
Other manufactures	22.0	12.9	6.6
Total manufactures	25.3	13.5	6.9

Source: Ianchovichina and Martin (2002).

able restructuring of this industry (Harwit 2001). We estimate that restructuring in the motor vehicle industry to achieve scale economies in final assembly could reduce production costs by about 20 percent (Francois 2002). Such restructuring would more than reverse the negative impact on output of the reduction in protection from 1997 levels, and would allow the industry to expand dramatically as China's growth and shifting comparative advantage shift resources into sectors such as motor vehicles. If the industry is restructured successfully, exports of finished motor vehicles would increase rapidly, resulting in an increase in total exports of vehicles and parts of more than US$4 billion a year.[8] Increases in the efficiency of the final assembly industry relative to the production of intermediate parts are likely to increase the demand for imported parts substantially, with their share of total parts rising from 39 percent to 52 percent.

Clearly, profound adjustments are in store throughout the auto industry. Considerable painful restructuring, such as the closure of inefficient plants in many cities, will be required. However, there seems to be no alternative if China is to move to an efficient and internationally competitive motor vehicle sector.

Policy Concerns. What are the likely effects of the large reductions in the barriers facing China's exports of textiles and clothing to Europe, the United States, Canada, and Norway? Because these barriers are implemented through export quotas—that is, an exporter is required to purchase an export quota, or to forgo the opportunity to sell quotas it has been allocated by the government—they impose a cost on exports that is analogous to an export tax. Based on detailed information on quota prices, this tax is estimated to be around 15 percent for clothing and 10 percent for textiles (see www.chinaquota.com). For particular products, the export tax equivalent of these measures is much higher.

The analysis by Ianchovichina and Martin (2002) focuses largely on tariffs (given the great uncertainty about the protective impacts of nontariff barriers such as designated trading, quotas, and licenses in China, and their limited remaining coverage[9]), although it also considers the export quotas on textiles and clothing. Omission of the effects of removing nontariff barriers means that the results give something of a lower-bound estimate of the

benefits of the liberalization associated with accession, and they downplay some important actual and potential elements of trade policy.

A key omission of the analysis is the possibility that antidumping and safeguard measures might be applied against China. Another is the increasing use of measures of this type by China. The introduction of the product-specific safeguards against China is particularly important in this respect because no such measure specifically targeted China before China's accession. The risk that China will increase its use of antidumping and safeguard measures beyond the currently high levels is also of concern for development policy. Such an action would be a triumph of a rules-focused approach to WTO implementation—"it is legal therefore, we should do it!"—over the sharp focus on development that has characterized China's trade reform agenda since the beginning of the reform era.

Services

Trade in services was a key area in China's WTO accession negotiations, and China's commitments represent perhaps the most thoroughgoing liberalization of the services trade ever undertaken in the WTO (Mattoo 2002). Its range of offers is extremely broad, although some commitments involve restrictions on ownership, business scope, or region. Critical sectors such as telecommunications, logistics, and finance are going to face renewed competition and are likely to see a burst of innovation and productivity growth as they are restructured. Many middle-income developing countries, such as Thailand, that have experience in dealing with these problems are likely to find substantial market opportunities.

An important feature of China's commitments is that they focus on market access and do not discriminate between domestic and foreign suppliers. However, China's commitments are carefully crafted: in cross-border trade and in services consumed abroad, the number of sectors with guaranteed unrestricted access is smaller than in most other countries, and in establishment trade it is essentially zero.

Restrictions on Service Activities. Restrictions on the form of business establishments, such as requirements for joint ventures, business scope, and geographic scope, have a long history in China, and have often been justified as a means to acquire technology or obtain a share of monopoly rents. As Mattoo (2002) points out, rules requiring businesses to form joint ventures may in fact inhibit the transfer of technology. A more thoroughgoing approach to the problem of monopoly rents would ensure that competition between firms, whether domestic or foreign, would eliminate these rents.

Many restrictions on the geographic scope of service suppliers, such as restrictions on the cities that can be served by insurance companies, date from an era when it was believed that experimentation with market-oriented approaches needed to be isolated because of the inconsistencies between, for example, planned and market prices. There seems to be much less need for such policies now that the operation of market economies is so much better understood in China. Restrictions such as those in the WTO agreement that confine foreign ventures to five cities for five years—insurance is one example—might encourage agglomeration of these activities in the favored cities, and that agglomeration will not be reversed when the restrictions are subsequently lifted. This situation may reduce the opportunities for other parts of China, such as interior cities with a potential comparative advantage in these activities, to get started in these activities.

There appear to be good developmental reasons for China to phase out its geographic restrictions more quickly than required by the WTO commitments, given the risks of exacerbating the already substantial inequalities between coastal and interior provinces. China's commitments do not prevent the authorities from moving ahead faster than required, as they have done frequently in the past.

Regulations on services may have various goals, including making competition work, improving the availability of information to consumers, and ensuring universal service. Making competition work is particularly important in network industries such as telecommunications, where the dominant incumbent firms frequently do not find it in their interests to allow new firms to interconnect to their networks. Improving the availability of information is particularly important in financial services, where lenders often do not have enough information on the prospects and repayment capacity of borrowers. Developing efficient provisions on universal service is important for ensuring

that all parts of China have access to telecommunications services.

Logistics. China's WTO commitments on logistics involve a range of General Agreement on Trade in Services (GATS) service sectors, including packaging and courier services, maritime and rail transport, freight forwarding, and storage and warehousing services. Logistics costs are disproportionately high in China, and service quality is lower than desirable, in part an enduring legacy of the planned economy (Findlay and Luo 2002). Logistics-related costs are widely seen as accounting for up to 30–40 percent of the wholesale costs of manufactured goods in China, as against 5–20 percent in the United States (see Findlay and Luo 2002 and Tanzer 2001). High logistics costs are a particularly important problem for people in the poorer parts of China. Their ability to trade and, consequently, their real incomes are significantly reduced by these excessive costs. China has committed itself to increasing competition in some key areas, including road transport, rail transport, warehousing, and freight forwarding. The breadth of these commitments also provides a much stronger basis for development of integrated third-party[10] logistics firms able to reduce the costs and increase the quality of logistics services in China.

China has made substantial progress toward meeting its commitments on logistics services. Findlay and Luo (2002) believe that the costs of a wide range of goods and services might be reduced by about 10 percent from current levels—a huge savings that would raise incomes substantially in China, increase opportunities for exports to China, and strengthen China's competitiveness in export markets.

Achieving the full potential of logistics in China will require not just freer trade but also regulatory reforms—to remove discrimination against particular types of enterprises, to separate local administrations from enterprises, and to eliminate local protectionism. In addition, substantial investments in infrastructure will be needed to improve the timeliness, and reduce the cost, of providing logistics services.

Telecommunications. China's commitments in telecommunications take on particular importance given that China is expected to be the largest market for telecommunications in the world by 2010

(Pangestu and Mrongowius 2002). These commitments allow foreign entry to a wide range of activities currently closed to foreign investment. Furthermore, this entry takes place in a sector that was monopolized by China Telecom until 1994 and is currently dominated by a small number of state-owned firms.

In basic telecommunications, China has committed to the disciplines of the WTO reference paper on the regulatory framework for telecommunications (WTO 1996). These disciplines aim to ensure a competitive environment that allows interconnection between systems under reasonable and nondiscriminatory conditions and that allows for universal service provisions. They also require the existence of a regulator independent of the telecom provider and set criteria for licensing of entry and allocation of scarce commodities such as the mobile telephone spectrum.

In the context of a basic telecommunications system governed by the WTO regulatory framework, China's other GATS commitments cover value added services such as voice mail and online information services; mobile voice and data services; and domestic and international services such as private leased circuit services. Most of these services are initially subject to a combination of ownership restrictions and geographic restrictions within China. Although the geographic restrictions will be phased out over several years, China has not committed to allowing more than 49 percent foreign ownership in important areas such as mobile telephone service. Allowing higher levels of foreign ownership would, of course, be consistent with China's GATS obligations.

Allowing the telecommunications sector to make its maximum contribution to China's development will require further reforms of the regulatory framework. Important issues will include ensuring the independence of the regulator, ensuring that interconnection works adequately, and making pricing regulations more flexible.

Financial Services. China's WTO commitments on financial services call for radical changes in the structure of the system. This was a remarkable outcome given that, prior to accession, China's financial sector was widely regarded as being far from ready for a major increase in competition from abroad.

The size of the Chinese financial market was significant, with deposits at banks reaching 150 per-

cent of the gross domestic product (GDP) in 2001, and China's securities market was the second largest in Asia, with a market capitalization approaching 45 percent of GDP. However, four large state banks accounted for 67 percent of deposits and 56 percent of total financial assets. A key problem in the financial sector was insolvency and a lack of profitability in the four big state banks, with more than a quarter of outstanding loans nonperforming. Although there have been improvements, these banks were widely regarded as having limited ability to make lending decisions based on repayment ability and credit risk. Furthermore, the administered spreads between deposit and lending rates were very narrow, reducing the profitability of the banks and their incentives to lend to many dynamic areas of the economy. Many foreign banks were active in China, but they accounted for less than 3 percent of assets and only 0.1 percent of deposits.

China's accession commitments allowed foreign banks to enter the foreign currency business immediately, the local currency business for enterprises after two years, and the local currency business for all clients after five years. In the securities markets, foreign securities were allowed immediate entry into trading in foreign currency–denominated securities and entry within three years to joint ventures trading in domestic shares. Insurance firms were allowed immediate entry into reinsurance and life insurance and entry after two years into health insurance, pension insurance, and annuities.

The objective of these radical reform commitments appears to have been the vital one of bringing about technical innovation that will reduce the cost of financial services and help to stimulate growth. It seems clear that considerable further reform, and probably some re-capitalization of the state banks, will be required if this goal is to be achieved without the collapse of the state banks or a broader financial crisis.

Impacts of Reforms on the Economy

Because the reforms undertaken by China in response to WTO accession are broad-ranging and their economy-wide interactions extensive, it is important to evaluate these reforms on an economy-wide basis. They need to be seen in the context of the dramatic changes already under way in

China's industrial structure, output, and trade patterns related to more capital- and skill-intensive goods—changes made in response to changes in demand for China's exports, high rates of investment, and rapid growth in educational levels.

Ianchovichina and Martin (2002) have analyzed the impacts of liberalization associated with WTO accession in agriculture, manufactures, and services.[11] For this analysis, they use a special variant of the Global Trade Analysis Project (GTAP) model (Hertel 1997), developed to take into account the importance to China of duty exemptions for inputs into export production (see Ianchovichina 2003). In this model, liberalization of trade reduces the costs of imports and the costs of production for the domestic market by reducing the costs of inputs and the costs of production of all types through reductions in the prices of nontraded goods and factors. The second type of cost reduction is frequently termed a real exchange rate depreciation.[12] Ianchovichina and Martin (2002) divide the impacts of

accession into two components: those associated with the liberalization undertaken between 1995 and 2001 in preparation for accession and those stemming from the liberalization to be undertaken after 2001 to meet China's accession commitments.[13]

Exports

The liberalization associated with WTO accession will speed the growth in China's trade relative to output. The total volume of exports is projected to rise by 17 percent as a consequence of the liberalization after 2001 (Table 1.3).

The fastest-growing exports are clothing, which are projected to double after 2001 in response to the abolishment of the export quotas on clothing. Exports of most agricultural products will also rise, reflecting the decline in input costs to agriculture and in the persistent difficulties workers face in migrating out of agriculture. Exports of plant-based fibers (predominantly cotton) are projected

TABLE 1.3   Impacts of Reduction in Protection Required by WTO Accession from 2001 Tariff Levels, China

	Output (%)	Employment (%)	Exports (%)	Imports (%)	Trade balance (millions of US$)
Rice	−2.1	−2.3	6.1	−7.1	64
Wheat	−2.0	−2.3	18.9	−10.1	174
Feed grains	−2.3	−2.6	−77.8	−2.4	−596
Vegetables and fruits	−3.4	−3.7	14.6	−6.3	214
Oilseeds	−7.9	−8.4	29.8	20.9	−789
Sugar	−6.5	−7.4	13.9	24.1	−73
Plant-based fibers	15.8	16.4	−51.8	7.7	−189
Livestock and meat	1.3	1.1	15.5	−8.9	837
Dairy	−2.0	−2.4	13.5	23.8	−143
Other food	−5.9	−6.4	11.4	62.6	−3,460
Beverages and tobacco	−33.0	−33.1	9.7	112.4	−14,222
Extractive industries	−1.0	−1.3	7.5	−4.4	2,088
Textiles	15.6	15.5	32.7	38.5	−10,366
Apparel	57.3	56.1	105.8	30.9	49,690
Light manufacturing	3.7	3.7	5.9	6.8	1,786
Petrochemical industry	−2.3	−2.3	3.1	11.8	−8,810
Metals	−2.1	−2.1	3.7	6.8	−1,893
Autos	1.4	−2.2	27.7	24.0	516
Electronics	0.6	0.4	6.7	6.8	453
Other manufactures	−2.1	−2.2	4.1	18.9	−11,291
Total	1.0	0	16.8	17.3	717

Source: Ianchovichina and Martin (2002).

to fall, reflecting the increased demand for cotton in the export production of textiles and clothing and the abolishment of export subsidies. Feed grain exports will also fall, because of abolishment of the export subsidy on exports of maize. Exports of automobiles will rise substantially, because auto production becomes more efficient as it exploits economies of scale and becomes more exposed to international competition

None of these projected increases in exports takes into account the possible benefits to China of being able to expand its market access through participation in WTO market accession negotiations, such as those currently under way as part of the Doha Development Agenda. The expansion in textile and clothing exports is, in fact, a delayed benefit from the Uruguay Round, previously denied to China as a nonmember of the WTO.

Imports

China's imports are projected to rise in a range of sectors in which trade barriers have been substantially reduced—including beverages and tobacco, processed food, textiles, clothing, oilseeds, dairy products, and sugar. Imports of beverages and tobacco will rise the most because of the sharp reductions in tariffs on these commodities. Imports of services are also projected to rise substantially, because trade liberalization in services is expected to reduce import barriers.

Employment

The projected movements of labor between sectors are generally quite small relative to the changes in trade patterns. The biggest postaccession change in employment is likely to be in clothing, with a rise of more than 50 percent after 2001. Employment in the textile sector and in plant fibers used in textile production will also rise to meet the demand from the clothing sector. Trade reform will lead to small reductions in employment in most agricultural sectors and in manufacturing sectors such as petrochemicals, metals, and automobiles.

Welfare Gains

Trade liberalization is a source of substantial overall welfare gains for China. The liberalization undertaken between 1995 and 2001 is estimated to yield a continuing gain of $30 billion a year. The smaller reduction in protection between 2001 and the end of the implementation period will generate a smaller gain of $10 billion a year.[14]

As for the distribution of the projected gains, the wages of skilled and unskilled urban workers will rise modestly, and the wages of unskilled farm workers will decline by 0.7 percent in real terms. The distribution of gains is examined further in the next section.

Effects of WTO Accession at the Household Level

The simplest approach to capturing the effects of WTO accession at the household level requires an assessment of the changes in the prices consumers pay; the changes in the prices that owners of labor, capital, and other factors receive for their resources; and the effects of accession on the government's ability to provide transfers or public goods. In addition, it is useful to assess the ability of households to adjust to the changes resulting from accession, perhaps by changing their activities.

Effects on Rural and Urban Households

Because ongoing work on trade and poverty has found that impacts felt through factor markets are consistently more important than impacts felt through consumer prices, it is certainly worthwhile to examine the impacts of trade liberalization on factor markets. This is particularly the case in China, with its large income differences between urban and rural workers and explicit policy barriers to the movement of labor between urban and rural sectors.

China's labor markets are affected adversely by a range of regulations that restrict the movement of workers from rural to urban areas. These include the *hukou* system of residence permits, which regulates movement between urban and rural employment. Another inhibiting feature is the restrictions on the sale of farmland usage rights. The effect of these rights is that farm families that move permanently out of agriculture may have to relinquish their land rights without compensation.

The earnings of rural and urban households differ substantially, even for households with labor of the same skill level (Sicular and Zhao 2002). The large barriers that exist between urban and rural labor markets, particularly for poorer households, depress income levels and make it more difficult for workers to respond to changes in economic opportunities. Even so, the barriers are not absolute: for labor supplied to nonagricultural activities by rural households, elasticities of supply with respect to wage rate differentials are on the order of two for unskilled workers and closer to three for skilled workers (Sicular and Zhao 2002).

Shi Xinzheng (2002) has examined the substantial differences between the earnings of urban and rural households and the extent to which these differences are caused by the formal barriers between China's urban and rural labor markets. Only between 30 and 40 percent of the total difference between rural and urban wage rates can be explained by the *hukou* policy. However, this policy component of the gap, which is a fundamentally important building block for assessments of the implications of liberalization, is difficult to estimate precisely.

A key political concern throughout the implementation period is likely to be the impacts of accession on the formerly favored workers in state-owned enterprises. These enterprises are experiencing greater competition from imports as a result of abolishment of the barriers that formerly discouraged competition from foreign firms in the domestic market.

Effects on Poverty

From a poverty perspective, it seems likely that the central issues of concern will be in rural areas. Poverty is most prevalent in the rural areas of China, and rural workers face barriers in moving into the sectors that are likely to expand as a result of China's ongoing growth and liberalization. Two studies evaluate the impacts of China's trade liberalization on poverty, and both find that the rural sector is more vulnerable than the urban sector to this reform.

In Chapter 8 of this volume, Chen and Ravallion consider the impact of WTO accession on income distribution and poverty.[15] They find a sharp contrast between the experience of urban and rural households. Most urban households, and particularly those who are relatively poor, gain from WTO accession. This is not the case for rural households, the poorest of which experience noticeable reductions in their living standards. These reductions

reflect a combination of falling rural wages and increases in the prices of goods consumed by these households.

Hertel, Zhai, and Wang (2002) also provide important insights into the impacts of trade reform on poverty.[16] Because of limitations on the availability of household data, they focus on Liaoning, Sichuan, and Guangdong, three relatively diverse provinces. Their scenario for agricultural tariffs is similar to that in the Ianchovichina and Martin (2002) study, but focuses on an agricultural policy determined by the tariff-rate quotas. In aggregate, their conclusions are much more optimistic than those of Chen and Ravallion in Chapter 8, showing virtually all households benefiting from trade reform. However, their results suggest that inequality worsens after accession: urban households benefit substantially more than rural households, and rural households with diverse income sources benefit more than those that depend only on farming.

The results of these quantitative analyses are highly stylized, because they assume that enterprises and households adjust successfully to the changes in incentives that are created by WTO accession. As OECD (2002b) has pointed out, to make these changes successfully China will have to strengthen its economic system in areas such as enterprise governance and reform of the banking system.

The vulnerability of the rural sector to trade reform arises from restrictions on the movement of labor out of agriculture when returns fall. These restrictions inhibit the adjustment needed after accession and increase the vulnerability of poor people to downturns in agricultural prices. Reform of these restrictions has now become urgent, because the partial liberalization of agriculture is increasing the pressures on workers to leave agriculture.

Hertel, Zhai, and Wang (2002) consider the implications of two key complementary policies that might be used to deal with the problems of poverty in rural areas: (1) reducing the barriers to mobility of rural labor into nonagricultural employment, and (2) improving the availability of education in rural areas. They conclude that reductions in the barriers to mobility of labor out of agriculture would be an important antidote to the increases in inequality between rural and urban sectors experienced after accession, with diversified rural households becoming the largest gainers from a policy package combining WTO accession with reductions in the barriers to rural labor mobility. And over the longer term there is another potentially important source of gains to the rural sector: China will have an opportunity to press for greater market access for its labor-intensive exports.

Expansion of educational opportunities could also have powerful beneficial effects in helping unskilled workers in both urban and rural areas (Hertel, Zhai, and Wang 2002; Ianchovichina and Martin 2002). And improvements in agricultural technology would potentially yield large benefits to poor rural households that are able to adopt the new production techniques (Ianchovichina and Martin 2002).

Social Protection

China's network of social protection measures is still quite underdeveloped, with a stark dichotomy between urban and rural systems, a focus on reducing absolute poverty, and a high degree of decentralization in financing. The system in urban areas is relatively comprehensive, but that in rural areas is seriously deficient. In many areas "the social safety net is full of holes" (Hussain 2002).

China's social welfare measures are likely to remain partial in coverage and are not a viable tool for large-scale poverty reduction. Even so, particular attention needs to be given to strengthening basic safety nets for rural residents. Here, a feasible first step might be to extend a mechanism like the urban unemployment insurance schemes to wage employees in township and village enterprises.

Conclusions

China's WTO accession agreement provides a comprehensive road map for many aspects of reform in China's trade regime. In particular, it calls for substantially reducing protection, for strengthening the protection of intellectual property rights, and for adopting a framework of trade rules at home and abroad. However, the agreement is not all-inclusive, and China needs to keep a strong focus on its development needs, maintaining the perspective that has guided the steady transformation of its trade regime and economy, generally, from planned to market.

A central concern in the accession agreement is the provisions on antidumping and safeguards. The

nonmarket economy provisions that countries are permitted to invoke against China for up to 15 years are likely to result in the imposition of antidumping duties substantially higher than those invoked against other countries—and in a situation in which China faces seven times as many antidumping actions per dollar of exports as the United States. The product-specific transitional safeguard provisions, applicable for the next 12 years against China alone, are a new form of protection. The associated provisions on trade diversion lack even basic procedural restraints and pose a potentially serious threat to China's export development. China may be tempted to retaliate, particularly with antidumping actions of its own, but retaliation would damage China more than its trading partners. A better option would be to seek reform of the WTO rules in these areas.

Our analysis suggests that agriculture is being liberalized less than was suggested by some earlier studies that began with the assumption that agricultural tariffs were being reduced from their statutory levels. However, significant liberalization has occurred in areas such as maize, cotton, and sugar, and it appears that there will be significant adjustment pressures in these industries. Yet opportunities will emerge to expand exports of some labor-intensive exports as part of a broader policy reform and by seeking increases in agricultural market access in the Doha negotiations.

The industrial sector will face substantial adjustment pressures in key sectors such as automobiles, beverages, and tobacco, where external protection is being substantially reduced. Restructuring of scale-intensive sectors such as the automobile sector will be essential, and it can generate substantial productivity gains. Overall, however, most of the adjustment in this industry has already occurred, and what remains involves an expansion in both imports and exports.

China's GATS commitments represent perhaps the most thorough-going liberalization of services trade ever undertaken in the GATT. Its range of offers is extremely broad, although some commitments involve restrictions on ownership, business scope, or region. Critical sectors such as telecommunications, logistics, and the financial sector will confront renewed competition, and they are likely to see a burst of innovation and productivity growth as they are restructured.

China's labor markets are affected adversely by a range of regulations, such as the *hukou* system of residence permits regulating movement between urban and rural employment. This system, and related labor market policies, inhibit the adjustment needed after accession and increase the vulnerability of poor people to downturns in agricultural prices. Other features of the labor market, such as the "tie" to the land where households have use rights to land but cannot sell it because property rights are not sufficiently well defined, restrict the mobility of labor out of agriculture.

The two studies described in this chapter of the impacts of trade reform on poverty both find that the rural sector is more vulnerable to this reform than is the urban population. One study concludes that WTO accession is generally beneficial to urban households but that most rural households lose in the short run. The other study provides a more upbeat picture, but one in which rural households are more subject to negative shocks such as those resulting from reductions in protection on some agricultural commodities. A major conclusion is that the key to mitigating these problems is reforms such as reduction of barriers to the movement of labor out of agriculture and investment in rural education.

The network of social protection measures in China is quite underdeveloped and a constraint on China's ability to grow while dealing with widely held concerns about the need to compensate the potential "losers" from the policy reforms. Policymakers should pay particular attention to strengthening the social welfare systems available to rural residents.

The dramatic increases in China's imports and exports associated with its accession create enormous opportunities for China's trading partners to benefit, both as suppliers of exports to this rapidly growing market and as beneficiaries of lower-priced and higher-quality imports. In addition, many countries with similar ranges of exports will face greater competition in third-country markets for many products, particularly textiles and clothing, where the removal of quotas in 2005 will lift an enormous burden from China's exporters.

Endnotes

1. See www.worldbank.org/trade for those studies and more detailed references to the literature.

2. For example, tariffs may be set at any level below China's tariff bindings. Or the Agreement on Trade-Related Aspects of Intellectual Property Rights (TRIPS) may be used in a way that stimulates the development of a knowledge-based and more productive economy, or simply in a way that results in transfers to industrial countries. Or, similarly, WTO rules on contingent protection may be used in a way that is extremely damaging to open trade and economic development, or they may be used (or not used) in a way that is more consistent with economic efficiency and equity.

3. See Gertler (2002) for an outline of these principles.

4. Although the implementation period extends to 2010, almost all of the reduction will have been completed by 2005.

5. For example, in agriculture, China had to accept a limit of 8.5 percent on de minimis domestic support, as opposed to the usual 10 percent limit for developing countries.

6. See Maskus (2002). His assessment of China's intellectual property regime considers the provisions for patents, trademarks, trade secrets, and copyrights. He compares China's rules on intellectual property rights with international benchmarks for middle-income developing countries, using data from interviews with market participants.

7. Huang, Chen, and Rozelle (1999), for example, estimated the protection applying to rice, wheat, and maize in the mid-1990s at 4, 20, and 25 percent, respectively. By contrast, Tuan and Cheng (1999) estimated these protection rates to be –29, 62, and 15 percent, respectively. Carter (2000: 80) relied on producer price data and found generally negative price distortions.

8. All dollar amounts are current U.S. dollars.

9. The frequency of import licenses, in particular, has fallen from about two-thirds of tariff lines in the late 1980s to less than one-twentieth in 2001 (Lardy 2002).

10. Service suppliers that are independent of both the sender and the recipient of the goods.

11. Ianchovichina and Martin (2002) approximate very crudely the estimated liberalization of services by halving the barriers to trade in these activities estimated by François (2002). They also analyze the opportunities that arise from the elimination of the quotas against China's (and other countries') exports of textiles and clothing. Their analysis takes into account China's important export-processing arrangements and builds on the labor market studies undertaken by Sicular and Zhao (2002) and by Shi (2002) and on the analysis of automobile industry restructuring undertaken by Francois (2002). The resulting changes in the specification of their model greatly increase the realism of their analysis and have important implications for their results.

12. The reduction in the price of nontraded goods is often called a real exchange rate depreciation. The analysis described in this chapter considers only the impact of liberalization on goods markets, and ignores possible impacts on real exchange rates operating through induced increases in investment, an issue addressed in Chapter 2. McKibbin and Tang (2000) conclude that this stimulus to investment associated with reductions in the cost of capital and expansion of exports may be sufficient to reverse the long-run tendency toward real exchange rate depreciation, and may actually require real exchange rate appreciation, during the first years after accession.

13. The choice of 1995 as a starting period is somewhat arbitrary, given that China reformed its trade regime through-

out the 1990s. Nevertheless, 1995 was an important turning point, when China had to forgo its hopes of resuming its seat in the GATT and apply as a newcomer to the World Trade Organization, under a process much more focused on the commercial implications of the accession package.

14. These projections of export and income growth are very lower-bound estimates, because they ignore the benefits from abolishing nontariff barriers, because they involve serious aggregation biases, and because models of this type appear to understate greatly the implications of major trade liberalizations (Kehoe 2002).

15. Their study draws on the simulation model results provided by Ianchovichina and Martin (2002) and uses a sample of 84,000 households—17,000 urban and 67,000 rural—from National Bureau of Statistics surveys. The price impacts from the GTAP analysis are applied to the households' initial income and expenditure shares, taking into account the impacts of these price changes on the prices households must pay for their consumption goods and purchases of inputs, and the prices they receive for their sales of goods and of labor and other factors. The loss of government revenue from falling tariffs is restored very simply in the model experiment by increasing the price of all consumption goods through a consumption tax used to maintain government revenues. This approach to measuring the impact likely overstates the extent to which tax rates would need to rise, because government revenues from tariffs as a percentage of the value of imports were only about half of the 8 percent that would have been implied by the statutory tariff rates.

16. Their model of the Chinese economy takes into account important features such as the duty exemptions for intermediate goods used in the production of exports.

References

The word *processed* describes informally reproduced works that may not be commonly available through libraries.

Anderson, K., and others. 1986. *The Political Economy of Agricultural Protection: East Asia in International Perspective*. Boston, London, and Sydney: Allen and Unwin.

Anderson, K., J. Huang, and E. Ianchovichina. 2002. "Impact of China's WTO Accession on Agriculture and Rural-Urban Income Inequality." Paper presented to conference on China's Accession to WTO, Policy Reform and Poverty Reduction, Beijing, June 28–29.

Anderson, S., and C. Lau. 2001. "Hedging Hopes with Fears in China's Accession to the World Trade Organization: The Transitional Special Product Safeguard for Chinese Exports." Powell, Goldstein, Frazer, and Murphy, LLP, Geneva. Processed.

Bhattasali, D., Li Shantong, and W. Martin, eds. Forthcoming. *WTO Accession, Policy Reform and Poverty Reduction in China*. Washington, D.C.: World Bank and Oxford University Press.

Carter, C. 2000. "China's Trade Integration and Impacts on Factor Markets." In *China's Agriculture in the International Trading System*. OECD (Organisation for Economic Co-operation and Development) Proceedings, April.

Chun, Chang, B. Fleisher, and E. Parker. 2001. "The Impact of China's Entry into the WTO: Overview." *China Economic Review* 11 (4): 319–22.

Fewsmith, J. 2001. "The Political and Social Implications of China's Accession to the WTO." *China Quarterly* 167 (September): 573–91.

Findlay, Christopher, and W. Luo. 2002. "Logistics in China: Accession to the WTO and Its Implications." Paper presented to Conference on China's Accession to WTO, Policy Reform and Poverty Reduction, Beijing, June 28–29.

Francois, Joseph F. 2002. "The Motor Vehicle Sector in China and WTO Accession." Paper presented to Conference on China's Accession to WTO, Policy Reform and Poverty Reduction, Beijing, June 28–29.

Gertler, J. 2002. "What China's WTO Accession Is All About." Paper presented to Conference on China's Accession to WTO, Policy Reform and Poverty Reduction, Beijing, June 28–29.

Gilbert, J., and T. Wahl. 2002. "Applied General Equilibrium Assessments of Trade Liberalization in China." *World Economy* 25(5): 697–731.

Harwit, E. 2001. "The Impact of WTO Membership on the Automobile Industry in China." *China Quarterly* 167: 655–70.

Hertel, T. W., ed. 1997. *Global Trade Analysis: Modeling and Applications*. Cambridge: Cambridge University Press.

Hertel, T. W., F. Zhai, and Z. Wang. 2002. "Implications of WTO Accession for Poverty in China." Paper presented to Conference on China's Accession to WTO, Policy Reform and Poverty Reduction, Beijing, June 28–29.

Huang, J., and S. Rozelle. 2002. "The Nature of Distortions to Agricultural Incentives in China and Implications of WTO Accession." Paper presented at Conference on WTO Accession, Policy Reform and Poverty Reduction in China, World Bank, Beijing, June 28–29.

Huang, J., C. Chen, and S. Rozelle. 1999. "Reform, Trade Liberalization and Their Impacts on China's Agriculture." Paper presented at International Agricultural Trade Research Consortium Symposium on China's Agricultural Trade Policy: Issues, Analysis and Global Consequences, San Francisco, June 25–26.

Hussain, A. 2002. "Coping and Adapting to Job Losses and Fall in Farm Earnings." Paper presented at Conference on WTO Accession, Policy Reform and Poverty Reduction in China, World Bank, Beijing, June 28–29.

Ianchovichina, Elena. 2003. "GTAP-DD: A Model for Analyzing Trade Reforms in the Presence of Duty Drawbacks." GTAP Technical Paper No. 21. Available at www.agecon.purdue.edu/GTAP/techpapr/index.htm.

Ianchovichina, Elena, and William J. Martin 2002. "Economic Impacts of China's Accession to the WTO." Paper presented at Conference on WTO Accession, Policy Reform and Poverty Reduction in China, World Bank, Beijing, June 28–29.

Johnson, D. G. 2000. "The WTO and Agriculture in China." *China Economic Review* 11: 402–4.

Kehoe, T. 2002. "How Well Did Computable General Equilibrium Models Predict the Effects of NAFTA?" Paper presented to Conference on General Equilibrium Modeling, Cowles Foundation, Yale University, April.

Lardy, Nicholas R. 2002. *Integrating China into the Global Economy*. Washington, D.C.: Brookings Institution Press.

Lin, J. Y. 2000. "WTO Accession and China's Agriculture." *China Economic Review* 11: 405–8.

Martin, William J. 2001. "Implications of Reform and WTO Accession for China's Agricultural Policies." *Economics of Transition* 9 (3): 717–42.

————. 2002. "Reforming Japan's Rice Policies: Comment." In R. Stern, ed., *Issues and Options for Japan-US Trade Policies.* Ann Arbor: University of Michigan Press.

Martin, William J., and Elena Ianchovichina. 2001. "Implications of China's Accession to the World Trade Organization for China and the WTO." *World Economy* 24 (9).

Maskus, Keith E. 2002. "Intellectual Property Rights in the WTO Accession Package: Assessing China's Reforms." Paper presented to Conference on China's Accession to WTO, Policy Reform and Poverty Reduction, Beijing, June 28–29.

Mattoo, Aaditya. 2002. "China's Accession to the WTO: The Services Dimension." Paper presented to Conference on China's Accession to WTO, Policy Reform and Poverty Reduction, Beijing, June 28–29.

McKibbin, W., and K. Tang. 2000. "Trade and Financial Reform in China: Impacts on the World Economy." *World Economy* 23 (8).

Messerlin, Patrick. 2002. "China in the WTO: Antidumping and Safeguard." Paper presented at Conference on WTO Accession, Policy Reform and Poverty Reduction in China, World Bank, Beijing, June 28–29, 2002.

OECD (Organisation for Economic Co-operation and Development). 2002a. *Agricultural Policies in OECD Countries: Monitoring and Outlook.* Paris.

————. 2002b. *China in the World Economy: The Domestic Policy Challenges.* Paris.

Pangestu, Mari, and D. Mrongowius. 2002. "Telecommunication Services in China: Facing the Challenges of WTO Accession." Paper presented to Conference on China's Accession to WTO, Policy Reform and Poverty Reduction, Beijing, June 28–29.

Panitchpakdi, Supachai, and M. Clifford. 2002. *China and the WTO: Changing China, Changing World Trade.* Singapore: John Wiley (Asia).

Schmidhuber, J. 2001. "Changes in China's Agricultural Trade Policy Regime: Impacts on Agricultural Production, Consumption, Prices, and Trade." In *China's Agriculture in the International Trading System.* OECD (Organisation for Economic Co-operation and Development) Proceedings, April.

Shi Xinzheng. 2002. "Empirical Research on Urban-Rural Income Differentials: A Case of China." Peking University. Processed.

Sicular, T., and Y. Zhao. 2002. "Employment, Earnings and Poverty in Rural China: A Microeconomic Analysis." Paper presented to Conference on China's Accession to WTO, Policy Reform and Poverty Reduction, Beijing, June 28–29.

Tanzer, A. 2001. "Chinese Walls." *Forbes.* November 12.

Tuan, F., and G. Cheng. 1999. "A Review of China's Agricultural Trade Policy." Paper presented at International Agricultural Trade Research Consortium Symposium on China's Agricultural Trade Policy: Issues, Analysis and Global Consequences, San Francisco, June 25–26.

WTO (World Trade Organization). 1996. "Negotiating Group on Basic Telecommunications." Telecommunications Services Reference Paper. Geneva, April 24.

Yu, Wusheng, and S. Frandsen. 2002. "China's WTO Commitments in Agriculture: Does the Impact Depend on OECD Agricultural Policies?" Paper presented at Fifth Annual Conference on Global Economic Analysis, Taipei. Available at www.gtap.org.

2

REGIONAL IMPACT OF CHINA'S ACCESSION TO THE WTO

Elena Ianchovichina
Sethaput Suthiwart-Narueput
Min Zhao

China's accession to the World Trade Organization (WTO) and deeper integration into the world economy present important opportunities and challenges for the East Asia region. China's role in the region is unrivaled. First, its economy is large in absolute terms—constituting half the economy of Asia, according to measures of purchasing power. Second, China has rapidly expanded its trade, almost tripling its share of global exports and more than doubling its share of global imports over the period 1990–2002 and absorbing a fast-growing share of exports from East Asia over the last decade. Third, although its capital account is not fully convertible, China is important both as an investment destination and as a lender in global capital markets. It is the world's largest host country for foreign direct investment (FDI) and the largest capital supplier among developing countries.[1] And looking ahead, China will remain an important driver of change in East Asia. With WTO accession, it will continue to open its markets to other countries' exports and improve its business climate.

The task of assessing the impact of China and its accession to the WTO on East Asia presents an enormous challenge because of the complexity of the changes stemming from accession and the difficulty in specifying clearly what would have happened had China not acceded to the WTO. Thus the goal of this chapter is less to predict detailed changes than to provide a framework for understanding the impact of WTO accession on the region's economies and to offer a broad assessment of this impact for different countries and country groupings. The findings are drawn from quantitative and qualitative analysis, including improved computable general equilibrium (CGE) modeling and partial equilibrium studies, which are detailed on the Web site associated with this volume.[2] Because the analysis is at an aggregated level, readers should supplement the findings here with information from subsectoral case studies before making policy decisions.[3]

Finally, although this chapter focuses on the economic impact of China's accession to the WTO,

The authors gratefully acknowledge helpful comments from Lu Ding of the National University of Singapore, Nattapong Thongpakde of the Thailand Development Research Institute, William J. Martin of the World Bank, and participants at seminars held at the Institute for Southeast Asian Studies of the National University of Singapore, the Thailand Development Research Institute in Bangkok, and the World Bank office in Jakarta, as well as helpful discussions with Arvind Panagariya of the University of Maryland at College Park and the excellent research assistance of Wallada Atsavasirilert.

the ultimate impact on the region will be driven not just by economics, but also by broader political economy considerations. China's accession to the WTO is a signal of its greater interdependence with the world and its increasing international presence, which also will have repercussions in the region. China's expanding influence as a regional power may be viewed with growing concern by its neighbors, and that influence raises issues about China's future leadership on economic matters in the region, a role traditionally played by Japan.

The chapter is organized as follows. The next section briefly describes the major channels through which the impacts of China's WTO accession will be felt, followed by a section assessing the impact of accession on the newly industrializing economies (NIEs) in East Asia—in particular, their growing opportunities in China's markets and the effects of the evolution of global production networks. The next section assesses the scope for East Asian middle-income developing countries to expand exports to China, as well as the challenges they face from competition with China in third-country markets. It also outlines how domestic markets are likely to be affected by increases in the supply of exports from China and by patterns of foreign direct investment. The impact of China's accession to the WTO on the lower-income coun-

tries of East Asia is the subject of the next section, and it is followed by our conclusions.

Channels of Impact

Over the next decade, China's growth and greater integration into the world economy will have major effects on the region. Other countries in East Asia will feel the impact of China's WTO accession through four main channels:

1. Expansion of markets in China for their exports
2. Increased imports from China into their domestic markets
3. Competition with China in third-country markets
4. Expansion of foreign direct investment in China and, potentially, outward foreign investment from China.

Increased Access to China's Domestic Markets

In the 1990s, exports to China spurred growth not only in the newly industrializing economies but also in the developing countries of East Asia (Figure 2.1). The countries of the Association of South East Asia Nations (ASEAN) have increased their exports to China by 390 percent and expanded their share in China's total imports from 6 percent to 9 percent.

FIGURE 2.1 Exports to China from East Asia Compared with Exports to Other Partners

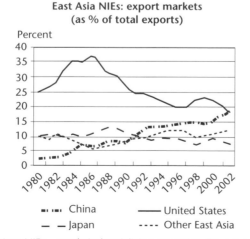

East Asia NIEs: export markets
(as % of total exports)

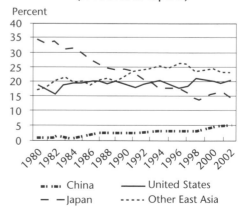

Developing East Asia: export markets
(as % of total exports)

Note: NIEs = newly industrializing countries. "East Asia NIEs" refers to Hong Kong (China), Rep. of Korea, Singapore, Taiwan (China).
Source: IMF, *Direction of Trade Statistics* (various years); data reported from exporter country accounts.

Note: "Developing East Asia" refers to Cambodia, Indonesia, Lao PDR, Malaysia, Mongolia, Myanmar, Philippines, Thailand, Vietnam.
Source: IMF, *Direction of Trade Statistics* (various years); data reported from exporter country accounts.

Continued growth in China's huge domestic markets will fuel further export growth for the world and the economies of the region. In many sectors, China's WTO accession only adds a little to the already vigorous projected growth of these markets (Figure 2.2). Nonetheless, accession will cause several significant shifts. China's substantial commitments to liberalize trade in *services* represent the most significant part of the accession package (Mattoo 2002), providing national treatment to foreign-funded firms and greater opportunities for exporters of services. In *manufacturing*, China's commitments to abolish nontariff barriers and reduce its import tariffs from 13.3 percent in 2001 to 6.8 percent by the end of the implementation period in 2010[4] will fuel further industrial restructuring. Some sectors such as the motor vehicle and high-end manufacturing will be affected significantly by rationalization and industrial restructuring. In *agriculture*, too, China's imports are projected to grow substantially, although the effect of WTO-related reforms on agricultural output and imports is much smaller than projected by earlier studies because protection of many farm products is expected to remain virtually unchanged by the end of the implementation period (Huang and Rozelle 2002).

Growth in the region's exports will also be fueled by the increased demand from those major trading partners that benefit directly from China's accession. The developing countries of East Asia will export more not only to China, but also to the newly industrializing economies in East Asia, whose own demand for imports has grown as a result of the accession. Both the direct and indirect effects of increased access to China's markets will be important for regional trade.

Increased Imports from China

China's accession to the WTO will be accompanied by cuts in its export prices, increasing China's appeal as an efficient supplier of intermediate inputs. China's preaccession reforms have already improved the competitiveness of its exports and benefited its closest trading partners. Trade intensity indexes for 1985 and 2001 (Ng and Yeats 2003) suggest that trade between individual East Asian countries and China has intensified sharply since 1985. Consequently, most East Asian economies are expected to benefit from further cuts in export prices as China continues to implement WTO-related reforms over the next few years. The benefits to these countries will be evident in both increased output and welfare.

A growing segment of imports from China will be inputs in production processes, not just finished consumer goods (Figure 2.3). China is increasingly a central player in production networks. Although Japan remains an important center of production-sharing operations in East Asia, originating about one-third of all regional exports of components for

FIGURE 2.2   China's Imports, 1995 and 2005

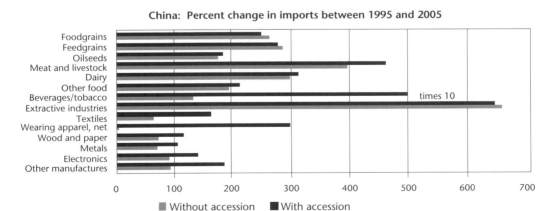

Note: This figure captures the effects of WTO accession, encompassing all reforms since 1995. Ianchovichina and Walmsley (2003), whose work has been drawn on for the remainder of this chapter, have estimated the effects of WTO accession for 2001–10.
Source: Ianchovichina and Martin (2001).

FIGURE 2.3   China's Growing Role in Production Networks

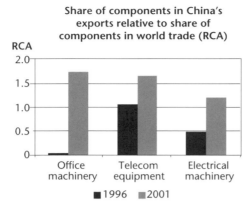

Share of components in China's exports relative to share of components in world trade (RCA)

■1996 ■2001

Note: RCA = revealed comparative advantage.
Source: Ng and Yeats (2003).

Parts and components imports from China, 2001

	Value of imports from China (millions of US$)	Share in total (%)
Japan	5,587	36.7
Hong Kong (China)	13,556	45.5
Korea, Rep. of	1,695	21.1
Singapore	1,989	11.9
Taiwan (China)	1,308	18.9
Indonesia	109	4.9
Malaysia	1,394	12.8
Philippines	170	2.4
Thailand	1,030	13.3

Source: Ng and Yeats (2003: Table 17.1).

assembly, China is finding niches; its exports of parts and components increased by almost US$20 billion[5] from 1996 to 2001. By 2001 China was exporting more than $20 billion in parts and components to others parts of emerging East Asia, representing up to 20 percent of those countries' parts and components trade (Ng and Yeats 2003). Thus imports from China represent an opportunity for the rest of emerging East Asia to benefit from China's growing role in global production networks.

To realize the full benefits of China's lower export prices, it will be important that countries resist pressures to protect their domestic producers and that they avoid imposing excessive safeguard measures for this purpose. Pressures to do so are growing in several countries. However, succumbing to them will only prolong the adjustments needed to realize regional comparative advantages, and will distract policymakers from facilitating the transition of workers by putting in place the appropriate labor market and safety net policies and programs.

Increased Competition in Third-Country Markets

Competition with China in third-country markets will intensify as a result of China's accession. This competition will present a challenge for many countries, especially those with a similar comparative advantage in labor-intensive goods.

Southeast Asia competes with China in world markets for manufactures, especially labor-intensive products, and increasingly in higher value added manufactures such as semiconductors and other high-technology products. Competition with China has brought unit prices down, but thus far other East Asian exporters have maintained their market shares in the United States and Japan. In Japan, developing East Asian countries have even managed to enlarge their market share slightly, while China has captured market share at the expense of the United States.

In the future, competition is set to intensify for two reasons. First, the United States, Canada, and the European Union (EU) will abolish their import quotas on Chinese textiles and apparel by 2005.[6] China will then become a formidable competitor, especially in the apparel sector,[7] pushing prices down in these important third-country markets. Second, China will lower its own import tariffs on inputs for manufacturing. The effect of these tariff reductions on the real exchange rate will be lower costs of both traded and nontraded inputs for China's manufacturers. This development will make China's products more competitive as imports, putting pressure on domestic producers in the countries that import them.

Shifts in Investment Patterns

WTO accession is likely to increase foreign direct investment in China, as trade liberalization lowers production costs and the price of capital goods and increases the rental rates, resulting in rising returns to capital in China.[8] Meanwhile, the liberalization of rules on investment should ease flows of foreign direct investment into previously restricted sectors such as services and automobile production. Given the substantial productivity gap that exists between local and foreign firms, the new FDI flows are likely to raise China's productivity. In apparel and footwear, for example, the adoption of foreign technology raises productivity by 30–62 percent in collective enterprises and 20–59 percent in state enterprises (Claro 2001).

China's accession is also likely to set off changes in regional trade and production patterns, the effects of which will be felt over the medium to long term. The question for other East Asian economies is whether their own FDI inflows will increase or decrease as a result. It is difficult to answer this question because much will depend on the policy responses of individual countries. In addition, some factors will work simultaneously to determine the net regional impact of China's WTO accession on FDI flows.

Although countries that lose competitiveness may see declining returns to capital and FDI diverted to China, several effects are likely to counteract this negative impact on FDI. First, increased productivity and trade liberalization in China both increase the country's demand for imports and raise investment and welfare in China's trading partners. Martin (1993) shows that a productivity shock in manufactures and services, for which there is a lot of two-way trade, is more likely to raise welfare in a country's trading partners than is trade liberalization. The technological advance accompanying China's liberalization will improve the country's competitiveness, but also increase the country's demand for imports.

Second, investment liberalization in China will make it possible for multinational firms to further rationalize their production processes within East Asia. The relief of local content requirements under trade-related investment measures (TRIMs) will encourage these firms to relocate some segments of their production from China to other countries in the region.

Third, in some sectors China's neighbors may receive FDI flows that complement those going to China. The scope for export specialization varies with the degree of complementarity between China and other countries of East Asia.

Fourth, as FDI creates more backward and forward linkages among countries in the region, the competitiveness of Asian products will depend not only on the competitiveness of the country that exports the final product, but also on those neighboring countries that contribute various components at different stages of the production process. This situation will create an incentive for locating investments in the countries that are part of the regional production network in which China is playing an increasingly central role.

Fifth, whereas in the past China drew heavily on the overseas Chinese community as a source of FDI, with WTO accession China is now able to draw on global capital markets for both FDI and portfolio investment. Therefore, competition between China and other countries in the region for FDI may actually weaken.

Last, but not least, the determinants of FDI are evolving over time. Agglomeration effects are becoming more important relative to the traditional determinants of FDI such as market size and labor costs (UNCTAD 2001). China resists easy definitions of its comparative advantage in terms of high-tech or low-wage manufacturing, and its comparative advantage also may change appreciably in response to WTO accession. Its current comparative advantage in labor-intensive products suggests that there is more scope for export specialization vis-à-vis the newly industrializing economies than the developing East Asian countries. However, this situation is likely to change as East Asia's export structure evolves.[9] Over time, China is also likely to shift and extend its comparative advantage from land- and labor-intensive products and low-end manufacturing to higher-end products as a result of trade-induced productivity gains and savings in transaction costs from the reforms spurred by WTO accession. Increased productivity from WTO-related liberalization and higher wages—initially in China's coastal regions—has been shown to reduce the competitive threat to the lower- and middle-income economies of Southeast Asia,[10] while increasing the threat to the newly industrializing and more advanced middle-income economies of East Asia.

According to a recent analysis, the impact of accession is significantly larger than the estimated static gain, if productivity increases in services and high-end manufacturing are taken into account. Every percentage point increase in productivity from expanded competition and foreign entry in China's services sector implies a welfare gain for China of

$10 billion (1997 US$) and an increase in its gross domestic product (GDP) of 2.2 percent—equivalent to the total estimated static gain from China's WTO accession (Ianchovichina and Walmsley 2003).

Impact of WTO Accession on Newly Industrializing East Asia and Japan

On balance, the industrialized and newly industrializing economies in East Asia will benefit from China's accession to the WTO.[11] As important suppliers of materials to China, these countries will see an improvement in their terms of trade.[12] In both Japan and the NIEs, most of the projected increase in production will be driven by expanded exports to China. Although these countries are well positioned to gain from China's accession to WTO, many of the trends that have developed from China's growing role in world trade are already evident.

Japan, Taiwan (China), the Republic of Korea, and Hong Kong (China) are expected to raise their output of textiles in response to increased demand from China's expanding garment industry. Their own garment industries will be squeezed, however, particularly in the markets—North America and the EU—where the quotas on Chinese textile and apparel exports are removed. The growth of their textile exports to India, the Philippines, Vietnam, and other South and Southeast Asian economies is also expected to slow as these countries' garment industries contract in the face of competition with China in third-country markets.

China's demand for intermediate inputs and final products is expected to drive the export growth of these products from its neighbors. Examples include metals and petrochemicals from Korea; electronics and other manufactures from Singapore; light manufactures, petrochemicals, machinery, equipment, and electronics from Taiwan (China); and metals, petrochemicals, oil, and other extractive industry products from Japan. In electronics, China is expected to seek its additional inputs from the countries that get the largest tariff reductions—India, the United States, and other South Asian countries, and to a lesser extent Hong Kong and Singapore—rather than from Korea, where tariffs on electronic products are already low.[13] The potential for specialization and complementary intraindustry trade could be significant. As shown in Figure 2.4, China already represents an important source of parts and components for the NIEs.

In automobile production, China's current plans for restructuring its industry will make it a more efficient assembler of motor vehicles and eventually

FIGURE 2.4   Impact of China's WTO Accession on Japan and East Asia's NIEs, 2001–10 (cumulative changes in output of selected sectors relative to baseline, millions of 1997 US$)

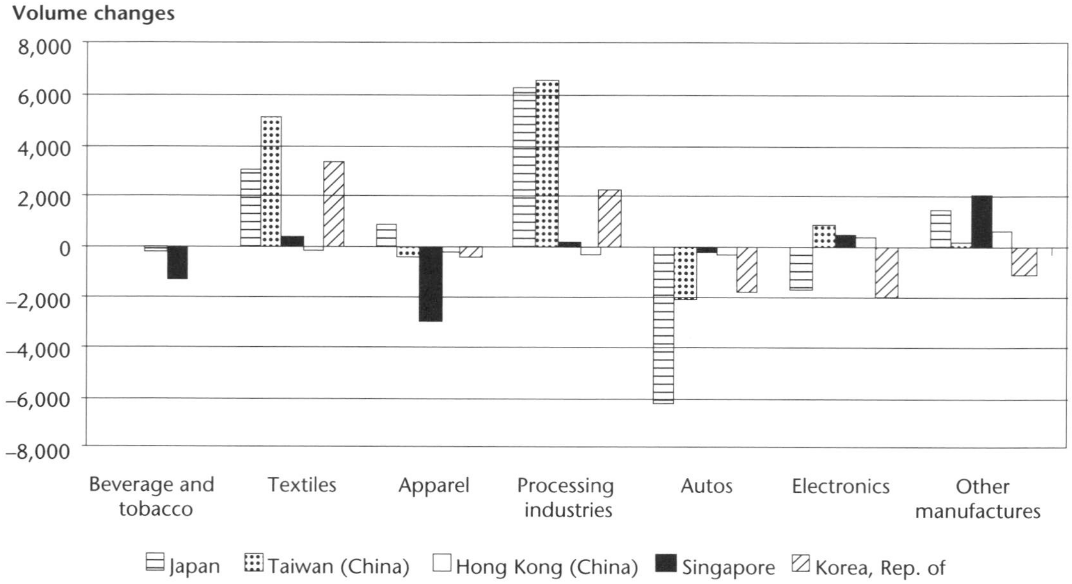

Source: Ianchovichina and Walmsley (2003).

an exporter (François and Spinanger 2002). This prospect could provoke a major reorganization of the industry across the region. Our analysis projects a contraction of automobile production in Japan and the NIEs.

The NIEs will benefit from China's increased demand for services. Indeed, accession is likely to increase demand for all types of services, including transport and communications, which these economies are well positioned to provide. And it will enhance the role of Hong Kong as a financial center serving the mainland's investment needs and providing investment services (Deutsche Bank 2001).

Investment flows into the NIEs are unlikely to fall as the result of China's WTO accession. The returns to capital in these countries will rise relative to the baseline (though not by as much as in China).The reason is that the NIEs are suppliers of raw materials to China, rather than competitors of China, and thus the prices received for their exports will tend to rise.

For Japan, the major impact of China's WTO accession is that China will become a more attractive destination for Japanese investments. After five years of strong growth, Japanese FDI to China dropped substantially in 1996–99 (Ministry of Finance, Japan), less because of Japanese firms' financial difficulties than because of a difficult market environment in China (Marukawa 2001). Some of the concerns about China's weak legal and

administrative environment for foreign investment are likely to be addressed in line with WTO accession, although competition in markets for goods and services is expected to intensify.

While the benefits to Japan and the NIEs from China's WTO accession are clearly positive, over time China's likely shift to extend its comparative advantage into higher-end products implies that these countries will face increasing competitive challenges, as is already happening in selected subsectors and regions.

Impact of WTO Accession on the Middle-Income Developing Countries of East Asia

Overall, China's trade liberalization and growth will have a mixed impact on these countries—Indonesia, Malaysia, the Philippines, and Thailand (Figure 2.5). Some factors are common to these countries. China's market presents sizable opportunities, including links with China as it plays an increasingly larger role in global production networks. At the same time, similarity in export structure suggests the threat of increased competition in third-country markets from increased exports from China, with the impact of accession itself concentrated in a few sectors—notably, apparel and textiles, where adjustments are likely. Generally, and increasingly over time, trade-induced changes in

FIGURE 2.5 Impact of China's WTO Accession on Developing Economies of East Asia, 2001–10
(cumulative changes in output of selected sectors relative to baseline, millions of 1997 US$)

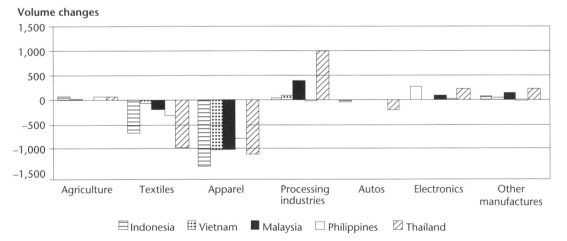

Source: Ianchovichina and Walmsley (2003).

China's productivity will make China a stronger partner and will ensure that the benefits from market opportunities outweigh third-country market competitive challenges. The details, however, will depend on the situation and response of the individual countries.

Indonesia

In the decade ahead, China's liberalization and economic expansion open several opportunities for Indonesia but also pose risks, both as an exporter and as a destination for investment. The challenge will be to manage the transition to realize those opportunities.

Indonesia's exports to China stand to benefit significantly from China's growth and liberalization.[14] Much of the tariff reduction under China's WTO accession will occur by 2004 (Table 2.1), but China is free to offer tariff rates below these bindings. For example, under the "Early Harvest" aspect of the Framework Agreement on China-ASEAN Comprehensive Economic Cooperation, which would establish an ASEAN-China Free Trade Area, a range of Indonesian exports will face lower tariffs than other countries' exports.[15]

Some of the top exports from Indonesia to China will also benefit significantly from reductions in nontariff barriers (Table 2.2). Nearly 20 percent of Indonesian exports to China are in products—especially palm oil, rubber, and processed oil—on which quantitative restrictions will be lifted (Table 2.2). Palm oil exports, in particular, should gain significantly from the relaxation of quantitative restrictions (QRs).[16] Palm oil, which was previously subject to an import license, is now subject to tariff-rate quotas (TRQs) with accession. Initial quota levels are set significantly above import levels prior to accession and are slated to increase significantly by 2005.[17] TRQs on rubber will take effect in 2004, when quotas are eliminated.[18] Urea also will be subject to a TRQ, with a final quota level in 2006 of more than 2.5 times the initial quota level and an in-quota tariff rate of 4 percent.[19] Most categories of timber will also be liberalized within three years of accession.

Indonesia's overall export volume will continue to grow. Demand from China will be compounded by increased import demand from China's closest trading partners—Japan, the NIEs, the EU, and the United States—which themselves have benefited from China's growth and WTO accession. However,

TABLE 2.1 Weighted Average Tariffs Facing Exports to China: Indonesia and Thailand, 2001–08 (percent)

	2001	2002	2003	2004	2005	2006	2007	2008
Indonesia	8.20	8.66	5.82	4.91	4.73	4.65	4.58	4.51
Thailand	10.19	8.91	8.41	4.86	4.63	4.43	4.25	4.05

Note: The weighted average tariff was calculated on the top 100 exported products to China, representing more than 85 percent of each country's exports to that country. The in-quota tariff rate is used for tariff-rate quota products.
Sources: UN Comtrade data; China's WTO accession agreement; authors' calculations.

TABLE 2.2 Shares of Exports to China Affected by Lifting of Quantitative Restrictions (QRs): Indonesia and Thailand (percent of total exports, 1995–99)

Country	Percent of exports facing QRs	Key products (% of total exports)
Indonesia	16.5	Palm oil (7.3), rubber (2.9), processed oil (0.6)
Thailand	30.6	Rice (9.24), rubber (11.8), cane sugar (5.8)

Sources: UN Comtrade data; China's WTO accession agreement; authors' calculations.

competitive pressures are likely to shift Indonesia's manufacturing structure. Exports from electronics and other manufacturing industries are projected to increase, as are exports of land-intensive products—food and feed grains and wood products—and other raw materials, including energy products.[20] Indonesia will also increase its exports of oilseeds, sugar, and cotton to China.

At the same time, the increasing similarity in export structure between China and Indonesia suggests a potential threat from competition in third-country markets.[21] Indonesia's apparel sector will have to adjust. Indonesian apparel is sold mainly in North America and Western Europe, where it will be particularly vulnerable to the abolishment of quotas on Chinese apparel exports. With a possible decline in apparel output, Indonesia's textile sector will also come under pressure, although there will be niches for its expansion.

The risk to exports to third-country markets was confirmed by a market-by-market and product-by-product analysis carried out for Indonesia. For this analysis, we identified "exports at risk" to the U.S. and Japanese markets based on their importance to the exporting country and the extent to which they compete with similar products from China.[22] Exports in product categories that are characterized by both a high share of Chinese imports (at least 5 percent) and unit values close to

those of competing imports from China were deemed to be most at risk. For Thailand and Indonesia, the results indicate that 15–25 percent of exports to the United States and Japan are at risk from growing competition from China (Tables 2.3 and 2.4).

Indonesian exports are more at risk in the United States than in Japan. Among Indonesia's exports to the United States in 1995–99, the top five products[23] accounted for more than 30 percent, and the top 100 products for 84 percent of total exports. Of Indonesian exports to the United States, almost half (47 percent) appear to have unit values close to those of competitor products from China, and 16 percent are in the at-risk categories—those in which unit values are close to those of China and in which China supplies more than 10 percent of imports (Table 2.3). Using the 5 percent threshold, nearly a quarter of Indonesian exports to the United States are at risk, including Indonesia's second and third most important export products to the United States.[24]

In the Japanese market, Indonesia's export structure has been even more concentrated than in the United States, with the top five products[25] accounting for more than 44 percent and the top 100 for more than 85 percent of total exports in 1995–99. About 11 percent of Indonesia's exports are in at-risk categories, with unit values close to

TABLE 2.3   Market-by-Market and Product-by-Product Analysis of Indonesian Exports: China's Market Share and Closeness of Unit Value (UV) as Proxies for Potential Risk

	China's import share			China's import share		
	< 10%	> 10%		< 5%	> 5%	
Share in U.S. market (%) *(n = 165 products)*						
UV close	30.5	**16.2**		22.8%	**24.0**	
UV not close	16.1	21.1		14.1%	23.1	
Share of market in analysis			83.9			83.9
Share in Japanese market(%) *(n = 188 products)*						
UV close	23.8	**11.0**		18.5	**23.0**	
UV not close	24.6	11.7		23.3	13.1	
Share of market in analysis			71.2			77.9

Note: The table shows calculations using two (arbitrary) threshold levels for Chinese imports: 5 percent and 10 percent of the total import market.
Sources: UN Comtrade data; China's WTO accession agreement; authors' calculations.

TABLE 2.4   Market-by-Market and Product-by-Product Analysis of Thai Exports: China's Market Share and Closeness of Unit Value (UV) as Proxies for Potential Risk

	China's import share			China's import share		
	< 10%	> 10%		< 5%	> 5%	
Share in U.S. market (%) (n = 150 products)						
UV close	23.9	**8.7**		18.1	**14.5**	
UV not close	22.1	16.4		19.2	19.4	
Share of market in analysis			71.1			71.1
Share in Japanese market (%) (n = 189 products)						
UV close	28.0	**20.8**		23.9	**24.9**	
UV not close	17.2	16.8		11.9	22.1	
Share of market in analysis			82.8			82.8

Note: The table shows calculations using two (arbitrary) threshold levels for Chinese imports: 5 percent and 10 percent of the total import market.
Sources: UN Comtrade data; China's WTO accession agreement; authors' calculations.

those of competing Chinese products and with China supplying more than 10 percent of imports. Using the 5 percent threshold, 23 percent of Indonesia's exports are potentially at risk; they include some of the most important exports to Japan.[26]

Indonesia is likely to adjust to the increased competition in apparel by increasing its specialization in wood and paper products and in light, high-end, and other manufactures. Exports of these products could increase, primarily in response to rising demand in China.

China's increased attractiveness for investors again provides both opportunities to Indonesia to expand its intraindustry trade and potential threats. One approach to assessing Indonesia's ability to prevent a decline in foreign direct investment is to look at the sectoral changes likely to occur. If the sectors that are expanding (contracting) are the ones that already account for a large share of FDI, then FDI is likely to increase (decrease) as well. Sectors that are growing less rapidly in Indonesia—apparel and textiles as well as assembly operations—have received foreign direct investment in the past, whereas any expansion in agriculture likely involves little FDI. Opportunities exist for Indonesia to participate in global production networks—cosmetics, machinery, and audiovisual equipment, for example—in which FDI may

expand in China and Indonesia simultaneously. And, like other ASEAN middle-income countries, Indonesia has the potential to develop its role as a supplier of specific parts to an automobile production network, given the restructuring of the industry now taking place in the region.[27]

Indonesia will need to tailor its strategy to grasp the opportunities for increases in trade and investment flows if it is to offset the declines that are projected in its exports to the EU, Japan, and the United States. Key elements will be measures to restore investor confidence and increase competitiveness. Meanwhile, Indonesia will have to avoid protecting its domestic producers with excessive safeguard measures in order to facilitate an adjustment in the manufacturing sector that responds to the opportunities in China's markets. Measures such as the recently introduced temporary safeguards against garment imports will only prolong the adjustments that Indonesia needs to make to realize its regional comparative advantages.

Malaysia

Among the developing middle-income countries in East Asia, Malaysia is likely to be the one most positively affected by China's accession to the WTO.[28] Overall, the effect on trade will be positive, as Malaysia becomes a more important trading partner to China. Flows of foreign investment will not be much affected, because the returns to investment in Malaysia are expected to rise only slightly over the accession period.

Malaysia's exports of wood products and other manufactures will likely increase as a result of WTO accession, relative to the baseline, in response to increased demand for these products in China and Taiwan (China).[29] Malaysia's overall volume of agricultural exports is not projected to change much, but exports of oilseeds, sugar, livestock, and cotton to China and Taiwan (China) are likely to increase as a result of China's WTO accession. Demand from China will be compounded by a higher import demand from China's closest trading partners—Japan, the NIEs, the EU, and the United States—which themselves have benefited from China's growth and WTO accession.

Just like the other developing economies of East Asia, Malaysia is expected to lose some of its share in the world apparel market as a result of China's accession.[30] In textiles, however, output will be little affected, and while the textile exports of all the other developing countries in the region will contract as a result of China's accession, Malaysia's exports will hold their ground, buttressed by increased demand from China's apparel industry. In this way, Malaysia is more similar to the NIEs in the region.

Malaysia's involvement in intraregional production networks and the improving quality of its labor and infrastructure position it well as a destination for foreign direct investment that complements investment in China. By 2001 Malaysia was already exporting $1.3 billion to China and importing $1.4 billion from China in parts and components (see Ng and Yeats 2003). During China's recent expansion, Malaysia received significant FDI in the information technology-related and electronics industries; FDI in electronics grew 40 percent from 1997 to 2001. In the automobile sector, Malaysia may position itself to benefit from participating in international production networks—for example, at present it is producing steering gears. Alternatively, it may maintain its more protectionist stand, which may harm its prospects to attract additional FDI.

The Philippines

Philippine exports to China stand to benefit from China's growth and liberalization.[31] With its accession to the WTO, China will demand more raw materials and land-intensive products, and the Philippines is well positioned to increase exports of food and feed grains, cottons, sugar, vegetables, and fruits in response.[32] Food grain exports, in particular, are expected to rise substantially as a result of China's accession. Output and exports of light manufactures are expected to grow faster with than without China's accession. Demand from China will be compounded by increased import demand from China's closest trading partners, which themselves will have benefited.

At the same time, because the Philippines has comparative advantages in many areas in which China is strong, China's WTO accession will intensify competition between the two countries. Competition with China will be particularly acute in apparel produced for North America and Western Europe because of the removal of quotas on China's textiles and apparel in these markets. Overall, the impact of accession on the Philippines' output of apparel and textiles will be negative. Even so, the Philippines occupies certain niches within the export market that may be less exposed to Chinese competition.

The impact of China's accession on the Philippines will also depend on investment flows. As in Indonesia and Thailand, the sectors that are growing less rapidly—apparel, textiles, and assembly operations—have been targets of FDI in the past. However, looking ahead, the Philippines is poised to take part in global production networks in electronics, machinery and equipment, processing, and light manufacturing, where FDI may well expand in China and the Philippines simultaneously. In 2001 imports from China and exports to China in parts and components totaled $170 million and $342 million, respectively. This represents only a 2 percent share of the total parts and components trade for the Philippines, suggesting considerable opportunity for expansion (Ng and Yeats 2003).

The Philippines' ability to move up the value chain and capture more benefits from China's accession will depend on what strategy the country adopts. Many of the sectors that will suffer from China's accession to the WTO use unskilled labor intensively, while those sectors that will expand use land or skilled labor more intensively. Wages of unskilled workers may well come under pressure. The potential impact on urban inequality and vulnerability in the short term will have to be carefully monitored and addressed, with increasing pressure to facilitate the adjustment process in the labor market.

Thailand

Thailand is well positioned to expand its manufacturing base, despite the fact that China's WTO accession may present a challenge to the Thai economy as competition in the textile and apparel sector strengthens.

The intensity of trade between Thailand and China (Ng and Yeats 2003) in 2001 suggests that the planned reductions in protection of China's markets offer some good opportunities for exporters. For Thailand, much of the tariff reduction will occur by 2004 (Table 2.1); it is receiving an average tariff reduction of more than six percentage points. These rates represent the statutory tariff bindings under China's WTO accession, but China is free to offer tariff rates below these bindings as agreed, for example, in 2003 under the "Early Harvest" aspect of the ASEAN-China Framework Agreement.

Thailand's agricultural exports to China stand to benefit significantly from the liberalization of nontariff barriers.[33] More than 30 percent of Thai exports to China are in products—especially rice, rubber, and cane sugar—on which quantitative restrictions will be lifted (Table 2.2).[34] And, under the WTO accession agreement, China confirms that tariff-rate quotas will be allocated with historical trade flows to end users in mind, and imports will be allocated to the full limit of the quota established for each calendar year based on demand in the Chinese market. Because Thailand's import share in many of the products subject to tariff-rate quotas has been high historically, it can expect to be allocated high quotas.[35] Thailand's food processing industries also are well placed to expand in China's markets.

Thailand's overall export volume will continue to grow. Demand from China will be compounded by increased import demand from China's closest trading partners—Japan, the NIEs, the EU, and the United States—which themselves have benefited from China's growth and WTO accession. However, competitive pressures are likely to shift Thai manufacturing increasingly into electronics and other manufactures, especially metals and petrochemical products. Exports from processing and electronics

industries are projected to increase, as are exports to China of land-intensive products—oilseeds, sugar, and wood products. Cotton production may expand as demand for cotton increases in response to the expansion of Taiwan's textile sector. China's accession will have a negative impact on growth in the apparel and textile sectors.[36]

The increasing similarity in export structure between China and Thailand suggests, however, a potential threat from competition in third-country markets. A market-by-market and a product-by-product analysis carried out for Thailand suggest that Thai exports are less at risk in the United States than in Japan.[37] In the U.S. market, the specific products that appear most at risk from Chinese competition do not include Thailand's most important export products to the United States.[38] Thailand's exports to the United States are heavily concentrated. Based on data for 1995–99, the top five products account for more than 25 percent of total Thai exports, and the top 100 products account for 81 percent. Less than 9 percent of Thailand's U.S. exports fall into the at-risk categories—that is, where unit values are close to those of Chinese products and where China's import market share exceeds 10 percent (Table 2.4).[39] For products in which China supplies 5–10 percent of U.S. imports, roughly 15 percent of Thai exports are at risk.

Thailand's exports to Japan are more vulnerable than those to the United States. They are less concentrated than those to the United States, with the top five export products[40] accounting for only 21 percent of total Thai exports and the top 100 for 76 percent. But nearly 21 percent of Thailand's exports are in the at-risk category—where the unit values of Thai products are close to those of their Chinese competitors and where China's share of imports is greater than 10 percent.[41] Four of Thailand's top 10 exports to Japan appear to be at risk on this basis.[42] Based on the 5 percent threshold, nearly 25 percent of Thailand's exports to Japan are at risk.

As for investment flows, the opportunities may outweigh the risks. Sectors that are now contracting in Thailand—apparel and textiles as well as assembly operations—have historically accounted for important shares of inward FDI. One-fourth of FDI has gone to the hotel and restaurant sectors, which have room for expansion. At the same, Thailand is poised to expand its role in global networks producing electronics, metals, petrochemicals, and other manufactures. In the electronics industry, when FDI flows to China gained momentum in the late 1990s, FDI flows to Thailand in these subsectors continued growing, reaching 27 percent of the FDI in Thai manufacturing in 1997–2001. In 2001 imports from China of parts and components already represented 13 percent (or more than $1 billion) of Thailand's total parts and components imports, and exports to China of parts and components totaled nearly $1 billion (Ng and Yeats 2003).

In Thailand as in the Philippines, many of the sectors with exports at risk use unskilled labor intensively, while the expanding sectors use land or skilled labor more intensively. This finding suggests that growth and change in China will have the effect of lowering the wages of unskilled Thai workers relative to those of skilled workers. The potential impact on urban inequality and vulnerability in the short term will have to be carefully monitored and addressed. As unemployment in the labor-intensive sectors rises, the pressure to facilitate the adjustment process in the labor market will increase.

The extent to which Thailand will exit from assembly-type production or upgrade its capabilities will depend largely on the policies it pursues—either embracing trade-induced competitiveness and productivity gains or submitting to short-term protectionist pressures. Manufacturers are already complaining about low-cost imports of electrical appliances and motorbikes from China. Also important are supply factors, including the local availability of engineering and sourcing capabilities, and government incentives for upgrading technology. Thailand's private business community is already exploring niche opportunities within labor-intensive sectors.

Impact of WTO Accession on the Low-Income Countries of East Asia

The impacts of China's accession to the WTO will vary widely among Cambodia, the Lao People's Democratic Republic (Lao PDR), and Vietnam. Cambodia is particularly vulnerable because of its heavy emphasis on apparel exports. Lao PDR, by contrast, is likely to be little affected in either China or third-country markets. Vietnam falls somewhere in between, with competitive pressures on its exports matched by growing market opportunities.

Regional arrangements are playing an important role in ensuring that the low-income countries of East Asia benefit from regional trade. For example, under the "Early Harvest" aspect of the ASEAN-China Framework Agreement announced in November 2002, China granted these countries most-favored-nation (MFN) status, even though they have not yet acceded to the WTO.

Cambodia

For Cambodia, it will be important to capitalize on any opportunities from China's growth. Cambodia will see some benefits from China's import tariff reductions,[43] but, most important, some of Cambodia's top exports—especially rubber and wood—will benefit from the reduction in quantitative restrictions (Table 2.5). The "Early Harvest" provision of the ASEAN-China Framework Agreement also gives Cambodia MFN treatment. Growth in China overall is expected to be a powerful source of external demand for Cambodia, including for cross-border activity that may not be well captured in official statistics.

China's accession to the WTO could pose a double threat to Cambodia: to its balance of payments,

TABLE 2.5 Share of Exports to China Affected by Lifting of Quantitative Restrictions (QRs): Cambodia and Lao PDR (percent of total exports, 1995–99)

Country	Percent of exports facing QRs	Key products (% of total exports)
Cambodia	11	Rubber (11); timber (2.9); plywood (4.64)
Lao PDR	0.6	Rice (0.6); timber (62.4)

Sources: UN Comtrade data; China's WTO accession agreement; authors' calculations.

from lost exports, and to many of its households, from lost jobs and lower wage incomes. Cambodia's exports are already highly correlated with China's, and many of Cambodia's leading exports are in the apparel and textile categories where China is currently quota-constrained.

The United States makes up 40 percent of Cambodia's export market. Cambodia's exports to the United States have been very concentrated, with 94 percent of them in textiles and apparel. Five products—all apparel—accounted for nearly half of total exports in 1995–99. It is true that a high proportion (68 percent) of Cambodian exports to the United States have unit values that are not close to those of their Chinese competitor products, and thus the share of exports that are at risk at the 10 percent share threshold appears low (9 percent) (Table 2.6). But this estimate significantly understates Cambodia's likely true exposure. Once the quota restrictions on China are lifted, its exports to the EU and North America are likely to capture more than 10 percent of these markets. If Cambodia's exports in these categories are viewed as being in a category with a high Chinese import share, the picture changes dramatically: Roughly 30 percent of Cambodia's exports show themselves to be at risk.

Cambodian manufacturers continue to hope they can compete in various niche markets. But they face some significant administrative hurdles and government interventions that tend to negate Cambodia's comparative advantage against its regional competitors, particularly in the context of low labor input costs.

Singapore is another important market. Cambodia's exports to Singapore are extremely concentrated, with natural rubber accounting for nearly 60 percent, and their exposure to Chinese exports is quite limited. Even at the 10 percent import share threshold, less than 3 percent of Cambodian exports appear to be at risk.

All this said, Cambodia faces major challenges in adjusting its economy. Reforms in governance and other areas need to be speeded up to ensure that alternative production networks develop.

Lao People's Democratic Republic

Lao PDR is less exposed than Cambodia to the impact of China's accession to the WTO. Although the effects of tariff reduction will be quite small,[44] the phase-out of quantitative restrictions associated with WTO accession will create market opportunities for Lao PDR. The main benefit of the QR liberalization will be felt in timber exports,[45] which make up 62 percent of total exports to China, but will also affect other key exports such as dried fruits, "other pharmaceutical plants," and coffee.

No appreciable losses are expected in Lao PDR's most important export market, Thailand, which absorbs one-fourth of its total exports.[46] Ten percent of Laotian exports go to Japan, and 45 percent of these are in a single product category—builders and joinery.[47] Only 4 percent of Lao PDR's exports to Japan are in at-risk categories, where unit values are close to those of competitor products from China and where China's import share is more than

TABLE 2.6   Market-by-Market and Product-by-Product Analysis of Cambodian Exports: China Market Share and Closeness of Unit Value (UV) as Proxies for Potential Risk

	China's import share			China's import share	
	< 10%	> 10%		< 10%	> 10% + all apparel, textiles
Share in U.S. market (%) (n = 64 products)					
UV close	22.0	9.5		2.4	29.0
UV not close	39.3	28.7		1.0	67.0
Share of market in analysis			99.4		99.4

Note: The figure shows calculations using two (arbitrary) threshold levels for Chinese imports: 5 percent and 10 percent of the total import market.
Sources: UN Comtrade data; China's WTO accession agreement; authors' calculations.

10 percent (see Table 2.7). (Using the 5 percent import share threshold, the exposure increases to 19 percent, but sensitivity analysis shows only an insignificant impact on the terms of trade.)

Although trade with China clearly represents opportunities for Lao PDR, the likely impact of China's WTO accession on the country may be limited. Its policymakers therefore have some breathing space to implement their broader development agenda.

Vietnam

China's WTO accession will present Vietnam with a combination of expanding market opportunities in China's growing market and serious competitive threats. The ability of the economy and particularly the private sector to react flexibly will be critical. Vietnam itself is preparing for integration with the rest of the world. The country has made a bold step toward trade reform by signing the Vietnam-U.S. Bilateral Trade Agreement. It is also in the process of implementing the ASEAN Free Trade Area (AFTA) and getting ready for accession to the WTO. Despite these reforms, however, its economy is still relatively closed (Ianchovichina 2001), and it is still in the process of establishing its export base.

On the positive side, increased access to China's domestic market will stimulate Vietnamese exports across most product categories and further intensify trade between the two economies.[48] China's accession will create opportunities for expanding rice production and increasing exports to China of oilseeds, sugar, and cotton, for example. Other sec-

tors likely to expand include food processing, light manufacturing, metals and petrochemicals, electronics, and other manufactures (Figure 2.5).

To date, Vietnam has been particularly successful at expanding its apparel and other labor-intensive exports—apparel is an important growth sector for Vietnam. By global standards, Vietnam's exports of garments are small,[49] but at the national level they are important. They account for more than 14 percent of Vietnamese exports and provide a livelihood for thousands of unskilled workers, many of whom are female. The country has exported apparel mainly to the EU and Japan. More recently, the Vietnam-U.S. Bilateral Trade Agreement has opened up the U.S. market to apparel from Vietnam,[50] but China's WTO accession calls into question how much of a share Vietnamese exporters will be able to capture in this market. Vietnam has two years to establish itself before the 2005 removal of the quota on Chinese imports. Estimates suggest that China's entry to the WTO will depress Vietnam's apparel output and exports relative to the baseline by 2010 and negatively affect its terms of trade (Figure 2.5).[51] Therefore, it is important for Vietnam to use the period 2002–05 to advance the reform process and smooth the structural adjustment that will need to take place.

For Vietnam, trade liberalization by China implies lower costs for Chinese imports, which represents an important opportunity to reduce the costs of Vietnamese manufacturing overall. At the same time, liberalization may represent tougher competition for its own manufacturers. Vietnam has already imposed temporary safeguard measures

TABLE 2.7 Market-by-Market and Product-by-Product Analysis of Lao PDR's Exports: China Market Share and Closeness of Unit Value (UV) as Proxies for Potential Risk

	China's import share			China's import share		
	< 10%	> 10%		< 5%	> 5%	
Share in Japanese market (%) (n = 11 products)						
UV close	67.3	4.0		52.2	19.1	
UVnot close	24.3	4.3		24.3	4.3	
Share of market in analysis			100.0			100.0

Note: The figure shows calculations using two (arbitrary) threshold levels for Chinese imports: 5 percent and 10 percent of the total import market.
Sources: UN Comtrade data; China's WTO accession agreement; authors' calculations.

on imports of motorbikes. Such measures can only prolong the adjustments that Vietnam needs to make to realize its regional comparative advantages.

Vietnam will have to greatly improve its business environment if it is to compete successfully for foreign investment with China and reap net gains from China's growing role in the region. Without such action, the net impact of China's WTO accession could be negative for Vietnam. It will be important to resist protectionist pressures from domestic producers and to act aggressively to establish its garment exports in the United States.

Conclusions

The biggest beneficiary of China's accession to the World Trade Organization is China itself, and most of the benefits are associated with China's own trade liberalization. China's accession and growing role in the world economy also have important implications for the rest of East Asia.

Emerging East Asia is in a good position to benefit from China's agricultural liberalization. China already is a major agricultural market for these countries, and the markets of most interest to developing East Asia—oilseeds, sugar, processed foods—are poised to open further. Although the initial protection in China's food grain sector might be less than other studies have suggested (e.g., for rice), import demand is still expected to increase considerably.

The potential for specialization and complementary intraindustry trade in the manufacturing sector could be significant. China is increasingly a central player in global production networks, including electronics and machinery. And its trade with the rest of East Asia in parts and components—both imports and exports—represents an opportunity for the rest of emerging East Asia to benefit from China's growing role. In the automobile sector, however, China's current plans for restructuring its industry will make it a more efficient assembler, leading to a contraction of production in Japan and the NIEs. Likewise, the abolishment of import quotas on Chinese textiles and apparel in key markets by 2005 will make China a formidable competitor, especially in the apparel sector, and will lead to restructuring, with a particularly significant impact on quota-dependent low- and middle-income countries.

Dynamic gains will swamp the static impact from China's WTO accession. The liberalization of China's services sector will lead to expanded exports of services such as transport logistics, communication, business, and tourism services, and the productivity from expanded competition and foreign entry in China's services sector will fuel China's economy and demand. Because trade intensity with China is high for all emerging East Asian economies, they stand to benefit from this dynamic growth. Growth in the region's exports will also be fueled by the increased demand from China's major trading partners that benefit directly from China's accession to the WTO.

China's accession and deeper integration into the world economy present the East Asia region with a range of opportunities and challenges. Given the complexity of the changes, this assessment of the impact on the region's economies is merely suggestive. However, it provides a framework for further understanding the likely changes, so that East Asian economies can position themselves to grasp the opportunities and manage the challenges.

Endnotes

1. It is difficult to judge the accuracy of the FDI data because they reflect "round-tripping" investments undertaken from China to take advantage of concessions enjoyed only by foreign investors. The outflows do not include flows through Hong Kong (China).

2. Descriptions of the CGE methodology and detailed results are given in the background paper by Ianchovichina and Walmsley (2003) at www.worldbank.org/eaptrade.

3. For information on individual sectors, see Yusuf, Altar, and Nabeshima (2003).

4. These are weighted average tariffs computed using trade weights for 2001; see Ianchovichina and Martin (2002). See www.worldbank.org/eaptrade for the estimated evolution of tariff rates by product group, 1997–2010.

5. Dollar amounts are current U.S. dollars.

6. China will be subject to additional textile safeguard quotas until 2007, but these will be applicable for only one year at a time, unlike the existing quotas that were put in place for an indefinite period.

7. This is a consensus finding supported by Deutsche Bank (2001), Ianchovichina and Martin (2003), Ianchovichina and Walmsley (2003), and Wang (2002). The textile industry in general will also be hurt, though not nearly as much as the apparel industry, because some of these countries will start exporting textiles to China and other NIEs.

8. McKibbin and Tang (2000) and Ianchovichina and Walmsley (2003) discuss in detail the effect of trade liberalization on rates of return to capital and foreign investment.

9. All East Asian economies saw increases in their share of manufactured exports during the first half of the 1990s, and all saw changes in the structure of manufactured exports. In

the 1990s the NIEs increased their share of electronics and information technology products and China increased its share of electronics and telecommunications exports.

10. Even though wage levels and productivity lag in China's hinterland, in the short to medium term the lagging regions may not be able to compete successfully with other less developed East Asian economies in attracting footloose export-oriented industries because of high transport and other infrastructure costs.

11. These results from CGE modeling are consistent with findings of other CGE modeling work. See Li and others (2000), Deutsche Bank (2001), Ianchovichina and Martin (2003), and Wang (2002).

12. See Appendix Table 2.3 in the technical appendix to this chapter at www.worldbank.org/eaptrade.

13. Differences in tariff cuts reflect differences in export composition by exporting country.

14. Ng and Yeats (2003) estimate a distance-adjusted trade intensity index of 1.36 for China and Indonesia.

15. This group of products includes roasted decaffeinated coffee, palm kernel or babassu oil, cocoa powder, soap, cathode ray tubes, and cane and bamboo furniture.

16. Between 1995 and 1999 Indonesia was the second largest exporter of palm oil to China after Malaysia. In 1999 it supplied China with 355,172 metric tons.

17. The initial quota for palm oil is 2.1 million metric tons, which will rise to 3.168 million metric tons in 2005. In 1999 Chinese imports of palm oil totaled 1.193 million metric tons. The in-quota tariff rate is set at 9 percent throughout the period, and while the initial out-of-tariff rate is as high as 63.3 percent, it is slated to decline constantly to 9 percent in 2006. Although TRQs will be allocated to both state and nonstate trading enterprises, the reduction in the proportion of state trading enterprises from 42 percent to 10 percent during the implementation period and the elimination of the tariff-rate quota on January 1, 2006, should facilitate development of the market.

18. For natural rubber imports, the total initial quota level is set at 429,000 metric tons, with an annual quota growth rate of 15 percent after 2004, when the quota will be eliminated. Phasing-out dates are as of January 1 of the calendar year specified. Natural rubber is a product subject to designated trading (Annex 2B of China's WTO accession agreement), which is slated to be liberalized within three years of accession. Under designated trading, the Chinese government authorizes only certain firms to engage in international trade. Initial and final tariff rates are bound at 20 percent.

19. Urea accounted for 1.3 percent of Chinese imports from Indonesia. Previously, urea was subject to both an import license and quota. These restrictions will be replaced by tariff-rate quotas upon accession. The initial quota for urea is about 1.3 million metric tons, increasing to 3.3 million metric tons in 2006. The out-of-quota tariff rate is 50 percent.

20. Indonesia could increase its oil sales. However, because Indonesia is a member of the Organization of Petroleum Exporting Countries (OPEC), its production is constrained by OPEC quotas.

21. During 1995–99, based on 2,700 products at the five-digit Standard International Trade Classification (SITC) level, the correlation between Indonesia's export structure and China's rose from 0.174 to 0.302.

22. In each major import market we looked at three variables. The first was imports in a particular product category as a share of total imports from that country (e.g., garment imports from Thailand as a share of total imports from Thailand). This vari-

able indicates the importance of exports in that product category to the sending country. The second variable was imports from China as a share of total imports in that product category (e.g., garment imports from China as a share of total garment imports in the United States). In the country-by country analyses, we looked at two (arbitrary) threshold levels for the share of Chinese imports—10 percent and 5 percent of total imports. The third variable was unit values of imports in the product categories in question. Product categories mask a variety of differences; unit values provide an additional indication of how similar products are and therefore how likely there is to be a terms-of-trade impact from competition. If the unit values of imports from both sending countries were on the same side of the average unit values for the product category in question, we deemed them to be "close."

23. These products are technically specified natural rubber (9 percent of exports); footwear with outer sole of leather (8.2 percent); video recording or reproducing apparatus (5.4 percent); plywood with outer ply of tropical wood (5 percent); and other rubber footwear (3.1 percent).

24. Footwear with leather soles and video recording or reproducing apparatus—which accounted for 8 percent and 5 percent of Indonesian exports to the United States, respectively.

25. Plywood with an outer ply of tropical wood (19.4 percent); frozen shrimp and prawns (11.5 percent); bituminous coal (7.1 percent); nickel mattes (3.5 percent); and nonalloyed aluminum (2.9 percent).

26. They are bituminous coal and cotton yarn other than sewing thread.

27. In 2001 Indonesia exported $313 million to China and imported $110 million from China in parts and components (Ng and Yeats 2003).

28. Although Malaysia faces some threats because of its high wages and heavy reliance on mid-range electronics, the economy-wide, medium-term analysis highlights equally important opportunities for gains.

29. See Appendix Table 2.2 in the technical appendix to this chapter at www.worldbank.org/eaptrade.

30. See Appendix Table 2.2 in the technical appendix to this chapter at www.worldbank.org/eaptrade.

31. Ng and Yeats (2003) estimate a distance-adjusted trade intensity index of 2.29 for China and the Philippines.

32. See Appendix Table 2.2 in the technical appendix to this chapter at www.worldbank.org/eaptrade.

33. The annual average value of Thailand's exports to China is $2.14 billion. Thailand's top exports to China include parts for automated data processing machines, rice, rubber, cane sugar, and plastics.

34. According to China's WTO Protocol of Accession, tariff-rate quotas will apply to grains, sugar, and cotton for which out-of-quota tariffs are quite high. Otherwise, after the phase-in period the tariffs will range between just 1 and 15 percent—representing substantial liberalization over 2001 levels (Anderson, Huang, and Ianchovichina 2002).

35. In 1995–99 Thailand supplied more than 84 percent of China's imports of rice and nearly 60 percent of its imports of natural rubber. Thailand supplied almost 33 percent of China's imports of raw cane sugar, but it is only one of 12 countries that have initial negotiating rights.

36 See Appendix Table 2 in the technical appendix to this chapter at www.worldbank.org/eaptrade.

37. See the description of the methodology in the earlier section on Indonesia for which a similar analysis was carried out.

38. The top export products include digital monolithic units (7.7 percent); frozen shrimp and prawns (7.5 percent); pre-

cious metal jewelry (4.1 percent); prepared and preserved crustacea (3.6 percent); and leather sole footwear (2.4 percent).

39. These shares denote minimum levels of exposure, because the analysis covers only the top 150 and 165 products.

40. They are smoked sheets of natural rubber (6.4 percent); frozen shrimp and prawns (5.7 percent); frozen poultry parts (3.7 percent); preserved and prepared crustacea (2.8 percent); and parts for automated data processing machines (2.5 percent).

41. Among the top 200 export products, unit value data are missing for 11. We focus on the remaining 189 products, which collectively accounted for 82.8 percent of Thailand's exports to Japan.

42. The four exports are frozen poultry parts; prepared and preserved crustacea; other frozen, dry, salted mollusks; and seats with wooden frames.

43. The weighted average tariff for the top 100 exports to China will decline from a relatively low level of 4.3 percent in 2001 to 2.6 percent in 2005.

44. The weighted average tariff for the top 100 exports to China will decline from 7.3 percent in 2001 to 6.0 percent in 2005.

45. Timber trading will be liberalized within three years of accession.

46. Nearly 62 percent of exports to Thailand are of wood and related products—categories in which a large Chinese export supply response is not expected.

47. Lao PDR exports 11 products to Japan—largely wood and wood products (74 percent), coffee (24 percent), and some cotton shirts and footwear (2 percent).

48. Trade intensity indexes in Ng and Yeats (2003) show that the intensity of trade between China and Vietnam grew markedly between 1985 and 2001.

49. In 1997 Vietnam had less than a 1 percent share of the global apparel market.

50. Vietnamese apparel exports to the United States have grown rapidly over the past couple of years. In 2001 articles of apparel and clothing accessories exported to the United States amounted to $57 million. In 2002 exports of these items exploded to nearly $900 million, and to more than $200 million in January 2003 alone (http://dataweb.usitc.gov/). In response, the U.S. government was prompted to imposed quotas on Vietnamese garment exports.

51. See Fan and Li (2000). Also see Appendix Table 2.3 in the technical appendix to this chapter at www.worldbank.org/eaptrade.

References

The word *processed* describes informally reproduced works that may not be commonly available through libraries.

Anderson, K., J. Huang, and E. Ianchovichina. 2003. "Impact of China's WTO Accession on Farm–Nonfarm Income Inequality and Rural Poverty." Policy Research Working Paper 3052, World Bank, Washington, D.C.

Claro, S. 2001. "Tariff and FDI Liberalization: What to Expect from China's Entry into WTO?" Paper presented at Eighth Annual Conference on Empirical Investigations in International Trade, Purdue University, November 9–11.

Deutsche Bank. 2001. *Quantifying the Impact of China's WTO Entry*. DB Global Market Research, December 14.

Fan, Z., and S. Li. 2000. "The Implications of Accession to WTO for China's Economy." Paper presented at Third Annual Conference on Global Economic Analysis, Monash University, Melbourne, Australia, June 28–30.

Francois, Joseph F., and Den Spinanger. 2002. "Market Access in Textiles and Clothing." Paper prepared for Informing the Doha Process: New Trade Research for Developing Countries, Cairo, May.

Hertel, T. W., T. L. Walmsley, and K. Itakura. 2001. "Dynamic Effects of the 'New Age' Free Trade Agreement between Japan and Singapore." *Journal of Economic Integration* 16 (4): 446–48.

Huang, J., and S. Rozelle. 2002. "The Nature of Distortions to Agricultural Incentives in China and Implications of WTO Accession." Paper presented at Seminar on WTO Accession, Policy Reform and Poverty Reduction in China, World Bank, Beijing, June 28–29.

Ianchovichina, Elena. 2001. "Trade Barriers in Vietnam and China: A Comparison." World Bank, Washington, D.C. Processed.

———. 2003. "GTAP-OD: A Model for Analyzing Trade Reforms in the Presence of Duty Drawbacks." GTAP Technical Paper 21, Purdue University.

Ianchovichina, Elena, and William J. Martin. 2001. "Trade Liberalization in China's Accession to the World Trade Organization." *Journal of Economic Integrations* 16 (4): 421–45.

———. 2003. "Economic Impacts of China's Accession to the WTO." Policy Research Working Paper 3053, World Bank, Washington, D.C.

Ianchovichina, Elena, and Terrie Walmsley. 2003. "The Impact of China's WTO Accession on East Asia." Policy Research Working Paper 3109, World Bank, Washington, D.C. Processed.

IMF (International Monetary Fund). Various years. *Direction of Trade Statistics.* Washington, D.C.: IMF.

Li, S., Z. Wang, Z. Fan, and L. Xu. 2000. *WTO: China and the World.* Beijing: China Development Press.

Martin, William J. 1993. "The Fallacy of Composition and Developing Country Exports of Manufactures." *World Economy* 16 (2): 159–72.

Marukawa, T. 2001. "Japanese Foreign Direct Investment and China's Industrial Development: Focusing on Automobile, Electronics, and Textile Industries." Paper presented at Conference on Japan and China: Economic Relations in Transition, Tokyo, January 18–19.

Mattoo, Aaditya. 2002. "China's Accession to the WTO: The Services Dimension." Paper presented at Seminar on WTO Accession, Policy Reform and Poverty Reduction in China, World Bank, Beijing, June 28–29.

McKibbin, W., and K. Tang. 2000. "Trade and Financial Reform in China: Impacts on the World Economy." *World Economy* 23 (8).

Ng, F., and A. Yeats. 2003. "Major Trade Trends in East Asia: What Are Their Implications for Regional Cooperation and Growth?" Policy Research Working Paper 3084. World Bank, Washington, D.C.

Spihauger, Den. 1999. "Textiles beyond the MFA Phase-Out." *World Economy* 22 (4): 455–76.

UNCTAD (United Nations Conference on Trade and Development). 2001. *World Investment Report 2001: Promoting Linkages.* Geneva.

Wang, Z. 2002. "WTO Accession, 'Greater China' Free Trade Area, and Economic Relations across the Taiwan Strait." Paper presented at Fifth Conference on Global Economic Analysis, Taipei, June 5–7.

Yusuf, Shahid, M. Anjum Altar, and Kaoru Nabeshima, eds. 2003. *Global Production Networking and Technological Change in East Asia.* Washington, D.C.: World Bank and Oxford University Press.

3

NEW REGIONALISM: OPTIONS FOR EAST ASIA

Mari Pangestu
Sudarshan Gooptu

Half of world trade is now conducted under preferential trade arrangements (WTO 2000a, 2000b), up from 40 percent in 1988–92 (Lloyd and Crosby, 2002). In East Asia, the past several years have seen a plethora of proposals for new preferential arrangements, both bilateral and regional. Although very few of these proposals have reached the negotiation stage or have been formalized, several economies in the region are seriously engaged in developing new preferential trade relationships. These include China and two countries, Japan and the Republic of Korea, that were formerly staunchly against the preferential route to trade liberalization.

The most significant of the new initiatives in terms of members is the ASEAN (Association of Southeast Asian Nations)-China Free Trade Area now under negotiation.[1] If agreement is reached, it will be the world's biggest free trade area, encompassing 1.7 billion people, a collective gross domestic product (GDP) of almost US$2 trillion,[2] and intraregional trade of $1.2 trillion. Other recent proposals include bilateral cooperation between Japan and Korea and between Japan and Singapore

and arrangements aimed at broader cooperation—for example, ASEAN + 3 (China, Japan, and Korea) and ASEAN + CER (Australia, New Zealand). New early warning systems for macroeconomic imbalances, as well as numerous technical assistance and information exchange arrangements, are also being considered.

Preferential trade arrangements are sharply at odds with previous East Asian preferences for a nondiscriminatory approach to reform.[3] In the mid-1990s economies in the region pursued a unilateral and nonpreferential route to trade liberalization—an approach that is embodied in the principles of the Asia-Pacific Economic Cooperation (APEC) forum and supported by evidence that such a commitment contributes to growth, development, and greater integration in economic terms and more broadly.[4] The East Asian economies, especially, undertook unilateral liberalization mainly on a most-favored-nation basis, encouraged by regional peer pressure and World Trade Organization (WTO) commitments, among other factors.

This chapter draws on background papers prepared for this study by Peter Lloyd and Mark Crosby (2002) and He Fan (2002), as well as other papers listed in the references. We have also benefited from the excellent research assistance that was provided by Qing Lani Wu from the Kennedy School of Government, Harvard University, during her internship at the World Bank.

Regional integration in trade should be viewed as only one element (but a critical one) of a broader set of policy and institutional changes currently taking place in East Asia and aimed at regional economic cooperation. The wider the country and sectoral coverage of regional trade agreements (RTAs), the greater will be the gains from removing intraregional barriers through them. Thus liberalization goals can be well served by moving on several fronts. The outcome will depend crucially on maintaining a common set of principles for each regional integration agreement that focus on trade facilitation measures, allowing the most liberal rules of origin, and yet at the same time act as a catalyst for multilateral trade liberalization.

Reasons for New Regionalism

The new regionalism in East Asia seems to be motivated by several factors. The first is the need to reduce the risks of financial contagion and unusual exchange rate instability, the damaging effects of which were made clear by the Asian financial crisis of 1997–98. The crisis showed that rapid depreciation of one country's currency could adversely affect the export competitiveness of other countries, especially neighbors producing the same products for the same export markets (Eichengreen 2001). The crisis initially propelled countries to explore options for monetary cooperation and macroeconomic policy coordination,[5] but, by highlighting the economic interdependence of the region, it has also given rise to proposals for regional cooperation in trade and investment (see Box 3.1.).

A second key factor in the new trend is the perceived need by other economies of the region for stronger cooperation with China, both as a growing import market and as a rising competitor in export markets. Over the decade 1990–2000, China experienced an average real rate of growth of 10 percent a year, and its exports quadrupled from some $62 billion to $250 billion. Meanwhile, investment flows to China increased dramatically, from some $3 billion to more than $40 billion (ASEAN-China Expert Group on Economic Cooperation 2001).

BOX 3.1   Forms of Regional Preferential Trading Arrangements

Statistics on regional trading arrangements notified to the WTO show that more than twice as many preferential trading arrangements (197) are in force today as 10 years ago (WTO 2002b). Nearly all WTO Members (97 percent) now participate in RTAs, and many belong to more than one. Some, like member countries of the European Union (EU) and Mexico, belong to more than 10 RTAs (Crawford and Laird 2000). EU-centered or -related RTAs make up about half of the RTAs in force. RTAs come in many forms:

- *Sectoral preferential trading arrangements*: preferential tariffs in selected sectors and goods. Examples are the European Coal and Steel Community and the ASEAN Preferential Trade Agreement scheme, which preceded the AFTA scheme.
- *Free trade area*: removal of tariffs and other trade regulations that restrict trade among the members (may apply to goods and services).
- *Customs union*: a free trade area plus harmonization of tariff rates and trade regulations that face third countries (may apply to goods and services).

- *Common market*: free trade area among members in goods, services, capital, and labor. Entails removal in those areas of all barriers and trade regulations that restrict trade among members.
- *Single market*: a common market plus harmonization of all laws, regulations, and taxes that affect market prices.
- *Economic union*: common market and unification of economic institutions and coordination of economic policy among member countries. Supranational institutions are established with decisions binding all members. Involves considerable surrender of national sovereignty.
- *Monetary union*: a single currency and a single central bank.
- *Fiscal union*: equal tax treatment in one country of enterprises and persons from anywhere within the RTA region.

Sources: Lloyd and Crosby (2002) and Chia (2002).

A third factor is the interest of business communities in getting preferential access to foreign markets, especially when these are imperfectly competitive markets in which some form of establishment is required. The benefits from being the first movers in such an environment are significant. The greater tradability of many services and the growth of foreign direct investment (FDI) have contributed to this focus in policymaking.

Other factors include the move by many economies, especially the more developed in the region, to lower their average tariffs; the growing recognition of the value of harmonizing standards and regulations, so that they do not impede trade; and the higher concentration of trade among regional partners, especially in East Asia. These changes have affected countries' assessment of the costs and benefits of entering into preferential agreements. Some countries are also seeking to forge new agreements as a defensive response to arrangements being created elsewhere.

Agreements on economic cooperation offer opportunities to build a sense of community or to repair past tensions between neighboring economies. Membership in regional trading arrangements and informal economic cooperation forums provides occasions for numerous meetings between senior officials, ministers, and leaders, and apparently it has served as a crucial component of the community building that has taken place in the region, especially in ASEAN. APEC meetings have also provided an important forum in which to discuss economic and, increasingly, noneconomic issues of concern to members without having to negotiate. The discussions and negotiations that do take place, including issues not yet covered in the WTO, are also seen as important capacity-building exercises.

Finally, countries cite their perceptions of a slow pace of progress in trade liberalization, or their expectations of poor prospects under WTO and existing regional cooperation mechanisms such as ASEAN and APEC and the example set by increased economic integration in Europe and North America.

Organization of This Chapter

The chances for a new WTO trade round are now brighter, and East Asia stands to gain from any breakthroughs in the multilateral trade liberalization presently being considered at the global level. There is concern that pursuit of a regional approach might deflect attention from the multilateral agenda, that it could hold East Asia back from reaching its full economic potential, and that it could increase economic and political tensions in the region. Experience shows that a haphazard and uncoordinated proliferation of preferential agreements can increase the costs of doing business.

With an eye toward helping the economies of the region make informed decisions on trade policy and economic integration, this chapter reviews current and proposed regional trading arrangements and discusses issues in their design. The first major section that follows outlines the agreements now in force and under discussion in East Asia. The next section examines what the literature reveals about the benefits and risks of such arrangements and draws out some policy implications for East Asian economies. It includes a look at whether a regional approach can complement a multilateral approach. The evolving relationship between China and ASEAN and the implications for their cooperation agreement now under negotiation are examined in the next section. It is followed by a discussion of regional financial cooperation and our conclusions.

Regional Trade Agreements in East Asia

Bilateral and multilateral trading arrangements in East Asia are proliferating and becoming more complex. Chia (2002) distinguishes between economic *regionalization* and *regionalism*. Regionalization refers to the greater economic interdependence that results from increased intraregional trade, investment, technology, and migration flows without any formal framework of cooperation. It is often termed *market-driven* integration because it occurs as each economy undertakes its own unilateral process of opening up, as well as fulfilling its multilateral commitments. Regionalism refers to *formal* economic cooperation and economic integration arrangements, and agreements between two or more countries that are designed to achieve economic growth through trade and investment liberalization and facilitation.

Market-driven integration or regionalization has been occurring in East Asia since the mid-1980s through increased trade and investment linkages. The process has been driven by unilateral reforms in individual economies and by the logic of the "flying geese" pattern of relocating production processes to cheaper areas abroad as domestic costs rise. Firms moved their production processes from Japan to the East Asian newly industrializing economies (NIEs) in the 1970s and early 1980s, to Southeast Asia in the mid-1980s to early 1990s, and to China in the mid-1980s to mid-1990s (Xu and Song 2000).[6] To support the vertical specialization and division of production along the value chain, intraregional trade has grown rapidly in components, parts, and inputs.

Table 3.1 lists actual and potential trading arrangements involving East Asian economies.[7] Most of these arrangements are still in the form of proposals and studies, or at the negotiation stage.

Some may never be implemented because many unresolved issues remain, and others may only become implementation agreements associated with APEC processes.

The arrangements mooted or under discussion are all free trade areas, not customs unions. Like regional trading arrangements elsewhere in the world, they extend beyond the traditional areas of trade policy—such as tariffs and nontariff measures—and into investment, services, and standards. These are areas covered by the WTO, but where the progress of WTO negotiations might be seen as too slow (e.g., in services), or where WTO coverage is very limited (e.g., the investment issues in goods production). All the discussions refer to WTO consistency as well as other rules such as open access and comprehensive coverage.

TABLE 3.1   Proposed and Actual Regional Trading Arrangements Involving East Asian Countries

	Type of agreement	Status	Year
Bilateral Asia Pacific			
China–Hong Kong (China)	Closer economic partnership	Signed	2003
Singapore–Australia	Free trade area	Signed	2003
Singapore–Canada	Free trade area	Under negotiation	2001
Singapore–Chile	Free trade area	Under negotiation	2000
Singapore–Japan	Free trade area	Signed	2002
Singapore– Korea, Rep. of	Free trade area	Proposal	
Singapore–Mexico	Free trade area	Under negotiation	1999
Singapore–New Zealand	Closer economic partnership	Signed	2001
Singapore–Taiwan (China)	Free trade area	Proposal/study	2002
Singapore–USA	Free trade area	Signed	2003
Korea, Rep. of–Australia	Free trade area	Official discussions	2000
Korea, Rep. of–Chile	Free trade area	Signed	2002
Korea, Rep. of–China	Free trade area	Proposal/study	
Korea, Rep. of–Japan	Free trade area	Official discussions/ study	1998
Korea, Rep. of–Mexico	Free trade area	Official discussions/ study	2000
Korea, Rep. of–New Zealand	Free trade area	Official discussions/ study	2000
Korea, Rep. of–Thailand	Free trade area	Proposal/study	2001
Korea, Rep. of–USA	Free trade area	Under negotiation	2001
Japan–Canada	Free trade area	Proposal/study	2002
Japan–Chile	Free trade area	Official discussions/ study	2000
Japan–China–Rep. of Korea	Free trade area	Proposal	2002
Japan–Mexico	Free trade area	Official discussions/ study	1998

TABLE 3.1 (continued)

	Type of agreement	Status	Year
Japan–Philippines	Free trade area	Proposal	2002
Japan–Taiwan (China)	Free trade area	Proposal	
Japan–Thailand	Closer economic partnership	Proposal/study	2002
Taiwan (China)–New Zealand	Free trade area	Proposal	
Taiwan (China)–Panama	Free trade area	Proposal	
Hong Kong (China)–New Zealand	Closer economic partnership	Official discussions	2001
Thailand–Australia	Free trade area	Under negotiation	2002
Thailand–Croatia	Free trade area	Proposal	2001
Thailand–Czech Republic	Free trade area	Proposal	2001
Thailand–India	Free trade area	Proposal	2002
USA–Philippines	Free trade area	Proposal	2002
USA–Taiwan (China)	Free trade area	Proposal	2002
Regional plus			
AFTA	Free trade area	Being implemented	1992
AFTA + CER	Closer economic relations	Official discussions/ study	2000
ASEAN + China	Free trade area	Official study/ negotiation	2001
ASEAN + India	Regional trade and investment agreement	Proposal	2002
ASEAN + Japan	Closer economic partnership	Official discussions	2002
ASEAN + Korea, Rep. of	Free trade area	Official discussions	2002
Singapore + EFTA	Free trade area	Signed	2002
ASEAN + 3	Free trade area	Official discussions/ study	2000
EU + ASEAN	Trans Regional EU–ASEAN Trade Initiative (TREATI)	Proposal	2003
New regional			
Japan–Korea, Rep. of–China	Free trade area	Official discussions/ study	2000
Pacific 5	Free trade area	Proposal	1997

Notes:
EFTA (European Free Trade Area): Switzerland, Iceland, Liechtenstein, and Norway.
Pacific 5: Singapore, Australia, New Zealand, United States, and Chile.
ASEAN: Brunei, Cambodia, Indonesia, Lao PDR, Malaysia, Myanmar, the Philippines, Singapore, Thailand, Vietnam.
ASEAN + 3: ASEAN plus Japan, Korea, and China.
AFTA = ASEAN Free Trade Area.
CER = Australia–New Zealand, already associated under the Australia-New Zealand Closer Economic Relations Trade Agreement (ANZCERTA).
Sources: Authors' compilations from various media sources.

Geographic proximity is not a key considera-tion. Some agreements are between close neigh-bors, but others are between trans-Pacific part-ners, such as Mexico and Singapore or Korea and Chile. Several take ASEAN/AFTA (ASEAN Free Trade Area) as their focal point and build upon AFTA.

ASEAN Free Trade Area

AFTA was until recently the only preferential regional trade agreement in East Asia. It now has 10 member economies with a combined population of nearly half a billion and a combined GDP almost as large as China's. AFTA became effective on January

1, 2002, for the original six ASEAN members. Longer timetables apply to the newer members: 2004 for Vietnam, 2006 for Lao People's Democratic Republic (Lao PDR) and Myanmar, and 2008 for Cambodia.

Formal economic integration under AFTA is confined mainly to tariff reductions, and intra-ASEAN trade already enjoys low tariffs. AFTA's target is for 0–5 percent tariffs for intra-ASEAN trade among the original six signatories. In fact, 90 percent of intra-ASEAN trade can already be conducted at tariffs in the 0–5 percent range. The average ASEAN common effective preferential tariff (CEPT) fell from 12.76 percent to 2.91 percent over the period 1993–2002. Because individual ASEAN economies were already liberalizing their trade before AFTA came into force, AFTA's common effective preferential tariff rates differ little from the most-favored-nation (MFN) rates, and indeed for two-thirds of the items in AFTA's inclusion list the two tariffs are the same. As a result, not much of intra-ASEAN trade has come in under the CEPT tariff (Soesastro 2001).

The integration of trade and investment—as well as, to some extent, services and factor movements—among AFTA members stems more from the unilateral liberalization that has been undertaken by individual members and from the market forces integrating their economies, especially those that are close neighbors, than to the agreement itself. Different AFTA members have different trade policy regimes: Some have chosen to multilateralize their AFTA commitments; others have chosen the same schedule of tariff reductions as AFTA but with a slightly higher end point on an MFN basis compared with the AFTA preferential rate.

AFTA has evolved more gradually than regional cooperation schemes in North America and Europe. Strong expressions of political commitment, and proposals to widen ASEAN cooperation, have not always been followed up with concrete and broad-ranging implementation.[8] A comprehensive and integrated framework to cover investment, services, trade and investment facilitation measures, competition policy, and antidumping has been proposed, but it has not progressed very far.

Proposed Regional Arrangements Involving China

Various initiatives have been discussed in the last few years to strengthen cooperation in trade, investment, and finance between China and northeast Asia, ASEAN, the economies of Hong Kong (China) and Macao (China), and East Asia more widely. At a recent meeting in Hong Kong, China announced the possibility of a Hong Kong, Macao, and China free trade area.[9] And there have been discussions of separate bilateral agreements between China and Asian countries such as Korea and Thailand. The recently completed ASEAN + 3 (China, Japan, and Korea) Bilateral Swap Arrangement of the Chiang Mai initiative (CMI) is perhaps a precursor to expanded trade arrangements and greater financial and macroeconomic cooperation and coordination.[10]

Proposals for northeast Asian economic cooperation involving China, Korea, and Japan face many obstacles such as agricultural protectionism and the complex and shifting political relations in northeast Asia.[11] Proposals such as a Northeast Asian Council and a Northeast Asian Development Bank have not gone far (He Fan 2002).

The most concrete proposal is for economic cooperation between China and ASEAN. In November 2000 the fourth meeting of the ASEAN + 3 leaders created a task force to study the possibility of establishing an ASEAN free trade zone, and in November 2001, "to everyone's surprise," ASEAN leaders and Chinese premier Zhu Rongji endorsed the establishment of a free trade area between China and ASEAN economies within 10 years in the context of the Framework Agreement on China-ASEAN Comprehensive Economic Cooperation (He Fan 2002).[12] Negotiations are ongoing, including on issues of product coverage.

The envisaged scope of the agreement is quite comprehensive. On trade in goods it goes beyond the removal of tariffs and nontariff barriers to include trade facilitation measures such as conformity of standards and procedures, and it also covers trade in services. The aim is to introduce tariff reductions for a certain group of products over three years beginning prior to January 1, 2004, and for other products over the agreed time frame of the free trade area—either to 2010 or to 2013.

Other ASEAN Proposals

In response to the proposed creation of the ASEAN-China Free Trade Area, other countries have now shown interest in free trade agreements with

ASEAN. Japanese prime minister Junichiro Koizumi recently suggested an ASEAN-Japan Comprehensive Economic Partnership, an arrangement that would include traditional as well as new elements related to facilitation, standards, and other forms of cooperation. Korea has made a similar proposal, and at the APEC 2002 meeting in Mexico, even the United States made a similar overture. President George W. Bush put forward a new trade initiative called the U.S. Enterprise for ASEAN Initiative, under which ASEAN could liberalize its trade with the United States. No timetable has been set.

In the last year or so, Thailand has begun a more deliberate pursuit of bilateral and regional arrangements. Observers are concerned, however, about how such arrangements will affect ASEAN economic regionalism and cooperation.

ASEAN is in a unique position at the hub of a series of proposed preferential arrangements, but probably because of its own internal weaknesses and lack of leadership it does not seem to be making the most of this position. Therefore, to achieve success ASEAN would be well advised to ensure that it has a clear vision of what it wants to achieve from regionalism and that it has a coherent framework for deciding which agreements to enter.

Regional Financial Cooperation

Since the Asian financial crisis, East Asian economies have accelerated cooperation in the financial sector and macroeconomic management.[13] The initiatives range from institutional—such as the creation of an Asian Monetary Fund, sparked by the initial dissatisfaction with the International Monetary Fund (IMF) bailout programs at the beginning of the crisis—to the currency swap lines of the Chiang Mai initiative. In practice, the efforts have focused more on stabilizing currencies than on coordinating macroeconomic policy or achieving overall financial stability.

Financial cooperation to date has focused on strengthening surveillance and supervisory measures within the region and on swap agreements. ASEAN + 3 established an ASEAN + 3 Surveillance Process in November 1999, based in the ASEAN Secretariat in Jakarta, to encourage the coordination of macroeconomic and financial policies. The following issues will be covered by finance ministers at their meetings: enhancing cooperation in

monitoring short-term capital flows, developing early warning systems, assessing regional financial vulnerabilities, and preventing a future financial crisis. The Asian Development Bank has dedicated a monitoring unit to undertaking this surveillance task as well as to providing training for central bank officials and promoting other regulatory and monitoring initiatives.

The most concrete initiative is the Chiang Mai initiative of May 2000. CMI expanded the existing ASEAN swap arrangements to include all ASEAN countries and set up a network of bilateral currency swap and repurchase arrangements among ASEAN + 3 countries. The aim of the initiative is to provide additional short-term hard currency for countries facing possible liquidity shortfalls. In addition, the CMI will seek to achieve better monitoring of capital flows, regional surveillance, and training of personnel (Henning 2002). The ceiling for withdrawal is not high and would not have been sufficient to prevent the liquidity shortfall during the 1997–98 financial crisis. Some bilateral agreements have reached their ceiling withdrawal of $3 billion. The maximum available for withdrawal under each bilateral swap agreement is to be negotiated between countries, because the terms of collateral and conditionalities need to be determined. By the end of March 2003, 12 bilateral swap agreements involving $39 billion had been concluded under the CMI. In addition, two more bilateral swap agreements proposed by Indonesia with China and Korea, respectively, were under way. The implementation of the CMI bilateral swap agreements is to be reviewed in 2004, at which time the ASEAN + 3 group of countries may decide to amend the CMI framework arrangement, to make it permanent, or to begin a process to transform it into a more formal institution for foreign exchange pooling.[14] The June 2003 APEC Summit launched the $1 billion Asian Bond Fund, a scheme that aims to reinvest a small portion of the reserves of Asia's central banks within the region.[15] It also endorsed initiatives to contain the economic damage from the severe acute respiratory syndrome (SARS).

According to He Fan (2002), China was not initially enthusiastic about financial cooperation in East Asia, but it has changed its attitude out of concern that if it does not play a positive role in the process, it will be kept out by other countries. The

Chinese government reportedly feels that trade and technological cooperation is more fundamental and should be preconditions for financial cooperation. According to McKinnon (2001), a U.S. dollar–linked currency standard can be used to achieve regional exchange rate stability. Mundell (2003) supports the idea of having an Asian "currency anchor," but believes that neither the Chinese yuan nor the Japanese yen is a suitable candidate at the present time. Meanwhile, Kuroda and Kawai (2003) note that a U.S. dollar–based exchange rate regime makes an economy susceptible to fluctuations in effective exchange rates (e.g., when the dollar-yen rate became volatile in 1995 and 1998). Such risks need to be managed as well. The ASEAN Task Force on ASEAN Currency and Exchange Rate Mechanism, which was established in March 2001, is discussing ways of coordinating exchange rate policies in the region.[16]

Costs and Benefits of Economic Regionalism

What can countries hope to achieve from preferential trade agreements (PTAs)? What does the literature say about the economic costs and benefits of these agreements?

The economic benefit of a preferential trade agreement is the gains in economic efficiency achieved from trade liberalization. A member country will allocate resources to sectors in which it has a comparative advantage vis-à-vis other members, and trade is created. The greater size of the combined market can also contribute to economies of scale and attract foreign direct investment, although because the benefits depend on the size of markets as well as on the producers in the RTA, they vary widely across countries.

Other than the traditional economic benefit of greater efficiency, countries enter into RTAs for many development-related reasons. Such arrangements offer the chance to create larger regional markets that are more attractive to foreign investors; to sequence liberalization by opening up in stages; to lock in place unilateral reforms; and to pursue structural change jointly with other members. Even though liberalization, trade facilitation, and structural reform are often thwarted by vested interests, regional cooperation for the joint promotion of these processes can make them easier to achieve. For smaller states, RTAs also offer the opportunity to build capacity in trade negotiations.

But preferential agreements also carry risks, one of which is that trade may be diverted away from more efficient nonmembers to less efficient members. If a preferential agreement diverts more trade than it creates, it will yield smaller gains in efficiency than would multilateral liberalization. The larger the difference between the preferential RTA tariff and the external tariff imposed on imports from nonmembers, the greater is the trade diversion effect. Trade also may be diverted if members of a free trade area impose rules of origin, because such rules may cause imports to be redirected through the member country that has the lowest external tariff.

The literature on the benefits and costs of regional trade agreements does not offer conclusive guidance on whether trade creation will outweigh trade diversion or on what such agreements will contribute to welfare.[17] The view of Srinivasan, Whalley, and Wooton (1993) is that quantitative assessments do not offer sufficient grounds for either vigorous support of or vigorous opposition to preferential agreements. They reviewed work in this field based on computable general equilibrium (CGE) models and found that the welfare effects of preferential trade agreements had probably been positive but not very large.[18]

Krueger (1995) found that trade diversion tended to occur less in those RTAs whose members had high levels of bilateral trade before entering the agreement. And Yeats (1998), looking at experience in MERCOSUR (Mercado Común del Sur/Southern Common Market Agreement), found that trade diversion can be minimized if external tariffs are low and if members become more open by further reducing their external tariffs as they enter the RTA.

Soloaga and Winters (1999), in a comprehensive study of nine arrangements over 17 years, found no indication that the rise in preferential agreements in the 1990s significantly boosted intrabloc trade. At the same time, for trade diversion they found significant effects only in the European Union (EU) and European Free Trade Area (EFTA).

Davis, McKibbin, and Stoeckel (2000) found that a joint free trade arrangement between AFTA and CER would yield worthwhile benefits[19]: for AFTA an extra $25.6 billion and for CER an additional $22.5 billion in GDP in net present value (that is, in discounted cash flow) terms. The real consumption gain, allowing for the ability to shift spending through time, would be 1 percent by 2005 for AFTA and 0.6 percent for CER.[20]

However, the same study also found that if APEC proceeds on schedule, the additional gains from the AFTA-CER arrangement would be relatively small: those to AFTA would be just over $10 billion, and those to CER members would be just under $2 billion. Two reasons are given for this finding: (1) trade between AFTA and CER is small compared with members' trade with APEC as a whole; and (2) APEC is not preferential, so that some of the APEC gains could in fact be attributable to the AFTA-CER connection, to the extent that this arrangement encourages further liberalization by APEC members.

Bayoumi and Mauro (2001) also examined the costs, benefits, preconditions, and implications of an ASEAN regional currency arrangement that is assumed to culminate in a regional currency. They are of the view that, on economic criteria, ASEAN appears less suited for a regional currency arrangement than Europe before the Maastricht Treaty, although the difference is not large.[21] The experiences of the European Monetary Union (EMU) indicate that the path toward a common currency is a difficult one. It requires a firm political commitment to ensure that an attempt to form a regional currency arrangement is not viewed as simply another fixed exchange rate regime open to speculative crises.

Clarete, Edmonds, and Wallack (2003) provide empirical analysis to show that the impact of PTAs on trade flows varies widely across PTAs. They also find that the establishment of APEC and the EU expanded trade significantly, both among members and to the rest of the world, providing evidence that PTAs can create rather than divert trade. Although they used export data in this analysis, their findings are consistent with those of Frankel (1997), who used total trade data (i.e., sum of exports and imports). Frankel attributed the strong positive effect on trade to the large share of total world trade accounted for by the APEC member countries. Meanwhile, Low (2003) concedes that bilateral and cross-regional trading arrangements are still "second best," and that broader regionalism and multilateralism are still superior. The Doha ministerial declaration has acknowledged that this

"theory of new regionalism" complements and supplements the World Trade Organization. The current initiatives in Asia and Asia-Pacific regionalism are responses to regionalism happening elsewhere in the context of globalization, information communication technology, and knowledge-based economies.

Free Trade or a Bloc-ed Up World?

The question of whether regional trade arrangements are stumbling blocks or building blocks in attempts to achieve a more open multilateral system arises often. RTAs have not always been effective in locking in unilateral reforms,[22] and it is not clear whether, when compared with a multilateral approach, they are able to achieve deeper and faster liberalization. Negotiations of RTAs have arguably been no more successful than multilateral negotiations in dealing with sensitive sectors and issues. Indeed, RTA negotiations, like multilateral negotiations, have tended not to cover sensitive sectors such as agriculture. Furthermore, regional arrangements may divert attention and resources away from multilateral and unilateral efforts to liberalize and facilitate trade. Especially in small economies, concentration on negotiating regional agreements could have dire implications if it slows down progress on these fronts.

These concerns aside, several recent studies have suggested that, under some circumstances, uncoordinated preferentialism could lead to global free trade. Their results are derived from special conditions—in which just one (differentiated) good or service is traded in oligopolistic markets—but they provide some guidance and focus for cooperation.

For one thing, consider the case in which, driven by producers' interest in getting access to rents in foreign markets, economies form a bloc to which others seek membership. If the bloc's constitution says that everyone who wants to join must be let in on the same terms as the original members, then the excluded economies continue to seek to join until everyone is a member.

Another possibility is the merging of blocs. Andriamananjara (1999), who considers the incentives to merge smaller blocs, starts with a situation in which each economy forms a bloc with one neighbor. In the next stage, the members of one agreement merge with those of one other agreement, and so on. Could this process continue until global free trade is reached, or will it stop before then? He finds that global free trade can be attained, but only if the general level of inter-bloc tariffs is low enough. When tariffs are low, the oligopolistic firms that populate this model can make greater profits with unrestricted access to all markets.

These two situations suggest that it would be worthwhile to introduce rules on the use of preferential agreements and, in particular, rules on accession to such agreements. When bloc members have discretion over who can join, they will stop letting in others before global free trade is reached. Therefore, without a rule on accession, free trade blocs will stop growing at a point short of universal free trade.

Network effects are a factor that could drive the outcome of a preferential approach further toward free trade. When direct network effects exist, the value of a product increases with the number of consumers who use a compatible product. Gandal and Shy (2001) show that when these effects are significant, the incentive to form a standards union disappears.

Freund (2000), by examining serial bilateralism, provides another perspective on the process of consolidation.[23] She finds that the benefits of a bilateral agreement include higher profits from preferential access to foreign markets and higher consumer surplus at home. These gains always outweigh the loss of profits in the home market and the loss of tariff revenue that results from offering foreign suppliers access at preferential rates. This is the case no matter what agreements are already in place and what other economies have done. The best strategy, then, is for each economy is to have a bilateral agreement with every other economy. In this model, in the presence of uncoordinated bilateralism the outcome is free trade.

In reality, as Freund points out, costs are associated with having a series of bilateral agreements, including those associated with complex rules of origin. The issue of sensitive sectors is also ignored. And the more dimensions there are to an agreement, the more scope there is to apply discrimination in a variety of ways and the more difficult it becomes to bolt different agreements together (Snape 1996a; Findlay 2001). Cooperation with one set of partners could make it more difficult to harmonize with other partners, and it could impede the signing of new preferential agreements. Such condi-

tions, in turn, could stop the proliferation of agreements before free trade is reached. The issues that are now on the trade liberalization agenda—for example, in services, standards, and investment—are likely to make preferential agreements increasingly complex. The outcome, in practice, is likely to be a host of different agreements between different groups of partners—the "spaghetti bowl" effect.

Latin America's overlapping preferential agreements have produced this effect. Experience shows that in these circumstances the costs of doing business increase, pushed up by inconsistencies among different agreements—for example, different schedules for phasing out tariffs; different rules of origin and exclusions, conflicting product standards, and differences in rules on antidumping and other regulations and policies. The more dimensions there are to the agreements and the more agreements there are, the wider is the scope for such inconsistencies. And if the costs of doing business increase, further trade diversion effects may arise.

Distribution of Benefits: Hubs and Spokes

Many of the proposed regional trading agreements in East Asia are of the so-called hub and spoke pattern.[24] The concern here is that the balance of advantages in hub and spoke arrangements will tend to favor the hub because of its stronger bargaining position and the greater attractiveness to investors of its central location. Agreements on contentious matters will also tend to be tailored to the demands of the hub. The spokes, for their part, having secured their preferential access, will have an incentive to oppose the admission of new members into the circle. The rest of this section summarizes the key findings of the substantial literature on hub and spoke arrangements.

Hub and spoke agreements do not provide equal market access to all participants. Even if tariffs were removed along each spoke, the spoke countries would still not have free access to each other's markets but only to that of the hub.

Snape (1996b) explains that in such systems there is an incentive to create tailor-made agreements to deal with products that the hub country regards as contentious. He also notes how small countries have incentives to join preferential agreements, especially as more and more countries sign up with the hub economy. Indeed, the hub and spoke system can "spread like a rash" (Baldwin 1997). The spoke economies may or may not have deals with each other—see, for example, Snape, Adams, and Morgan (1993); Anderson and Snape (1994); Wonnacott (1996); Snape (1996b).

Compared with all the other spokes, the hub economy benefits from its preferential access to each spoke economy. Only firms based at the hub get duty-free inputs from each spoke. The hub country also gains if it diverts investment from each of the spokes; its favored position gives producers access not only to the domestic market but also to those of all the spoke economies. Furthermore, producers based in the hub are likely to be able to get more inputs at low or zero tariffs than those based in the spokes, because they can source both from the hub and from any of the spokes. An inefficient pattern of investment may be perpetuated, as a result of inertia, even if a hub and spoke system evolves into a free trade area (Wonnacott 1996).

A spoke economy does not gain from free trade with other spokes; it could be damaged by discrimination in other spoke markets; and its ability to compete in all markets against firms that are based in the hub might be reduced (Wonnacott 1996). It can respond in three ways:

1. It could organize equivalent agreements with other spoke countries. But doing so may be costly, and the risk is that a series of such agreements, negotiated one after the other, could simply add to the layers of discrimination as each pair deals with its own set of difficult issues.
2. It could make one bloc with all the other spokes. Realistically, however, because the original membership of the set of spokes was the result of pressures from interest groups in the hub, it may be difficult for this group to agree subsequently and simultaneously on how to deal with a now larger set of contentious issues.
3. It could unilaterally cut tariffs to the rest of the world. Depending on the extent of these cuts, such an initiative could offset the investment diversion effects. The spoke agreement would then be part of a transition to free trade, but an expensive one. In hindsight, a giant leap to free trade is preferable to a couple of small steps.

Hub and spoke mechanisms can lead to greater resistance to multilateral liberalization. Snape

(1996b) argues that each spoke country has paid a price for its preferential access to the hub country, and that it will resist further reductions of tariffs on an MFN basis that erode the value of its special deals on sensitive products.

At the least, the trade policy of the hub could become a source of conflict among current and prospective members of the arrangement (Andriamananjara 1999). Spokes may seek to have new members come in with fewer and fewer benefits. This objective may stem not only from domestic interests in the spoke countries, but also from foreign investors who have invested in these countries in order to gain access to the hub. (These investors may be originally from the hub country, and they will not be without influence in their old home.)

In short, the hub and spoke structure is fraught with many risks. Economies that are large enough have strong incentives to assume the role of hub economy and to dominate a group of complementary economies in their region. But doing so leads to a structure of layers of discrimination and potential conflict. A hub economy that is already dominant in economic terms can easily be perceived as trying to acquire political dominance by biasing the rules of the new trading system in its favor (Wonnacott 1996).

Assessing the Alternatives

What type of regional arrangements will best serve the East Asia region? First, they should not become a "stumbling bloc" to multilateral liberalization. Second, they should focus less on easing market access and more on facilitating trade measures and achieving cooperation on external issues of common interest and mutual benefit, such as some of the negotiating issues in the WTO. Third, they should contribute positively to the multilateral trade liberalization process—for example, by including standstill provisions on further barriers to trade and investment; by implementing a simultaneous program of reduction of barriers to nonmembers; by allowing the most liberal rules of origin possible; and by avoiding the spaghetti bowl outcome for other issues.

ASEAN and China

Adjustments in industrial trade and investment resulting from China's accession to the WTO are likely to occupy the East Asian economies for the next decade. ASEAN member countries can count on both increased export competition with China and new opportunities within China. This section briefly explores some of the issues this scenario raises for a preferential agreement between ASEAN and China.

At the outset it is important to emphasize that among the ASEAN economies, three of the poorest—Vietnam, Lao PDR, and Cambodia—are not yet WTO Members and, as a result, do not have MFN status to export to China. It is a priority to ensure that these three members are integrated into the WTO system as soon as possible to avoid unbalanced market access outcomes.

Now that China has acceded to the WTO, the new pressure from competition will further sharpen China's competitiveness and its ability to win market shares, including in the domestic markets of ASEAN member countries. This enhanced competitiveness is already affecting labor-intensive products such as textiles, garments, electronics/electrical appliances, footwear, and toys. Furthermore, China will now have the same MFN treatment as all other ASEAN member countries. With this status, it becomes a more stable supplier—a desirable feature from the point of view of importing firms.

The planned removal of quotas on textiles and garments, if fully implemented by 2005, will also mean that the ASEAN economies will have to compete openly with China in third-country markets, and it is likely that ASEAN, and other developing Asian economies in South Asia, will lose market share to China. In the U.S. market for textiles and clothing, for example, ASEAN countries have up to now managed to maintain and sometimes slightly increase their share, aided by the quota allocations in this market.[25] But in Japan's more openly competitive market, they have been losing ground to China; 62 percent of Japan's imports of textiles and apparel now come from China and only 8 percent come from ASEAN.[26]

China is also increasingly competitive in high-tech products. There are predictions that by 2006 chip manufacturing in Shanghai will be as big as that in Taiwan (China), positioning China as an important competitor to both Taiwan and Singapore. Taiwan is fully aware that, politics aside, it must integrate economically with China. The only

way it can remain competitive in the global market is to relocate production plants in China, as it has been doing for some time. This trend will now accelerate and could have serious implications for ASEAN. Singapore may find it difficult to compete with high-tech exports produced in China.

Like other countries, ASEAN members will also have access to the more open and growing Chinese market, where import tariffs on ASEAN manufactured products will continue to come down, from 15 to 10 percent over the next five years. Quotas and quantitative restrictions will be removed and replaced by tariff-rate quotas. These developments will be important for ASEAN agricultural products such as palm oil, rice, and sugar. Other nontariff barriers and investment-related measures, such as local content and trade-balancing requirements, also will be removed, immediately or gradually. Under its accession commitment, China will open up its services sector over the next five years. Especially important for ASEAN economies will probably be professional services, tourism, and the possibility of some professional labor migration.

China's demand for imports from ASEAN is likely to increase. Products likely to benefit include oil and gas, wood, rubber, food and other agriculture-based products, as well as some manufactured products such as electrical machinery. It is up to ASEAN member economies to ensure their competitiveness in supplying these products to China.

Other than greater market access, the hope is that China's WTO accession will result in greater transparency and certainty in laws and regulations and their implementation. Surveys of businesspeople in Malaysia and Singapore have revealed some of the common problems experienced by ASEAN and other investors in doing business in China. They cite unpredictable laws, uncertain product standards, a weak legal infrastructure, insufficient trade facilitation measures, inefficient bureaucracy, low quality of work, poor protection of intellectual property, financial market restrictions, and poor enforcement legislation.

China's accession will eventually benefit ASEAN as a whole. China's restructuring is providing an impetus for the establishment of new regional production networks, initially in electronics, which promote more productive firms. For now, these production networks are oriented toward export to developed countries, but the growing markets within East Asia provide a potential complementary source of demand.[27] The Framework Agreement on China-ASEAN Comprehensive Economic Cooperation, with its "Early Harvest" provisions, provides another avenue through which the poorer countries in the region, including non-WTO Members,[28] can benefit from trade opportunities in the region.

ASEAN-China Economic Relations

ASEAN and China have strengthened their mutual trade and investment ties in the last decade, propelled by the dynamic growth in China, and in ASEAN before the financial crisis; by the liberalization undertaken by individual countries; and by their geographic proximity.

ASEAN as a region is China's fifth largest trading partner, after the United States, Japan, the EU, and Hong Kong. ASEAN's share of China's trade is still quite small, at around 8 percent, even though it has been growing by 20 percent a year during the last decade. Between 1991 and 2000 ASEAN increased its share of China's exports from 5.7 to 6.9 percent and of China's imports from 6 to 9.9 percent.

ASEAN exports to China still consist mainly of resource- or agriculture-based products (minerals, pulp, wood, vegetable oil, rice, and sugar). However, a growing share consists of machinery and electrical components for assembly into final goods in China. These exports are linked to trade-related investments and are part of the multinational regional production structure as well as the regional pattern of sourcing (ASEAN-China Expert Group on Economic Cooperation 2001; Yusuf, Altaf, and Nabeshima 2003). Intraindustry trade also takes place in textiles and fibers.

Investment relationships between ASEAN and China also have been growing stronger. Investments have flowed from ASEAN countries into China in the last decade, with varying degrees of success. Singapore was one of the first Southeast Asian countries to enter when China opened up to foreign investment in the late 1970s; reflecting ancestral links, the investments went mainly to small businesses in Guangdong and Fujian. By the end of 2001, Singapore was the fifth largest investor in China, with a cumulative realized investment of $18.6 billion in that country.

Recently, China itself has begun a vigorous outward investment drive, and the government has encouraged Chinese companies to invest in and contract for major engineering and construction projects (*Far East Economic Review*, March 28, 2002). This go-abroad policy appears to be designed to expose Chinese firms to international business practices as well as to achieve resource security, given this high-growth economy's demands for fuel, minerals, and other resources. For example, the Chinese state-owned offshore oil company, CNOC, recently acquired the Spanish oil company *Repsol-YPF* for its Indonesian oil and gas assets.[29] Other gas purchase deals between Indonesia and China are being negotiated. But because of the sluggish growth of most economies in the group, ASEAN in general remains a less attractive destination for Chinese investment than Latin America, the United States, or Europe. Thus far, it accounts for 20 percent of China's outward investment.

ASEAN and China have important relationships in services, especially tourism, finance, and telecommunications. China's growing prosperity means that an increasing number of Chinese tourists are visiting ASEAN countries. Indeed, 2.2 million visited ASEAN countries in 2000, particularly Malaysia, Singapore, Thailand, and Vietnam. For their part, ASEAN tourists are visiting China in increasing numbers. One drawback to investment and the attractiveness of tourist destinations in ASEAN members is the discriminatory treatment of ethnic Chinese minorities in some of these countries, especially Indonesia. This problem needs to be overcome and properly managed because of its sensitive nature.

Proposed ASEAN-China Free Trade Area: The Goals and Means to Achieve Them

In 2001 China and ASEAN agreed to establish the ASEAN-China Free Trade Area within 10 years. The stated motivation behind this initiative is to take advantage of complementarities and build on existing strengths, to make the region collectively more efficient and competitive, and to attract investment. The aim is to use the enhanced efficiency to compete in third-country markets, as well as to provide members with preferential entry to each other's markets (China being the largest). The experience of the ASEAN Free Trade Area and other RTAs that have been introduced recently suggests that any kind of

ASEAN-China free trade area must go beyond liberalization of cross-border barriers. The proposal prepared by the expert group is in fact comprehensive and covers trade and investment liberalization in goods and services, trade and investment facilitation, capacity building and technical assistance, and cooperation in various areas (ASEAN-China Expert Group on Economic Cooperation 2001).

Certainly the agreement promises big economic benefits. Estimates based on the study by the expert group indicate that the ASEAN-China agreement would augment trade on both sides by 50 percent and increase GDP by 0.9 percent for ASEAN and by 3 percent for China. China's exports to ASEAN countries would be 55 percent greater with the agreement than without it, and ASEAN countries' exports to China would be 48 percent greater.[30]

For ASEAN, the agreement would provide first-mover advantages in the Chinese market before it is opened on an MFN basis (Box 3.2). As well as provide opportunities for the "Early Harvest," it is hoped the agreement will address various nontariff barriers of concern to ASEAN members, such as quotas on palm oil and other agricultural products; China's complex import procedures (whereby, for example, only state-owned enterprises are allowed

to import palm oil); and issues of testing, standards, and labeling requirements, investment promotion and protection, visa facilitation, and infrastructure development. The agreement may also provide opportunities to build up the capacity of ASEAN's less developed members.

But the idea is not yet widely accepted by ASEAN member countries, and some of them have indeed expressed concern about their ability to compete with China and about whether a free trade area would be mutually beneficial. Thailand and Singapore seem to be the most supportive of the idea, with Indonesia and the Philippines taking a moderate position, Malaysia adopting a careful stance, and the lower-income economies within this group—Cambodia, Lao PDR, Myanmar, and Vietnam—expressing the most concern about their ability to compete and mutually benefit from such an arrangement. China, for its part, has an interest in the reduction of ASEAN tariffs and trade barriers on products of special export interest, including motorbikes and vehicle components.

As He Fan (2002) suggests, it may be that China wants to assuage ASEAN countries' fear of the "China threat" by opening up its markets to them. Other than the relatively comprehensive economic

---

BOX 3.2 "Early Harvest"

"Early Harvest," which refers to provisions of the Framework Agreement on China-ASEAN Comprehensive Economic Cooperation, would liberalize tariffs in priority sectors of interest and implement other trade and investment facilitation measures that are deemed to generate immediate benefits to the ASEAN and Chinese business communities. These measures could include:

- Development and technical assistance to build capacity among countries, particularly for the new members of ASEAN, in order to improve their competitiveness
- Trade and investment facilitation measures
- Trade policy dialogue
- Business sector dialogue
- Facilitation of visa arrangements for business-people
- Standards and conformity assessment

- Measures enhancing market access opportunities for specific products or services of interest to ASEAN and China, such as agricultural and tropical products, textiles and clothing, machinery and electronic products, footwear, oils and fats, foodstuffs, forestry and aquaculture products, and energy (the list of products and services will be determined by mutual consultation)
- Extension of MFN treatment of China's accession commitments to non-WTO members of ASEAN in compliance with WTO rules
- Any other measures delivering immediate mutual benefits.

Source: SEOM-MOFTEC Inputs on Forging Closer ASEAN-China Economic Relationship, Second SEOM-MOFTEC Meeting, Brunei Darussalam, October 28, 2001.

integration proposed, such an agreement and cooperation would enhance the sense of community within the region, reduce tensions, and contribute to stability. It may also enhance members' cooperation on the external front. For China and ASEAN alike, the process of getting to know each other is important, and it is hoped that a trade agreement will provide a basis for developing a cooperative stance on external issues of common concern such as the global financial architecture. In the near term, given that ASEAN's share of China's trade is still small, the political impact of the ASEAN-China free trade area may be more important than the economic impact.

Progress in implementing the agreement is likely to be slow, even though it is known that the wider and deeper the coverage, the greater will be the benefits. The agreement will probably be confined initially to eliminating tariffs on goods. Sensitive sectors such as agriculture will likely be excluded, and progress will be slow in other areas such as the removal of nontariff barriers, liberalization of services, investment, and other New Age RTA issues such as treatment of workers, environmental standards, and the movement of labor. But if the ASEAN-China Free Trade Area is to be a building block for deeper economic integration within the region, the framers of the RTA would be well advised to focus not just on the nitty-gritty of item-by-item tariff lines and exclusions, but also on ways to increase competition and efficiency and real economic benefits.[31] In this regard, Elek (2000) suggests focusing on trade facilitation through, for example, simplifying customs procedures and harmonizing standards.

To become viable suppliers to the Chinese market and to compete successfully with China in their own and export markets, ASEAN member countries need to anticipate and prepare for the structural changes that will happen in China. Meanwhile, their own comparative and competitive advantages need to be continually strengthened. Companies in ASEAN must focus on specialization and product differentiation, including in terms of quality. Each member country should devise a comprehensive program to achieve such goals as well as an action plan that anticipates the institutions, human resources, and infrastructure needed to support the program. (In fact, such a program is likely to be a more helpful response to the China challenge than is a regional trade arrangement per se.)

Other than restructuring and maintaining their competitive edge, individual ASEAN countries should continue on the current track of unilateral liberalization and reforms, while exploring regional cooperation such as that being proposed through the ASEAN-China initiative.

Conclusions: The Way Forward

Regional economic cooperation arrangements in East Asia raise complex issues, and decisionmakers need to understand and assess the options carefully, especially in view of the limited resources and capacity of some of the region's economies.

East Asian economies seek increased economic efficiency and competitiveness rather than economic integration in the manner of Europe, and they can pursue these goals through enacting unilateral reforms and through ensuring an open, rules-based multilateral trading system.

The role of regional trade arrangements is to facilitate and build toward this outcome. The way forward in the first instance is to ensure that unilateral reforms are continued, that commitments to the multilateral process are faithfully met, and that economies are preparing themselves to maximize the benefits from future developments in the multilateral trading system.[32] In the process of accession to the WTO, for example, China had to concede on many sectors and issues. In the forthcoming negotiations, China will now be able to press for market access for products and services of importance to its economy, and for discipline and fairness in the rules of the game as well.

Progress on involving a large group of economies can be expected to occur through functional cooperation in the financial and monetary area. The tasks to be carried out seem likely to be confined to surveillance, technical assistance and capacity building, information sharing, and limited swap arrangements. Joint macroeconomic policy coordination or currency union seems unlikely in the near future.

Given the limited experience with regionalism in East Asia to date, progress on an inclusive regional trade agreement is likely to be slow. The ASEAN Free Trade Area lacks scope and depth, as noted earlier, and the ASEAN-China Free Trade Area being negotiated is likely to suffer from the same problems because it is based on AFTA. But it is possible that ASEAN-China cooperation can extend to forging common positions for international negotiations, such as in the WTO.

Both in the formal regional arrangements such as AFTA and in the informal regional processes such as APEC the goal up to now has been more to stimulate and support unilateral reforms and contribute to multilateral liberalization than to achieve greater regional integration or intraregional trade and investment. In such arrangements in East Asia, it may be that the process of regional cooperation is more important to the participants than outcomes. If this is so, the agreements should be evaluated not just on the basis of whether they achieve free trade and investment, but also according to the process whereby each country actually makes progress in unilateral reforms.[33] And it may be that the informal process needs to be nurtured more systematically so that it will evolve into a more institutional one. Whether this means creating an East Asian secretariat needs further debate and deliberation.

Is ASEAN/AFTA the natural locus for regional cooperation? Some analysts believe that it is not in a strong position to serve this important role because of weaknesses within ASEAN itself, which have resulted partly from lack of leadership and slow progress on new areas of cooperation (Soesastro 2001). It has been suggested that to strengthen ASEAN the implementation of AFTA must be accelerated and the ASEAN economies must rethink their vision of regionalism.

To conclude, broader liberalization on a multilateral basis will lead to greater net benefits, but East Asia is likely to realize net gains if it pursues complementary regional approaches simultaneously with multilateralism. One further benefit from stronger regional cooperation could be a more effective stance at the WTO on issues of common interest—for example, in achieving further discipline on antidumping. China would play a critical role in this regard because of its growing economic dominance in the East Asian region, if not the world, and thus the type of regional cooperation arrangement in which it chooses to participate will have a lasting impact on the course of events and pace of development in the region. Economic development in China can only strengthen the perception of East Asia as a "good neighborhood" and place to be within the global community.

Endnotes

1. ASEAN has 10 members: Brunei, Cambodia, Indonesia, Lao People's Democratic Republic, Malaysia, Myanmar, the Philippines, Singapore, Thailand, and Vietnam.
2. All dollar amounts are current U.S. dollars. This GDP is half of Japan's, but if current growth rates are maintained, it will catch up with Japan's in the next 5–10 years. In purchasing power parity (PPP) terms, China's GDP now exceeds that of Japan (World Bank 2002).
3. Until a few years ago, apart from the ASEAN Free Trade Area (AFTA), East Asia had no formal regional cooperation agreements. A proposal by Malaysian prime minister Mahathir Mohamad in December 1990 to form an East Asian economic grouping elicited strong protests from U.S. Secretary of State James A. Baker III, and support of the proposal from Japan or China was not forthcoming. There was in general a strong sentiment against institutionalizing regional cooperation or regionalism. See also Munakata (2001).
4. The texts of most regional trade agreements (RTAs) can be found on the Web site of the RTA secretariat (e.g., the ASEAN Secretariat at www.aseansec.org or the European Union Secretariat at europa.eu.int) or of the relevant administering government department in one or more member countries (e.g., the Singaporean Ministry of Trade and Industry at www.mti.gov.sg or the New Zealand Ministry of Foreign Affairs and Trade at www.mfat.govt.nz). The texts of all agreements in the Americas are available on the Web site of the Organization of American States (www.sice.oas.org). Useful reviews of developments under particular RTAs also are available. See, for example, Pelkmans (1997), Thanadsillapakul (2001), Lloyd (2002), Mahani (2002), and Low (2003). The Asian Development Bank (2002: Part III) reviews RTAs in the Asia-Pacific area, and Estevadeordal (2002) provides an excellent comparison of some features of RTAs in the Americas. See also the WTO's *World Trade Report* (2003: 46–66) on recent developments in the realm of RTAs.
5. Kaminsky and Reinhart (1999) have shown that output losses are much more significant when a currency crisis is accompanied by major financial sector problems.
6. The distinct period for each group of economies is also the period in which flows of foreign direct investment, especially intraregional FDI, accelerated into that group.
7. This section provides only an introductory overview of the various regional and multilateral trade arrangements in East Asia, and the following questions may need further research: How large is intra-ASEAN Free Trade Area (AFTA) trade relative to AFTA's total trade? How much intra-AFTA trade is excluded because of "sensitive sectors"? How would these numbers change if China were added? How much variance is there among AFTA and ASEAN members in how much of their trade is covered? The answers to these questions will influence how different countries and groups approach others and their approach to liberalizing in other geographic areas.
8. There is evidence that some AFTA members have fallen behind in their reform schedules. One example is delays in including the automotive and petrochemical sectors in the AFTA by Malaysia and the Philippines, respectively.
9. The main reason is that because of China's WTO accession these three have separate customs territories, and so China cannot give preferential treatment to Hong Kong or Macao unless they are members of a free trade agreement.

10. Eichengreen (2001) finds that unlike in the EU countries and those under the North American Free Trade Agreement (NAFTA), in East Asia monetary and financial cooperation has tended to precede cooperation in trade.

11. Such as the role of China in the Korean Peninsula situation and Japan's alleged support for Taiwan.

12. Agreement was also reached at the November 2000 meeting on reviewing the possibility of an East Asian economic zone. The fact that the ASEAN-China economic cooperation has forged ahead faster than East Asia-wide cooperation (or a similar earlier idea for cooperation between Japan and ASEAN) indicates, some would say, the current lack of vision and strategy shown by Japanese leaders about Japan's leadership in the region (www.Asahi.com, November 2001). The main issue in Japan is resistance to opening up its agriculture sector.

13. For details, see Yusuf and others (2003: Chap. 5).

14. Henning (2002) and Kuroda and Kawai (2003) provide details on recent bilateral swap agreements under the CMI and discussions of related issues.

15. Asia's official reserves account for over half of global reserves. See "APEC Declining Relevance" (2003).

16. See Kuroda and Kawai (2003). Manupipatpong (2002) reviews the development of regional surveillance and self-help mechanisms through the ASEAN Surveillance Process and the Chiang Mai initiative.

17. Much depends on the assumptions made and the methods used to measure trade creation and diversion, and whether the effects measured are dynamic or static. Some authors find a positive net trade creation effect (Salazar-Xirinachs 2001), while others argue that in some cases there has been a serious net trade diversion effect, such as in North America (Panagariya 2000). The balance between positive and negative effects also may differ between members and nonmembers of an RTA. For example, dynamic benefits might outweigh positive effects for members, but nonmembers might still be adversely affected by trade diversion as a result of their exclusion. Yeats (1998) found net trade diversion in the case of MERCOSUR (Mercado Común del Sur/Southern Common Market Agreement), where a contributing factor seems to have been the high margins of preference. However, for some pairings the cost in terms of trade diversion may be relatively small when trade barriers are already low. The preferential trade agreement route then looks like a low-risk option.

18. CGE models have the advantage of providing more options for good choices of base scenarios and for capturing more of the detail of preferential policies. The models are becoming increasingly sophisticated and able to incorporate scale effects, imperfect competition, and capital accumulation. Panagariya (2000), however, identifies some problems in the modeling approaches. Appendix C of "The Angkor Agenda" (available from www.aseansec.org/aem/angkor_agenda.pdf) also lists some empirical papers.

19. They use the APG-cubed model (18 countries and 6 sectors), which permits the identification of dynamic gains and allows for allocative efficiency effects, terms of trade changes, and capital accumulation for goods and for services, as well as endogenous productivity effects.

20. These gains are nearly three times as great as those found by an earlier study that excluded services liberalization and the productivity effect.

21. On the basis of the theory of optimum currency areas, the benefits emanate mainly from the greater economic integration, reduced transaction costs, and higher levels of trade and investment that may result from exchange rate stability within ASEAN. The costs come from the loss of monetary autonomy involved, which limits the macroeconomic policy options available to deal with unexpected macroeconomic shocks (Bayoumi and Mauro (2001). See also Lloyd (2002).

22. There is some evidence that this has worked effectively in some cases in the Western Hemisphere, but in other cases unilateral reforms have been delayed as economies held back moves to open up until they entered into RTA and WTO negotiations.

23. Freund uses the same segmented oligopolistic market model as Andriamananjara (1999), but now governments maximize welfare—that is, the sum of producer and consumer surplus, plus tariff revenue. The outcome of unilateral policymaking is that each government sets the optimal tariffs on imports from other economies, taking those economies' tariffs as given. In this setting, when bilateral agreements are possible, each country wants to sign an agreement with every other country.

24. Suppose there are three countries: A, B, and C. Country A concludes separate agreements with B and C, but B and C do not have an agreement with each other. Country A is the hub, and B and C are the spokes. Lloyd and Crosby (2002), using this example, point out that the entity at the hub could itself be a regional trading agreement.

25. James, Ray, and Minor (2002). Before its WTO accession, China was not eligible to take advantage of growth in the U.S. quotas.

26. For example, from 1996 to 2001 China's share of Japan's market for cotton knit apparel increased from 47.3 to 77.3 percent, and for manmade fiber knit apparel it increased from 59.1 percent to 80.4 percent. Japan does not impose bilateral quotas, and thus its market reflects more open competition.

27. China's domestic market is the largest of these, but recent trends show Korea, Thailand, and other economies growing on the strength of domestic consumption demand.

28. Vietnam, Lao PDR, and Cambodia are not yet WTO Members.

29. This acquisition, for $584 million, is the biggest foreign acquisition of Indonesian oil and gas assets in the last decade (*Far East Economic Review*, March 28, 2002).

30. He Fan (2002: 14), quoting Zhou Keren, the Chinese vice minister of foreign trade and economic cooperation.

31. According to Chirathivat (2002), the ASEAN-China FTA has "contributed to the rethinking of East Asia, not for only a geographical concept, but more strongly as an institutional arrangement." However, both ASEAN and China remain highly dependent on outside markets "rather than a self-fulfilling grouping among themselves" to further stimulate their economic growth.

32. For both the Maastricht Treaty and North American Free Trade Agreement (NAFTA), crucial unilateral domestic decisions that reflected the pressures of rising openness preceded the negotiations. For the Maastricht Treaty, French and Italian financial market liberalization was a prerequisite, and for NAFTA, Mexican trade liberalization was a necessary precondition (Milner 1998).

33. For example, APEC had the purported role of helping to break the deadlock in the Uruguay Round negotiations in 1993.

References

The word *processed* describes informally reproduced works that may not be commonly available through libraries.

Anderson, Kym, and Richard Snape. 1994. "European and American Regionalism: Effects on and Options for Asia." *Journal of the Japanese and the International Economies* 8 (4): 454–77.

Andriamananjara, Soamiely. 1999 "On the Size and Number of Regional Integration Arrangements: A Political Economy Model." Policy Research Working Paper 2117. World Bank, Washington, D.C.

"APEC Declining Relevance." 2003. *Oxford Analytica Brief.* June 18.

ASEAN (Association of Southeast Asian Nations)-China Expert Group on Economic Cooperation. 2001. *Forging Closer ASEAN-China Economic Relations in the 21st Century.* Report submitted to the ASEAN SEOM-MOFTEC, October.

Asian Development Bank. 2002. "Preferential Trade Agreements in Asia and the Pacific." *Asian Development Outlook.* Available at www.adb.org/Documents/Books/ADO/2002/pta0000.asp.

Baldwin. R. 1997. "The Causes of Regionalism." *World Economy* 20 (7).

Bayoumi, Tamim, and Paolo Mauro. 2001. "The Suitability of ASEAN for a Regional Currency Arrangement." *World Economy* 24 (7): 933–54.

Chia Siow Yue. 2002. "East Asian Regionalism." Paper presented at East Asian Cooperation: Progress and Future Agenda, Institute of Asia-Pacific Studies (Chinese Academy of Social Sciences, CASS) and Research Center for APEC and East Asian Cooperation (CASS), Beijing, August 22–23.

Chirathivat, Suthiphand. 2002. "ASEAN-China Free Trade Area: Background, Implications and Future Development." *Journal of Asian Economics* 13: 671–86.

Clarete, Ramon, Christopher Edmonds, and Jessica Seddon Wallack. 2003. "Asian Regionalism and Its Effects on Trade in the 1980s and 1990s." *Journal of Asian Economics* 14: 91–129.

Crawford, Jo-Ann, and Sam Laird. 2000. "Regional Trade Agreements and the WTO." Paper prepared for meeting of North American Economic and Finance Association, Boston, January 6–9.

Davis, Lee, Warwick McKibbin, and Andrew Stoeckel. 2000. "Economic Benefits from an AFTA-CER Free Trade Area: Year 2000 Study." Centre for International Economics, Canberra and Sydney, June.

Eichengreen, Barry. 2001. "Hanging Together? On Monetary and Financial Cooperation in Asia." University of California, Berkeley. Processed.

Elek, Andrew. 2000. "Sub-Regional Trading Arrangements among APEC Economies: Managing Diversity in the Asia Pacific." Pacific Economic Papers No. 309. Australia-Japan Research Centre, Australian National University, November.

Estevadeordal, A. 2002. "Traditional Market Access Issues in RTAs: An Unfinished Agenda in the Americas?" Paper presented at WTO Seminar on Regionalism and the WTO, Geneva, April 26.

Findlay, Christopher. 2001. "Old Issues in New Regionalism." Pacific Economic Papers 311. Australia-Japan Research Centre, Australian National University, January.

Frankel, J. 1997. "Regional Trading Blocs in the World Economic System." Institute for International Economics, Washington, D.C.

Freund, Caroline. 2000. "Spaghetti Regionalism." International Finance Discussion Paper No. 680. Federal Reserve Board, September. Available at www.federalreserve.gov/pubs/ifdp/.

Gandal, N., and O. Shy. 2001. "Standardization Policy and International Trade." *Journal of International Economics* 53: 363–83.

He Fan. 2002. "Regional Economic Cooperation: China's Perspective." Background Paper for EAS Country Unit. World Bank, Washington, D.C., June.

Henning, Randall C. 2002. "East Asian Financial Cooperation." *Policy Analyses in International Economics* 68 (September). Institute for International Economics, Washington, D.C.

James, William E., David J. Ray, and Peter J. Minor. 2002. "Indonesia's Textile and Apparel Industry: Meeting the Challenges of the Changing International Trading Environment." Report for Ministry of Industry and Trade, Republic of Indonesia, USAID/ECG, Jakarta, July.

Kaminsky, Graciela, and Carmen Reinhart. 1999. "The Twin Crises: The Causes of Banking and Balance of Payments Problems." *American Economic Review* 89 (3): 473–500.

Krueger, Anne O. 1995. "Free Trade Agreements versus Customs Unions." NBER Working Paper No. 5084. National Bureau of Economic Research, Cambridge, Mass., April.

Kuroda, Haruhiko, and Masahiro Kawai. 2003. "Strengthening Regional Financial Cooperation in East Asia." Pacific Economic Papers. Australia-Japan Research Centre, Australian National University, Canberra, May.

Lloyd, Peter. 2002. "New Bilateralism in East Asia." *World Economy* 25 (9): 1279–96.

Lloyd, Peter, and Mark Crosby. 2002. "China's Options for Regional Integration and Cooperation: Conceptual and Theoretical Framework." Background Paper for EAS Country Unit. World Bank, Washington, D.C., June.

Low, Linda. 2003. Multilateralism, Regionalism, Bilateral and Crossregional Free Trade Arrangements: All Paved with Good Intentions for ASEAN. *Asian Economic Journal* 17 (1): 65–86.

Mahani, Zainal-Abidin. 2002. "ASEAN Integration: At Risk of Going in Different Directions." *World Economy* 25 (9): 1263–77.

Manupipatpong, Worapot. 2002. "The ASEAN Surveillance Process and the East Asian Monetary Fund." *ASEAN Economic Bulletin* 19 (1): 111–22.

McKinnon, Ronald. 2001. "After the Crisis, the East Asian Dollar Standard Resurrected." In Joseph Stiglitz and Shahid Yusuf, eds. *Rethinking the East Asian Miracle.* Washington, D.C.: World Bank and Oxford University Press.

Milner, Helen. 1998. "Regional Economic Cooperation, Global Markets and Domestic Politics: A Comparison of NAFTA and the Maastricht Treaty." In William D. Coleman and Geoffrey Underhill, eds., *Regional and Global Economic Integration: Europe, Asia and the Americas.* London and New York: Routledge Publications.

Munakata, Naoko. 2001. "Focus on the Benefits—Not Threats—of Regional Economic Integration." PacNet Newsletter, November 16. Centre for Strategic and International Studies, Washington, D.C.

Mundell, Robert. 2003. "Prospects for an Asian Currency Area." *Journal of Asian Economics* 14: 1–10.

Panagariya, Arvind. 2000. "Preferential Trade Liberalization: The Traditional Theory and New Developments." *Journal of Economic Literature* 38 (June): 287–331.

Pelkmans, J. 1997. *European Integration: Methods and Economic Analysis.* New York: Longman.

Salazar-Xirinachs, José M. 2001. "Implications of Proliferating Sub-Regional Trade Agreements: Lessons from the Latin American Experience." Pacific Economic Cooperation Council (PECC), Trade Policy Forum, Seminar on Regional Trade Agreements, Bangkok, June12–13.

Snape, Richard. 1996a. "Trade Discrimination—Yesterday's Problem?" *Economic Record* 72 (December): 381–96.

————-. 1996b. "Which Regional Trade Agreement?" In Bijit Bora and Christopher Findlay, eds. *Regional Integration and the Asia Pacific.* Melbourne: Oxford University Press.

Snape, Richard, Jan Adams, and D. Morgan. 1993. *Regional Trade Agreements: Implications and Options for Australia.* Report for the Australian Department of Foreign Affairs and Trade, AGPS, Canberra.

Soesastro, Hadi. 2001. "Whither ASEAN Plus Three?" Paper presented to Pacific Economic Cooperation Council (PECC) Trade Policy Forum, Seminar on Regional Trading Arrangements, Bangkok, June 12–13.

Soloaga, I., and A. Winters. 1999. "Regionalism in the 1990s: What Effect on Trade?" Discussion Paper No. 2183. Centre for Economic Policy Research (CEPR), London.

Srinivasan, T. N., John Whalley, and Ian Wooton. 1993. "Measuring the Effects of Regionalism on Trade and Welfare." In Kym Anderson and Richard Blackhurst, eds. *Regional Integration and the Global Trading System.* London: Harvester Wheatsheaf for the GATT Secretariat.

Thanadsillapakul, L. 2001. "Open Regionalism and Deeper Integration: The Implementation of ASEAN Investment Area and ASEAN Free Trade Area." Processed.

Wonnacott, Ronald. 1996. "Trade and Investment in a Hub-and-Spoke System versus a Free Trade Area." *World Economy* 19 (3): 237–52.

World Bank. 2002. *World Development Indicators 2002.* Washington, D.C.: World Bank.

WTO (World Trade Organization). 2000a. "Synopsis of 'Systemic' Issues Related to Regional Trade Agreements." WT/REG/W/37. Note by the Secretariat, March 2.

————. 2000b. "Committee on Regional Trade Agreements, Mapping of Regional Trade Agreements." WT/REG/W/41. Note by the Secretariat, October 11.

————. 2002. "Regional Trade Integration under Transformation." Paper prepared for the World Trade Organization's seminar Regionalism and the WTO, Geneva, April 26.

————. 2003. *World Trade Report.* Geneva, August.

Xu, X., and L. Song. 2000. "Export Similarity and the Pattern of East Asian Development." In P. Lloyd and X, Zhang, eds., *China in the Global Economy.* Cheltenham, UK: Edward Elgar.

Yeats, Alexander. 1998. "Does Mercosur's Trade Performance Raise Concerns about the Effects of Regional Trade Agreements?" *World Bank Economic Review* 12 (1):1–28.

Yusuf, Shahid, M. Anjum Altaf, and Kaoru Nabeshima, eds. 2003. *Global Production Networking and Technological Change in East Asia.* Washington, D.C.: World Bank and Oxford University Press.

Yusuf, Shahid, with M. Anjum Altaf, Barry Eichengreen, Sudarshan Gooptu, Kaoru Nabeshima, Charles Kenny, Dwight H. Perkins, and Marc Shotten. 2003. *Innovative East Asia: The Future of Growth.* Washington, D.C: World Bank and Oxford University Press.

4

MARKET ACCESS BARRIERS AND POVERTY IN DEVELOPING EAST ASIA

Bijit Bora
with additional material by
Paul Brenton and Takako Ikezuki

A central element of any poverty alleviation strategy is to improve market access for exports in which the poor have a comparative advantage. This chapter analyzes market access barriers to agricultural exports produced by the poor in East Asia. The effects of trade liberalization on the poor are the subject of intense debate,[1] but there is general support for freeing market access for products of export interest to the poor. The discussion takes as a starting point the premise that increased exports of products of interest to the poor will help to reduce poverty.[2]

This first section of this chapter identifies the key export products and major markets of East Asian exporters likely to be of interest to the poor, with a focus on agricultural and agroprocessing products. The next section analyzes market access barriers for those products. A concluding section suggests priorities.

Identifying and removing barriers to international trade are, however, only part of the process of alleviating poverty. Policymakers need to consider market access barriers in conjunction with issues such as downstream integration and coordination between producers and retailers.[3] The value chain between the production of commodities by the poor and the final product that reaches the markets of developed and developing countries is central to improving market access for products of the poor (see Chapter 9 in this volume for approaches to such improvements).

Products and Markets of Export Interest to the Poor

Reducing the trade barriers in agriculture is particularly important for reducing poverty in East Asia.[4] Although agriculture is no longer a major source of exports and income for many economies of East Asia,[5] it is the main livelihood for poor households in both low-income and middle-income countries in the region. According to statistics compiled by the World Bank, agriculture represents the main source of income for over 90 percent of poor

The views in this paper are expressed in a personal capacity and should not in any way be associated with the World Trade Organization, World Bank, or their member states. I am grateful to Zheng Wang for her excellent research assistance and to Aki Kuwahara, Daniel Morales, and Jurgen Richtering for extracting and processing the tariff data. The paper also benefited from comments from Florian Alburo and other participants in the seminar held at the Institute for Southeast Asian Studies, Singapore.

households in Cambodia and Vietnam, and over two-thirds of poor households in Indonesia, the Philippines, and Thailand.[6]

Determining the exposure of the poor to international markets is a first step in identifying products of export interest to the poor. Research using a framework developed by Winters shows that their exposure is largely indirect (see McCulloch, Winters, and Cirera 2001). Poor households tend to produce primary products such as fruits and vegetables, fish and fish products, and commodities such as jute and coffee. Those in these households also work for wages in low-skill jobs such as in textiles, clothing, footwear, and travel goods. In each of these cases, output is sold to wholesalers, who then make international transactions. This chapter focuses on agricultural and agroprocessed exports.

Analytical modeling suggests that the gains from agricultural liberalization are reasonably large, as shown in Figure 4.1. This figure reveals that the East Asia region stands to benefit substantially from agricultural liberalization in high-income countries, and perhaps three times as much from agricultural liberalization in low- and middle-income countries. Full global agricultural liberalization would bring benefits to East Asia of almost US$300 billion,[7] an amount comparable to the gains from further liberalization in manufactured goods. Some of the gains would come from a better allocation of resources associated with agricultural liberalization

and from improved market access. But the majority of the gains, about three-quarters, would come from productivity improvements as farmers gain unrestricted access to export markets and specialize in higher value added crops. China would be one of the main beneficiaries, and, indeed, China has taken a position of unilaterally opening its markets for agriculture, thereby obtaining some of the potential benefits for itself. But as shown in Chapter 1, China is likely to become a major importer of oilseeds, sugar, beverages, tobacco, plant fibers, and other food products in which regional East Asian economies have strong comparative advantage. Thus some of the gains from agricultural liberalization can be generated through regional arrangements, even if global negotiations do not make significant progress.

Agricultural and Agroprocessed Exports

Within the East Asia region, there is significant diversity of products through which the poor are exposed to international markets. Using an approach described in the technical appendix to this chapter,[8] we examined the structure of exports, which suggests some important priorities despite this diversity.

The agricultural exports of the East Asian developing countries are quite concentrated.[9] The top four products account for between 30 percent and

FIGURE 4.1   Real Income Gains in Developing East Asia from Agricultural Liberalization

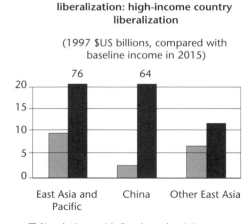
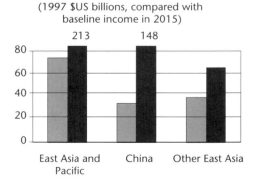

Source: World Bank (2002: Table 6.1).

90 percent of the total agricultural exports of each country. In Indonesia, for example, four products account for more than half of agricultural exports: palm and coconut oil account for 40 percent, and coffee and cocoa beans add another 14 percent. Myanmar represents an extreme case, where fresh vegetables account for more than half of agricultural exports and nearly a quarter of total exports. Rice is Myanmar's next most important export, accounting for 20 percent. Similar concentration effects can be found for Cambodia, Lao People's Democratic Republic (Lao PDR), and Vietnam.

Table 4.1 identifies the top products for developing East Asia based on the number of times particular types of products appear on the list of top agricultural exports for the individual countries. The most frequently listed products are spices plus cereal and other food preparations, followed by

fruits and vegetables and then other products.[10] For the poorer developing countries, fruits and vegetables and coffee appear to be relatively more important.[11] Among the agroprocessed products exported by the least-developed countries in East Asia, those such as fish and fish products are important, as well as leather and rubber products.

Markets for the Key Agroproducts

The major markets for the key agroproducts of the least-developed countries in East Asia are summarized in Table 4.2.[12] Not surprisingly, the main feature of the results is the concentration of exports to Association of Southeast Asian Nations (ASEAN) members, China, the European Union (EU), Japan, and the United States. Myanmar is the exception, with India and Pakistan in its list of destinations.

TABLE 4.1   Frequency of HS4 Lines in Top 30 Exports of Developing East Asia by Value

Number of appearances in East Asian top 30 agricultural exports	MTN category for agriculture		Harmonized system nomenclature (HS 1996)
	MTN category	Description	
86	15	Spices, cereal, and other food preparations	0407–10, 0904–10, 1101–04, 1107–09, Ch. 19, 2102–06, 2209
83	12	Fruit and vegetables	Ch. 07, Ch. 08, 1105–06, 2001–08
76	23	Other agricultural products	Ch. 05 (except 0509), 0604, 1209–10, 1212–14, 1802, 230110, 2302–03, 2307– 09, 290543–45, 3301, 3501–05, 380910, 382460, 4101–03, 4301, 5001– 03, 5101–03, 5201–03, 5301–02
40	20	Beverages and spirits	2009, 2201–08
37	13	Coffee, tea, maté, cocoa, and preparations	0901–03, Ch. 18 (except 1802), 2101
37	18	Oilseeds, fats and oils, and their products	1201–08, Ch. 15 (except 1504), 2304–06, 382360
29	17	Animals and products thereof	Ch. 01, Ch. 02, 1601–02
27	19	Cut flowers, plants, vegetable materials, etc.	0601–03, 1211, Ch. 13, Ch. 14
21	22	Tobacco	Ch. 24
18	14	Sugars and sugar confectionery	Ch. 17
15	16	Grains	Ch. 10
11	21	Dairy products	0401–06

Notes: Ch. = harmonized system chapter; HS4 = harmonized system to four digits. MTN = Multilateral Trade Negotiations.
Source: World Trade Organization.

TABLE 4.2 Key Markets for East Asian Agricultural Exports

Reporter	Export value (US$)	Agricultural exports/agricultural imports	Agricultural exports/total exports	Largest export markets (percent of total)				
				1st	2nd	3rd	4th	5th
Brunei Darussalam	1,007,143	0.004	0.04	Other ASEAN (90.3)	EU (6.2)	Yemen (1.4)	Australia (0.8)	Areas, n.e.s. (0.8)
China	11,946,201,904	1.3	4.79	Japan (28.9)	Other China[a] (16.3)	ASEAN (12.3)	EU (11.1)	Korea, Rep. of (10.4)
Hong Kong (China)	4,046,168,687	0.5	2	China[a] (71.7)	ASEAN (13)	USA (4.7)	Japan (3)	EU (2.5)
Indonesia	4,048,359,304	1	6.52	EU (23)	Other ASEAN (20.7)	India (13.5)	USA (11.6)	China[a] (8.3)
Japan	1,628,656,355	0.04	0.34	China[a] (41.3)	USA (20.5)	ASEAN (11.2)	Korea, Rep. of (10)	EU (7.7)
Malaysia	4,918,276,068	1.4	5.01	Other ASEAN (27.2)	China[a] (12.8)	India (12.2)	EU (10.7)	Pakistan (6.1)
Mongolia	62,917,847	1	14.83	China,[a] (75.0)	Russia Fed. (13.2)	EU (5.5)	Areas, n.e.s. (4.5)	Japan (1.6)
Myanmar	199,419,463	2.2	44.38	India (23.7)	Other ASEAN (23.7)	Pakistan (13.3)	Japan (8.1)	Sri Lanka (6.5)
Taiwan (China)	1,016,346,249	0.2	0.68	Japan (34)	China[a] (19.4)	USA (18.3)	ASEAN (11.3)	EU (4.4)
Philippines	1,496,655,871	0.6	3.93	USA (29.4)	Japan (20)	EU (19)	China[a] (11.2)	Other ASEAN (9.1)
Korea, Rep. of	1,591,817,483	0.2	0.92	Japan (48.6)	China[a] (17.1)	USA (10)	ASEAN (7.1)	Russian Fed. (4.6)
Singapore	2,829,032,672	0.7	2.05	Other ASEAN (40.6)	Japan (14.6)	China[a] (11.0)	EU (6.9)	USA (3.8)
Thailand	6,088,003,412	2.3	8.85	Other ASEAN (20)	Japan (19.6)	EU (15.1)	China[a] (12.3)	USA (8.2)

a. Includes China, Hong Kong (China), Taiwan (China), Macao. Areas, n.e.s. = all other areas not specified.
Source: UN Comtrade data.

Regional agricultural markets are large. Notably, China (with Hong Kong and Taiwan) is the first or second largest market for all economies with the exception of Brunei, Singapore (where China is third largest), Indonesia (fifth largest), and the Philippines (fourth largest). ASEAN is also a large and important market, with the rest of ASEAN being the first or second largest market for all the ASEAN economies. For the northern Asian economies of Japan, Republic of Korea, and China, ASEAN is the third or fourth largest market. This implies that many of the mutual gains from agricultural liberalization depend on the policies of countries in the East Asia region.

There also is a clear distinction between markets in which preferential access through the ASEAN Free Trade Agreement (AFTA) is important, and those in which most-favored-nation (MFN) rates apply. Some countries have nonreciprocal preferences through the Generalized System of Preferences (GSP). Cambodia, as a least-developed country, is eligible for a specific set of preferences.

Market Access Barriers

This section examines the implications of some of the market access policies of importing countries in sectors of central interest to East Asian developing countries. In agriculture, governments use a variety of policies beyond tariffs that not only protect their markets but also distort them so that efficient producers are not the main suppliers of products (ABARE 2000).

Domestic Support

Hoekman, Ng, and Olarreaga (2002) make an important point that guides the analysis here. Comparing the impact of a 50 percent cut in domestic support by an importing, not exporting, country with a 50 percent cut in tariffs, they find that developing countries as a group would receive a larger benefit from the cut in tariffs.[13] For one thing, domestic support payments are concentrated in few products in which developing countries directly compete, and tariff cuts have a more direct effect on world market prices than do cuts in domestic support programs. This section therefore focuses on the different types of border measures and the identification of relevant nontariff mea-

sures where possible. This is not to suggest that support payments in importing countries are unimportant to developing country exporters, but rather that these payments should be considered in relation to the export potential of specific countries. According to Hoekman, Ng, and Olarreaga (2002), domestic subsidy payments are concentrated in a few sectors such as meat, dairy products, and cereals (Table 4.3).

Most products important to the poor of East Asia, such as fruits, vegetables, and spices, together account for only 7 percent of domestic support payments. The major exception is rice. Within cereals, rice accounts for nearly half of all direct support commitments, totaling $46 billion driven by the $36 billion attributable to Japan (see Box 4.1). Because of the dominance of East Asia in rice production and trade, many of the mutual gains from agricultural liberalization depend on the policies of countries in the East Asia region. Coordinated regional action could contribute to an increase in the share of rice traded and thereby to an increase in the reliability and stability of rice markets, which have been at the core of concerns of East Asian policymakers.

Tariff Barriers

Because several different types of measures are known collectively as tariffs, it is useful to clarify the measures analyzed here. First, bound and applied MFN tariffs differ. Bound tariff rates, which are negotiated in the World Trade Organization (WTO), are the ceilings that apply to tariffs. Applied tariffs are the actual duties applied at customs on an MFN basis.[14] They can be raised in a manner consistent with a country's WTO obligations so long as the increase is not above the bound rate. This chapter looks at the applied rates. Second, it is important to identify the prevalence of specific tariffs as well as ad valorem duties. Data presented in this section show the prevalence of specific tariffs on the exports of developing Asian countries.

Table 4.4 provides an overview of the simple average of tariff rates applied on products of interest to the poor in East Asian countries.[15] These figures have been calculated using only ad valorem lines. Many countries do not report ad valorem equivalents for specific tariffs or tariff-quota schemes, so these figures may largely reflect the barriers posed

TABLE 4.3   Commitments and Average Direct Domestic Support Levels, 1995–98

HS2 Product	Direct support (millions of US$)		As % of total	
	Commitment	1995–98	Commitment	1995–98
01 Live animals	250	63	0.1	0.1
02 Meat and edible meat offal	60,155	14,907	22.3	18.5
04 Dairy products; birds' eggs; honey	39,372	11,557	14.6	14.3
06 Live trees and other plants; bulbs, cut flowers	0	14	0.0	0.0
07 Edible vegetables and roots and tubers	10,326	3,975	3.8	4.9
08 Edible fruit and nuts; melons	7,879	3,474	2.9	4.3
09 Coffee, tea, maté, and spices	1272	50	0.5	0.1
10 Cereals	104,109	27,953	38.5	34.6
11 Milled products; malt; starches	421	142	0.2	0.2
12 Oilseed, oleaginous fruits	8,577	447	3.2	0.6
13 Lac; gums, resins, other vegetables	0	0	0.0	0.0
15 Animal/vegetable fats and oils and products	1,899	1,050	0.7	1.3
17 Sugars and sugar confectionery	12,370	5,304	4.6	6.6
18 Cocoa and cocoa preparations	16	0	0.0	0.0
20 Prep. of vegetable, fruit, nuts products	892	529	0.3	0.7
21 Miscellaneous edible preparations	0	0	0.0	0.0
22 Beverages, spirits, and vinegar	4,306	1,172	1.6	1.5
23 Residues and waste from food industry	382	192	0.1	0.2
24 Tobacco and manufactured tobacco products	2,662	735	1.0	0.9
50 Silk	416	14	0.2	0.0
51 Wool, fine/coarse animal hair nest	124	17	0.0	0.0
52 Cotton	3,411	655	1.3	0.8
53 Other vegetable textile fibers and yarns	34	71	0.0	0.1
98 Nonproduct-specific	11,276	8,392	4.2	10.4
Total agricultural products above	270,151	80,714	100.0	100.0

Notes: Direct domestic support is defined as the sum of World Trade Organization DS4 to DS9 categories. HS2 = harmonized system to two digits.
Source: Hoekman, Ng, and Olarreaga (2002). Based on WTO Secretariat (2000).

by ad valorem tariffs only.[16] The table does show reasonably high numbers in the key agricultural categories (categories 12–23)—in particular, fruits and vegetables (category 12); coffee, tea, and cocoa (category 13); and cut flowers (category 19). Average tariffs are also high on agroprocessing products of traditional export interest to the poor: leather, rubber, footwear, and travel goods (category 3) and fish and fish products (category 11).[17] The data here are based on MFN trade barriers and do not take into account the preferences that East Asian countries are granted in these markets.

This table confirms two general points about the landscape of protection. First, developing countries in general impose considerably higher overall aver-

age tariff rates than developed countries. Second, industrial countries apply above-average tariffs on agricultural products of particular interest to developing countries. These products tend to face tariffs that are double the average rates in the United States, Japan, and the EU.

Specific tariffs are quite prevalent. Table 4.5 summarizes the structure of the trade policies of the EU, Japan, and United States affecting market access for East Asia as a whole.[18] The data here are based on MFN trade barriers and do not take into account the preferences that East Asian countries are granted in these markets. Yet they suggest that, for individual countries, *specific tariffs* can affect a very large proportion of agricultural exports,

BOX 4.1   Global Trade in Rice

Over 90 percent of rice production and consumption occurs in Asia. Much of Asian rice is subject to monsoon climates, resulting in uncertain rice yields and rice supplies. Only 6.8 percent of global rice production is traded, a smaller share than other major grains and oilseeds. The price variability of rice is also the largest of all food crops, with a coefficient of variation of 47 compared with 34–35 for wheat and maize. However, its price variability is much less than that of other commodities such as sugar and oil with a coefficient of variation over 70.

The major types of distortion in world rice markets are import tariffs and tariff-rate quotas (TRQs) in key importing countries and price supports in key exporting countries. In 2000 the global trade weighted tariff on all rice was 43.3 percent. Global trade weighted average rice tariffs for japonica rice markets were much higher than those on indica rice—217 percent compared with 21 percent—because of the TRQ and quotas in the major japonica rice–importing economies of Japan, the Republic of Korea, and

Taiwan (China). Protection in other countries of East Asia is more moderate. The greatest degree of protection is in medium and short grain rice, and thus very few rice-exporting countries produce this type. Most global rice trade is in long grain rice, which is characterized by tariff escalation, notably in the European Union and Central and South America. This pattern of protection depresses world prices for high-quality, milled long grain rice and discriminates against the milling sectors of exporting nations such as Thailand and Vietnam.

Protectionist policies have contributed to the thinner global markets by encouraging greater reliance on domestic production for domestic consumption. At the same time, the variability in global markets has been a motivation for heavier protection. If collective action were taken in East Asia to address transition and vulnerability concerns, it is estimated that trade liberalization would result in a 73 percent increase in global trade of short and medium grain rice, which in turn would contribute to the stability and reliability of global markets.

notably to the EU and the United States. These tariffs contribute to a lack of transparency about the magnitude of the overall extent of protection.

In *agriculture,* more than 94 percent of East Asian countries' exports to Japan are subject to duties at the border (ad valorem or a specific tariff). Almost three-quarters of their agricultural exports to the EU and just over 46 percent of those to the United States are subject to duties. Specific tariffs are prevalent in the United States, affecting more than one-quarter of all East Asian exports of agricultural goods and more than half of the East Asian agricultural exports that are subject to duties. In the EU, specific tariffs affect about one-quarter of total agricultural exports from East Asia and more than one-third of those that are subject to MFN duties. For example, almost two-thirds of Thailand's agricultural exports to the EU are subject to specific duties, and 45 percent of total agricultural exports from the Philippines to the United States are subject to specific duties. Within the East Asia region, however, specific duties are very rarely used as a means of trade protection.[19] Specific duties are less com-

mon in Japan, affecting only about 10 percent of agricultural exports from East Asia.

The incidence of specific duties likely falls particularly heavily on the least-developed countries exporting relatively low-value products, where the computed ad valorem equivalents of specific duties are subsequently often high.[20] The reason is that the methodology for conversion depends on the per unit value. In many cases, the per unit value of products from the poor is lower than those from higher-income producers, resulting in a high ad valorem rate. Thus paradoxically, low-quality goods, and cheap goods from low-income countries, are subjected to higher rates of border taxation for their exports to Europe and the United States.

Tariff Escalation

High tariffs are only part of the market access picture for developing countries. Tariff escalation, whereby tariffs imposed on processed products are relatively higher than those on raw materials, reduces the incentive for producer countries to

TABLE 4.4 Simple Average MFN Applied Tariff Rates by MTN Category, Selected Asian Countries and Major Trading Partners (percent)

MTN Category	Description	Brunei	China	HK (China)	Taiwan, (China)	Indo-nesia	Japan	Malay-sia	Myan-mar	Philip-pines	Korea, Rep. of	Singa-pore	Thailand	EU	Canada	USA
1	Wood, pulp, paper, and furniture	4.1	14.1	0	4.6	7.9	1.3	10.9	6.5	8.9	5.9	0	13.8	2.2	1.5	0.8
2	Textiles and clothing	0.6	26.8	0	9.4	14.0	7.6	13.5	10.6	12.6	10.1	0	25.4	8.5	12.2	9.4
3	Leather, rubber, footwear, and travel goods	3.0	17.7	0	5.9	10.7	6.7	14.0	5.3	7.7	8.0	0	26.3	4.2	6.1	4.4
4	Metals	0.0	9.8	0	6.0	8.5	1.4	9.3	3.0	5.9	6.1	0	12.5	2.5	2.3	2.2
5	Chemicals and photographic supplies	0.4	11.4	0	3.7	6.6	2.6	3.6	2.3	4.2	7.3	0	10.4	4.9	3.0	3.4
6	Transport equipment	13.7	23.3	0	11.6	12.1	0.0	18.5	3.9	8.2	5.5	0	23.6	4.1	5.5	3.2
7	Nonelectric machinery	6.3	14.4	0	4.9	2.3	0.0	3.7	1.6	3.5	6.4	0	9.2	1.7	1.4	1.2
8	Electric machinery	14.2	16.1	0	5.3	7.7	0.2	6.7	4.2	5.0	6.1	0	13.2	2.5	2.3	1.9
9	Mineral products and precious stones and precious metals	0.5	12.1	0	4.2	6.0	0.8	8.8	4.3	5.5	5.9	0	10.0	2.0	1.7	1.9
10	Manufactured articles not elsewhere specified	5.0	18.0	0	4.8	10.3	1.1	5.1	6.4	5.5	6.8	0	15.0	2.6	2.8	2.1
11	Fish and fish products	0.0	21.5	0	27.1	5.0	5.9	2.4	8.1	9.0	16.2	0	57.6	11.2	1.1	1.1
12	Fruits and vegetables	0	22.6	0	28.7	5	8.4	2.9	13.1	10.4	55.6	0	58.9	9.8	2.7	7.8
13	Coffee, tea, maté, cocoa, and preparations	0.9	26.1	0	13.8	4.9	11.6	9	14	18.9	55.3	0	60	5.8	1.4	2.6
14	Sugars and sugar confectionery	0	27.9	0	27.3	3.8	10.1	2.8	5.6	18.9	20.1	0	46.3	11.4	4.0	6.2
15	Spices, cereal, and other food preparations	0	31.4	0	20.2	5.2	12.5	2.6	8.1	9	111.8	0	42.5	5.0	3.7	3.1
16	Grains	0	54.4	0	2.8	2	1[a] [23.8]	0	0.9	18.5	192.5	0		5.4	11.5	2.2
17	Animals and products thereof	0	20.7	0	26.3	4.6	7.8	0.5	11.4	27.1	24.7	0	50.3	5.3	4.4	3.4
18	Oilseeds, fats and oils and their products	0	31.1	0	8.2	4	2.1	1.7	1.7	6.3	14.3	0	28	3.2	3.1	9.1

19	Cut flowers, plants, vegetable materials; lacs, etc.	0	12.4	0	9.2	5.7	1.3	0	4.5	3.2	28.1	0	38.5	2.4	0.7	1.2
20	Beverages and spirits	0	50.6	0	28.1	80	14.7	9.4	24.2	10.7	29.1	0	0	11.3	4.4	1.8
21	Dairy products	0	40.3	0	18.6	5	26	3.6	3.3	5	72.2	0	35.8	7.7	7.4	13.5
22	Tobacco	0	56.7	0	25.4	10.7	4.2		25	8.4	33.2	0		39.7	7.3	:204.2
23	Other agricultural products	0.1	12.3	0	3.7	4.4	1.1	0.7	3.1	3.2	10.1	0	29.1	1.3	0.8	0.8

Notes: MFN = most-favored nation; MTN = Multilateral Trade Negotiations, World Trade Organization.
a. Excluding tariff-rate quotas, which are high on rice. Brackets indicate value with ad valorem equivalents calculated using Stawowy (2001).
Source: WTO IDB.

TABLE 4.5   Trade Policy Structure of European Union, Japan, and United States for Imports from East Asian Countries (percent)

	Share of duty-free imports	Share of dutiable imports	Share of dutiable imports subject to specific tariffs	Share of products subject to specific duties in total imports
Agriculture				
EU	25.65	74.35	33.26	24.72
Japan	5.81	94.19	10.88	10.25
United States	53.32	46.68	56.30	26.28
Manufactures				
EU	34.21	65.79	0.75	0.49
Japan	59.59	40.41	10.56	4.27
United States	46.14	53.86	13.31	7.17

Note: For details, see the appendix tables to this chapter at www.worldbank.org/eaptrade.
Source: UNCTAD TRAINS database.

process products before exporting them. This has been a contentious issue in trade negotiations.

To put the tariff escalation issue in perspective, consider coffee in Vietnam. By processing its coffee, Vietnam could capture a higher proportion of total value added in the production chain. But it is difficult to perceive how Vietnamese producers, despite their phenomenal success in coffee production, would be able to integrate downstream. As indicated earlier in this chapter, the world market for coffee is highly concentrated, with processors exercising monopsonistic powers. Simply lowering an import tariff on processed coffee would ease market access, but it would not be sufficient to induce investment that ensures competitive exports of processed coffee from the coffee-producing country.

For this study, tariff escalation was analyzed in five products of interest to developing countries: coffee and tea, tomatoes, dried vegetables, crustaceans, and leather products (Table 4.6). For coffee, Canada does not discriminate between unprocessed and processed products, whereas both the EU and the United States do to quite a large degree, with a difference in duties of about 10 percent. This difference translates into much higher effective protection of coffee processing. The MFN duties applied by developing Asian countries on coffee are much higher and differ significantly between processed and unprocessed products.[21] For most of the other four products, the pattern is similar.[22]

Thus East Asian exporters appear to face significant tariff escalation in their main overseas markets. Within East Asia, however, it is clear that as the ASEAN Free Trade Area is fully implemented, the problem of high tariffs on regional trade and tariff escalation among ASEAN countries will be considerably reduced.

Preferential Rates

Although this chapter focuses on multilateral market access, nonreciprocal preferential arrangements are discussed briefly in this section because for certain exports from certain countries these preferences may make the multilateral market access barriers less relevant.[23] However, evidence suggests that the limited coverage and rules of origin in various schemes limit their impact on barriers to products important to the poor of East Asia.

Because the U.S. Generalized System of Preferences (GSP) scheme effectively excludes the agricultural exports of most poor East Asian countries, most of their exports enter the U.S. market at MFN rates. As for the EU, the least-developed countries' access for agricultural products is formally more open, because under the Everything but Arms (EBA) agreement these countries have duty- and quota-free access to the EU market. Yet their access to the EU market does appear to be constrained by restrictive rules of origin. Agricultural products, with some exceptions, are covered by the EU's EBA

TABLE 4.6   Tariff Escalation for Selected Products in Selected Markets and ASEAN Free Trade Area

HS6 category (four-digit code)	Quad countries (MFN)				ASEAN countries (AFTA commitments)[a]									
	Canada	EU	Japan	USA	China	Cambodia	Indonesia	Lao PDR	Malaysia	Myanmar	Philippines	Taiwan (China)	Thailand	Vietnam
Agriculture														
Coffee														
Unprocessed (0901)	0.0	0	12.0	0.2	25	30	5 (0)	40 (0)	0	5 (4)	51 (5)	5.3	40 (5)	25 (5)
Processed (2101)	0	9.5	18.7	12.2	50	35	5 (5)	20	11.6 (2)	15	35 (5)	22.5	47 (5)	50
Tomatoes														
Unprocessed (0702)	0.0	Entry prices[b]	0.0	Specific and seasonal[c]	13	7	5(0)	40 (0)	0	15	10 (5)	10	60 (5)	30 (5)
Processed (2002)	11.5	14.4	12.6	11.9	25	35	5 (0)	30	5.8 (0)	15	11.6 (4)	24	30 (5)	50
Vegetables														
Unprocessed (0713)	2.5	3.2	11.2	1.2	7.2	7	5 (5)	40(0)	0	0	4 (4)	12	60 (5)	30 (50
Processed (1106)	6.0	15	15.9	6.9	25	35	5 (0)	5 (0)	5 (0)	4	10 (3)	20	60 (5)	20 (5)
Nonagricultural products														
Crustaceans														
Unprocessed (0306)	5	11.07	3.8	7.5	30.2	15	5.0 (5)	10 (0)	8 (2.5)	10 (3)	10.8 (5)	36.5	60 (5)	30 (5)
Processed (1605)	4.35	19.04	5.9	7.1	25	35	16 (0)	10 (0)	20 (2.5)	15	5 (5)	30.0	40 (5)	50 (5)
Leather														
Unprocessed (4104)	3.3	0–5.5	24	3.4	8.7	35	0 (0)	20	0	7.5 (5)	4 (3)	2.5	5	5
Processed (6403)	18	7.7	7.2	10	25	24	15 (5)	10 (0)	30 (0)	2 (2)	15 (5)	5	40 (5)	50

Notes: MFN = most-favored nation; ASEAN = Association of Southeast Asian Nations; AFTA = ASEAN Free Trade Area; HS = harmonized system.

a. The commitments made by AFTA members are in parentheses. No parentheses indicate that no commitment has been made.

b. The tariff comprises an ad valorem component and a specific duty that increases the lower the prices. The duties are also seasonal. For example, the ad valorem component ranges from 8.8 to 14.4 percent.

c. The specific duty ranges from 2.8 to 3.9 cents per kilogram, depending on the season.

Source: WTO IDB.

scheme, but the reduction on specific duties is only 30 percent. Furthermore, when the MFN duty has both an ad valorem and a specific component, the specific component is not reduced.

The GSP is highly relevant to the exports of the least-developed countries and Vietnam to the EU. Almost 100 percent of Cambodia's EU exports, 93 percent of the Lao PDR's EU exports, and 83 percent of Vietnam's EU exports are eligible for preferential access to the EU. For other East Asian countries, the GSP is less important, and poor households in these countries do not benefit. For example, less than 30 percent of China's exports to the EU are eligible for preferences, and only 15 percent of Malaysia's exports are eligible.[24]

An important feature of many nonreciprocal preference schemes is their low level of utilization for products actually exported by developing countries. For example, although almost all of Cambodia's exports to the EU were eligible for preferences, Cambodia took advantage of these preferences for only 36 percent of those exports.[25] For the other East Asian developing countries, the take-up of preferences never exceeds two-thirds of the value of exports eligible for preferences. A major reason is the prevalence of stringent rules of origin. Poor countries, with underdeveloped institutions, find it hard to comply with the complex bureaucratic requirements needed to prove the origin of their exports and so take advantage of tariff reductions.

Nontariff Measures

Data on nontariff measures (NTMs) are very difficult to collect, but they remain an important barrier in agroproducts. Unfortunately, despite the important role that nontariff measures play in the market access of agricultural products, very little work has been done to quantify their impact. One possible methodology for assessing the extent of NTMs is the use of frequency data. Such data are available, but they are limited in their ability to quantify the trade distortive element of NTMs (see Bora 2002). Qualitative data are more helpful, but those available are not comprehensive. Case studies are the best way to deal with these kinds of issues.

The qualitative data that are available, such as the analysis by Cerrex (2002) reproduced as Table 4.7, show that for the products of concern to the poor countries of East Asia, the key issues are health

and safety regulations, notably maximum pesticide residue levels; difficulties with understanding and administering standards; lack of technical assistance; and, in some cases, seasonal tariffs. For example, health and safety standards are a major barrier for fresh fruit, vegetables, fish, sweet biscuits, and other foodstuffs and drinks. Organic products face high costs in complying with EU standards and definitions and problems of certification.

Conclusions

Agriculture is the predominant source of income for poor households in East Asia. In products of special importance to these poor households—agricultural and agroprocessing products—important barriers remain in developed and developing country markets.

In contrast to the move toward increased transparency and reduced protection in trade policy for manufactures, agriculture and agroprocessing remain more heavily protected, distorting global markets and affecting production patterns and the efficient adoption of technology in poor countries. For this reason, agricultural liberalization offers great potential for welfare gains. And because poor households are heavily engaged in agricultural activity, they would benefit most from greater market access in agricultural products. For East Asia, liberalization in both developed and developing country markets is important, the latter even more so than the former. And there is greater potential for realizing these gains through regional arrangements, especially between ASEAN and China, given the political complexity surrounding multilateral agricultural liberalization and given the existing marketing links within the region in agricultural products.

Fortunately, East Asian farmers do not participate much in those markets most distorted by the domestic support programs used in high-income countries, with the notable exception of rice. But each major market has significant barriers, which vary according to the product and market. First, the EU and the United States levy above-average ad valorem tariffs on agricultural products and use specific tariffs to a large extent, thereby reducing transparency and creating higher effective protection against low-value goods, often from poorer coun-

TABLE 4.7   Nontariff Measures Affecting Products of Interest to Developing East Asia Economies

Product	HS number	Particular problems
Fresh fruit		Health/safety: pesticide residue levels; difficulties in complying with EU standards (i.e., expense, lack of technical knowledge, difficulty with interpretation of directives).
		Common Agriculture Policy (CAP) levies; quota/license requirements; seasonal preferences; continuing high residual tariffs. Generally no tariff preference for GSP suppliers.
Processed fruit/ fruit-vegetable juices	Except 20.07 to 20.09	Same as above, especially high residual tariffs. No concession for GSP.
Jams and jellies	Except 20.07	Preference given, although residual duty remains very high.
Natural honey	04.09	No preference for GSP; high residual duties.
Rice	10.06	Quotas and licensing and levies: very complicated tariff structure.
Vegetables		Health/safety regulations: maximum pesticide residue levels; difficulties with understanding and administering standards; lack of technical assistance.
		Seasonal preferences for some products; no preference generally for tomatoes.
Organic products	Misc.	High costs of complying with EU standards and definitions; problems with certification; lack of subsidies from national governments; costs of meeting phytosanitary standards.
		Mixture of tariff preferences (e.g., no GSP preferences for chicken or pork); minimal GSP preference for sausages.
Walnuts	Except 08.02	Tariff quotas may apply.
Fish	Except Ch. 3	High residual tariffs often granting GSPs no preference; and 16 problems of origin rules; cost of meeting and administering health regulations; difficulties and cost of testing procedures.
Chocolates		Origin rules and sugar levies.
Sweet biscuits	19.05	Difficulties meeting health/phytosanitary standards; sugar levies; quotas.
Fresh flowers		
Orchids and rose stems	06.03	Difficulties in meeting environment and social standards; CAP levies and duties; quota/license requirements.
Wine	Except 22.04	Subject to continuing high duties; specific excise duties; removal of GSP preference for certain countries.
Cocoa	Except 18	A mixture of the effect of sugar levies. Origin rules for chocolate, quotas, and the number of preferences available (up to 28) make this the most complicated chapter in the tariff.
Foodstuffs and drinks, electrical and engineering goods	Passim	Standards.
Wheat gluten	11.09	Quotas may apply; no preference for GSP countries.
Refined palm oil	15.11	CAP levies and duties may apply; quota restrictions.
Frozen vegetables	Chs. 7 and 20	Need for financial assistance for freezing capacity.
Essential oils and perfumes	33.01 and 33.03	Operation of excise duties to the disadvantage of cheaper products.

Notes: This list is not meant to be a fully comprehensive one of the products or of the problems. The information given is as of mid-2001. HS = harmonized system; GSP = Generalized System of Preferences; Ch. = harmonized system of chapter.
Source: Cerrex (2002).

tries. Second, domestic support and tariff-quota schemes remain an important element of protection in Japan, notably for rice. Third, tariff escalation on agroprocessed goods in the EU, North American, and Japanese markets results in high effective protection rates and discourages diversification into processing activities as well as the capture of more value added by producing countries. Fourth, standards are increasingly a major barrier, with East Asian exporters facing difficulties in meeting health and safety standards, for example.

The results of the analysis in this chapter suggest that reducing trade barriers to agriculture-based products important to the poor of East Asia should be a central trade policy objective. Because no single trade protection element dominates in barriers to these products—and because each trade protection element is important in at least one major market—the approach toward trade policy needs to be broad. Thus the targets for this trade policy should cover all of the following:

- Reducing the above-average tariff rates
- Reducing the extent of tariff escalation and providing additional routes for product diversification and export growth in developing countries
- Reexamining health and safety regulations and procedures for administering them
- Improving the transparency of tariff schedules by converting non–ad valorem rates to ad valorem rates.

Deciding on the arena in which to pursue these objectives is another issue. The chapter has stressed that many of the poorer countries have adopted nonreciprocal market access as a central component of their export strategy. However, these schemes remain beyond the scope of multilateral negotiations for reasons that are beyond the scope of this chapter. Nevertheless, an opportunity for improvements in market access conditions clearly exists through further clarification and simplification of rule of origin procedures, clearer and more streamlined applications of standards, and, in the case of some developed markets, a broadening of the coverage of such schemes.

An opportunity also exists to address some of the market access barriers discussed in this chapter through the current round of multilateral negotiations. Negotiators have been given a clear mandate to address barriers specifically for products of interest to developing countries. Such steps would include reducing tariff barriers, converting non–ad valorem lines to ad valorem rates, reducing domestic support, and disciplining export subsidies. The type of result that emerges from the negotiations, however, depends on the effective participation of developing countries in the negotiations.

Yet another possible avenue for pursuing enhanced market access is through the ASEAN Free Trade Area process and other regional arrangements. The current implementation schedule has resulted in fewer barriers in the more advanced ASEAN members. This is an important step because evidence suggests that many products are produced on a regional basis. A more liberal regional trading landscape will encourage further processing and specialization in a regional context, which could enhance opportunities for exporting the types of products discussed here.

Endnotes

1. See Rodriguez and Rodrik (1999) for a general discussion of these issues, as well as Rodrik (2001).
2. Much has also been written about the need for developing countries to move from labor-intensive and low-technology exports into higher technology and higher value added products. Indeed, such a transition is crucial from a general development perspective. But because agricultural products and labor-intensive products remain of key interest to poor households, this chapter focuses on these products.
3. For example, consider coffee in Vietnam. Since 1990 Vietnam's coffee production has increased more than tenfold—mainly from small farms. Farmers sell their coffee cherries to wholesalers, but all they can do is try to ensure that their crop meets minimum quality standards. Four companies purchase half of the world's coffee production, and fewer than 20 percent of the world's population drinks 65 percent of the coffee. Traders who mediate between farmers and the major buyers are responsible for the rest of the production process. Some coffee retailers buy some supplies directly from farmers, but the coordination costs of dealing with millions of farmers are high. The U.S. retail chain Starbucks, for example, buys only about 10 percent of its total coffee purchases directly from farmers. This discussion is based on Stern (2002).
4. See Bacchetta and Bora (2002) and Bora (2002) for a general discussion of this topic.
5. Agriculture's share of official exports is only significant for Myanmar, as shown in Table 4.2 (44 percent). Agriculture's share of GDP exceeds 25 percent in only a few countries such as Mongolia, Lao People's Democratic Republic (Lao PDR), and Cambodia.
6. World Bank, Poverty Projections Toolkit, 2002 estimate.
7. All dollar amounts are 1997 U.S. dollars.
8. The technical appendix to this chapter can be found at www.worldbank.org/eaptrade.

9. The top 30 agricultural exports of each least-developed country in East Asia were identified for this study. Lists are available from the author upon request.
10. It should be noted that the frequency count could overstate the importance of a particular category. For example, countries such as Malaysia have fairly diverse exports, but export value is heavily concentrated in a few products.
11. See last column of Appendix Table 4.1 of this chapter at www.worldbank.org/eaptrade.
12. The major markets were identified for each of the key four-digit products on the basis of aggregated overall agricultural exports. ASEAN served as one group, given the similarity of members' protection profiles in the ASEAN Free Trade Area. In that way, further attention could be focused on non–ASEAN markets such as Canada, Japan, the European Union, and the United States.
13. The reasons for this are the high incidence of domestic support for products that are of relatively low importance to developing countries and the fact that tariffs affect world prices more strongly than do subsidies. This is not to say that support payments in importing countries are unimportant to developing country exporters, but rather that one needs to consider these payments in relation to the exports of specific countries.
14. A distinction can also be drawn between the applied rate of duty as in a nation's tariff schedule and the rate of duty that is applied at the customs point.
15. See the technical appendix to this chapter at www.worldbank.org/eaptrade.
16. See the technical appendix to this chapter at www.worldbank.org/eaptrade.
17. China's tariff profile does not take into account its final WTO accession commitments, which have yet to be fully implemented.
18. For details, see the appendix tables 4.4 and 4.5 to this chapter at www.worldbank.org/eaptrade.
19. See Appendix Table 4.3 to this chapter at www.worldbank.org/eaptrade.
20. For example, in the EU market in 2001 the specific duty of 128 euros per 1,000 kilograms on imports of broken rice translated into an ad valorem tariff of 24.75 percent for imports from China and 28.92 percent for imports from Vietnam. In the U.S. market, specific tariffs on certain nuts exported from East Asian countries can translate into ad valorem equivalents in excess of 12 percent.
21. Lao PDR is an exception, imposing a lower duty on processed coffee than on unprocessed.
22. In certain cases, the tariffs on processed agricultural products can be very complex. For example, in the EU processed food products such as biscuits are subject not only to a tariff on the product itself (of about 9 percent) but also to specific tariffs on both the milk and sugar content of the product. Such tariffs can represent very high levels of protection.
23. For developing Asian countries, two important issues surround preferential rates: the nonreciprocal preferences they are granted in the industrial country markets and the reciprocal granting of preferences in the context of regional integration. As discussed elsewhere in this volume, an important question for these countries is whether improved market access at the regional level could be an intermediary step toward multilateral liberalization. In industrial markets, the issue is whether preferences remove or limit the impact of the above-average tariffs and the extensive use of specific tariffs on products of particular relevance to the poorest countries.
24. Further details of preferential access arrangements for poor East Asian countries to the EU and the United States are given in the technical appendix to this chapter at www.worldbank.org/eaptrade.
25. Brenton (2003) shows that, even with duty-free access on paper, Cambodia faced an average tariff equivalent to 7.7 percent on its exports to the EU.

References

The word *processed* describes informally reproduced works that may not be commonly available through libraries.

ABARE. 2000. *The Impact of Agricultural Trade Liberalization on Developing Countries.* Canberra: Australian Bureau of Agricultural and Resource Economics.
Bacchetta, M., and B. Bora. 2002. "Industrial Tariffs and the Doha Development Agenda." World Trade Organization, Geneva. Processed.
Bora, Bijit. 2002. "LDC Market Access Issues and the Doha Development Agenda." World Trade Organization, Geneva. Processed.
Brenton, Paul. 2003. "Integrating the Least Developed Countries into the World Trading System: The Current Impact of EU Preferences under Everything But Arms." Policy Research Working Paper, World Bank and forthcoming in *Journal of World Trade.*
Cerrex. 2002. "Making EU Trade Agreements Work." Study prepared for the UK Department for International Development. Processed.
Hoekman, Bernard, F. Ng, and M. Olarreaga. 2002. "Reducing Agricultural Tariffs versus Domestic Support: What's More Important for Developing Countries." World Bank, Washington, D.C. Processed.
McCulloch, Neil, L. Alan Winters, and Xavier Cirera. 2001. *Trade Liberalization and Poverty: A Handbook.* London: Centre for Economic Policy Research.
Rodriguez, Francisco, and Dani Rodrik. 1999. "Trade Policy and Economic Growth: A Skeptic's Guide to the Cross-National Evidence." NBER Working Paper No. 7081. National Bureau of Economic Research, Cambridge, Mass.
Rodrik, Dani. 2001. "The Global Governance of Trade: As If Development Really Mattered." United Nations Development Programme, New York, October. Processed.
Stawowy, V. 2001. "A Method for Calculating Ad Valorem Equivalents." United Nations Conference on Trade and Development (UNCTAD), Geneva. Processed.
Stern, Nicholas. 2002. "Crisis in a Coffee Cup." *Fortune.* December 9.
World Bank. 2002. *Global Economic Prospects and Developing Countries: Making Trade Work for Poor.* Washington, D.C.
WTO (World Trade Organization) Secretariat. 2000. *Domestic Support.* WTO document G/AG/NG/S/1, Secretariat Background Paper 13. World Trade Organization, Geneva, April.

PART II

DEVELOPMENT ORIENTATION FOR A BEHIND-THE-BORDER AGENDA

5

TRADE AND LOGISTICS: AN EAST ASIAN PERSPECTIVE

Robin Carruthers
Jitendra N. Bajpai
David Hummels

Why focus on logistics? The reason is simple. Reducing the cost and improving the quality of logistics and transport systems improve international market access and lead directly to increased trade—and through this to higher incomes and a wider scope for significant reductions in poverty.

East Asia's progress on logistics has failed to keep pace with its growth in trade. Developing countries in other regions are now catching up, so faster progress on logistics development will be crucial to sustaining East Asia's competitive advantages. High logistics costs for East Asian countries stem from poor transport infrastructure, underdeveloped transport and logistics services, and slow and costly bureaucratic procedures for dealing with both exported and imported goods. The balance among these three factors varies among countries, but in each country a complementary approach to addressing all of them will be needed to produce a sustainable improvement in competitiveness.

Recent studies have indicated the importance of efficient ports (in terms of both operational efficiency and document facilitation) for trade competitiveness (Wilson and others 2002), but the arguments presented in this chapter show that ports are only one aspect of the connection between logistics and trade growth. A look at the total cost of getting products from producers to markets reveals that land transport to ports accounts for a higher proportion of the cost than processing within the port or the maritime voyage itself, and improvements in land access offer the greatest scope for increasing trade competitiveness.

Countries that have moved beyond exporting basic agricultural and mining commodities find that logistics requirements have become more onerous, not less onerous. Manufacturing firms, especially those integrated into global production chains, seek not only low transport costs but also fulfillment of a host of sophisticated logistical needs: short transit times, reliable delivery schedules, careful handling of goods in cold storage chains, certification of product quality, and security from theft. Basic transport infrastructure does not meet the logistics needs of manufacturing firms. Thus the requisite policy agenda extends broadly to stimulating the evolution of transport services,

The authors are grateful to Dr. Jose Tongzan for his comments at the seminar at the Institute for Southeast Asia Studies, Singapore.

promulgating product standards, licensing imports, and encouraging foreign investment.

This chapter reviews the logistics issues facing East Asia and proposes a policy agenda to address them. We first briefly outline the macroeconomic connections between logistics and trade, and, because the economies of the region differ fundamentally in their levels of development, the extent of openness and composition of trade. We then discuss the logistics needs specific to each of three broad groupings of economies. This discussion is followed by a description of the benefits that flow from improvements in logistics, and the channels through which these benefits are produced. We then review the current situation in different aspects of logistics across the region and offer policy recommendations.

Trade and Logistics Nexus

The literature offers substantial evidence linking improvements in transport and logistics directly to improvements in export performance. The effects are especially strong when importers have access to multiple suppliers of highly substitutable commodities. Comparing sales by manufacturers of similar products, Hummels (1999) estimates that exporters with 1 percent lower shipping costs will enjoy a 5–8 percent higher market share. Limao and Venables (2001) estimate that differences in infrastructure quality account for 40 percent of the variation in transport costs for coastal countries and up to 60 percent for landlocked countries. Fink, Mattoo and Neagu (2002) estimate that liberalizing the provision of port services and regulating the exercise of market power in shipping could reduce shipping costs by nearly a third.

A World Bank study (Wilson and others 2002) shows that member countries of the Asia-Pacific Economic Cooperation (APEC) forum differ substantially in the quality of their logistics and trade facilitation across a broad range of measures, including ports infrastructure, customs clearance, regulatory administration, and e-business use. They find that these differences are related significantly to differences in trade performance, and conclude that substantial growth in trade within the APEC bloc could be accomplished by bringing lagging countries up to median performance levels.

Furthermore, improving access to international markets raises incomes. Frankel and Romer (1999) found that countries closer to world markets enjoy higher levels of trade, and that a 1 percent rise in the ratio of trade to gross domestic product (GDP) increases income per person by at least 0.5 percent. Redding and Venables (2002) estimate that more than 70 percent of the variation in per capita income across countries can be explained by the geography of market and supplier access. Better access to coasts alone raises incomes by 20 percent.

As for income differences within countries, internal and effectively landlocked regions have systematically lower levels of income than coastal regions. Comparing China's regions, Wei and Yi (2001) show that trade levels, trade growth, and income growth rates all drop as one moves inland from coastal areas.[1] The evidence on inland regions makes an especially strong case for the importance of access to international markets, because within-country differences control for institutional characteristics that cross-country regressions cannot.

Country Group Perspective

A useful way to organize thinking about logistics in East Asia is to place economies on a graph of trade openness and accessibility (Figure 5.1). Those lying above the horizontal axis score high on measures of openness. The economies to the right of the vertical axis are accessible to world markets in the sense of having superior logistics and low transport costs.[2]

The combination of these two measures groups economies on the basis of their current logistics status, as well as on the basis of the value of improved openness and logistics services in the future—that is, economies with fewer political barriers to trade can enjoy greater returns to logistics investments than those whose tariff structures would prevent much trade growth even with world-class infrastructure. Similarly, accession to the World Trade Organization (WTO) may be of limited value if logistics services are too weak to support trade growth.

Figure 5.1 suggests two additional correlates: per capita incomes and the commodity structure of trade. The economies in the upper-right quadrant enjoy higher incomes than those in the lower left, and their exports are high-technology manufactures rather than resource-based commodities. Causality probably runs both ways. Economies like those of Singapore and Hong Kong (China) have

FIGURE 5.1   Potential Contribution of Transport to Economic Growth in East Asia

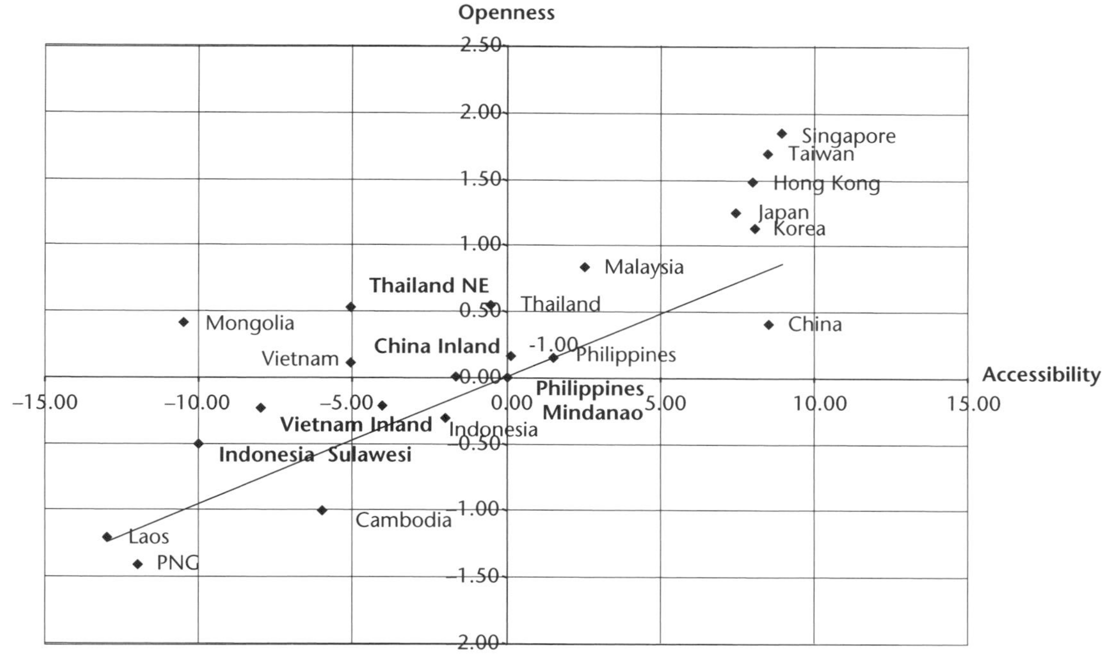

Source: Carruthers and Bajpai (2002).

TABLE 5.1   Availability of Transport Infrastructure

	Total roads (km/ 1,000 km^2)	Percent of roads paved	Railways (km/1,000 km^2)	No. of airports with paved runways longer than 1,523 m/ 1,000 km^2
Cambodia	78.6	11.6	3.3	22.1
China	146.3	28.3	7.1	27.4
Indonesia	178.5	46.3	3.4	32.8
Lao PDR	59.1	24.0	0.0	25.3
Korea, Rep. of	888.9	74.7	31.7	375.7
Malaysia	196.1	75.3	5.5	63.7
Mongolia	46.1	2.2	1.2	4.5
Philippines	606.5	19.8	3.0	113.3
Thailand	125.7	97.5	7.9	75.9
Vietnam	283.1	25.1	9.5	45.5
Argentina	78.6	29.5	12.3	32.8
Brazil	234.0	9.3	3.6	21.3
Mexico	167.9	29.7	9.3	64.8
USA	695.4	90.1	23.2	190.7
France	1,621.8	100.0	58.1	138.1
Poland	1,218.6	65.6	74.9	236.7

Note: The *World Development Report 1994* (World Bank 1994) provided a broad assessment of the basic infrastructure of 132 countries. The consultants for this report expanded and updated the data. UN ESCAP provides
an even more comprehensive and current transport database for Asia at
www.unescap.org/tctd/data/index2.asp.
Source: Policy Research Corporation (2003).

grown rich in part because their past investments in superior logistics have facilitated trade. Meanwhile, Mongolia, Lao People's Democratic Republic (Lao PDR), and Cambodia still suffer from poor basic road access (Table 5.1). Similarly, while sophisticated logistics facilitate the move up the manufacturing quality ladder, demands from advanced manufacturers may push the private sector to improve logistics. Figure 5.1 also presents data for inland regions of China, Thailand, and Vietnam as well as for the islands of Mindanao in the Philippines and Sulawesi in Indonesia, because these areas have very different access to international markets compared with the coastal metropolitan areas or principal islands in the same countries.

Using Figure 5.1, we divided the economies of the East Asia region into three groups:

1. Outward-oriented, highly accessible: Hong Kong, Rep. of Korea, Singapore, Taiwan (China)
2. Outward-oriented, accessible: China, Indonesia, Malaysia, the Philippines, Thailand
3. Less open and accessible: Cambodia, Lao PDR, Mongolia, Papua New Guinea, Samoa, Vietnam.

Group 1: Outward-Oriented, Highly Accessible

In the higher-income economies—Hong Kong, Korea, Singapore, and Taiwan—exports have shifted toward high-technology manufactures and services. Logistics costs are at very competitive levels, transport volumes are high, and multimodal linkages are well developed. Given the strength of global competition, however, these economies need to keep their logistics costs competitive and improve quality in line with the evolution in technology and with recently introduced security requirements.

Hong Kong and Singapore have specialized in providing logistics services as transshipment hubs for neighboring states. Singapore has been the main transshipment stop for much of Southeast Asia, and Hong Kong has specialized in direct shipment to and from neighboring Guangdong Province, the manufacturing region that produces nearly 40 percent of China's exports. But these two megaports now face competition from emerging regional ports: Singapore from Tanjung Pelepas in Malaysia and Laem Chabang in Thailand, and Hong Kong from the rapidly expanding container ports of the

Pearl River Delta on China's southern coast. The major success factors for these and other newly emerging ports are their transaction cost and time cost advantages. Other advantages include their efficient auxiliary services (particularly customs and freight forwarding), less congested road and rail access, and better links to national and international transport networks. Relative to Singapore, the competitive advantage of Tanjung Pelepas will increase as Malaysia expands its rail network and links the port to Cambodia, Thailand, and Vietnam. Likewise, the growth in traffic through ports in southern China is expected to accelerate with the dismantling of restrictions on the direct imports of goods from the United States and Taiwan.

Group 2: Outward-Oriented, Accessible

The countries that fall in this category—China, Indonesia, Malaysia, the Philippines, and Thailand—face daunting problems in addressing the logistics impediments to higher pro-poor economic growth. They are still in the early stages of designing national policies and institutional structures that encourage rather than inhibit the growth of the multimodal transport services that they need for increased external and domestic trade. Many parts of these countries have inadequate and inefficient port and shipping facilities, transport services, and land infrastructure. Poor rural roads cause long transport times and high transport costs, which in turn hamper the development of domestic markets and lead to substantial interregional price differences, particularly within China, Indonesia, and the Philippines. Local authorities and other agencies charge quasi-legal and illegal road tolls, often in a desperate attempt to raise revenue, but always to the detriment of market access.

In the countries of this group, the form of contracts used for international trade and transport discourages multimodal use. It is common for the purchaser of exports to contract free on board (FOB) in the port of the exporting country, and the seller (producer) is responsible for contracting landside delivery to the specified port. Because no one agent assumes responsibility for the whole logistics chain, the full advantages of multimodal transport are not realized. Third-party logistics (3PL), in which an industry contracts out its logistics functions to specialized suppliers of logistics services, are uncommon in Group 2 except in Thailand. In some cases, however, such as large international agroproduct companies in the Philippines, large exporters have developed their own well-integrated logistics. Trade documentation is a particularly difficult hurdle for international trade with an inland origin or destination. Customs and health authorities are very reluctant to allow inland clearance.

Interviews with freight forwarders in the interior of China suggest that inland transport costs can account for about two-thirds of the total transport costs from Chinese producers to overseas markets. In the context of WTO requirements, customs fees will be reduced. China's recent liberalization process has led to an influx of foreign shipping services (foreign carriers transported almost 60 percent of export trade cargo in 2002). In some cases, shipment costs for exports are subsidized by imports.[3]

Group 3: Less Open and Accessible

These mostly low-income countries—Cambodia, Lao PDR, Mongolia, Papua New Guinea, Samoa, Vietnam—are either former centrally planned socialist economies or small island states, dependent on a small number of commodities and tourism. Their regimes, recent history, and geographic position are largely responsible for the small role that international trade plays in their national economies. Except for Vietnam, they have low population density, small domestic markets, and primarily subsistence agrarian economies.

Many logistical constraints hamper the economic growth of these countries, the most fundamental being lack of adequate infrastructure. Roads are often closed and services suspended, and the state of infrastructure requires the use of small, inefficient vehicles and vessels, which have high operating costs. In Cambodia, for example, truck rates for distances over 100 kilometers vary from about $.034–$.116 per ton-kilometer, depending on road conditions. In Lao PDR, almost 40 percent of villages are more than 6 kilometers from a main road, half are inaccessible during the rainy season, one-quarter of the district centers lack year-round road access, and a quarter of provincial and local roads cannot be used during the rainy season. This situation not only makes it difficult to get outputs to markets, but also increases the import costs of essential consumer products and inputs such as fertilizers. In Papua New Guinea, the

Highlands Highway, the prime road corridor used for the export of minerals and coffee, is inadequate for container movement by trucks; it suffers from poor maintenance and frequent closures, causing enormous losses in trade.

Government policies in the realm of logistics tend to lack stability, consistency, and transparency, creating many additional problems for the processing, storage, transport, grading, marketing, and sale of products. Policy coordination between central and provincial authorities is poor. Many countries in this group suffer from highly distorted prices as a remnant of their previously centrally planned economies. National standards on product quality, packaging, storage, and transport conditions are often rudimentary, and farmers lack management, marketing, and logistics capabilities. In Vietnam, overall port, cargo handling, trucking, and rail tariffs may not be excessive, but relative inefficiencies impose high costs in terms of inventory and the unproductive times of vessels and road vehicles.

The intermodal transport systems of most of these countries are poorly integrated, with no streamlined procedures to support the seamless movement of containers between coastal and inland areas. Many countries lack container freight stations, yards, and trucks in their inland regions. Container tracking capability is particularly poor, with shippers often unaware of their containers' whereabouts. The potential impact of improved multimodal transport is well illustrated in a recent study on the time and costs of container movements from Lao PDR to Europe. The study showed that alternative multimodal routes could reduce the present high door-to-door cost from Lao PDR to Europe (through Danang and Singapore) by almost one-third (Banomyong and Beresford 2000).

Border procedures are also cumbersome and time-consuming in these countries. One reason is excessive and ad hoc regulatory requirements. In Cambodia, which experiences enormous competitive pressures from its neighbors, customs clearance takes 8 days for imports and 10–14 days for exports. Informal payments are needed to handle vessels after 5 p.m. in its main port, Sihanoukville. Port charges at Sihanoukville are the highest in the region, almost four times those at the comparably sized port of Songkhla in Thailand (Cambodia Ministry of Commerce 2001). For landlocked countries, land border crossings invariably involve delays and costs arising from the inefficient application of national regulations, difficulties in cargo and document clearance, unnecessarily long storage, high insurance premiums, and long waiting times. For example, Mongolian rail freight arriving at the border with China often waits for days for Chinese rail wagons so that it can complete its journey to the port of Tianjin. Because of a lack of qualified staff at the relevant ministries or government departments, documentation is often inadequate. Border delays lead to extra storage charges, which cannot always be properly controlled. Detailed customs statistics are often collected at a high cost to traders, but data that might be of use to them are not compiled, published, or analyzed.

Remote Regions within Countries

Many East Asian countries have vast remote areas with poor connections to other domestic markets, as well as to international sea and air gateways. The problem begins with low population density and geographic remoteness, but it is worsened by the lack of basic transport infrastructure. Of course, where markets are distant and trade volumes are low, it is difficult to justify building and maintaining even basic infrastructure. But this situation creates a vicious cycle, resulting in transport costs so high

that these remote areas become nearly autarkic. Remoteness is not limited to landlocked regions. In the Philippines, Mindanao has few connections with population centers, and containerized cargo services are limited. Inland transport costs of moving goods from some remote regions of China to external markets are large multiples of the inland transport costs at the other end (Table 5.2).

Logistics difficulties associated with remoteness extend beyond the frequency and cost of transport. For example, connections are poor between the main cities and many of the outlying counties and villages in the Chinese provinces of Hunan and Yunnan. In such interior regions, it is difficult to maintain road access and harder still to maintain supporting facilities such as warehouses, cold storage rooms, intermodal terminals, and information structures to control flows. As a consequence, cargo consolidation is limited, harvests cannot be stored, and perishable products do not survive shipment.

Inland regions are squeezed on two sides—by higher prices for their imported consumption items and by lower net revenues (and therefore lower wages) for their exported output.[4] In Lao PDR, for example, regions that enjoy more days of road access have much lower rates of poverty. Figure 5.2 charts poverty rates across Lao provinces against road access in the rainy season.

FIGURE 5.2   Poverty and Accessibility in Lao PDR

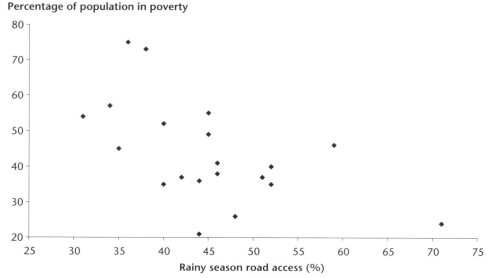

Source: D. Hummels's calculations, based on Arnold (2003).

Similar arguments apply across countries. A country with high logistics costs is, in a broad economic sense, far from international markets in that it pays high prices for its imports and receives low prices for its exports.[5]

Benefits from Improved Logistics

What are the specific channels through which investments in logistics can improve welfare in developing economies? This section reviews examples and evidence taken both from academic studies and from a series of recent country studies by the World Bank.

Reduced "Wedge" between Consumer and Producer Prices

Reducing the cost of moving goods between markets reduces the prices paid by consumers and increases the prices received by producers. On the consumer side, this effect can be seen most clearly by examining the price of goods at the port relative to the price of goods inland. Producers will not ship goods inland unless the price they receive, net of shipping, is at least as high as the price at the port. As a result, inland consumers bear the full burden of shipping costs for any good that is not produced locally. This burden can be substantial. Data from Mongolia, for example, reveal substantial price differences between Ulaanbaatar and outlying regions, with as much as 67 percent of the higher costs in outlying regions attributable to transport.

A similar logic applies to exports. International markets will not pay more for goods produced in inland regions, and so the ex factory or ex farm prices are reduced by the full inland logistics costs of access to the port.

Insurance against Regional Price Fluctuations

Agricultural output sometimes varies because of unpredictable weather—one region may experience drought and food shortages, while another enjoys sufficient rainfall and ample harvests. If the regions are separated by poor logistics and transport systems, consumers in the shortfall region will face very high food prices, and producers in the surplus region will face a market glut. Regional variations in agricultural prices are especially pro-

nounced in countries such as Cambodia, Lao PDR, and Vietnam, where agricultural production is a large portion of national output and where interior regions are poorly connected or inaccessible.

Good internal logistics facilitate commodity shipments from surplus to shortfall regions, smoothing price variations between them and providing a kind of insurance against shortage and glut. Better market access appears to dampen price volatility for a broad range of products. According to Engel and Rogers (1996), the volatility in goods prices between city pairs rises with the distance between the cities, and is especially large for city pairs across national borders. Essentially, arbitrage is necessary to narrow price differentials across locations, but such an objective is much harder to achieve when logistics are poor.

Reduced Inventory Costs

Better transport and logistics systems not only lower the costs of delivery, but also make the timing of delivery more reliable. Because producers cannot manufacture goods without the inputs they need and retailers cannot sell goods they do not have in stock, firms must hold large inventories of goods if delivery times are uncertain. Gausch and Kogan (2001) found that inventory holdings in manufacturing are two to five times higher in developing countries than in the United States, and they estimated that halving inventories could reduce unit production costs by 20 percent.

One reason for long and uncertain delivery times is poor infrastructure—roads may be impassable and railways nonexistent, or roads may inflict damage on trucks that involves high costs and long delays. Another reason is peak load congestion, a severe problem in areas where population and manufacturing intensity have grown faster than infrastructure capacity. In Vietnam's Ho Chi Minh City, for example, the government bans trucks heavier than 2 metric tons in the inner city between 6 a.m. and 6 p.m. to combat growing traffic congestion. Delivery trucks sit idle during that period, forcing manufacturers to maintain large inventories all day. By contrast, under modern just-in-time techniques, deliveries are continuous, and the transport capital stock is in constant use.

But leaner production techniques require a substantial flow of information. Manufacturing firms

TABLE 5.2   Composition of Logistics Costs of Container Transport from Inland China (Chongqing) to U.S. West Coast

Activity	US$ per TEU	Percent of total cost
Land access to port	2,300	63
Port handling	200	5
Maritime transport	750	21
Port handling	150	4
Land access to final destination	250	7
Total	3,650	100

Note: A TEU is a 20-foot equivalent unit, the size of a standard container.
Source: Carruthers and Bajpai (2002).

can run with small inventories of inputs only if they are certain where and when the next shipment will arrive—a situation that requires sophisticated electronic data interchange. Table 5.5 shows that in many countries in the East Asia region systems for this purpose are far from competitive.[6]

More Developed Markets

Well-developed logistics increase consumers' choices and producers' sources of supply, and bring more markets within the reach of producers. According to Evenett and Venables (2002), 40 percent of the growth in trade in East Asia arises from offering new product lines and extending exports of existing product lines to new trading partners.

Product diversification benefits both agricultural- and industrial-based economies. For both, specialization in a narrow range of products can be dangerous because of price volatility. Recent studies have shown that most of the differences in trade levels between small and large economies can be attributed to differences in the range of goods traded, and that much of the growth in imports that results from lowering trading costs arises from expanding the set of products available.[7] Romer (1994) shows that the welfare benefits from expanded product variety can dwarf those from standard calculations of the gains from trade. And manufacturing firms are consumers as well. Feenstra and others (1999) find that expanding the variety of inputs in Taiwan and Korea is associated with productivity growth in manufacturing.

Better logistics allow expanded variety in two ways. First, they may directly lower the fixed costs of expansion. The scale advantages to providing transport hubs, warehousing, and logistics services

that many firms can share are significant. Second, by lowering the marginal costs of serving markets, firms can increase sales and spread entry costs over more units.

The diversification argument also applies across markets, because reliance on a single export destination leaves firms subject to significant risks from business cycles. The market destinations for East Asia's exports are mainly the industrial countries, and intraregional trade is limited. This situation stems in part from the pattern of logistics costs and the institutional barriers to land-based trade that make many countries in the region effectively closer to industrial countries than their own geographic neighbors. Thus, although the proposed conversion of the Association of Southeast Asian Nations (ASEAN) to a free trade area would do much to remove tariff barriers, the signatory countries will have to make a corresponding change in their implementation of customs and other restrictions on trade, supported by a reduction in logistics costs, if they are to realize the full benefits of tariff reductions.

Moving Up the Value Chain

As countries move up the value chain from resource extraction to sophisticated manufacturing and higher value added agriculture, they must develop their logistics capabilities accordingly. As the value-to-weight ratio of a country's exports rises, logistics and transport costs will fall, but only if the nature of logistics and transport services stays unchanged. In practice, the more sophisticated exports generally impose much greater demands on logistics and transport services. For example, iron ore and bulk grains may be heavy and difficult to move over land for long distances, but their shipment is otherwise uncomplicated. High-value agriculture (flowers, fruits, and seafood) requires careful handling, timeliness, and product standardization. Electronics manufacturing requires all this, as well as tightly integrated supply chains.

Regional Transport and Logistics Issues

Despite two decades of improvement, East Asia has significant scope for further reducing its transport and logistics costs.[8] The rest of this section reviews problems and opportunities in specific areas, as a prelude to the policy recommendations offered later in this chapter.

Maritime Issues

Ninety percent of the world's trade in manufactured goods is now carried by containers, and the use of containerized shipping has increased throughout East Asia (Table 5.3). During the 1990s, total container movements increased by nearly 10 percent a year, with the fastest growth occurring at the ports of China and new ports in Malaysia and Thailand (Frenkel 1998). The rapid growth in container usage represents both a revolution in maritime technology and a significant logistics challenge to economies in the region.

Although regional container ports are becoming more efficient at handling containers, they are not keeping pace with the rapidly growing demand for berth space. Although the capacity of the container fleet on the East Asian routes increased by more than 20 percent a year between 1980 and 2000, the capacity of container berths to handle those ships increased by less than 8 percent a year. Countries are responding to the shortage by adding new berths, converting general cargo berths to container handling, and developing new ports (Vitasa and Seprato 1999).

Expanded container capacity requires the availability of additional land for container storage, road and rail links, and associated services. These issues are discussed later in this section.

Higher East Asian trade volumes have led liner services to introduce large container ships that require deeper access channels, which often can be provided only through voluminous dredging. As a result, ports in river estuaries (such as Bangkok, Haiphong, Saigon, and Shanghai) may become less competitive than coastal deepwater ports (such as Laem Chabang and Hong Kong). Some existing

TABLE 5.3   Container Movements at Selected East Asian Ports, 1995–2001

Port	1995	1996	1997	1998	1999	2000	2001	Annual growth (%)
Hong Kong (China)	**12,550**	**13,460**	**14,567**	**14,582**	**16,211**	**17,800**	**17,900**	**6.1**
Singapore	**11,846**	**12,944**	**14,135**	**15,136**	**15,945**	**17,040**	**15,520**	**4.6**
Shanghai	1,196	1,305	2,527	3,066	4,206	5,613	6,310	31.9
Port Klang	1,134	1,410	1,685	1,820	2,550	3,206	3,759	22.1
Laem Chabang	—	729	1,036	1,425	1,756	2,195	2,424	27.1
Qingdao	603	810	1,031	1,213	1,540	2,100	2,639	27.9
Tianjin	702	822	935	1,018	1,302	1,708	2,010	19.2
Guangzhou	515	558	687	848	1,179	1,430	1,628	21.1
Taichung, Taiwan	447	695	842	880	1,107	1,130	1,069	15.6
Total (East Asia)	54,433	57,836	65,119	68,155	75,155	83,422	94,267	9.6
Hong Kong and Singapore (%)	45	46	44	44	43	42	35	

— Not available.
Source: Containerization International, March 2002.

estuarial ports are already looking for new developments on the coast to overcome this disadvantage.

Because the scope for further reducing costs by increasing vessel size is limited, the next development is likely to be more direct services from what are now feeder ports. With higher volumes and more efficient smaller vessels, such a step could overcome the high cost penalty of transfers in the hub ports. This trend is already reflected in the slower growth rates of the two regional megaports, shown in Table 5.3.

Multimodal Transport

Much of East Asia uses containers only for the maritime part of trips, loading and unloading them in the ports rather than at the origin and destination of their cargo. This approach, however, eliminates the main cost savings advantages of container use. The countries most successful at encouraging door-to-door movement of containers using multimodal transport will be the ones best equipped to compete and to bring trade benefits to their more remote regions. To achieve this integration, they will need to:

- *Match inland infrastructure with maritime infrastructure.* One important reason that containers do not move inland from container ports is that road and rail infrastructure lack the appropriate carrying capacity and vehicle dimensions for the transport of loaded containers.
- *Simplify trade documentation.* Examples include the use of through waybills and single invoices for all modes. In customs clearance times, those of the East Asian economies are quite similar to those of other developing countries (Table 5.4), but, taken together, developing countries are significantly slower than developed countries. Another regulatory change—allowing containers to be cleared for tariffs, customs, health, and taxation charges at inland locations away from the ports—would help to reduce port congestion, but could raise additional security concerns.
- *Develop an efficient freight forwarding industry.* As noted earlier, third-party logistics is not a well-advanced concept in East Asia. In industrial countries, almost a third of logistics turnover is contracted to 3PL providers, but even in several industrialized East Asian economies, barely 10 percent of trade-related transport services is provided in this way. In some countries, pro-

gression to the earlier stage of second-party logistics—in which companies unify their internal transport and warehousing functions and create their own internal logistics departments—is still under way.

- *Develop effective communications systems.* Such systems will allow freight forwarders to take advantage of the shipping alternatives available and inform clients about the status and location of their freight.

Some of the least accessible countries have improved the quality and scope of their information systems (Table 5.5), but few have been able to develop freight forwarding agencies that perform as well as those in the more accessible and trade-open countries. The efficiency of logistics services correlates closely with the efficiency of other trade facilitation procedures. Countries that have poorly integrated trade services, such as customs requirements that are badly coordinated with those of taxation and health agencies, also tend to have poorly developed logistics services. Evidence from some East Asian countries, particularly Thailand, suggests that the presence of a strong logistics industry can be effective in bringing about efficiencies in these other trade facilitation procedures.

Some evidence also suggests that even those countries with the least developed logistics systems have recognized the need to catch up. According to a recent report on logistics in China,[9] the development of hypermarkets and other large retail customers with significant bargaining power is creating a demand for better logistics services that was not obvious even a few years ago. At the same time, the Chinese government is encouraging companies to outsource their logistics services, and as part of the agreement on WTO accession, it is in the process of rapidly opening its logistics services to foreign competitors and participants.

Ports and Land Access

The high costs of land access to ports, reinforced by the effects of production agglomeration, have caused an excessive concentration of export-related activities in port cities and essentially have restricted the benefits of trade growth to the areas immediately surrounding ports. In China, for example, more than 90 percent of foreign direct

TABLE 5.4   Customs Clearance Times

Country	Average no. of days for customs clearance		
	Air	Sea LCL	Sea FCL
France	1	4	2
Germany	1	1	1
Greece	1	1	1
Netherlands	1	2	2
Spain	2	2	2
Sweden	1	2	2
USA	2	3	3
Average, sample of developed countries	1.3	2.1	1.9
China	4	30	5
Hong Kong (China)	2	4	3
Indonesia	3	4	4
Malaysia	4	4	4
Philippines	4	5	3
Singapore	2	3	3
Taiwan (China)	4	10	7
Thailand	5	5	5
Vietnam	5	7	7
Average, sample of East Asian counties	3.7	8.0	4.6
Argentina	7	15	12
Brazil	10	10	10
India	8	10	12
Mexico	4	7	4
Mozambique	5	8	8
Russia	10	12	15
Zimbabwe	4	5	5
Average, sample of other developing countries	6.9	9.6	9.4

Note: LCL = less than container load; FCL = full container load.
Source: International Exhibition Logistics Associates (www.iela.org).

investment in export-oriented activities has gone to the four main coastal provinces (Fujian, Guangdong, Jiangsu, and Shanghai). Similarly, the multiplier effect of the textile export boom in Cambodia has been limited largely to areas that have easy access to the deepwater port at Sihanoukville.

If the benefits of trade are to be more widely distributed, the penalties of inaccessibility have to be addressed. Such action could stimulate trade-induced growth in currently inaccessible regions, and, if successful, could slow the growth of trade-induced urban congestion and pollution in port cities.

The social costs of the concentration of manufacturing activities in port cities can be significant.

Traffic congestion costs, in particular, can be enormous. A recent study in Bangkok estimated that moving port-related activities out of the downtown area would result in a 10 percent reduction in peak-hour trips and would entail benefits of up to US$400 million[10] annually (UN ESCAP 2000). Reductions in port access costs depend on having available adequate infrastructure, the appropriate vehicles, and the logistics technology that allows both to be used efficiently (Box 5.1.)

As container ports expand, municipalities find it increasingly difficult to accommodate both the added space requirements and the road congestion that results from the high volumes of truck traffic servicing the ports. In some instances, the only fea-

TABLE 5.5   Electronic Data Interchange and Transport E-Commerce in Selected Countries

Country	Port operators MIS	Traders in port EDI system	Customs agency MIS	Traders in customs EDI system	All parties electronically linked	Electronic trade in transport services
Japan	X	X	X	X		
Singapore	X	X	X	X	X	X
Korea, Rep. of	X	X	X	X	X	X
Thailand	X	X	X	X	X	X
Philippines	X	X	X	X		
Indonesia	X	X	X	X		
Vietnam	None					
Lao PDR	None					
Cambodia	None					

Note: MIS = management information system; EDI = electronic data interchange.
Source: Based on UN ESCAP (2002).

BOX 5.1   Successful Integration of Ports and Land Transport Networks: Republic of Korea

The ports of the Republic of Korea benefit from one of East Asia's most developed land access networks. Major road and rail links run to the ports of Pusan and Kwangyang from Korea's major manufacturing regions. Kwangyang, which is alongside a major steel mill and industrial complex, is now in its second stage of development, with a potential capacity of 2.4 million TEU (20-foot equivalent unit). Pusan has developed a new port area away from the downtown area. This location has reduced traffic congestion and air pollution, and improved logistics efficiency has made the new port easier to reach from the city's industrial areas and the rest of Korea (www.pusanconsulting.co.kr/En-aboutPusan.htm).

The Yangsan inland container terminal has been constructed to relieve port-generated traffic congestion and environmental problems resulting from the massive transport movements that the port generates. Another inland container terminal is being developed in the center of the Korean peninsula to serve the growing industrial zones on the west coast and in the center of the country. Together with the ports, these terminals are part of a logistics system based on an advanced electronic data interchange and information service.

---

sible response is to build a new port. A less costly response is to move port activities out of downtown urban areas, while retaining the employment and business activities that the ports attract. For example, one of the principal reasons for developing the Waigaoqiao container terminal and Luojing coal terminal outside Shanghai was to move port-based traffic out of the urban area. This goal was achieved between 1996 and 1998. The port traffic handled at terminals within the city was reduced by about 13 million metric tons, and that in the new terminals outside the city was increased by about the same amount. However, the urban traffic associated with the existing port must be reduced even further, and this need is part of the justification (together with the limited depth of the access channel) for the development of a new deepwater port away from the urban area. Based on two offshore islands, the new port will require new 30-kilometer access roads, including a bridge, and is conservatively estimated to cost up to $4 billion just for the first stage.

When the depth of the maritime access channel is not a constraint on growth, the urban congestion problems of port growth can often be solved by moving the nonmaritime port activities (mostly value-adding production and packaging services) inland, closer to the industries that the port serves, and building rail links to avoid generating extra road traffic (Rafferty 2003).

Air Freight

Air freight accounts for only about 1 percent of East Asia's international trade by volume, but more than 35 percent by value. More than for other regions, air freight is important for East Asia. For one thing, the distance from the region's major markets—the United States and Europe—makes quick delivery of sea freight impossible. And, for another, a high proportion of the region's manufactured exports require timely delivery. (Because these manufactures have high value-to-weight ratios, the ad valorem cost of their air transport is comparatively low.)

A ranking of cargo volumes by airport reveals the importance of air freight to East Asia. Of airports outside the United States, those in East Asia took 10 of the top 30 places for air freight volume in both 2000 and 2001, and accounted for more than 30 percent of air freight at the top 30 airports worldwide (Table 5.6).

Good air freight facilities are important in attracting fast-growing, high value added industries. Competition is, therefore, growing between airports in the region to act as a hub for major logistics companies. The smaller, newer airports

that can offer better services are growing faster than the larger ones.

Airlines and traditional freight forwarders both compete and cooperate with each other to provide air transport-based freight services. The progress of air freight forwarding and air freight logistics in Hong Kong, Japan, Korea, and Singapore compares favorably with that in the United States and Europe. Some countries in the region still depend on a few multinational air carriers for efficient air freight logistics.

Policy Recommendations

Against this background, governments in East Asia need to take action to improve trade-related logistics on several fronts if they are to increase their trade competitiveness.

Domestic Integration

For the less open and less accessible group of countries, and for landlocked regions and remote regions in China, Indonesia, the Philippines, and Thailand, the development of more tightly integrated domestic markets and logistics systems is a high priority. Besides promoting an appropriate mix of modes—roads, waterways, and rail—institutional actions must be taken to extend better transport services to remote areas and to establish

TABLE 5.6 Ranking of Major Freight Airports in East Asia, 2001

Global ranking	Airport	Code	Amount of cargo handled (metric tons)
3	Hong Kong (China)	HKG	2,099,605
5	Tokyo	NRT	1,680,938
8	Singapore	SIN	1,529,930
15	Inchon	ICN	1,196,845
16	Taipei	TPE	1,189,874
18	Osaka	KIX	871,161
19	Bangkok	BKK	842,588
23	Tokyo	HND	725,124
27	Seoul	SEL	598,620
28	Beijing	PEK	586,704
	Total East Asia		33,210,120
	Percent of total top 30		34.1

Source: Airports Council International, 2002.

better conditions for market development through, for example, postharvest services, cargo consolidation through farmer or business associations, information on prices and market demand, access to credits, and human skills.

Private Sector

Transport of the outputs of very simple extractive industries may not require advanced logistics abilities, but high-value products call for services such as freight forwarding, third-party logistics, warehousing, storage, packaging, e-business, and trucking.[11]

Logistics needs of this kind tend to be better served by the private sector than by the public sector. The governments of many countries may be well advised to halt providing logistics services directly and turn instead to creating an environment conducive to competition and private investment. Such an approach may entail legalizing and deregulating freight forwarders and allowing new entrants, including the international companies that can be a major source of the capital, technology, and new management practices needed to develop sophisticated services. Even areas traditionally managed by government, such as port management and operations, may benefit from private services.[12] Countries throughout East Asia are likely to reap a very high payoff from a well-developed private logistics industry.

Given the fixed costs of entry, private operators are reluctant to provide services where trade volumes are low. One solution supported by the World Bank is to provide initial public funding for the development of facilities where the economic benefits indicate earlier development than the financial returns would support. The initial public investment in facilities such as inland container terminals in potentially high-growth regions distant from ports can be recovered through later concession revenues or outright sales.[13]

Regulatory Environment

Transport. Lack of regulatory coordination across transport modes is a common problem in East Asia. One regulatory agency monitors ports; another monitors roads; and a third monitors rail. And each may have different plans, standards, and reporting requirements. This situation presents problems for

firms seeking seamless freight movement across modes. A transparent, uniform regulatory and legal regime for private sector participation, safety, environment, traffic rules, vehicle weight, and dimension is a prerequisite for an effective transport ministry. An obvious solution is regulatory consolidation so that businesses face consistent rules.

Improved transport infrastructure in trade corridors is an important part of a regional poverty reduction strategy that seeks to attract foreign direct investment and trade-based growth away from port cities. Although infrastructure development in competing modes can stimulate intermodal competition, it can be costly in the early stages of trade corridor expansion. Government should promote an integrated planning framework for developing these corridors, with an established hierarchy of modal interfaces (inland terminals, container stations, cargo clearance facilities for customs, health inspections, and tax payments). Coordination between the agencies responsible for different modes is essential here.

A further problem is that access to publicly administered transport may not be allocated according to an efficient market-based pricing model. In central China, for example, some bulk commodities are allowed queuing priority on rail lines. Such a practice reverses the priorities that would exist if queuing were determined by market prices. Often some public or private monopolies[14] are unable to provide satisfactory services despite their high service charges.

Countries already within the WTO, such as China, and those likely to join in the near future, such as Cambodia, Vietnam, and Lao PDR, need to review their transport regulations and policies. This review would be aimed at bringing them into line with WTO and General Agreement on Trade in Services (GATS) rules on nondiscrimination between foreign and local service providers, transparency of rules and regulations, and elimination of quantitative restrictions.

Cross-Border Facilitation. Cross-border facilitation is a key intervention in lowering overall export and import transaction costs. It promises high returns for all East Asian countries, although less for those that are relatively advanced. It can be best achieved by harmonizing and simplifying customs procedures, sharing information, modernizing information and communications technology and customs administration, and establishing transparent transit rules and postentry compliance audits. Plans for improvements must take into account the interests of related public and private communities—including customs, freight forwarders, shippers, port operators, shipping lines, insurers, and bankers.

Urban Land Use and Management. Urban governments need to exercise market-responsive land use policies for locating logistics infrastructure, especially ports. This is perhaps more difficult than it sounds because of unpriced externalities. Firms move production into clusters because there they enjoy positive productivity externalities—information spillovers, access to intermediate inputs, and specialized human capital—but they do not take into account the effect that clustering has on already severe congestion. Government efforts to relieve congestion or relocate facilities must take into account the trade-offs between the positive externalities (agglomeration economy) and negative externalities (congestion, pollution) of the businesses or facility to be displaced, such as a port or container depot. Unfortunately, these externalities, especially the positive spillovers, remain difficult to measure.

Security

The September 11, 2001, terrorist attacks on the United States heightened the importance of efficient and secure trade facilitation in supporting trade-led growth. The increased transport costs related to security have already begun to affect trade volumes and the competitiveness of ports. According to an estimate by the Organisation for Economic Co-operation and Development (OECD), trading costs excluding the increased inventory and other "behind the border" costs have risen by about 1–3 percent, resulting in a loss of about $75 billion in aggregate welfare.

The increased costs and challenges of trade facilitation will depress the level of trade of countries that cannot manage them successfully. All the international agencies involved directly in international trade are helping exporting countries to achieve higher security as expeditiously as possible. They are providing funding for the procurement of equipment, technical assistance in drafting regula-

tions, and training for customs and security staff. The solutions that countries select are likely to vary according to country conditions (human skills and resources, technology, quality of facilities), risk profiles, and types of trade transactions. The World Customs Organization Task Force on Security and Trade Facilitation is expected to develop appropriate processes and identify the related needs for capacity building.

Because security and facilitation are two sides of the same coin, an integral approach to supply chain management would be appropriate, although now the focus is on limiting the security risks of imports by improving a few discrete points in supply chains (customs). Security initiatives are now targeting containers as well as air cargo and passenger movements.[15] For security initiatives to succeed, the relevant technologies and information systems must be shared among government agencies, shippers, and corporations.

Regional Cooperation

Such sharing is best achieved through a regional dialogue—a dialogue that is also central to the harmonization of national, regional, and international rules and policies related to trade facilitation. Cooperation is especially important in assisting landlocked countries, such as Mongolia and Laos PDR, and those with long land borders, mostly in the Mekong River region.

Ongoing regional and subregional initiatives (ASEAN, APEC, Mekong River Commission, and Greater Mekong subregion) provide regular opportunities to cooperate on country-specific investments and reforms to address the regional needs.[16] The World Bank's country-specific programs—and more specifically the Global Trade Facilitation Partnership[17] among more than 100 international, public, and private agencies—can also assist countries through investments and technical assistance on trade facilitation issues, while serving as a major source for knowledge sharing in global best practices and capacity building.[18]

Endnotes

1. Gallup, Sachs, and Mellinger (1999) point out that "core" coastal regions worldwide contain 10 percent of the world's population but contribute 35 percent of the gross world product.

2. The measures of openness are based on those indicated in the *Global Competitiveness Report 2001–2002* (World Economic Forum 2002). Values for countries not included in that report have been added using World Bank staff assessments of the three indices (see Carruthers and Bajpai 2002). All values have been normalized for the countries of East Asia. The measures of accessibility are based on the cost of transporting a standard container from the metropolitan region of the largest port to Hamburg, Germany. For inland regions, the land transport cost to the metropolitan region has been added.

3. For example, in Thailand the inbound rate for a 20-foot container is about $380 compared with $168 for an outbound container.

4. Transport cost incidence is a primary candidate for explaining why incomes drop as international market access drops, as shown by Wei and Yi (2001) for China and by Frankel and Romer (1999) and Redding and Venables (2002) for the situation worldwide.

5. A manufacturer in Thailand claimed to be closer in time and cost to the United States than to Vietnam because of the poor land access facilities from Thailand to Vietnam.

6. Certainty in delivery also requires that shipments be secure from theft and pilferage. This problem is likely to be most serious for products that are of high value but sufficiently homogeneous that gray markets exist for resale. Firms' strategies to avoid theft can result in higher transport costs and uncertainty in delivery times. For example, manufacturers of integrated circuits in the Philippines reduce hijacking of shipments by using irregular and therefore costly transport schedules.

7. See Hummels and Klenow (2001) for cross-sectional comparisons of small and large economies, and Hillberry and McDaniel (2002) for an examination of how trade liberalization affects trade growth.

8. An assessment of the issues at the country and specific trade flow levels is provided in country studies undertaken for the World Bank in 2002. See Arnold and Villareal (2002); Arnold, Banomyong, and Ritthironk (2002); Infrastructure Consulting Ltd. (2002); International Trade Institute of Singapore (2002); and Nomura Research Institute (2002).

9. See Shaw and Wang (2002). Other articles in this series of the *McKinsey Quarterly* also confirm the growing importance of multimodal transport arrangements.

10. All dollar amounts are current U.S. dollars.

11. Domestic providers of such services may not be up to international standards. For example, because of concerns about the quality of local freight forwarders, Japanese manufacturers in Vietnam insist on working with freight forwarders that are joint venture partners with familiar (Japanese) logistics providers. Part of the reason may be a need for the superior technology that the foreign logistics providers can offer, and part may be the long-standing relationship between the manufacturer and logistics provider. Freight forwarders that fail to provide reliable delivery times and careful handling jeopardize contracts not only in Vietnam but also back in Japan.

12. See Fink, Mattoo, and Neagu (2002) for the Latin American experience with port privatization.

13. This approach is being applied in the China Container Transport Project supported by the World Bank.

14. Such as the Philippines Ports Authority, the private shipping cartels Vinamarine and Vinalines in Vietnam, and the traders' cartel for freight forwarding in Lao PDR.

15. See Reddy (2002). Traditional security methods result in processes that increase the cycle time for activities, such as queuing to go through metal detectors and physical inspections. Reddy argues that the preferred approach from both the security and efficiency perspectives is for goods and raw materials to be secured after inspection at the point of origin. If this approach can be implemented for the 1 percent of shippers that account for more than 60 percent of all container movements at the point of origin, then national security agencies can focus on a more thorough examination of the remaining 40 percent of containers. The overall result should be to minimize the impact on the flow of international trade. A key to this approach is the security of containers once they have left their country of origin. Some technologies already available allow a container to be tracked and monitored at all times between its origin and destination.

16. Including for cross-border transport links, improved customs processing, and harmonization of rules dealing with customs, vehicle standards, border crossings by vehicles registered in neighboring or third countries, movement of hazardous material, insurance coverage, safety and treatment of transit traffic.

17. The Global Facilitation Partnership for Transport and Trade (GFP) seeks to pull together all interested parties, public and private, national and international, that want to help achieve significant improvements in transport and trade facilitation in World Bank member countries. The partners will together agree to design and undertake specific programs toward meeting this objective, making use of their respective comparative advantages in the subject matter in a coordinated fashion (http://wbln0018.worldbank.org/twu/gfp.nsf/).

18. For example, by means of distance learning and toolkits on customs modernization, supply chain management, and port modernization.

References

The word *processed* describes informally reproduced works that may not be commonly available through libraries.

Arnold, John. 2003. "Logistics Development and Trade Facilitation in Lao PDR." Working Paper No. 3, East Asia Transport Unit. World Bank, Washington, D.C.

Arnold, John, and Theresa Villareal. 2002. "Philippine Logistics Study." Study prepared for the World Bank, Washington, D.C.

Arnold, John, Ruth Banomyong, and Nipawis Ritthironk. 2002. "Logistics Development and Trade Facilitation in Lao PDR." Study prepared for the World Bank, Washington, D.C.

Banomyong, R., and A. K. C. Beresford. 2000. "Multi-Modal Transport Systems: The Case of the Laotian Garment Industry." Trois-Rivieres, France. Processed.

Cambodia Ministry of Commerce. 2001. "Integration and Competitiveness Study—Part B." Pilot study prepared under Integrated Framework for Trade-Related Technical Assistance.

Carruthers, Robin, and Jitendra N. Bajpai. 2002. "Trends in Trade and Logistics: An East Asian Perspective." Working Paper No. 2, Transport Sector Unit. World Bank, Washington, D.C.

Engel, Charles, and John. H. Rogers. 1996. "How Wide Is the Border?" *American Economic Review* 86 (5): 1112–25.

Evenett, Simon J., and Anthony J. Venables. 2002. "The Geographic Spread of Trade: Evidence from Twenty-Four Developing Countries." European Research Workshop in International Trade (ERWIT), Munich, June 14, 2002.

Feenstra, Robert C., Dorsati Madani, Tzu-Han Yang, and Chi-Yuan Liang. 1999. "Testing Endogenous Growth in South Korea and Taiwan." *Journal of Development Economics* 60 (2): 317–41.

Fink, Carsten, Aaditya Mattoo, and Ileana Cristina Neagu. 2002. "Trade in International Maritime Services: How Much Does Policy Matter?" *World Bank Economic Review* 16: .81–108.

Frankel, Jeffrey, and David Romer. 1999. "Does Trade Cause Growth?" *American Economic Review* 89 (3): 1–16.

Frenkel, E. G. 1998. "China's Maritime Developments." *Maritime Policy Management* 25 (3): 235–49.

Gallup, John Luke, and Jeffrey Sachs with Andrew D. Mellinger. 1999. "Geography and Economic Growth." *International Regional Science Review* 22 (2): 179–232.

Gausch, Luis J., and J. Kogan. 2001. "Inventory in Developing Countries: Level and Determinants, a Red Flag on Competitiveness and Growth." World Bank, Washington, D.C.

Hillberry, Russell, and Christine McDaniel. 2002. "A Decomposition of North American Trade Growth since NAFTA." *International Economic Review* (May/June): 1–6.

Hummels, David. 1999. "Towards a Geography of Trade Costs." Graduate School of Business, University of Chicago. Processed.

Hummels, David, and Peter Klenow. 2001. "The Variety and Quality of a Nation's Trade." NBER Working Paper No. 8712. National Bureau of Economic Research, Cambridge, Mass.

Infrastructure Consulting Ltd. 2002. "Mongolia Trade Competitiveness." Study prepared for the World Bank, Washington, D.C.

International Trade Institute of Singapore. 2002. "Logistics Development, Trade Facilitation and Its Impact on Poverty Reduction in China's Lagging Provinces." Study prepared for the World Bank, Washington, D.C.

Limao, Nuno and Anthony Venables. 2001. "Infrastructure, Geographical Disadvantage, Transport Costs and Trade." *World Bank Economic Review* 15: 51–479.

Nomura Research Institute. 2002. "Vietnam Logistics Development and Trade Facilitation." Study prepared for the World Bank, Washington, D.C.

Policy Research Corporation. 2003. "East Asia Transport and Logistics Strategy: Measuring Progress." Working Paper No. 9, East Asia Transport Unit. World Bank, Washington, D.C.

Rafferty, Laura. 2003. "East Asia Ports in their Urban Context." Working Paper No. 7, East Asia Transport Unit. World Bank, Washington, D.C.

Redding, Stephen, and Anthony, J. Venables. 2002. "Economic Geography and International Inequality." Discussion Paper No. 2568. Centre for Economic and Policy Research (CEPR), London.

Reddy, Ram. 2002. "Friction over Security Gaps." October 8. Available at www.intelligententerprise.com/.

Romer, Paul. 1994. "New Goods, Old Theory, and the Welfare Costs of Trade Restrictions." *Journal of Development Economics* 43: 5–38.

Shaw, Stephen, and Feng Wang. 2002. "Moving Goods in China." *McKinsey Quarterly.* No. 2.

UN ESCAP (United Nations Economic and Social Commission for Asia and the Pacific). 2000. "State of the Environment in Asia and the Pacific." ST/ESCAP/2087. Bangkok.

———. 2002. "Review of Developments in Transport and Communications in the ESCAP Region, 1996–2001." Bangkok.

Vitasa, H.R., and N. Seprato. 1999. "Maritime Sector Developments in ASEAN Countries." Paper presented at United Nations Development Programme (UNDP) Conference on Trade and Development, Jakarta, October.

Wei, Shang-Jin, and Yi Wu. 2001. "Globalization and Inequality: Evidence from China." NBER Working Paper No. 8611. National Bureau of Economic Research, Cambridge, Mass.

Wilson, John S., Catherine Mann, Yuen Pau Woo, Nizar Assanie, and Inbom Choi. 2002. "Trade Facilitation: A Development Perspective in the Asia Pacific Region." Working paper presented to APEC (Asia-Pacific Economic Cooperation). World Bank, Washington, D.C.

World Bank. 1994. *World Development Report 1994: Infrastructure for Development.* Washington, D.C.: Oxford University Press and World Bank.

World Economic Forum. 2002. *Global Competitiveness Report 2001–2002.* Geneva.

6

PROTECTING INDUSTRIAL INVENTIONS, AUTHORS' RIGHTS, AND TRADITIONAL KNOWLEDGE: RELEVANCE, LESSONS, AND UNRESOLVED ISSUES

Manjula Luthria
Keith E. Maskus

In recent years, the increasingly intensive use of knowledge and innovation in international trade flows and foreign direct investment has brought the issue of intellectual property rights (IPRs) into the mainstream in global trade discussions.[1] The debate leading up to the Agreement on Trade-Related Aspects of Intellectual Property Rights (TRIPS), adopted by Members of the World Trade Organization (WTO) in 1995, was a contentious one between developed countries, which were lobbying for stronger intellectual property rights, and developing countries, which largely considered such across-the-board upgrading to be premature, given their positions as users rather than producers of technological innovations. Subsequent and ongoing negotiations at the global and bilateral levels are attempting to address some of these tensions.

Intellectual property rights are a form of domestic business regulation that sets background incentives for innovation and the diffusion of new information into consumption and competition. The interests of innovative businesses need to be delicately balanced with those of the users of new products and technologies.[2] It is possible to establish intellectual property standards that are too weak to support local innovation and product introduction, but it is also possible to adopt standards that are excessively protectionist, limiting the access that consumers and rivals have to new technologies. Both of these problems can limit a country's long-term economic growth prospects. It is evident that the interests of countries that are primarily technology importers and adapters could differ significantly from those of the more industrialized developing economies, which are moving rapidly into technology development and exports.

To assist new adopters of IPR protection, this chapter discusses national case studies of patent

This chapter draws on background reports prepared by Jaeyong Song, Yonshei University, Seoul, Korea, and Timothy Swanson, University College, London, UK. The authors gratefully acknowledge helpful comments from Myrna Austria and other participants in the seminar held at the Institute for Southeast Asian Studies of the National University of Singapore and in the Fourth Asia Development Forum in Seoul as well as seminars held at the Thailand Development Research Institute in Bangkok and the World Bank office in Jakarta.

and copyright protection and also looks closely at the issues involved in the protection of traditional knowledge. The idea is to examine how these three forms of intellectual property protection are being implemented in countries of widely different development levels and technological capacities. We then attempt to draw basic conclusions about the development aspects of different forms of IPRs across countries.

The first case study is retrospective: it considers the impacts of past patent reforms in the Republic of Korea, an advanced developing economy. Patents have been studied in the literature on the economics of innovation for nearly four decades, and the repercussions of patent protection are generally well understood. Patents are usually of relevance for countries importing or creating cutting-edge technologies and innovations, and they are becoming relevant more broadly because the TRIPs agreement mandates stronger patent protection in all its signatory nations.

The second case study is contemporary: it summarizes the results of a survey of copyright-sensitive firms in Indonesia, a lower-income developing country that is in the process of upgrading its protection. Copyrights have been studied much less than patents, but they have recently taken center stage as economic incentives in areas such as software and the entertainment industries.[3] Copyrights affecting the software, publishing, film, and music industries are relevant to a broad range of middle- to low-income nations.

The final case study is prospective: it analyzes the difficulties poor countries will face in developing appropriate regimes for protecting traditional knowledge. This knowledge is concentrated in lower-income nations, and its protection is generally expected to have direct effects on poverty reduction.[4] As some industrial countries attempt to patent the products they have developed based on traditional knowledge, developing nations perceive themselves as doubly disadvantaged—their indigenous resources are being used without compensation and the resulting products are coming to them at a higher price because of the associated patents. Protection of traditional knowledge is a relatively new issue, and the policy dialogue would benefit from more analytical work to improve understanding of the conceptual issues underlying this debate.

Did Korea's Stronger Patent Laws Contribute to Its Success in Foreign Patenting?

Governments often strengthen IPRs in the hope that by establishing exclusive rights to use and sell newly developed technologies they will promote investments in knowledge creation and business innovation, including by foreign investors who will introduce advanced technologies. A rise in innovative activity, or in the amount of productive research and development (R&D), signals an acceleration of technological change and a positive outlook for productivity growth. If increases in patenting, and in the innovation that gives rise to them, can be attributed entirely to changes in IPR laws, there are important implications for the design of public policy. Specifically, policymakers need to better understand the complementary roles of broader public policies that promote innovation and of private corporate sector strategies in facilitating technological catch-up. To shed light on these issues, we examine the determinants of Korea's dramatic success in patenting in the United States.

The Republic of Korea is a premier example of a nation that has achieved rapid structural transformation and industrialization in recent decades. As such, it illustrates an economy that was poised to achieve dynamic gains from stronger protection at the time of its major policy regime shift. In a series of new laws enacted from 1985 to 1992, the government expanded patent coverage, increased the scope of claims, lengthened the duration of protection, and made other changes. Although there was significant opposition to these policies, which seemed to many to have been imposed externally via pressure from the United States, some industrial concerns had already established competence in research and product development.[5] Thus Korea is a good candidate for a case study of a country with an industrial structure and resource base that would be able to react positively overall to stronger domestic patent protection. Our interest is in ascertaining whether the patent regime change itself might be responsible for rising rates of innovation as measured by Korean patent applications in a major foreign market, the United States.

Before beginning this analysis, we note that other factors entered into Korea's ability to expand its innovation stream. For example, an important element was Korea's success in educating and training rapidly rising numbers of technical personnel for deployment in industry during this period. Between 1980 and 1996, the number of researchers per million inhabitants in the country rose from 484 to 2,193.[6] Such factors are discussed further in the next section.

Factors Contributing to the Rise in Korean Patenting

The number of U.S. patents filed by Korean firms has risen dramatically in recent years (Figure 6.1). Patenting activity might rise because of either an increase in the *propensity* to patent or an increase in the *ability* to patent. The former could be framed as the demand side view and the latter as the supply side view. Four factors might explain Korean patenting success. On the demand side, the factors are

• *Fertile technology pull.* In this view, patenting was spurred by a global surge in discovery and innovation in emerging, "patent-intensive" industries such as semiconductors and biotechnology.[7]
• *Friendly court pull.* By making courts more prone to grant and enforce patents, the stronger intellectual property protection regime adopted

by Korea may have increased the propensity of inventors to seek patent protection.

The supply side factors are

• *Industrial upgrading push.* In this view, upgrading of Korean industry shifted the output mix to more patent-prone, high-technology industries.
• *Corporate management push.* Large Korean business groups (*chaebols*) placed ever more emphasis on innovative capabilities, and they improved R&D management and productivity. This view postulates that changes in the corporate management of R&D have contributed to increased patenting activity.

The rest of this section examines each factor in turn. The analysis relies on aggregate data on international patent applications by technology class and assignee of patents in the United States; patent citation data of Korean firms; and aggregate measures of research effort. We also use information from in-depth, firm-level interviews.

Fertile Technology Pull. If a surge in innovation is driven by breakthroughs in specific technologies, we should expect to see an uneven increase in

FIGURE 6.1 Comparison of Patenting Trends, Republic of Korea and Major Developing Countries, 1978–99 (Registration counts in U.S. Patent Office)

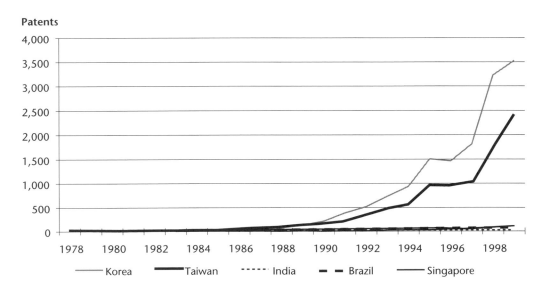

Source: U.S. Patent Office.

patenting across technologies. When the techno-logical revolution is more widespread, we should expect a general increase in patenting activity worldwide. Korean semiconductor patents, in par-ticular, show a growth pattern similar to the general increase in patenting activities in the semiconduc-tor industry worldwide (Figure 6.2).

Is Korea simply enjoying the benefits of a world-wide technology explosion in semiconductors? A comparison with other industrial and industrializ-ing countries suggests instead that Korea is an out-lier (Figure 6.3).

Pair-wise t-tests support this conclusion, show-ing that Korea's semiconductor patents have prolif-

FIGURE 6.2 Comparison of Korean Semiconductor Patents with Worldwide Semiconductor Patents, 1976–99 (Registration counts in U.S. Patent Office)

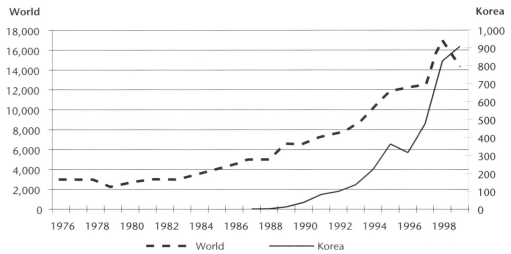

Source: U.S. Patent Office.

FIGURE 6.3 Comparison of Korean Semiconductor Patents with Semiconductor Patents of Major Advanced Countries, 1976–99 (Registration counts in U.S. Patent Office)

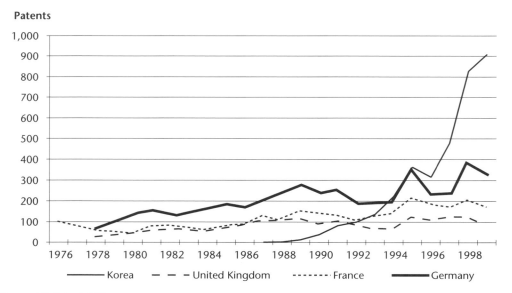

Source: I.S. Patent Office.

erated much faster than those of advanced countries such as Germany, Japan, and the United States. However, there is no statistically significant difference between the growth rates of semiconductor patents in Korea and Taiwan (China).[8]

Friendly Court Pull. What was the role of intellectual property protection regimes in patenting activities at home and abroad? We examine important changes in IPR protection within Korea to understand whether it increased access to foreign knowledge at home (through foreign patents) and provided a testing ground for domestic innovators before they attempted patenting abroad. If Korean courts become more patent-friendly, both foreign and domestic firms should find patenting in Korea increasingly attractive, and thus patent registration data should be relatively uniform across both foreign and native residents.

Three major changes have affected Korean IPRs since the 1970s:[9]

- 1980–82: Revision of the patent law in 1980 in compliance with the Paris Convention for the Protection of Industrial Property and revision of the patent law in 1982 in compliance with the Patent Cooperation Treaty
- 1986: Revision of the patent law to introduce substance (product) patents for pharmaceutical and chemical materials
- 1995–97: Revision of the patent law in 1995 in compliance with TRIPs as well as to reform the appeals/trials system. The patent law was revised again in 1997 to introduce opposition to the granting of patents after registration.

Trends in foreign and total patent applications in Korea seem to support the view that IPR changes have spurred increases in patenting. Foreign patent applications in Korea had two major inflection points in the 1980s. The first jump took place in 1983 just after the major changes in Korean IPRs in 1980–82. The second jump occurred in 1986–87, just after the introduction of substance (product) patent eligibility for pharmaceuticals and chemicals. In the 1980s, when the major IPR changes were made in Korea, patent applications by foreigners rose faster than those by local residents, although patent applications by the latter also increased steadily. Paired t-tests confirm that

between 1983 and 1991 Korea's patent growth rate was significantly faster than that of either Japan or Germany.[10]

Industrial Upgrading Push. Did improvements in Korean industry shift the output mix to more patent-intensive industries? If so, the industrial composition of Korean patents in both the United States and Korea should more closely match the industrial composition of Korean exports to the United States than the industrial composition of U.S. patents at large. Analysis shows that the industrial composition of Korean patents in the United States correlates very highly with that of Korean exports but not with that of overall U.S. patents. This finding strongly suggests that Korean patenting in the United States has been influenced more by Korea's industrial upgrading than by specific industry-level propensities for patenting.[11]

The highly significant positive correlation between patenting and exporting suggests that industries that develop strong innovative capabilities (reflected in subsequent patenting) tend to achieve strong revealed comparative advantages and thereby to export more. At the same time, export-driven industries tend to invest more in innovative R&D activities and file for patents abroad more aggressively, both to build and maintain their global competitiveness and to protect their newly developed technologies and products in their main export markets. Thus export-driven industrial upgrading and patenting through building innovative capabilities seem to be mutually reinforcing trends, even though we cannot infer cause and effect here.

Corporate Management Push. Increases in patenting activity may have been caused by increases in R&D and its productivity. To test this proposition, we compared the R&D productivity of Korean firms with that of selected advanced countries, using the number of U.S. patents per US$1 billion[12] spent by each country on R&D. We allowed for a five-year time lag between R&D investments and patent registrations.[13] Research productivity was lower in Korea than in Japan and the United States, but substantially higher than in Germany, the United Kingdom, or France (Table 6.1). U.S. firms have a clear home advantage in patenting in the United States, and the other four

TABLE 6.1   Research Productivity of Selected Countries

	U.S. patent counts in 1999	R&D expenditures (billions of 1994 US$)	U.S. patent count/ R&D expenditures
Korea, Rep. of	3,529	12.8	275.7
USA	75,014	169.3	443.1
Japan	32,666	75.1	435.0
Germany	8,121	37.3	217.7
France	3,150	26.5	118.9
UK	2,351	21.7	108.3

Sources: Patent counts from our U.S. patent database; R&D expenditures from OECD (1999).

countries account for about 70 percent of total U.S. patents of foreign origin. Thus Korea's research productivity, measured by U.S. patent counts per amount of R&D expenditure, seems to be the second highest in the world, just behind Japan's.[14]

Private corporations, particularly the five largest *chaebols*, accounted for most of the Korean patents granted in the United States in the 1990s.[15] The increased productivity of R&D in Korea has essentially been driven by the good R&D management and productivity of the five largest *chaebols*, especially the Samsung Group. The largest *chaebols* increased their R&D expenditures dramatically in the 1980s, and in that decade Korea's investment in private sector R&D per unit of gross domestic investment was higher than that of any other country.[16] In 2000 the four largest *chaebols*—Samsung, LG, Hyundai, and SK—spent 4.731 trillion won (about $4 billion) on R&D, and in 2001 their R&D spending continued to increase, even in the wake of the global recession.[17]

Over time, R&D investments have become more concentrated in the top 20 companies. According to the Korean Ministry of Science and Technology, the top 20 companies in Korea (all industries) accounted for 49.8 percent of R&D spending in 1992 and 51.7 percent in 1993, and that percentage climbed steadily to reach 56.5 percent in 1996 and 65.8 percent in 1998. The top five corporate spenders on R&D accounted for 31 percent of Korea's R&D spending in 1993. In manufacturing, Korea's top 20 spenders on R&D undertook 64 percent of research spending in 1996. This concentration is significantly higher than comparable figures for the United States, at 43 percent, and Japan, at 44 percent (Korea Ministry of Science and Technology, 1998).

In 1997 the private sector accounted for 77 percent of Korea's R&D expenditures, and since then, private corporations' share of R&D expenditures has continued to rise. In 2000 they increased their R&D expenditures by 20 percent, while government research institutes and universities increased theirs by only 9 percent and 3 percent, respectively. Private R&D laboratories proliferated, especially in the late 1990s, as the government's policy of nurturing high-technology start-up firms began to pay off.[18]

The *chaebols* were also able to hire the best R&D researchers. After they began investing heavily in the high-tech industries, they aggressively sought to lure experienced ethnic Korean engineers from major companies and universities abroad, especially in the United States (Song, Almeida, and Wu 2002). The returned engineers played an important role in speeding up the learning process of Korean companies and enhancing the productivity of their research. Koreans residing abroad also served in R&D posts for Korean companies and as counselors to the Korean government in helping to shape the direction of policy support in Korea.

Technology Trajectory

How do Korea's firms compare with the world's leaders in the technology fields in which Korea has large numbers of patents? And why has Korea's private sector been so successful in one fast-growing technology field, semiconductors, but not in another, biotechnology, where world patenting is rising dramatically?

Innovation Performance: Korean Firms and Worldwide Leaders. All new claims for patenting must contain a reference to a previous invention on which the current invention builds. This is known as a citation. Patent citation trends were examined to see whether Korean companies have established their own country-specific or firm-specific technological paths.[19] Among U.S. patents granted to Korean private corporations, the ratio of Korean patent citations to total patent citations has increased steadily, reaching almost 8 percent by 1999 (Figure 6.4). The ratio for U.S. patents granted to government research institutes (GRIs) is substantially lower. This result may indicate that private corporations have developed better technological bases or more solid technological paths over time than government research institutes.

Next, trends in self-citations were traced to measure the path dependence of firms and countries in innovations.[20] Self-citation occurs when a patent filed by an organization (or a country) cites another patent from the same organization (or country).[21] Generally, the self-citation rate is high for a firm or a country that has developed strong innovative capabilities over time. The self-citation rate in patent applications by private corporations has risen steadily over time (Figure 6.5). By the late 1990s, half of the patent citations by Korean private firms were self-citations.

The patenting trends of representative Korean companies were compared with those of leading overseas companies in several individual industries.[22] The leading Korean companies are still, in general, substantially behind the leading global companies in terms of numbers of both patents and self-citation rates.[23] The exception is in semiconductors, where Samsung Electronics has emerged as one of the leading innovators in the industry worldwide.

Why Semiconductors and Not Pharmaceuticals or Chemicals? Compared with its performance in the semiconductor industry, Korea's innovation performance in chemicals and pharmaceuticals has been particularly poor (Figure 6.6). Figures on revealed comparative advantage confirm the disparity between the semiconductor and chemical industries in Korea.[24]

Interviews with senior researchers and R&D managers in these industries revealed that the electronics/semiconductor industry is a more engineering-driven, assembly-oriented industry than either the chemical or pharmaceutical industries, both of which are more science-driven. In electronics/semiconductors, technical progress has been very fast, and companies have often experienced major technological discontinuities that offered good entry opportunities for latecomers like Korea.[25]

By contrast, companies in the chemical and pharmaceutical industries must master cumulative know-how that is acquired mainly by time-consuming trial-and-error learning—a particularly

FIGURE 6.4   Citations of Korean Patents as a Proportion of Total Patent Citations, by Types of Patent Applicants, 1986–99

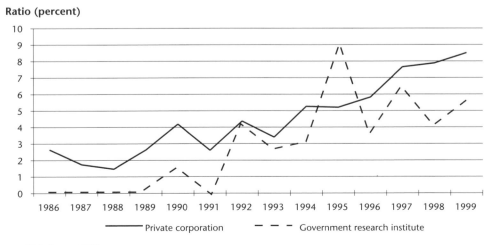

Source: U.S. Patent Office.

FIGURE 6.5   **Self-Citation Rates of Korean Private Corporations, 1980–99**

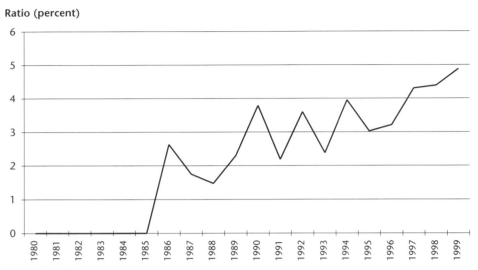

Source: U.S. Patent Office.

FIGURE 6.6   **Korean Patents Granted in the United States, Selected Industries, 1981–99**

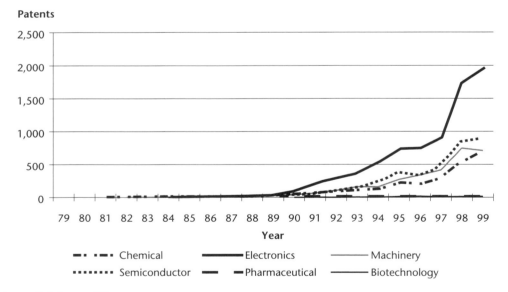

Source: U.S. Patent Office.

slow process for a country with a relatively short period of industrial experience. Even in firms that are industry leaders, new drugs take several years to develop, entail huge costs, and come with a high chance of failure.[26] And—given the heavily regulated nature of the drug approval and distribution processes—even if Korean companies develop potentially valuable drugs or new chemical entities, they must rely on the multinational pharmaceutical

giants for global clinical trials, drug approvals, and worldwide distribution.

Korea's government and companies placed their bets on electronics and information technology, which they perceived as easier industries in which to catch up technologically. As a matter of industrial policy, both the investments and the number of researchers in the chemical, pharmaceutical, and biotechnology industries have been small compared with those in the electronics/semiconductor industry.[27] Historical industrial policy in Japan and Korea have favored engineering-based industries as opposed to science-based ones, presumably because of the greater uncertainties associated with the latter type of research. An additional factor may be that Korea's close proximity to and trade relationships with Japan fostered the expansion of Korea's electronics sectors through the use of Japan's OEM (original equipment manufacturer) technologies.

Conclusions

Korea's success in innovation has required much more than a tightening of intellectual property rights. Industrial upgrading, exports, a big push in R&D from the *chaebols*, and selective targeting of the electronics/semiconductor industry have all played a role.

Korean firms have become much more innovative in the short span of a decade, but the self-citation patterns of patents registered by Korean firms reveal that most have yet to attain the status of global leaders in technology. The focus thus far in Korea has been on inventing processes and not on developing generic technologies. As the innovation process becomes more sophisticated, it may become more difficult for Korea to compete successfully in broader-based inventions. Thus the next stage of its R&D effort will likely have to focus on inventing standard-setting technologies that can earn substantial royalties in international markets.

To comply with the TRIPs agreement, many countries will have to introduce stronger patent protection. Given Korea's experience, other countries wishing to boost innovative activity among their private firms should not expect too much from simply adopting a new patent regime, and they may wish to design packages of complementary "behind-the-border" policies. Korea has used a variety of instruments for this purpose, many of which could be emulated by developing countries.

Will Stronger Copyright Protection Encourage the Development of Copyright-Sensitive Businesses in Indonesia?

This section examines the effects of copyright law on business development in Indonesia. Using data from field interviews and surveys of copyright-sensitive firms, we draw some general lessons for the design of copyright policy.[28]

From the standpoint of economic development, the main reasons for a developing country to adopt and enforce stronger copyright laws are to encourage creative activity by local artists and firms and to support the transformation of that activity into products for the domestic and export markets. Stronger copyright regimes can generate significant income streams for creative people and firms. Yet at the same time these new rights can be expected to raise the prices of copyrighted goods by reducing the supply of pirated versions. The higher prices will hurt consumers, although they benefit from having higher-quality products and support services on the market. Stronger copyright regimes also may also hinder the progress of education and scientific and technical advance. Copyright strengthening will likely cut the sales of imitation products over time, and, to the extent that imitators and their employees are domestic, the impact may be higher unemployment and adjustment costs in the labor market.

To the extent that workers in the pirating firms are poor, stronger copyrights can worsen poverty, at least in the short term. In many developing nations, fear of the short-term effects of stronger copyright laws on employment and prices is widespread. For stronger copyrights to reduce poverty, they must open new economic opportunities for poor artists and innovators, including those in the software, film, music, and print publishing industries, to develop, record, and sell their products. Furthermore, mechanisms must be in place to ensure that these artists and innovators realize higher incomes from the commercialization of their works.

On this subject, Indonesia is an interesting country to study for two reasons. First, the citizens of this lower-income economy may have strong preferences for unimpeded abilities to purchase unauthorized copies of software and entertainment products. Second, Indonesia has a wealth of cultural interests, particularly in music, and a growing base of intermediate skills. Thus considerable scope exists for developing local copyright sectors, which would prefer somewhat stronger protection. A conflict may therefore exist in perceived interests, raising interesting policy trade-offs.

Legal Structure and Enforcement

On paper, Indonesia has a strong copyright regime, and one Indonesian official has declared that, of the countries in Southeast Asia, Indonesia has the strongest degree of compliance with the WTO TRIPs agreement. Indeed, Indonesia's 1997 copyright law was virtually in compliance with that agreement. It was replaced by a new copyright law in early 2003, which established a regime of neighboring rights (consistent with the Rome Convention) and significantly increased the civil and criminal penalties for infringement.[29]

As might be expected, the gap between legislation and actual protection is significant, because Indonesia's capacity to enforce the copyright law is relatively limited for several reasons:

- The piracy, largely of recorded movies and music, is extensive. The incentives to copy and distribute these and similar goods are enormous, and piracy has become such a significant industry that even a well-funded enforcement agency would find it difficult to make much of a dent in its scope.

- Funding for the police is extremely low. According to one police official in Jakarta, his department's budget for copyright enforcement is about $200 per action, but each case costs perhaps $1,000–$1,500. The police therefore accept payments from complainants (for example, music recording companies) to defray their costs. This practice limits the incentives for legitimate complaints and is questionable from the standpoint of honest and efficient enforcement.

- Very few customs authorities and police personnel work on IPR issues, because these officials may have higher priorities. The copyright office itself devotes some effort to making raids and raising awareness, but it is seriously understaffed. And, like many developing countries, Indonesia has far fewer qualified judges, prosecutors, and IPR lawyers than it needs for effective enforcement. Computerized systems are virtually nonexistent.

- Centralized authorities in Jakarta and Bandung find it impossible to undertake enforcement activities in Indonesia's widely flung urban and rural areas and coastlines. They rely on local governments to manage the problem, and those

governments may have other priorities or interests in weak enforcement.

Despite these limitations, the government is making some progress in combating piracy. A new law requires registration of the pressing machinery for compact discs, digital video discs, and video CDs—all of which is imported. The number of copyright enforcement cases increased from 44 in 1999 to 109 in 2001 and to 1,999 by early June 2002.[30] Virtually all such cases involve pirated movies and music, with enforcement actions against both production facilities and retail shops.

At the time of this writing, no copyright cases have involved software copying, probably because of a significant limitation in the law. To sustain a claim of infringement, complainants must provide original software code to the courts so that the authorities can compare the code with that of the defendant. Many software companies prefer not to reveal their machine language in an environment in which it may be released to rivals. However, in two cases in 2001 the local agent for a major foreign software firm sued five firms for having loaded the firm's products into personal computers without authorization. The agent was able to do so under Indonesia's consumer fraud statutes and achieved judgments against all defendants.[31]

Effects of Copyright Law on Specific Industries

This section describes particular copyright-sensitive industries in Indonesia and the changes they might experience in the event of stronger copyright enforcement.[32] Across the board, survey respondents overwhelmingly preferred stronger government efforts to reduce piracy. This finding is not surprising, because it would remove some costs for these industries while expanding demand for their products.

Software. In Indonesia, software and databases are protected by copyrights providing protection for 50 years, and computer programs may be patented. According to at least two Indonesian officials, the government views copyrights as an inducement to innovation in software development, an industry it has identified as central to economic growth and recovery. This decision is based on the fact that writing code for programs and games is fairly straightforward and labor-intensive, offering prospects for absorbing large numbers of reasonably well-educated young people into the labor force. Indeed, as several interviewees commented, Indonesia has a good base of semiskilled workers for the software industry. Software is viewed as a dynamic industry that should experience rising global and domestic demand over the long term, particularly as the Indonesian economy makes greater use of information technologies. The government has established incubator programs that provide incentives for software developers. The programs are too new to assess, but they seem to be well structured for this purpose.

The software industry has considerable scope for expansion in both the domestic and export markets. Copyright protection will be one element in realizing this potential. In this relatively young industry, firms perceive the threat of software piracy as a significant entry barrier. Other major entry barriers cited are strong competition, shortages of skilled labor, existence of dominant producers, and concern about weak copyrights in neighboring countries. For firms considering expansion, the most significant problems are a weak telecommunications infrastructure and Internet services, shortages of skilled labor, and concern about unauthorized copying. Of the 25 software firms surveyed, 24 indicated an intention to expand output over the next two years. Twenty-two firms cited uncertainty about the economy as a "very important" or "somewhat important" barrier to expansion. At least over the medium term, better copyright enforcement seems to offer only moderate potential for encouraging additional business activity in software development in Indonesia.

Virtually all the survey respondents found piracy endemic and would like to see stronger efforts to reduce it. Of the small firms surveyed, only one said it would expand its output and investment if rights were strengthened. Medium-size enterprises would be more likely to expand their activity and develop new products, as would larger enterprises. Presumably, that expansion would increase net incomes for software developers and employees in the industry, even as it reduces employment opportunities in copying.

It is possible to be more optimistic about the longer term. Given the country's human capital resources and the small size of the software industry in relation to Indonesia's economy and population, stronger copyright protection should improve the software industry's prospects to some degree.[33] However, the industry is unlikely to grow significantly before the economy overcomes its current sources of instability and uncertainty and improves its infrastructure for telecommunications services.

Recorded Music. Among the copyright-sensitive industries in Indonesia, the recorded music industry probably suffers the most damage from poor copyright enforcement. The industry is largely devoted to local cultural and pop music and the domestic audience. It is made up mainly of small firms, and, as in software, they are remarkably few in number for an economy of Indonesia's size. The current system yields revenues for a very small number of musicians. A more sophisticated system, including professional rights management and collection societies, could help to improve this situation considerably. The primary prospect for expanding income opportunities for poor artists lies in the expansion the recording companies say they would undertake in response to better copyright protection; the companies also would invest more in artist development.

Virtually all the recording companies said the government is doing "far too little" to stop piracy, and claimed unambiguously that their businesses would grow considerably if copyright enforcement were more transparent and effective. Both large firms, all 11 of the medium-size firms, and 9 of the 11 small firms said they would expand, either modestly or significantly. Ten of the small firms and all the medium-size firms would invest more in developing new songwriters and recording artists. Again, given Indonesia's size, there is reason to believe that expansion now will pay off considerably in the long run.

Film. Indonesia's film industry is small but growing. Film producers with small companies are particularly concerned about domestic copying and could benefit from stronger copyright enforcement. Like those in the recorded music business, the great majority of firms said the government is doing far too little to reduce piracy. However, stronger copyright enforcement is not expected to have as dramatic an impact on film as on music.

Among the film companies, 9 of 16 said they would attempt to expand modestly or significantly, while 6 of the small firms anticipated no impact or a small contraction. At the same time, 14 of 16 firms (including 6 small firms) said they would invest in more filmmaking capacity in the event of stronger copyrights. Thus, although the signals are somewhat mixed, there does seem to be a reasonable indication that the film industry would expand as copyrights become more strongly enforced.

Print Publishing. Indonesia's publishers believe book piracy is fairly widespread, but their industry is suffering only modest damage and would not expand much as the result of stronger protection. They believe that the major problem in starting a print publishing business in Indonesia is a shortage of financial backing.

Conclusions

Indonesia's copyright law is TRIPs-compliant, and in some ways it goes beyond the TRIPs requirements. An assessment of whether the extra protection is really appropriate for Indonesia's economy might be useful.[34] For some time into the future, enforcement is likely to continue to suffer from weak capacity, chronic underfunding, limited access to enforcement procedures, and a lack of transparency.

As rights are more successfully enforced, copyright-sensitive industries will see opportunities for expansion and more income. These gains would be felt in the medium term and would have to be assessed against the short-term hardship that would result for the firms and workers now engaged in unauthorized copying and distributing. The extent of this hardship cannot be predicted with confidence, but it seems probable that employment in copying and selling pirated versions of music, movies, and software is significant in the larger cities.

If copyright enforcement is likely to remain ineffective for the foreseeable future, what might Indonesia do to improve the marketing prospects of local artists, software developers, and publishers? First, the government could accelerate its programs to improve telecommunications and private Internet services, which initially could be used to raise awareness abroad of Indonesian products. Second,

it could encourage development of a larger base of technological and creative personnel through education and training incentives. Finally, to the extent that other barriers to entry in these sectors exist, they could be diminished.

What Are the Problems in Protecting Traditional Knowledge in Genetic Resources?

Genetic resources, including plants and herbs, and understanding of their properties for nutrition and medicines are known collectively as biologically based traditional knowledge. Typically, that knowledge derives from generations of collective and experimental use of naturally occurring plants and soils. This section addresses the problems encountered in converting such knowledge into marketable products.

Other forms of traditional knowledge arise in music, designs, and folklore. For example, traditional designs of carpets and clothing are often shared by numerous villages in particular regions of developing countries. Although many of the problems discussed in this section arise in these cultural contexts as well, the scientific and biological basis of genetic resources makes them unique and the center of current controversy. Thus we focus on issues that emerge particularly in the latter area.

Innovations in agriculture and pharmaceuticals are drawing increasingly on traditional or indigenous knowledge, and the market value of pharmaceutical derivatives from traditional medicine has been estimated at about $43 billion a year worldwide (IPBN 1995). The trial and error required to bring about a successful innovation can be drastically reduced when researchers consult the practitioners of traditional knowledge. In medical research, bio-prospectors have increased the success ratio of clinical trials from 1 in 10,000 samples to 1 in 2,000 (Prakash 1999). Given that roughly 90 percent of the world's genetic resources and traditional knowledge is held in developing countries, and roughly an equal percentage of the world's R&D activity takes place in industrial countries, there is scope for mutually beneficial bargains between a gene-rich, technology-poor South and a gene-poor, technology-rich North.

The proper means for establishing the documentation, ownership, compensation, and exploitation of traditional knowledge remain unclear. The TRIPs agreement touches on these issues, but essentially leaves them to interpretation or further negotiations. This is an area in which developing nations could benefit from advances in thinking and stronger policy options. This section outlines the analytical and practical issues that need attention to spur progress on protecting traditional knowledge or compensating its ownership. For this purpose, it begins by discussing the complexities in research and development in the biological sciences.

A Framework for R&D in the Biological Sciences

All technological advances take place in three distinct stages. In the primary stage, known as invention, a new idea is observed or occurs. In the secondary stage, the idea, by being embedded in a product or process, is transformed into an innovation. In the tertiary stage, the innovation is diffused.

Each of these stages has features peculiar to the biological sciences. In the primary stage, observation and experimentation, which must rely on a combination of physical, human, and natural capital, are needed to capture exogenous information. In the biological sciences, the dependence on natural capital (plants and soils) at this stage is unique, and issues related to the valuation of natural capital become central. In the secondary stage, traditional knowledge and natural capital are combined into physical and human capital. Innovations that are fully embodied in a physical product can be sold, and few externalities exist in appropriating the returns to investment. But innovations that are disembodied—that is, not contained in a physical product but rather held as knowledge, say, by a farmer or researcher or by a social system—are subject to such externalities. A large part of biological innovation is disembodied, and, in particular, traditional knowledge is almost always held within social systems. The tertiary stage, diffusion of the new innovation, also varies in character, depending on whether the innovation is embodied or disembodied. When the innovation is embodied, its diffusion takes place through the marketing of the product, albeit at a cost. The diffusion of disembodied innovations is more complicated. Because diffusion occurs mainly through the exchange or movement of human capital, it often takes place more efficiently in a nonmarket setting.

Much of the new knowledge in the biological sciences is acquired through observation of natural phenomena, combined with trial and error—as, for example, when farmers observe weather-resistance or disease-resistance in certain crops and then create hybrids that have the desirable characteristics. Finding new solutions to problems therefore depends on maintaining a diverse gene pool, and, in turn, the conservation of biodiversity per se is the key to solving the agricultural and health problems of tomorrow. Because the destruction of biodiversity is irreversible, preservation of the stock of genetically rich lands and resources is vital.

The economic question at the crux of the debate on protecting traditional knowledge is how to ensure that both the primary and secondary stages of R&D, and their associated capital inputs, receive enough compensation to generate incentives for their continuing efficient operation. How is natural capital to be valued? How are the returns to innovations to be appropriated and apportioned?

About half of the yield gains in agriculture can be ascribed to traditional genetic resources, according to estimates from models using the standard Cobb-Douglas production function. But when models have attempted to quantify firms' willingness to pay for such resources, shockingly small values have emerged.[35] The explanation for these small values lies in the potential redundancy of solutions in the biological sciences. The more ephemeral a solution promises to be (and thus the lower the revenue it promises to yield), the smaller the private investment. However, public health and food security concerns would dictate that the less durable the solution, the greater the investment needed in R&D. Therefore, some form of public intervention is warranted that rests on the understanding that resources that are not valuable now may be valuable later.

Proper arrangements for the appropriation of returns and compensation of contributors are preconditions for an optimal R&D effort and supply of the factors needed for innovation. Property rights provide these preconditions. The literature suggests that the property rights assignment matters very much if contracting within the industry is costly, and that property rights should be placed at the levels that most encourage investment in the assets concerned (Swanson and Goeschl 1999).

Evolution in R&D Management

The international R&D management regime for genetic resources has evolved through three eras:

1. *Equal access/common heritage.* This first era emphasized the accumulation of already available information and its widest possible diffusion. The aggregation of traditional knowledge and genetic resources occurred within national academic and governmental institutions, and almost wholly by virtue of publicly funded investments. The emphasis was on the public good nature of this information, and rapid diffusion was subsidized by means of the universal recognition of the doctrine of free access to collected resources.

2. *Private investment/property rights in end products based on genetic resources.* The second era arose with the recognition that the traditional knowledge base could be developed and expanded with investments of other forms of capital. Scientific method and physical capital could be combined with natural forms of capital (genetic resources) to create more information and more useful information. Public investors were probably the first movers, but they were joined rapidly by private investors whose involvement required the development of institutions for compensating private investments. In the pharmaceutical industry, these investments could be compensated through existing patent laws. In agriculture, it was necessary to extend IPR law in a new direction—that is, toward granting exclusive rights for the use of naturally occurring organisms.

   This second era of R&D management revolved around developing property rights in *end products based on genetic resources*; the fundamental notion that naturally occurring genetic resources were a common heritage remained undisturbed. The problem was seen as one of compensating other forms of capital (human, physical) that were combined with natural capital (genetic resources) to produce innovative end products, even when those products were biological and thus capable of natural reproduction.

   It became increasingly clear, however, that the useful genetic resource base was not static,

and that investment was needed to maintain and expand that base. Thus the assumption that property right mechanisms should not extend to natural forms of capital was brought into question. Once it was recognized that information in the biological sector must be optimally produced as well as diffused, it became important to move away from the doctrine of common heritage and free access.

3. *Private investment/property rights in base genetic resources.* The third era of R&D management is taking a harder look at claiming exclusive rights in the *base genetic resources*. Both physical and human capital are now directed at analyzing and manipulating the base resources themselves, with the object of developing genetic characteristics that are useful in and of themselves. In this way, the various forms of capital are all combined (natural, human, and physical), and the end product becomes the understanding or creation of a genetically generated characteristic that is useful in itself. The property right is then claimed in the genetic trait and its claimed use. Thus the third era of R&D management has moved the property rights debate down a level, to that of the genetic trait rather than the biological resource.[36]

A Brief History of Global Policies Affecting Genetic Resources

Historically, traditional knowledge and genetic resources were treated under the doctrine of the common heritage of mankind. They were therefore available without restriction.

This view changed in the 1930s in the United States and Europe, where plant breeders first sought to protect the results of their selective breeding programs. In 1961 the International Convention for the Protection of New Varieties of Plants (UPOV) established a harmonized system for international recognition and establishment of plant breeders' rights.

The Convention on Biodiversity (CBD), which came into force in 1992, established the doctrine of national sovereignty over genetic resource inputs, abrogating the doctrine of common heritage. It also established an approach to property rights in genetic resource inputs based on bilateral benefit-sharing agreements. This bilateral contract approach to property rights in genetic resources has had little impact to date, however, because of the practical difficulties of implementation. Under the terms of the CBD, either the state or the local community that hosts the resource can refuse access. If it allows an outside party to have access to its genetic resources, it can require an agreement setting out the terms on which access is given. But doing so successfully requires the passage of access legislation for the resources, as well as a means for deciding among competing rights of ownership and establishing the mechanism for consent and transfer. Few states have adopted and implemented the access legislation required for this task. It is also clear that establishing such claims and providing legal consent would be difficult.

By contrast, the TRIPs agreement attempts a global standardization of IPR regimes. In particular, the agreement requires WTO member states to adopt some form of plant breeders' rights, while it specifically permits countries to exclude from patentability all life forms emanating from essentially biological processes. The wording of the TRIPs agreement requires all member states of the WTO to adopt either some form of patent system for improved plant varieties or a *sui generis* regime for the protection of the same. Pressure has mounted for the adoption of uniform systems of IPR for plant varieties and other genetic resources (microorganisms) and for countries' mutual recognition of the rights they confer for such resources. The TRIPs agreement is essentially silent on the issues of traditional knowledge.

Thus CBD and the TRIPs agreement are in conflict. CBD emphasizes the importance of sovereign rights in indigenous genetic resources and the knowledge associated with them. The TRIPs agreement requires the adoption of IPR systems for improved plant varieties, but not for resources emanating from essentially biological processes.

Reconciliation of these two approaches would require, for genetic resources, some manner of recognition of rights to innovations, both at the industry end and potentially for some of the base genetic resources used as inputs. Such a regime would incorporate the rights of states that provide the natural inputs (as required under the CBD) and also those that provide the final outputs (as required under the TRIPs agreement). But how might such a regime operate?

Is There an Optimal Property Rights Institution?

To be practicable, a system of property rights in the biological sciences must take into account how this diverse (because it depends on so many different forms of capital) and globally dispersed R&D sector is managed. An intellectual property rights regime would seek to facilitate R&D management by providing some form of exclusive marketing rights so that the optimal level of investment is generated in various parts of the industry.

Broadly, the options for IPRs are the following: property rights only at the primary stage of R&D; property rights only at the secondary stage; or property rights at both the primary and secondary stages. We examine the pros and cons of each in turn.

1. *Property rights only at the primary stage of R&D.* This option would be inadequate. Property right institutions could not pertain only to the primary stage of R&D—that is, at the level of the products of the natural capital—because it would be impossible to capture the benefits emanating from the other (non-natural) forms of capital employed within the sector. The latter are usually employed at a later stage in the industry, and the property right pertaining to the first stage would be incapable of managing the end markets. Also, it is not clear that a property rights mechanism at this level would dramatically increase the levels of investment in reserves. The mechanism selected would need to operate at several different levels of knowledge, (embodied, disembodied, expressed) in order to create and share profits among suppliers of traditional knowledge. This scenario might be possible, but at the cost of introducing distortions (for example, exclusive dealing arrangements) that would introduce their own costs.

2. *Property rights only at the secondary stage of R&D.* The sector could be managed with a single property right at the secondary stage of R&D, but it would require substantial amounts of contracting between the industry developing end-use products and the providers of traditional knowledge and genetic resources. In essence, a single property right at the secondary stage would permit its owner to appropriate the full value of the information inherent in the final product, but complete contracting would be

needed to ensure that these rents are distributed efficiently across all components of the vertical industry. Given the diverse and widely distributed nature of the R&D sector, it would be costly to engage in this sort of structured contracting.

3. *Property rights at both the primary and secondary stages of R&D.* R&D could also be managed with the placement of a property right mechanism at both the primary and the secondary stages. Such an approach would create an institution focused on the efficient distribution of the industry's profits, but at the cost of creating multiple levels of monopoly within the same vertical industry. Multiple constrictions on output (to generate rents) would reduce the welfare generated within the industry. Successive monopolies would introduce successive distortions within the industry, which might result in more welfare reduction than enhancement.

The choice between the second and third options depends on their comparative institutional costliness. Having a single property right at the secondary stage (option 2) would result in substantial contracting costs and thus significant residual inefficiency in the distribution of rents. Having multiple property rights in the single vertical industry (option 3) would address this problem, but it would result in successive distortions in the market.

Practical Concerns

Even if the conceptual and analytical issues just outlined were somehow addressed, some practical concerns would remain about the valuation, appropriation, and distribution of returns from traditional knowledge.

First, intellectual property rights are individualistic, but traditional knowledge is normally held collectively and developed by members of an indigenous community over several generations, making it extremely difficult to identify individual inventors of such knowledge. Although the fact that the knowledge is passed down over generations should, in principle, add to its value, the problem arises that the information may be said to exist within the public domain.

Second, patent applicants must supply evidence of a single act of discovery. This would be extremely difficult to establish. The patenting of indigenous

practices might be supported if it were possible to provide written documentation of local and traditional practices, but traditional knowledge has usually been passed on orally.

A third problem concerns the description of traditional knowledge and ownership claims made from it in a written application. Specifications for a patent must be written in technical language that demarcates its limits and establishes the relationship of the innovation to existing knowledge and innovations. A particular use of a characteristic of a plant or animal may be well known to an indigenous community, but it must be stated in a form that distinguishes it from other biochemical or genetic information or usefulness. Much traditional knowledge is disembodied and subject to the problems of appropriating benefits from disembodied information.

Finally, to be protected from unauthorized use, traditional knowledge must first be placed in public registries. In principle, such registries would establish the sources, ownership, and characteristics of the included knowledge. In practice, the operation of registration systems poses at least two complex questions:

- How would traditional knowledge be registered? Before any valuation or distribution issues are tackled, traditional knowledge must be documented. Should the burden be on local communities to disclose and register what they know in the event that this knowledge becomes precious to the scientific community in the future? Would communities that do not do so be penalized?
- How would such registers operate? To establish a claim of prior possession and therefore preclude patenting by others, these registers would have to be made public. Putting them in the public domain could prejudice future protection of the knowledge documented in them.

To illustrate these problems and to understand one case in which they have been addressed, consider recent legislation in the Philippines (Box 6.1). This nation, which is composed of many indigenous peoples, has been a leader in instituting legislation for access and compensation of indigenous knowledge. Indeed, the country is viewed as a laboratory for evaluating solutions to the property

---

BOX 6.1   Protection of Indigenous Knowledge in the Philippines

The Philippines recently developed and implemented legislation on the protection of biological resources. Two noteworthy attempts have been Executive Order 247 (EO247) adopted in 1995 and the Indigenous Peoples' Act (IPRA) of 1997.

EO247 covers the prospecting of all biological resources in the public and private domains and requires anyone, whether a national or foreign entity, who wishes to access biological resources to enter into a formal research agreement with the government after obtaining the informed consent of the appropriate local community.

Although this approach has increased the involvement of the indigenous community, the actual practice has been criticized for being more of a procedural checklist than a substantive process in that access requires no more than notification to the local community. Also, EO247 does not elaborate precisely how benefit sharing with the local communities comes about. Notably, this legislation has been used as a basis for a model law on access and benefit sharing for national systems in Asia by the Association of Southeast Asian Nations (ASEAN).

IPRA gave indigenous peoples rights over their ancestral lands as well as rights to use and develop the natural resources found in their ancestral domains. It did so by creating the National Council for Indigenous Peoples, which is responsible for overseeing the issuance of permits for access to indigenous peoples' lands on the basis of prior informed consent. IPRA seeks to extend the system of controlled access beyond biological and genetic resources to their "sciences, technologies, and cultural manifestations" by recognizing the concept of "community intellectual property rights."

Although IPRA remains in its infancy, it is expected to provide impetus for significant changes to IPR law in the Philippines. Hurdles related to implementation need to be worked out—and one of the most challenging ones is to define and implement community-based IPRs.

For details on progress in the Philippines on legislating protection of traditional knowledge, see www.worldbank.org/eaptrade, which provides background papers and technical annexes.

---

rights problems that are affecting the R&D sector globally.

Conclusions

The historical tendency to treat genetic resources as constant and freely available is an anachronism in an era of private property rights for the products emanating from those resources. Thus a better approach to the management of these resources is needed, and some public intervention is required. Given international externalities, this public intervention should ideally be global in scope. In fact, rights acquired in countries of origin alone will not mean much unless they are extended to major markets where derived and patented products are marketed.

It is therefore appropriate to discuss the protection and compensation of traditional knowledge in international forums. The TRIPs agreement establishes the principle that some genetic resources should be subject to intellectual property rights, but it does not resolve the conflicts between WTO member states; it merely transfers the debate to this new forum. Complex problems—conceptual and practical—will have to be sorted out before progress can be made in linking traditional knowledge issues to WTO agreements or other mechanisms for managing R&D in the biological sciences.

In summary, the application of property rights to traditional knowledge raises important problems, but there is probably no one regime that could serve as a solution. In compensating communities that hold traditional knowledge, other institutional devices should also be considered, such as geographical indications, copyrights, and trade secrets. In selecting a second-best approach to managing R&D in the biological sciences, the comparative costliness of the various approaches will have to be the guide.

Overall Conclusions and Lessons

The development aspects of IPR regimes differ across the three forms of intellectual property protection examined here—patents, copyrights, and traditional knowledge—for countries of widely different development levels and technological capacities. Yet for each form, issues of balance and complementary policies are prominent.

Within the more advanced emerging economies and parts of China, stronger IPR regimes, successfully enforced, could stimulate innovation in technology, provided other conditions are favorable. Retrospective analysis of Korea's strengthened IPR regime suggests that it played a role in the country's dramatic success in patenting, but so did industrial upgrading, a big push in research and development from the *chaebols*, and the government's selective targeting of the electronics/semiconductor industry, where Korea has emerged as a leading innovator worldwide. The successes of these innovative businesses helped to offset the impact of stronger patent protection on the users of new products and technologies in Korea. Because impending TRIPs-related obligations mandate stronger patent protection, it will be worthwhile for other, more advanced emerging economies to identify such complementary policies to boost innovative activity among private firms in their economies.

For a broader range of middle- to low-income East Asian economies, copyrights might offer opportunities for gains, but again balance is critical. Contemporary analysis of Indonesia's copyright protection suggests that considerable scope exists for developing local copyright sectors—given the talents of software developers, musicians, artists, and authors—which would prefer somewhat stronger protection. Yet these gains would have to be assessed against the short-term hardship faced by the firms and workers who are now engaged in unauthorized copying and distributing. In addition, enforcement is likely to remain ineffective for the foreseeable future because of a weak capacity. In the interim, complementary policies might be considered to improve the marketing prospects of local artists, software developers, and publishers, such as improvements in telecommunications and private Internet services which could be used initially to raise awareness abroad of Indonesian products.

Traditional knowledge happens to be concentrated in lower-income nations, and its protection is generally expected to have direct benefits for poverty reduction. Prospective analysis suggests that treating genetic resources as constant and freely available is an anachronism in an era of private property rights in the products emanating from those resources through R&D activity, which is heavily concentrated in industrial countries. In East Asia, the Philippines is experimenting in this field with existing and pending legislation on indigenous knowledge. However, rights acquired in countries of origin alone will not mean much unless they are extended to major markets where derived and patented products are marketed. Thus a broader approach to the management of protection of traditional knowledge is needed, and some public intervention is required—ideally global in scope—to balance the interests of the communities holding traditional knowledge, those carrying out the R&D activity, and the ultimate users of these derived products.

Much of the debate on IPR has focused on the impact of more stringent rights on East Asia as a user of technology created elsewhere, but strengthened IPR regimes also play a role in local technology generation by compensating inventors and creators. We are mindful of the complexities of design for each form of IPR, and for countries at each stage of development, and the need to identify complementary policies. Nonetheless, if managed carefully, the scope for dynamic gains in innovation should be considerable.

Endnotes

1. A host of instruments are available for protecting different kinds of intellectual property: patents and trade secrets to protect industrial inventions; copyrights to protect authored works; trademarks to protect industrial logos and symbols; and geographical indications to certify that a product was made in an area that has specific characteristics (such as soil conditions, climate, or design traditions) underlying the quality of the good.
2. Maskus (2000a) discusses these trade-offs extensively.
3. An essential form of intellectual property protection, copyright gives creative artists and firms the right to control the copying and distribution of particular expressions of music, art, film, and literature. Copyrights and patents operate differently, primarily because copyrights control the use of an idea's expression, while patents control the use of the idea itself. In recent years, copyright protection has been extended in many countries to such industrially useful expressions as software, data compilations, performances, television broadcasts, and satellite transmissions, and it also has been applied to the use of electronic copies downloaded from the Internet. For these reasons, copyrights deserve greater analytical attention than in the past.
4. For example, if means can be found for villagers in poor countries to register their collective knowledge, whether of medicinal uses for biological materials or of other forms, for purposes of licensing its commercial use, they might benefit from substantial royalty income.

5. See Maskus (2000a) on the regime changes and World Bank (1993) on the economic structure.

6. Data from the United Nations Education, Scientific, and Cultural Organization (UNESCO). Available at http://portal.unesco.org/uis/TEMPLATE/html/SandTec/Table_III_1_Asia.html.

7. Patent-intensive industries are those that rely heavily on patenting to protect proprietary knowledge. Reliance on patents varies by industries because, by definition, patents must reveal what they need to protect. Upon revelation, some knowledge is easier to imitate than other—for example, highly coded knowledge (such as chemical formulas) is relatively easy to duplicate once it leaks out.

8. For the results of these tests, see Appendix Table 1 of this chapter at www.worldbank.org/eaptrade.

9. In essence, these are the changes being requested of most developing countries within the next two to four years.

10. We conducted paired t-tests of the growth rates of Japanese and German patents in Korea and the United States between 1983 and 1991. These tests confirm that the patent growth rate in Korea was significantly higher than that in the United States for both Japanese patents (t-value of 2.213) and German patents (t-value of 1.835), at the significance level of p = 0.10.

11. For the results of this test, see Appendix Table 2 of this chapter at www.worldbank.org/eaptrade.

12. All dollar amounts are current U.S. dollars.

13. Recent increases in patents per unit of R&D in many developed countries have also been attributed to an increase in "defensive" patenting—that is, innovations that a firm normally would not commercialize and protect, but it does so only to prevent others from patenting them later. In this way, the firm increases the portfolio of patents it owns to improve its negotiating power in technology purchase deals.

14. This is likely to be the outcome of a combination of factors such as more patentable inventions per unit of R&D, as well as a higher propensity to patent eligible inventions for the strategic reasons just described. See also Kim (1997).

15. Of the U.S. patents granted to private Korean corporations, 90 percent were awarded to the five largest *chaebols*, especially the Samsung Group.

16. It was 32 percent, compared with 16 percent in Taiwan and 9 percent in Japan (Kim 1997).

17. In 1998 the ratios of R&D expenditures to total sales for the flagship companies of the largest *chaebols* were Samsung Electronics, 7 percent; Hyundai Electronics, 8 percent; Hyundai Motor, 12 percent; and SK Telecom, 2 percent. These percentages were generally comparable to or higher than those of the global leaders in their respective industries.

18. As of February 2002, Korea had 9,208 private R&D labs, up sixfold from 1,435 a decade earlier (Korea Industrial Technology Association).

19. In the United States, under law a patent application must specify any and all of the "prior art" known to the applicant. Thus it is possible to track knowledge-building across people, firms, countries, and regions, and time. Recent studies have analyzed patent citations to trace the sources of original knowledge underlying patented innovations. See Jaffe, Tranjtenberg, and Henderson (1993); Almeida (1996); Almeida, Song, and Grant (2002); Song, Almeida, and Wu (2002).

20. Sorensen and Stuart (2000), Rosenkopf and Nerkar (2001), and Song, Almeida, and Wu (2002) have used self-citations to evaluate the extent of path dependence in innovation activities.

21. For example, if a patent application granted to Samsung Electronics in 1996 cites a patent granted to Samsung Electronics in 1990, it is regarded as a self-citation. If the ratio of self-citation to total citations is high, it means that a firm or a country has already established its own technological path or trajectory and will tend to pursue subsequent innovations along this path (Song, Almeida, and Wu 2002).

22. For detailed results, see the technical appendix to this chapter at www.worldbank.org/eaptrade.

23. This observation supports the finding that Korea invents in areas that have smaller citation peaks, which may imply newer technologies (Hu and Jaffe 2001).

24. Revealed comparative advantages for Korea, Japan, and the United States were 275, 253, and 133 for the electronics industry and 21, 45, and 170 for the chemical industry, respectively. Revealed comparative advantage is an index of the country's share of patents in those industries divided by the country's share of total patents, computed for the 1981–99 period.

25. A good example is the Korean advances in emerging digital technologies. Koreans lagged behind Japan and the United States in the conventional analog-based technologies in the electronics industry. However, when the technological base in the electronics industry recently moved to more digital-based technologies, Korean companies such as Samsung Electronics and LG Electronics seized golden opportunities to catch up with industry leaders in the European Union, Japan, and the United States by investing heavily in digital technologies early on. For both companies, a substantial number of U.S. patents are now for technologies related to emerging digital appliances, and some of them are more basic product patents than traditional process patents.

26. About 10 years are usually devoted to the discovery, animal testing, clinical trials, and approval of a new drug.

27. According to the Korea Industrial Technology Association, as of December 1999 the number of researchers in the electronics industry was 65,028, or about 38 percent of the researchers in Korea, whereas researchers in the chemical industry numbered only 15,807. The ratio of R&D expenditures to sales for Korean electronics companies was 4.54 percent in 1997, or more than twice the average for manufacturing firms.

28. In 2003 extensive interviews of government officials and enterprise managers were carried out, and a survey was administered to 70 Indonesian enterprises in these copyright-sensitive sectors, commissioned by the World Bank.

29. The new law also improves procedures for arbitrating and resolving disputes, and it clarifies that copyright cases can be appealed in a streamlined fashion to the commercial court. It also increases the authority of the police to undertake enforcement actions on their own initiative. Perhaps most significant, it makes end use piracy a criminal offense, with a maximum five-year prison term. Another provision of the new law permits copyright owners from outside Indonesia to retain Indonesian legal representation. Under past law, a complainant had to come to court in Indonesia to claim infringement. Foreign companies (and certainly individual artists) often found this was not worth the time and effort. Indonesia has adopted the World Intellectual Property Organization (WIPO) Copyright Treaty and intends to ratify the WIPO Performance and Phonograms Treaty. Among other things, these changes will make it illegal for Internet users to circumvent electronic protection devices on binary files and transmission protocols.

30. This increase seems to have come at the expense of fewer trademark cases. These data are from the national police force.

31. The money the agent received from the resulting fines was contributed to a program to purchase computers for schools.

32. Details of the survey results and descriptions of the industries appear in the technical appendix to this chapter at www.worldbank.org/trade.

33. The median estimates from the survey were that Indonesia has 230 software firms, employing some 5,800 workers. By contrast, survey work in Lebanon in 1997 estimated that the country was home to some 490 software companies employing about 3,000 workers (Maskus 2000b). Clearly, the Indonesian market potential is far larger than that of Lebanon.

34. Indeed, it may be that some aspects of Indonesia's intellectual property regime—in particular, the limitations on fair use and the provisions for patenting software—are overly restrictive from the standpoint of the country's development needs. In software, the tighter copyright law to be introduced in 2003 may substantially limit fair use provisions. In addition to the prior restraint that the user of a computer program may make only one archival copy, educational users of software and printed materials will be permitted only one copy for their use before they are required to attain licenses for multiple copies. The new law outlaws the decompilation (reverse engineering) of computer code.

35. For example, a hectare of land in West Ecuador and the Amazon—biodiversity hot spots of the world—is valued at $20.63 and $2.59, respectively (Simpson, Sedjo, and Reid 1996).

36. It is now possible to claim a patent in any or all of the following steps toward identifying useful biological activity: genetic sequence, cloning method, expression of protein from sequence, biological activity of protein, and method of action.

References

Almeida, Paul. 1996. "Knowledge Sourcing by Foreign Multinationals: Patent Citation Analysis in the US Semiconductor Industry." *Strategic Management Journal* 20: 251–59.

Almeida, Paul, Jaeyong Song, and Robert M. Grant. 2002. "Are Firms Superior to Alliances and Markets? An Empirical Test of Cross-Border Knowledge Building." *Organization Science* 13 (2): 147–61.

Hu, Albert G. Z., and Adam Jaffe. 2001. "Patent Citations and International Knowledge Flow: The Cases of Korea and Taiwan." NBER Working Paper No. 8528. National Bureau of Economic Research, Cambridge, Mass.

IPBN (Indigenous Peoples' Biodiversity Network). 1995. "Indigenous People, Biodiversity, and Health." COURTS Canada IPBN Factsheet, November.

Jaffe, Adam B., Manuel Trajtenberg, and Rebecca Henderson. 1993. "Geographic Localization of Knowledge Spillovers as Evidenced by Patent Citations. *Quarterly Journal of Economics* 108: 577–98.

Kim, Linsu. 1997. *Imitation to Innovation: The Dynamics of Korea's Technological Learning.* Cambridge, Mass.: Harvard Business School Press.

Maskus, Keith E. 2000a. *Intellectual Property Rights in the Global Economy.* Washington, D.C.: Institute for International Economics.

————. 2000b. "Strengthening Intellectual Property Rights in Lebanon." In Bernard Hoekman and Jamel Zarrouk, eds., *Catching Up with the Competition: Trade Opportunities and Challenges for Arab Countries.* Ann Arbor: University of Michigan Press.

OECD (Organisation for Economic Co-operation and Development). 1999. *Main Science and Technology Indicators, 1999.* Geneva.

Prakash, S. 1999. "Towards a Synergy between Biodiversity and Intellectual Property Rights." *Journal of World Intellectual Property* 2 (5).

Rosenkopf, Lori, and Atul Nerkar. 2001. "Beyond Local Search: Boundary-Spanning, Exploration, and Impact in the Optical Disc Industry." *Strategic Management Journal* 22: 287–306.

Simpson, R. D., R. A. Sedjo, and J. W. Reid. 1996. "Valuing Biodiversity for Use in Pharmaceutical Research." *Journal of Political Economy* 104 (1): 163–85.

Song, Jaeyong, Paul Almeida, and Geraldine Wu. 2002. "Learning-by-Hiring: When Is Mobility Useful in Inter-firm Knowledge Transfer?" In Linda Argote, B. McEvily, and R. Reagens, eds., *Management Science* (Special Issue on Knowledge) 49 (4): 446–63.

Sorensen, Jesper B., and Toby E. Stuart. 2000. "Aging, Obsolescence, and Organizational Innovation." *Administrative Science Quarterly* 45: 81–112.

Swanson, T., and T. Goeschl. 1999. "Ecology, Information, Externalities and Policies: The Optimal Management of Biodiversity for Agriculture." In G. H. Peters and J. von Braun, eds., *Food Security, Diversification and Resource Management: Refocusing the Role of Agriculture.* Brookfield, Vt.: Ashgate.

World Bank. 1993. *The East Asian Miracle.* New York: Oxford University Press.

7

TRADE AND COMPETITIVENESS ASPECTS OF ENVIRONMENTAL AND LABOR STANDARDS IN EAST ASIA

Keith E. Maskus

Rapid economic growth is often blamed for the widespread deterioration of the natural environment in East Asian economies through deforestation, urbanization, and industrialization. Put differently, it is claimed that domestic and multinational companies gain a competitive advantage from the willingness of public authorities to permit environmental resources to be used indiscriminately or without charge. Similarly, it is claimed that a permissive government attitude toward the protection of workers' rights permits firms to suppress wages and working conditions, generating a cost advantage on the labor side. A particular concern is that labor and environmental standards may have been weakened in the aftermath of the Asian financial crisis of 1997–98, or because of additional trade liberalization in the late 1990s, and that this weakening has boosted exports since the crisis. Poor environmental stewardship and a failure to support at least core labor rights raise issues of human rights, health maintenance, educational attainment, and sustainability.

This chapter reviews theoretical and empirical analysis to help clarify these issues. Three competing hypotheses are influential in the literature. One is that foreign direct investment (FDI) and trade respond at least in part to country standards. If weak environmental and labor standards provide cost advantages that motivate domestic and foreign firms to locate in areas with such standards, the standards may stimulate growth in exports. If weak or ineffective standards are an important spur to competitiveness and export growth, and firms at least implicitly demand such weakness through their location decisions, governments may compete to offer low standards in a "race to the bottom." Now that many countries have significantly reduced their tariffs and other border restraints on trade, standards that raise costs have presumably increased their influence on trade.

An alternative hypothesis is that exceptionally weak environmental and labor standards restrain economic competitiveness, exports, and growth.[1] Unchecked or untreated discharges of chemicals into water supplies can harm agricultural production and workers' health status and limit productivity. Widespread reliance on child labor limits educational enrollments and the development of labor skills, and potentially restricts both the modernization of the output mix and growth rates. To the

---

The author is grateful to Kanemi Ban for helpful comments at the seminar at the Tokyo office of the World Bank.

extent that firms require high productivity, low absenteeism, and clean resources, weak standards can deter investment and restrict exports. In this view, competitiveness flows more readily from higher social protection than from lower.

Both of these hypotheses suggest that competitiveness, trade, and FDI depend on the effects of environmental and labor protection regulations (and their enforcement) on costs. A third claim reverses this causation, arguing that the optimal standards for a country depend on factor endowments, development levels, technology, and national preferences (Anderson 1996; Antweiler, Copeland, and Taylor 2001). In this context, regulations are endogenous to changes in openness to trade and FDI. Openness may either worsen or improve the natural environment, depending on prevailing conditions, but to the extent that openness raises incomes, demand for stronger environmental protection may be expected to rise. Similar comments apply to rules on the protection of workers. These higher demands for stronger environmental protection and protection of workers have been observed in recent decades in Japan, the Republic of Korea, Taiwan (China), and Singapore as development has proceeded, in part because of export-led growth.

These hypotheses cannot be tested conclusively. One reason is that the relationships between labor standards or environmental standards, on the one hand, and international trade, on the other, are complex and involve causality in both directions. Another reason is that it is difficult with the available information to capture the subtleties of labor rights or environmental conditions for statistical analysis. Even so, by reviewing the balance of evidence it is possible to draw useful guidelines for policy. The next section considers general issues in the area of labor standards and trade, and it is followed by a discussion of the situation in East Asian nations. The next sections repeat this structure for environmental regulation. They are followed by a review of environmental protection issues arising in the Doha round of multilateral trade negotiations. A concluding section offers policy recommendations.

Labor Standards: Background and Institutions

The literature on relationships between labor market regulations and international competition is huge, reflecting the complexity of the subject.[2] This section summarizes important institutional questions and the available evidence.

Many different kinds of regulations provide workers with rights in labor markets:

- *Basic rights* include prohibition of slavery and physical coercion, elimination of discrimination, and a ban on the exploitative use of child labor.
- *Civic rights* include freedom of association, collective bargaining, and expression of grievances. Together, these provisions constitute the so-called core labor standards, which embody principles that are supposed to be universally respected as a matter of human rights.[3]
- *Survival rights* provide for a living wage or minimum wage, limited hours of work, information about working conditions and job hazards, protection from occupational hazards, and compensation for employment-related accidents.
- *Security rights* include protection against arbitrary firing, rights to severance payments, and access to health and retirement benefits and survivors' compensation.

These various rights are granted by governments to workers through regulations on employer practices.[4] Such regulations vary considerably across countries, and even within countries.

An important distinction may be made between core labor standards and other rights. To a considerable degree, core labor standards may be interpreted as policies buttressing the basic freedoms in the workplace. The elimination of coercive forms of labor and discrimination gives workers and firms wider choices, and costly distortions in labor markets are removed (Maskus 1997; Martin and Maskus 2001). Recognition of the rights of workers to associate freely and engage in collective bargaining allows worker groups to counter the distortionary impacts of single employers. By contrast, survival rights and security rights award workers benefits that might not otherwise emerge in competitive labor markets. But they also raise the costs and reduce the flexibility of firms. Moreover, as the strength of such mandates rises, firms may find themselves less able to compete.[5] This problem might be particularly difficult for minimum wage laws, which can contribute to unemployment in the event of an economic crisis or political collapse, as suggested by a recent study of Indonesia (Suryahadi and others 2003).

In addition to regulating employers' practices, governments may directly support workers through public services. Such services consist of social safety net programs, including temporary unemployment compensation, and programs to improve workers' ability to function in labor markets, including job training, wage subsidies, employment services, job creation through public works projects, and education.

Table 7.1 compares the policies of key East Asian economies on workers' rights and support programs by indicating their decisions on ratification of the eight "fundamental" conventions of the International Labour Organisation (ILO) that cover the core labor standards. In the table, the many ratifications since 1996 are indicated by boldface, and they suggest that worker protection standards have improved since the Asian financial crisis. These data reveal that legislated labor standards have not been reduced in the East Asian region

since 1997; indeed, there is some evidence of a general trend toward raising them.[6] Nevertheless, a review of legislation finds that Korea is the only country to have significantly strengthened its regulatory framework for labor protection. China has done little to improve its formal recognition and protection of union rights. Meanwhile, allegations persist that governments in the region are raising roadblocks to union activities, and enforcement of labor laws is often thought to be weak.[7]

Workers in the informal sector are not directly affected by changes in labor legislation. They have few rights and may work in conditions that are less sanitary and more dangerous than those in formal employment (Maskus 1997). Child labor tends to be concentrated in the informal sector. Employment in the informal economy depends on many factors (including the effects of labor regulations on costs in the formal economy), but especially on the rate of overall growth in the economy.

One impact of the Asian financial crisis was a shift toward informal employment in many East Asian economies (Betcherman and Islam 2001),

TABLE 7.1   Ratifications of Fundamental ILO Conventions Covering Worker Rights, Selected East Asian Countries

	Convention (convention number)							
	Minimum age (138)	Worst forms of child labor (182)	Forced labor (29)	Abolition of forced labor (105)	Equal remuner-ation (100)	Nondis-crimin-ation (111)	Free dom of associ-ation (87)	Collective bargaining (98)
Cambodia	Yes	No	Yes	**Yes**	**Yes**	**Yes**	**Yes**	**Yes**
China	**Yes**	No	No	No	Yes	No	No	No
Hong Kong (China)	**Yes**[a]	n.a.	**Yes**[a]	**Yes**[a]	No	No	**Yes**[a]	Yes[a]
Indonesia	**Yes**	Yes	Yes	Yes	Yes	**Yes**	**Yes**	**Yes**
Korea, Rep. of	**Yes**	**Yes**	No	No	Yes	Yes	No	No
Malaysia	**Yes**	**Yes**	Yes	No	**Yes**	No	No	Yes
Philippines	**Yes**	**Yes**	No	Yes	Yes	Yes	Yes	Yes
Singapore	No	**Yes**	Yes	No	**Yes**	No	No	Yes
Thailand	No	**Yes**	Yes	Yes	**Yes**	No	No	No
Vietnam	No	**Yes**	No	No	**Yes**	**Yes**	No	No

n.a. Not applicable.
Note: Words in boldface indicate ratification decisions since 1996.
a. Indicates Hong Kong's intention to comply with the conventions indicated, even though Hong Kong is not a member of the International Labour Organisation (ILO).
Sources: OECD (2000) and www.ilo.org.

which suggests that working conditions deteriorated on average. Although the shift was temporary in much of the region, it has persisted in Indonesia and the Philippines.[8]

Evidence on Labor Standards, Trade, and Competitiveness

Because the provision of workers' rights affects the costs of hiring workers, it may influence international price competitiveness. For example, the ability of firms to require employees to work long hours without a premium for overtime, or to discharge workers with little notice or severance pay, presumably reduces their labor costs per unit of output, which may be significant in labor-intensive products. Extensive government support programs for training and employment services can reduce average labor costs, depending on how such programs are financed. Unfortunately, it is quite difficult to ascribe changes in trade performance to such actions, both because they are difficult to measure (particularly at the firm level) and because the relationships are complex. This section considers these relationships and reviews some general evidence.

Effects of Openness on Labor Standards and Conditions of Work

Table 7.2 gives an aggregate index of the strength of labor standards across several developing countries in the late 1990s (Verite 2002). Among East Asian economies, China, Indonesia, and Malaysia rank near the bottom of this scale. Regulations in the labor market depend on several influences, including economic openness, which vary across countries and over time (Freeman 1994; Fields 1995; OECD 1996; Maskus 1997).

As the table suggests, a primary determinant of labor standards is the level of income per person or per family in an economy. The poor may be little able to refuse dangerous work. Clearly, extensive poverty is the main factor underlying high rates of child labor participation (Grootaert and Kanbur 1995). As incomes rise, the treatment of labor improves for several reasons. First, the contribution of children to household income becomes less important, and schooling becomes a higher-valued alternative as parents become more capable of investing in their children. The child labor supply in

many East Asian countries fell dramatically as those economies became richer (U.S. Department of Labor 1994). Second, richer households gain greater access to credit markets, permitting them to invest more in acquiring skills. This investment can play an important role in decisions by rural households to keep their children in school, but it is also important for increasing adult productivity, which supports better working conditions. Third, the demand for tighter labor protection increases. This demand reflects both the impact of rising real wages—which make workers demand more protection to safeguard their incomes from dismissal or injury—and the nature of labor standards as public goods that become more affordable as incomes increase.

Another important determinant of labor rights is the endowment and output mix of the economy. In countries with abundant unskilled labor, firms in labor-intensive sectors may view workers as easily replaceable and have few incentives to train them. In economies with greater endowments of skilled labor and training, workers offer more differentiated—and more valuable—skills that make employers more concerned about retaining them and about avoiding the output losses associated with occupational injuries. Rapid growth emanating from the accumulation of human capital tends to increase the demand for better working conditions.

Yet another determinant of labor rights is the nature of competition in both the product and labor markets. A firm that is the sole or main employer in a local labor market can suppress wages or working conditions.

A government's willingness to legislate and enforce better labor standards depends on the political-economic situation. A strong positive correlation exists between democracy and the rights of workers to freely associate (OECD 2000), as corroborated by the last column of Table 7.2. In countries without effective political competition, it may be difficult to establish stronger standards, even where economic efficiency could be improved by doing so or where much of the public would prefer such standards.

Effects of Changes in a Country's Trade and Investment Regulations on Labor Standards

Tariff cuts could have several distinctive impacts on workers, depending on the economic circumstances of each country:

TABLE 7.2   Overall Ranking of Labor Standards

Country	Labor Standards Index, late 1990s[a]	Fundamental ILO conventions		PPP per capita GDP, 1999 (US$)	Freedom House Index, 1998–99[b]
		1995	1999		
Chile	83.3	3	7	8,720	5.5
Argentina	80.8	6	7	12,258	5.0
South Africa	78.0	1	5	8,994	6.5
Korea, Rep. of	71.3	0	3	15.778	6.0
Brazil	67.8	5	5	7,130	4.5
Philippines	63.8	5	6	3,803	5.5
Thailand	63.0	2	3	6,095	5.5
Colombia	62.0	6	6	5,821	4.5
Peru	59.0	6	6	4,626	3.5
Venezuela	56.0	7	7	5,586	5.5
Mexico	55.3	5	5	8,329	4.5
Turkey	55.0	5	8	6,374	3.5
India	46.5	3	3	2,250	5.5
Malaysia	46.3	2	4	8,215	3.0
Indonesia	44.5	3	7	2,873	3.0
Egypt	44.0	6	7	3,423	2.0
Pakistan	40.0	5	5	1,813	3.5
China	36.3	1	2	3,620	1.5
Correlations with Labor Standards Index				0.71	0.77

Note: PPP = purchasing power parity.
a. This index is a weighted average of four broad categories: ratification of the fundamental International Labour Organisation (ILO) conventions (see Table 7.1); a comparison of national labor laws with ILO standard recommendations; an evaluation of each government's capacity to implement its laws and policies; and an assessment of the level of compliance with or violations of the core labor standards.
b. This index is the average of the figures for political rights and civil liberties from the Freedom House Web site (www.freedomhouse.org). Here they have been scaled so that a figure of 1 means the least political freedom and a figure of 7 means the most political freedom.
Sources: Labor Standards Index (VERLS) from Verite (2002); GDP data from World Bank (2001c).

- Relative price changes from trade liberalization would tend to push capital and labor into products in which the country has a comparative advantage. This situation could either worsen or improve net working conditions in the economy, depending on whether conditions in the expanding industries are worse or better than those in other sectors.[9]
- In labor-abundant countries, tariff cuts ordinarily would raise the real wages of less skilled labor and increase aggregate income. These impacts should induce workers to demand stronger labor standards. As a result, over time employers should be willing to provide better working conditions.

- Trade liberalization can increase poverty under certain circumstances.[10] Wages in formal manufacturing may fall significantly for workers whose incomes had previously been protected. Workers who are laid off could end up in the informal economy, pushing down wages there. Trade liberalization increases the prices of export goods, which may have a large weight in household consumption baskets. To the extent that openness to trade reduces wages and increases poverty, labor standards and worker protection will deteriorate. This impact would be especially problematic in those regions that are not competitive in producing exportable goods. In East Asian developing economies, however, greater openness to trade has increased incomes, reduced poverty, and improved working conditions.[11]

• As the product markets of different countries become more integrated through trade liberalization, firms may seek out locations with weaker standards. Studies of practices in developed countries have found no evidence of a "race to the bottom" in labor standards (Maskus 1997; OECD 2000). Unfortunately, it appears that no studies have been done of competition in labor standards among developing countries that produce similar goods for export.

Labor Standards in Export Processing Zones

Some analysts view export processing zones (EPZs), or free trade zones, as examples of competitive standard setting.[12] In many instances, workers within EPZs have been denied the rights to unionize and bargain collectively, and safety and health conditions are poor (Moran 2002). This complaint has been leveled at some of the EPZs in China, Indonesia, and the Philippines, suggesting that East Asian countries may be competing in this way. However, no evidence was found that standards in EPZs had been weakened in the aftermath of the Asian financial crisis or because of additional trade liberalization in the late 1990s.

By contrast, there is evidence that the operations of multinational enterprises, even within EPZs, tend to improve working conditions and wages relative to those in the rest of the economy.[13] It is not difficult to understand why multinational firms pay higher-than-average wages in developing countries. First, these firms invest much more in advanced industries, such as electrical equipment, electronics, industrial machinery, and automobile parts, than in the less advanced industries such as garments, textiles, footwear, and toys. Jobs in the advanced industries require higher skills and pay considerably higher wages than those in the less advanced industries. Second, these firms tend to produce for export, which requires sustained quality, specific skills, and limited absenteeism, and they are willing to pay higher wages in return. Third, multinational firms typically bring superior technologies to the factory floor, which raise productivity and wages relative to those of domestic firms. In this regard, openness to foreign direct investment is

generally a force for raising labor standards rather than the other way around.

Evidence on the Effects of Labor Standards on Trade Performance and FDI

Have weak labor standards in East Asian developing economies contributed positively or negatively to the export performance of these economies and to their attractiveness for inward FDI? This is a difficult question to answer. First, economic theory cannot establish a clear relationship between weakness in labor standards and international trade competitiveness.[14] Second, labor standards and working conditions are only two of numerous determinants of relative costs, and it is virtually impossible to isolate their impacts using aggregate data. A truly informative answer would require detailed survey work at the firm level and would track the dynamics of labor use over several years. Third, available aggregate measures of labor rights are crude and cannot capture the subtleties of cost impacts or enforcement efforts, nor can they control adequately for other influences on trade. Evidence on this subject must be treated with caution.

As for the relationship between *labor standards* and *international trade performance*, Aggarwal's (1995) study of manufacturing sectors in developing countries found that workers in export-oriented firms received higher wages and benefits than those in less export-oriented firms. And countries with weak labor rights did not have higher import penetration ratios in the United States than countries with stronger labor rights. Rodrik's (1996) cross-country econometric analysis found no relationship between basic measures of labor standards and international trade flows. Similarly, the Organisation for Economic Co-operation and Development (OECD 1996) found no relationships between labor standards and measures of export performance. Nor could the OECD authors detect any correlations between measures of revealed comparative advantage and attempts to suppress labor union rights, or any association between individual countries' core labor standards and the prices of their exports of textiles and apparel to the United States. They concluded that differences in core labor standards have no detectable effects on patterns of specialization, competitiveness, or exports.

Van Beers (1998), analyzing OECD trade data, found a weak association between stricter labor standards and lower exports of labor-intensive goods. His index of labor standards included such measures as maximum working hours, conditions of employment contracts, and minimum wages, suggesting that strong security rights can negatively affect trade performance in richer nations. It may be, however, that inflexible labor market mandates reduce competitiveness rather than fundamental labor standards.[15]

As for the relationship between *labor standards and FDI,* Aggarwal (1995) found no association between U.S. foreign direct investment and poor labor standards; if anything, FDI from the United States was less concentrated than expected in countries with low standards. Rodrik (1996) found some indication that FDI from the United States was lower than expected in countries with limited core labor standards. OECD (2000) reported that larger inflows of FDI are associated with stronger labor rights. This study also reported growing evidence that export processing zones with poor working conditions are less likely to attract sustained, long-term FDI than those with better conditions. Kucera (2001) regressed aggregate flows of FDI into many developing countries on several indexes of labor standards. He found no statistical indication that weak labor rights attract FDI, and some of his coefficients suggested that the opposite result holds.

The analysis just described suggests that weak labor standards are capable of expanding exports most readily in labor-intensive goods such as apparel, textiles, footwear, and miscellaneous manufactures such as toys and sporting goods. The Asian financial crisis may have reduced the relative costs of production in labor-intensive exports for several reasons. First, even if legislated labor standards were not diminished during this period, authorities may have signaled a reduced commitment to enforcing workers' rights within labor-intensive industries. Second, the costs of acquiring inputs from subcontractors may have fallen quite sharply during the crisis if wages fell in the subcontractors' firms. Third, exchange rate changes may pass through more quickly to competitive sectors. Under such circumstances, one would expect effectively weaker labor standards to have raised the share of labor-intensive manufactures in total exports between 1995 (before the crisis) and 1999 in East Asia.

At best, however, the data simply do not support this notion. Data on the shares of labor-intensive products in total manufactured exports show that, except perhaps in China and Indonesia, the output mix shift has, over time, shifted away from labor-intensive goods.[16] The export data cannot reveal much about how labor standards affected changes in trade shares, because numerous other factors could have driven these changes.[17] But data on labor conditions in this period provide useful complementary insights (ILO 2002). Despite the large increases in unemployment between 1995 and 1999 in Hong Kong (China), Indonesia, Korea, Malaysia, the Philippines, and Thailand, there was virtually no change in reported hours worked per week. Moreover, in these countries the number of reported injuries per 100,000 fell sharply during 1995–99. Thus, at least on these simple indicators, firms (in the formal sector) were not pressuring workers to work harder or more dangerously.

For a more formal test of the hypothesis that labor standards have affected East Asian exports of labor-intensive goods, and did so more strongly after the onset of the financial crisis, an econometric analysis was undertaken.[18] The underlying models are estimated for 1995 and 1999 to see if any differences may have arisen during the crisis in terms of the impact of standards on exports. (If weak labor rights were a factor raising exports of labor-intensive manufactures, one would expect to find a negative coefficient in both years. But if the negative coefficient was larger in 1999 than in 1995, it would suggest that differential labor rights provided a stronger impetus to exports in the latter year.) This is at best a partial and crude test of the notion that labor rights were effectively weakened during the crisis and that they helped to boost exports in the post-crisis period.

Three measures of labor standards were used: an index of the strength of freedom of association (FA) rights in the exporting countries; the index of four labor standards developed by Verite (2002—VERLS, see Table 7.2); and the number of the eight fundamental ILO conventions that were ratified by the exporting countries by 1995 or 1999 (see Table 7.1).

For two of these three measures of labor standards, the results suggest that bilateral export volumes in labor-intensive goods actually rise as worker protection is increased—a finding that is particularly true within East Asia (Table 7.3).[19] The

TABLE 7.3 Impacts of Labor Standards on Labor–Intensive Exports from Developing Countries

Variable	Model 1 (1995)	Model 1 (1999)	Model 2 (1995)	Model 2 (1999)	Model 3 (1995)	Model 3 (1999)
NAFTA	2.37***	3.53***	2.52***	3.62***	2.07***	2.86***
Political freedom	–0.30***	–0.19***	–0.82***	–0.91***	–0.27***	–0.11**
East Asia	1.05*	3.13***	2.80***	4.28***	1.59***	0.05
South Asia	8.18***	5.46***	16.9***	6.11***	–0.09	–1.56
Latin America	2.37**	1.34	1.55*	6.18***	0.69	0.72
FA rights	0.60***	0.66***				
	(1.37)	(1.59)				
FA rights • East Asia	0.94***	–0.32				
	(2.13)	(1.32)				
FA rights • South Asia	–2.42***	–1.52***				
	(0.71)	(1.15)				
FA rights • Latin America	–1.18**	–1.03**				
	(0.27)	(0.57)				
VERLS			0.09***	0.14***		
			(5.28)	(8.22)		
VERLS • East Asia			0.01	–0.02		
			(5.41)	(7.81)		
VERLS • South Asia			–0.21***	–0.04		
			(3.31)	(7.94)		
VERLS • Latin America			–0.03**	–0.11***		
			(4.56)	(5.57)		
ILO-F					–0.16**	–0.52***
					(–0.62)	(–2.69)
ILO-F • East Asia					0.38***	0.42**
					(–0.10)	(–1.93)
ILO-F • South Asia					0.85***	0.71***
					(–0.23)	(–2.25)
ILO-F • Latin America					–0.19**	–0.27
					(–0.92)	(–3.27)
No. of observations	1,700	1,700	1,700	1,700	1,700	1,700
R–squared	0.74	0.76	0.75	0.77	0.74	0.77

* Significant at 10 percent level.
** Significant at 5 percent level.
*** Significantly different from zero at 1 percent level.
Notes: FA = freedom of association; ILO-F = fundamental International Labour Organisation conventions. The coefficients come from gravity models of bilateral exports from 17 developing countries to 20 OECD importers listed below.
Each equation is estimated as an augmented gravity model with controls for importer and exporter GDP, importer and exporter population, bilateral distance, and industry fixed effects. Standard errors are robust to heteroskedasticity. Figures in parentheses are elasticities calculated at sample means.
Export values are included for the set of labor-intensive industries listed below.
The regressions include standard gravity variables (logs of importer and exporter GDP levels, logs of importer and exporter population levels, and the log of distance between trading partners), a dummy variable for NAFTA when the exporter is Mexico and the importer is either the United States or Canada, an index of political freedoms from the Freedom House Web site (www.freedomhouse.org), industry fixed effects, regional fixed effects, a measure of labor standards, and interaction terms between labor standards and regional dummies. Data on GDP (in billions of U.S. dollars in purchasing power parity terms) and population (in millions) are from World Bank (2001c). Distance is the number of kilometers (in thousands) between capital cities. The index of political freedoms is the simple average of the "political freedom" and "civil liberties" indicators from Freedom House (www.freedomhouse.org), rescaled so that an increase in the index here signifies an increase in political rights. Labor-intensive industries are defined as ISIC (International Standard Industrial Classification) 321, 322, 323, 324, and 390.
Exporters are Argentina, Brazil, Chile, Colombia, Mexico, Peru, Venezuela (Latin America); India, Pakistan (South Asia); China, Indonesia, Republic of Korea, Malaysia, the Philippines, Thailand (East Asia); Egypt, and South Africa.
Importers are Australia, Austria, Canada, Denmark, Finland, France, Germany, Greece, Japan, Ireland, Italy, the Netherlands, New Zealand, Norway, Portugal, Spain, Sweden, Turkey, United Kingdom, and United States.
Source: The author.

balance of evidence does not support the view that weak labor rights promote exports in these goods, nor does it suggest decisively that during the financial crisis weak labor rights translated into stronger labor-intensive exports.

The policy message that emerges is that East Asian developing countries need not delay in introducing core labor standards. Doing so will not reduce their competitiveness in labor-intensive manufactured exports and could well increase it. However, they should exercise caution in implementing stronger measures that could limit flexibility in formal labor markets.[20]

Environmental Protection: Background and Institutions

It is beyond the scope of this chapter to attempt a comprehensive review of environmental regulatory regimes. All the major East Asian economies have some form of regulatory regime and institutions aimed at protecting the environment or promoting sustainable resource use. But these regimes vary considerably in terms of resource commitments, enforcement capacity, and regulatory mechanisms (Esty and Cornelius 2002).

Did the onset of the financial crisis affect environmental use and policy in the region? Reports suggest that the crisis did alter various indicators of environmental damage, though in different ways. In many cities, the short-term effect of economic collapse was improved air quality as industrial production slackened and as vehicles were used less in reaction to lower product demand and, in some cases, sharply higher fuel prices (World Bank 1999). By 1999, however, air pollution indexes were regaining and perhaps exceeding their previous levels. Water quality is relatively insensitive to short-term changes in industrial activity and household consumption, and so water quality measures changed little. But sanitation conditions deteriorated markedly in many locations because growing amounts of industrial and toxic waste were not being disposed of properly. Industrial pollution worsened somewhat in some countries, perhaps because of weaker regulatory control and reduced compliance by firms. In several countries such as Indonesia, some urban dwellers responded to the financial crisis by returning to the countryside, which placed more stress on natural resources and

farming communities. The collapse also seemed to speed deforestation in Indonesia and Vietnam, although a reduction in export demand in Japan and Korea offset this problem initially (Marinova 1999; World Bank 1999, 2001b). Finally, there are indications that fishing stocks and coral reefs have come under greater stress as a result of rising unemployment, although most such pressures are long term rather than cyclical (World Bank 1999; World Resources Institute 2002).

Like for labor standards, there is little indication that governments actively reduced their legislated or formal environmental regulations during the crisis period. In fact, since 1997 some economies have adopted stricter regulation or greater incentives for conservation:

- China tightened its industrial point source pollution control and deforestation regulations in the late 1990s (World Bank 2001a), and it has increased pollution discharge fees to levels at least as high as treatment costs (APEC 2001).
- Hong Kong is subsidizing projects to develop green production technologies, develop new waste treatment systems, and promote ISO 14000 environmental standards. Vietnam has announced a reforestation program (World Bank 2001a).
- Korea's Ministry of Environment has expanded its programs for pollution prevention, including certification of enterprises, and it has begun requiring compliance with certain OECD standards. It also has expanded tax incentives and procurement policies for recycling (World Bank 2000). Korea adopted a new law in December 1998 that revises the Waste Management Act. The new law clarifies and increases landowners' liabilities for abandoned waste, which has become a significant and costly problem to clean up. By 1999 Korea had eased up on its regulations in the textile dyeing industry, despite a large drop in output. However, perhaps related to the financial crisis, Korea decided to delay revising some air quality standards in 1997. And recently the government has shifted toward deregulation of onerous mandates and self-certification and voluntary compliance by businesses.
- Thailand recently implemented a series of plans for enhancing and conserving national environ-

mental quality (APEC 2001). This approach includes both tighter pollution control, implementing the "polluter pays" principle, and programs to promote the development of new technologies.

However, in the countries affected strongly by the slowdown, the associated fiscal problems have reduced public expenditures on environmental protection (World Bank 1999, 2001a).[21] This reduced spending has been a significant problem in Indonesia, where the administrative and regulatory framework does not encourage sustainable use of the environment. It is likely that the collapse of central government authority exacerbated Indonesia's fiscal difficulties. Forest loss has continued, land use management problems remain severe, and inadequate wastewater treatment and the dumping of hazardous wastes have not abated. Some commentators view Indonesia's ongoing devolution of administrative authority to local governments as damaging for environmental protection, because these governments may not have effective capacities or budgets for the job and may be particularly prone to weak and nontransparent enforcement. In the Philippines, fiscal stringency has had a mixed effect on incentives for environmental resource use (World Bank 1999). Environmental budget cuts were reported, but fiscal pressures also resulted in reductions in subsidies to coal production and fuel consumption, with associated increases in user prices.

Remarkably little research has been done on the relationships among the environment, the financial crisis, and trade in East Asia. The following research agenda, which could be pursued by national authorities, international organizations, or research institutions, would substantially improve understanding of the processes at work:

- How the Asia financial crisis affected the use of environmentally damaging agricultural inputs and whether changes in such use were needed to sustain trade flows
- Whether exchange rate changes associated with the crisis altered demand for imported inputs that might have limited toxic discharges
- Whether multinational firms had a greater or lesser propensity than domestic firms to ignore cost-increasing environmental regulations.

Evidence on Environmental Protection, Trade, and Competitiveness

The links between declines in economic activity and environmental degradation are complex and not easily predicted. The same is true for the links between openness to trade and FDI and use of the environment. These impacts presumably work in both directions and depend on circumstances.

How Does Openness Affect Environmental Protection and Use?

Grossman and Krueger (1993) describe the impacts of changes in an economy's fundamental variables—endowments, prices, technologies, and policies—on the aggregate use of the environment.[22] Drawing on their framework, I use the word *emissions* as a proxy for all forms of environmental use, including air and water pollution, deforestation, habitat destruction, and waste deposits. In the simplest terms, the amount of emissions an economy generates depends on three essential factors: the size of the economy, the share of output produced by emission-intensive ("dirty") sectors, and the degree of emissions intensity in those sectors.

Any change in pollution emissions can therefore be decomposed into three effects. The *scale effect* refers to an increase in emissions associated with a larger gross domestic product (GDP), holding constant the relative mix of outputs and pollution intensities across sectors—that is, a 10 percent increase in all productive factors, everything else held constant, should raise pollution by 10 percent.[23] The *composition effect* refers to a change in the share of dirty goods in the GDP, which may come about because of a price change. With a constant scale of the economy and no change in emissions intensities per industry, a rise in the share of dirty goods would increase total pollution. The *technique effect* refers to a change in the amount of emissions per unit of output across sectors (an "emissions-intensity" change)—for example, as producers change technologies in response to a higher pollution tax.[24] This typology can be used to analyze the impacts of trade liberalization and FDI on the environment.

Trade liberalization reduces impediments to imports and exports[25] and affects use of the environment through its effects on prices, which then filter through to production and consumption. For example, suppose that an East Asian developing economy has abundant labor and therefore has a comparative advantage in labor-intensive goods. Freeing up trade would raise the price of labor-intensive goods in this economy and shift capital and labor into production of these goods. If these goods are produced with cleaner technologies on average, overall emissions will fall as the composition of output shifts away from dirtier goods. (Note that emissions could rise if the goods that a country exports are dirtier; comparative advantage is an important factor.) The shift in the composition of output after trade liberalization raises the aggregate productivity in the economy, and thereby raises real GDP. The scale effect of trade liberalization is thus to increase pollution. Finally, as aggregate and per capita incomes rise from freer trade, so does the demand for a cleaner environment.[26] Thus the technique effect of trade liberalization is to improve the environment by reducing emissions per unit of output.[27]

The same framework can be used to assess the effects of an increase in foreign direct investment on environmental quality. If multinational firms exist disproportionately in dirtier industries, their arrival in a country has an effect like an increase in the capital stock that worsens the environment through the composition effect. But if they exist disproportionately in cleaner industries, their arrival can improve the environment. By expanding economic activity, multinational firms would generate a scale effect that increases the effects of firms' activities on the environment.[28] Perhaps most fundamentally, the operations of multinational firms can generate beneficial technique effects. For a variety of reasons, they are likely to transfer cleaner technologies, developed in their home economies, to recipient countries (Moran 2002). If they pay higher-than-average wages without generating offsetting unemployment, the impact would be higher per capita incomes and an induced demand for stronger environmental protection. Thus, even if multinational firms do not alter much the composition of output, one would expect their operations to improve environmental stewardship. In this context, economies that are more open to FDI, other things being equal, would tend to have stronger environmental standards and cleaner technologies. However, this is an empirical issue.

Important evidence is available on the effects of trade liberalization on the environment, and what follows is only a selective and brief review.

The most prominent study is by Antweiler, Copeland, and Taylor (2001), covering the effects of trade liberalization on air pollution in 44 countries.[29] They find that international trade generates relatively minor changes in concentrations of air pollution when it alters the composition of output, but that the associated technique and scale effects reduce pollution. Overall, they find that within their sample greater openness to trade actually reduces air pollution on average.

Beghin and others (2000) consider the relationships between trade liberalization and pollution in Chile. In their computable general equilibrium model, unilateral liberalization substantially worsens air pollution by providing cheaper and dirtier energy sources. But if this trade policy were combined with an appropriate tax on emissions, Chile would reap significant welfare gains.[30]

Dean (2002) analyzes the impacts of trade liberalization on water pollution in Chinese provinces during 1987–95, a period in which there was both an extensive pollution levy system and a significant opening to trade. She finds that trade liberalization has aggravated environmental damage, because China has a comparative advantage in pollution-intensive goods, but that greater openness has also raised per capita incomes, mitigating the environmental costs through stronger regulation. She also finds that emissions per unit of industrial output in China would have been much higher without trade reform, so that China's opening to trade was beneficial for the environment overall.

Arunanondchai (2001) assesses the impacts that cuts in tariffs and export taxes on logging and timber products would have on Indonesian and Malaysian exporters. She finds that trade liberalization would not necessarily raise log production, because it might not raise net producer prices, but that foreign tariff cuts in plywood and sawn lumber would generate significant gains for Indonesia. She also finds that removal of export taxes on logs would reduce world log prices, tending to worsen the joint welfare of exporting nations.

APEC (1999) assesses the effects of selected nontariff restraints on trade in forest products. The authors find that multilateral removal of taxes and subsidies would generate some gains for timber exporters, but they claim that the data were insufficient to assess the environmental impacts of such liberalization.

In summary, the literature suggests it is not possible to predict the implications of trade liberalization for use of the environment and economic welfare in general, but the balance of econometric and empirical evidence suggests that it can be beneficial. Studies of the effects of FDI on environmental damage are surprisingly scarce.[31] Moran (2002) has provided some anecdotal evidence that multinational firms are associated with improvements in use of the environment, but such improvements depend on the industry.

Evidence on Environmental Standards and Competitiveness

The "pollution haven hypothesis" has attracted much study. What is the evidence that weak environmental protection either generates an export advantage or attracts FDI? In principle, one might expect weak regulation to be more strongly identified with trade performance and FDI for the environment than for labor standards. After all, unlike workers, the environment cannot complain or shirk when it is treated badly. Therefore, the ability to exploit it without regulation could reduce costs, at least up to the limits from congestion.

Past Evidence. This prediction is borne out in a 24-country study of environmental standards and trade by Wilson, Otsuki, and Sewadeh (2002).[32] Their results suggest that more stringent environmental laws reduce net exports of pollution-intensive goods. Thus weak environmental regulation is associated with higher trade performance. Moreover, they find that a hypothetical trade agreement to harmonize environmental protection laws at levels higher than those in developing countries would reduce trade by up to 11 percent a year.

Their study is unique in its findings, however. Earlier studies discovered no evidence that a country with stricter environmental standards would have lower exports of pollution-intensive goods (Tobey 1990; Low and Yeats 1992; Xu 1999). Most observers have concluded that, because environmental controls typically amount to a small percentage of total costs, they are relatively unimportant in determining trade patterns.

Levinson and Taylor (2001) find that in the United States during the 1970s and 1980s, the largest relative increases in sectoral net imports were in those industries experiencing the largest increases in environmental control costs. Thus trade flows do react to such regulation. Unfortunately, because there are no comparable measures in developing countries, it is impossible to determine whether this result holds more widely.

The literature gives little support for the hypothesis that FDI responds to international variations in environmental costs. For example, Eskeland and Harrison (1997) find almost no evidence that multinational firms investing in developing countries are attempting to escape higher environmental costs in their home countries. They also find that foreign-owned plants in developing countries are less polluting than comparable domestic plants. Wheeler (2001) discusses why the "race to the bottom" idea in environmental standards makes little sense in terms of attracting FDI. He finds that indexes of air pollution actually improved markedly in the major cities in China, Brazil, and Mexico during an era of extensive investment inflows. Smarzynska and Wei (2001) examine firm-level data in 24 transition economies, controlling for corruption levels, and find little support for the pollution haven idea (see also Jaffe and others 1995). Levinson (1996) finds no evidence that differences in environmental standards across states affect the location choices of manufacturing plants.

This view is not universal, however. Lucas, Wheeler, and Hettige (1990) claim that increasingly strict environmental regulations in OECD countries led to the displacement of pollution-intensive industries. List and Co (1999) find that FDI in the United States was negatively related to regulatory expenditures per firm. Mani, Pargal, and Huq (1997) discover that in India spending on environmental damage abatement was higher in more pollution-intensive industries and was a factor in plant location decisions. Keller and Levinson (2002) point out problems with endogeneity in such measures. The issues are inherently empirical.

Evidence from East Asia. Available measures suggest that environmental protection regulations are not very stringent in East Asia. Table 7.4 lists two indexes of environmental regulation in several developing countries. The first is an environmental sustainability index, which is a compilation of several categories involving resource use, pollutant concentrations, and infrastructure. The correlation of environmental sustainability with per capita GDP is positive and significant at 0.37, but well below unity. The environmental sustainability index is correlated positively with the political freedom ranking in Table 7.2, but only weakly. The second environmental policy index measures the stringency of environmental regulations. This index too is positively correlated with per capita GDP, but it is not correlated with the measure of political freedom.

One might expect a reduction in costs resulting from weaker, or more weakly enforced, environmental standards to be reflected in increases in the share of pollution-intensive goods in manufactured exports for East Asian economies. But, in fact, trends in shares of pollution-intensive exports vary widely across these economies.[33] Indonesia provides the most straightforward support for the idea that the financial crisis pushed the composition of output toward pollution-intensive sectors—a shift toward dirtier industries took place in its total exports and its exports to the European Union and the United States. This shift is consistent with the fact that Indonesia's output of dirty goods rose relative to that of other goods during the crisis (World Bank 2001b). The export share of dirty industries also rose in Korea from 1997 to 1998 before falling again in 1999, and there is some indication of similar increases in the Philippines and Thailand in 1999.[34]

To investigate further the relationship between environmental protection and exports of pollution-intensive goods, I undertook an econometric analysis based on models whose essential structure is the same as those applied earlier to the labor

TABLE 7.4 Environmental Policy Indexes

Country	Environmental Sustainability Index, 2001	Environmental Regulatory Regime Index, 2001[a]	PPP per capita GDP, 1999 (US$)
Argentina	62.9	−0.732	12,258
Brazil	57.4	−0.077	7,130
Chile	56.6	0.177	8,720
Colombia	54.8	−0.416	5,821
Peru	54.3	−0.722	4,626
South Africa	51.2	−0.029	8,994
Venezuela	50.8	−1.079	5,586
Malaysia	49.8	−0.127	8,215
Egypt	46.4	−0.224	3,423
Turkey	46.3	n.a.	6,374
Mexico	45.3	−0.602	8,329
Thailand	45.2	−0.389	6,095
Pakistan	43.4	n.a.	1,813
Indonesia	42.5	−0.758	2,873
India	40.7	−0.759	2,250
Korea, Rep. of	40.3	−0.121	15,778
China	37.5	−0.348	3,620
Philippines	35.6	−1.014	3,803
Correlation with GDP per capita	0.37	0.41	
Correlation with Freedom House Index, 1998–99	0.17	−0.03	

n.a. Not applicable.
Note: PPP = purchasing power parity.
a. Most values are negative because the measure is scaled across all countries (including OECD members) to be zero for the average regime.
Sources: Sustainability and regulatory regime indexes are from Esty and Cornelius (2002). GDP data are from World Bank (2001c).

standards.[35] The two measures of environmental standards used are the environmental sustainability index and the environmental regulatory regime index shown in Table 7.4. Also included are the index of political freedom, a dummy for joint importer-exporter membership in the North American Free Trade Agreement (NAFTA), and regional fixed effects. The results are shown in Table 7.5.

Overall, it is difficult to reach any confident conclusions from the results of the numerical analysis. From the changes in export shares by country, it appears that those countries hardest hit by the Asian crisis tended to shift more output and exports into pollution-intensive sectors. But the econometric analysis provides little evidence that weaker environmental standards are associated with higher exports of pollution-intensive goods.

TABLE 7.5   Impacts of Environmental Standards on Pollution-Intensive Exports from Developing Countries

Variable	Model 1 (1995)	Model 1 (1999)	Model 2 (1995)	Model 2 (1999)
NAFTA	2.38***	2.33***	2.33***	2.82***
Political freedom	0.38***	−0.82	−0.35***	−0.08
East Asia	15.8***	25.7***	−2.12***	−1.25***
South Asia	−237.4***	−247.6***	0.18	−0.09
Latin America	21.2***	29.8***	−2.44***	−2.95***
Environmental sustainability (ES)	0.46*** (21.6)	0.61*** (28.7)		
ES • East Asia	−0.30*** (16.1)	−0.51*** (19.3)		
ES • South Asia	5.85*** (51.9)	6.17*** (60.6)		
ES • Latin America	−0.46*** (13.2)	−0.64*** (16.9)		
Environmental regime (ER)			16.0*** (8.32)	14.9*** (7.75)
ER • East Asia			−16.3*** (5.01)[a]	−14.1*** (4.44)[a]
ER • South Asia			−13.1*** (7.57)	−10.9*** (7.00)
ER • Latin America			−14.2*** (5.44)	−13.9*** (4.87)[a]
Number of observations	2,880	2,880	2,880	2,880
R–squared	0.55	0.58	0.56	0.58

* Significant at 10 percent level.
** Significant at 5 percent level.
*** Significantly different from zero at 1 percent level.
Note: Each equation is estimated as an augmented gravity model, with controls for importer and exporter GDP, importer and exporter population, bilateral distance, and industry fixed effects. Standard errors are robust to heteroskedasticity.
Figures in parentheses are elasticities calculated at sample means.
Pollution-intensive goods are ISIC (International Standard Industrial Classification) 332, 341, 351, 352, 353, 356, 371, and 372.
Exporters are Argentina, Brazil, Chile, Colombia, Mexico, Peru, Venezuela (Latin America); Bangladesh, India (South Asia); China, Indonesia, Republic of Korea, Malaysia, the Philippines, Thailand, Vietnam (East Asia); Egypt, and South Africa. Importers are Australia, Austria, Canada, Denmark, Finland, France, Germany, Greece, Japan, Ireland, Italy, the Netherlands, New Zealand, Norway, Portugal, Spain, Sweden, Turkey, United Kingdom, and United States.
a. Not significantly different from zero at the 10 percent level.
Source: The author.

At best, there is no strong or systematic indication that the crisis significantly augmented exports based on pollution havens in East Asia.

Environmental Protection and the Doha Round

The Doha Round of multilateral trade negotiations at the World Trade Organization (WTO) would be the first round to consider linkages between environmental protection and trade. Many developing countries have raised concerns about the potential implications of environmental protection for their trade opportunities. This section reviews the environmental provisions of the Doha Declaration and the scope of the upcoming negotiations, and comments on potential obligations for East Asian economies.

The Doha Declaration calls on countries to

- *Clarify relationships between WTO rules and trade obligations under various multilateral environmental agreements (MEAs).*[36] Further clarification is needed about whether trade sanctions issued under the Montreal Protocol, the Convention on International Trade in Endangered Species (CITES), and other agreements are consistent with WTO obligations. To date, such sanctions have been effectively exempted from the WTO, and this exemption is likely to become a formal interpretation in the Doha Round. It is conceivable that a broad interpretation could limit export opportunities in certain goods in the future, even as it gives East Asian countries greater scope to limit imports. However, according to the Doha Declaration, negotiations on such linkages must be undertaken without altering the WTO rights of countries that are not members of an associated MEA. Thus there should be little reason for concern about facing trade restrictions by virtue of not joining MEAs.

  As for toxic waste disposal, developing countries need to know whether current or potential WTO rules allow them to ban imports of toxic wastes and products. A clarification of restraints under the Basel Convention and WTO obligations is needed. Under the Basel Convention, which was ratified or acceded to by all major East Asian economies by 2000, transboundary movements of hazardous wastes or other wastes can take place only after prior written notification by the exporting country authorities to the competent authorities of the importing country and to countries through which they might transit. Each shipment of hazardous waste must then be accompanied by documentation or be deemed illegal. Exports of toxic wastes to certain countries are banned outright. Cross-border movements can take place, however, if the exporting nation lacks the capacity to manage or dispose of the hazardous waste in an environmentally sound manner. The Basel Convention clearly anticipates that importing governments may closely regulate the disposal of hazardous wastes because they must agree to the documentation and may monitor execution of the transaction. The convention falls short of permitting individual countries to ban such imports, though a proposed amendment provides for countries to ban exports. Whether importers could issue such bans presumably depends on a legal interpretation of Article XX of the General Agreement on Tariffs and Trade (GATT), which permits trade restraints in order to protect environmental and human health. However, such regulation must be consistent with national treatment, so that imported waste is not treated worse in the commercial sense than is domestic waste. In poor countries, waste treatment tends to be weakly regulated, suggesting that import limitations could be problematic under WTO rules.

- *Reduce or eliminate trade barriers to environmental goods and services.* Such barriers raise costs to countries that must import technology if they wish to mitigate environmental problems. Obligations to cut import tariffs and open service markets may run into political economy concerns, but they can effectively complement domestic environmental policy.

- *Clarify rules on the effects of environmental regulatory measures on market access.* These rules seem to be aimed mainly at efforts by developed and middle-income countries to restrict trade in order to achieve (indirectly) some environmental goal.[37] It remains to be seen whether such clarification would expand the scope of unilateral action to restrict trade or whether it would impose additional obligations on countries that limit imports.

- *Identify cases where reducing trade restrictions and economic distortions would benefit the environment, trade, and economic development.* Prominent examples would be subsidies to coal and other forms of carbon-based energy and to water use in agriculture. Reductions in such subsidies bear considerable promise for improving use of the environment while raising market access to new technologies and agricultural products (Anderson 1996). Negotiations on this point should give East Asian economies an opportunity to rationalize their trade policy with resource subsidies and other policies.

- *Clarify provisions of the intellectual property agreement in the WTO that could affect the trade and transfer of environmental technologies.* There are concerns that stronger private property rights that exclude unauthorized use—including by governments—of technologies, products, and services able to reduce environmental problems might make environmental management more costly.

- *Consider the scope for environmental labeling requirements on products.* Effective labeling requirements could be beneficial in restraining the use of blunter trade restrictions, although meeting the costs of labeling could be high.

Finally, the declaration pledges that *developed countries will commit to increasing technical and financial assistance for meeting international environmental needs.*

This set of negotiating objectives aims to address the existing inconsistencies in and shortcomings of the trading system rather than permit the introduction of extensive new trade control regimes. Therefore, East Asian developing economies should not be overly concerned about the introduction of environmental issues into the WTO, because those issues are already included in various ways. The scope of negotiations as set out in this section would not raise much concern about market access, although developing country members should perhaps be particularly wary about labeling requirements.

Policy Implications

The analysis in this chapter finds little evidence that East Asian governments have relaxed their standards on working conditions or on environmental

stewardship. If anything, it finds a continuing trend toward stronger regulation. However, public expenditures devoted to social safety nets for workers and to enforcement of environmental laws suffered in some countries affected by the 1997–98 financial crisis, and there is anecdotal evidence of declines in working conditions and environmental protection during the crisis.

Unfortunately, it is quite difficult to trace whether these processes have boosted exports. Economic theory and evidence from past studies suggest that weak labor rights are not correlated with export performance, even in labor-intensive goods, and that they are negatively correlated with an economy's attractiveness to foreign direct investment. They also suggest that weak environmental regulations are not a significant determinant of exports or FDI in most circumstances. Given this background, it is not surprising that the econometric work performed for this study finds no indication that weak labor rights or environmental standards are positively correlated with export performance. There is evidence on the labor side that stronger rights are associated with higher exports of labor-intensive goods, although that finding depends on the measure of labor standards used. Environmental protection indexes also seem to be positively but weakly correlated with East Asian exports in pollution-intensive goods. In summary, although it is difficult to be confident about such inferences, I could find no significant evidence in the data that weak labor rights or environmental standards boost East Asian exports.

If the results are taken seriously, important policy messages emerge. East Asian developing countries have weaker measured labor and environmental standards, relative to per capita income, than do other developing regions. To the extent that these policies have supported flexibility in labor markets, they may be beneficial for export competitiveness. However, these countries have considerable room for improving their protection of fundamental labor rights and environmental standards. Doing so would not reduce their ability to export labor-intensive goods or pollution-intensive goods; indeed, export growth can be compatible with raising core labor standards and environmental protection. In short, the developing economies of East Asia can feel comfortable in applying greater weight to social considerations in setting their policies without significant fear of deterring export growth.

Endnotes

1. Such a situation can arise directly if, for example, absence of collective bargaining by workers permits monopsonistic employers in particular regions to restrain wages and output (Martin and Maskus 2001).
2. For extensive reviews, see Maskus (1997), OECD (1996, 2000), and Elliott (2001).
3. The right to strike is not generally considered a core labor standard.
4. Many such benefits may be provided by employers voluntarily or through collective bargaining arrangements. Thus government regulation may simply provide a floor for these rights.
5. An across-the-board set of requirements might be offset by depreciation of the home currency, with little net impact on international competitiveness (Sykes 1995). The claim that strong civic and security rights may raise costs is not universally accepted; institutional labor economists argue that such rights increase the attachment of workers to firms and skills, which can lower costs. It is an empirical question.
6. Note, however, that ratification signals only an intention to comply with a convention, not a country's actual labor market policies. The ILO has little scope for enforcing these rights. Conversely, a decision not to ratify does not mean that the inherent rights in a convention are denied. Governments may provide such rights while objecting to the language of a particular convention. The United States, for example, has ratified only two of these conventions (105 and 182), but its practices largely comply with ILO expectations. A review of labor standards in eight East Asian countries appears in the technical appendix to this chapter at www.worldbank.org/eaptrade, the Web site for this volume.
7. According to information on the ILO Web site, between 1997 and 2001 unions issued two complaints about government practices in China, one in Hong Kong, one in Cambodia, one in Indonesia, two in Korea, one in the Philippines, one in Thailand, and none in Malaysia, Singapore, or Vietnam.
8. In the Philippines, the gross primary school enrollment rate, which is strongly and negatively correlated with child labor, fell from 99.2 percent in 1997–98 to 98.1 percent in 1998–99 (Lim 2000). Overall, however, there is no evidence of a significant increase in child labor use during the crisis in the Asia-Pacific region.
9. In export-oriented, labor-intensive sectors in labor-abundant countries that have weak labor standards, conditions of work would deteriorate. However, if the effect of trade liberalization is to draw workers from the informal sector, net conditions could improve. Overall, whether the informal sector expands or contracts would depend on the circumstances (Maskus 1997).
10. See Dollar and Collier (2001) and McCulloch, Winters, and Cirera (2001) for an extensive discussion.
11. Dollar and Collier (2001) and Dollar and Kraay (2002) are two of many sources on the effects of more open trade on East Asia. The child labor force participation rate in the East Asia–Pacific Region fell from 21.5 percent in 1995 to 19 percent in 2000, despite the economic crisis (UNICEF 1999; ILO 2002). Although for various reasons these estimates may not be strictly comparable, they do not suggest that child labor use significantly increased during the crisis. Edmonds and Pavcnik (2002), who studied household surveys in Vietnam, discovered that an increase in the real price of rice in the 1990s, associated largely with a decision to phase out the export quota on rice, raised net incomes of rural households enough to reduce the use of child labor sharply. By their estimates, a 30 percent increase in the price of a kilogram of rice led to a decline of nine percentage points in the use of child labor. The children, especially secondary school–age girls, were able to go to school instead.
12. EPZs are regions within an economy that offer firms—often multinational enterprises (MNEs)—tax advantages, free importation of inputs (or duty drawbacks), infrastructure development, and other inducements to locate there and produce goods for export (Madani 1999; Moran 2002).
13. Romero (1995) reports extensive evidence that wages are significantly higher in manufacturing jobs within EPZs than in similar positions outside. Moran (2002) provides ample anecdotal evidence that MNEs pay wages 20–25 percent higher than those paid by domestic firms for similar jobs. He also describes a process of continuing improvements in the 1990s in safety conditions, minimum wages, and benefits packages within several EPZs, including two (Mactan and Baguio City) in the Philippines (also see Jacobson 1999). Drezner (2001) reviews theories of why multinational firms are likely to be a force for raising standards.
14. See the discussion in the technical appendix to this chapter at www.worldbank.org/eaptrade.
15. Mah (1997), who studied 45 developing countries, found that the ratio of exports to gross domestic product (GDP) correlated negatively with decisions to ratify fundamental conventions on freedom-of-association rights and rights to nondiscrimination. But the lack of control variables in the equations estimated renders these results questionable.
16. Figures on the shares of labor-intensive manufactured exports in 1995–99 for eight East Asian economies are in Appendix Figure 1 of the technical appendix to this chapter at www.worldbank.org/eaptrade.
17. For example, the growth in volume of exports of apparel and textiles to key markets may have been constrained by quotas. It is also possible that the price impacts of depreciating exchange rates were relatively greater for labor-intensive goods, tending to reduce their values if not volumes.
18. Details of this analysis appear in the technical appendix to this chapter at www.worldbank.org/eaptrade.
19. The results using the third measure differ from those using the first and second ones. Close consideration of the three measures provides insight. The OECD measure of freedom-of-association rights is directly keyed on a central and fundamental basic labor right, and the Verite Labor Standards Index (VERLS), though it combines four approaches, incorporates enforcement and effective recognition of four core labor standards, and thus also focuses on basic rights. Both of these measures are suited to analyze the impacts of core labor protection on export performance, and these impacts appear to be positive. On its face, the third measure—the number of ILO ratifications—should also be an indicator of core labor rights, but, as explained earlier, it is a questionable measure of a country's actual commitment to improved working conditions.
20. Hasan and Quibria (2002) reach a similar conclusion, although their focus is on the determinants of poverty reduction rather than trade competitiveness.

21. The Korean government reduced its environmental expenditures from 2.5 percent of total expenditures in 1997 to 2.3 percent in 1998, although this reduction was not especially severe in relation to those for other programs (World Bank 2000).

22. Copeland and Taylor (2001) provide a clear presentation of this framework.

23. It is assumed that net output (total output less resources devoted to pollution abatement) is produced with constant returns to scale.

24. One important reason that a government would increase the pollution tax (or generally increase environmental regulation) is that voters demand a cleaner environment as incomes rise, justifiably assuming that environmental health is a normal good. Thus in the applied literature, the term *technique effect* generally refers to the idea that anything that raises per capita income generates an endogenous increase in environmental taxes, thereby reducing the pollution intensity of production. In this sense, the term is related to the so-called Kuznets environmental curve. However, it also refers to autonomous improvements in environmental technologies.

25. It could also mean domestic deregulation of services and changes in other policies, such as intellectual property rights, the effects of which are left aside here.

26. Per capita income would be higher despite changes in the distribution of income.

    Three comments are relevant here. First, the impacts of openness to trade are less clear when account is taken of input flows. Because inputs themselves may be dirty or clean, there is an additional comparative advantage effect to consider. (For example, if trade liberalization increases access to imported coal and petroleum, the net effect may be expanded output of dirty final goods even if there is a direct comparative disadvantage in them. Moreover, tariff cuts could expand the consumption of cheaper imported fuels.) Second, many analysts suggest that as incomes rise there will be an incentive to improve environmental technologies endogenously as a result of the higher demand for environmental protection associated with rising incomes. One direct means by which this could come about is the greater access that more open economies have to foreign technologies. In this context, trade openness provides an endogenous technique effect that could be decisive in improving environmental stewardship. Third, for the standard technique effect to operate, citizen demand for a cleaner environment must be mediated effectively through an increase in the cost of polluting the environment. In some cases, this mediation takes place through informal pressures (Wang and Wheeler 1999), but, generally, the government must respond to citizen preferences and raise environmental charges as incomes grow. Therefore, once again the openness and efficiency of the political process matter for environmental policy, as they do for labor standards. Barrett and Graddy (2000) find that increases in political freedoms significantly improve environmental quality.

27. It is conceivable that trade openness in rich countries contributes to better environmental quality in developing country exporters by moving workers out of environmentally harmful rural activities. However, this hypothesis has not been tested.

28. Not all would agree that FDI expands economic activity as much as it eliminates domestic competition.

29. Using data on sulfur dioxide concentrations in 293 sites in 44 countries from the Global Environment Monitoring Project over the period 1971–96, they decompose emissions into scale (GDP), composition (capital-labor endowment ratios), and technique (real income) effects, interacting each with a measure of openness to trade.

30. This insight underscores an important observation about the nexus between trade policy and environmental policy. In general, if environmental distortions are internalized efficiently, open trade enhances welfare.

31. It is possible they exist, but I could not locate any.

32. They regressed net exports in five pollution-intensive industries on measures of factor endowments and environmental laws in 24 countries (6 OECD countries, including Korea, and 18 developing countries) over the period 1994–98.

33. Figures on shares of pollution-intensive manufactured exports are in Figure 7.1 in the technical appendix to this chapter at www.worldbank.org/eaptrade.

34. Grossman and Krueger (1993) found no contribution of U.S. pollution intensity to U.S. imports from Mexico.

35. It is noteworthy that those countries experiencing the greatest stress from the crisis—Indonesia, Korea, the Philippines, and Thailand—registered these increases in export shares. This tendency was not evident in Malaysia and Taiwan (China). Again, such calculations are only suggestive, because many factors other than declining environmental costs or weak environmental standards could explain such changes in export shares.

36. Details of this analysis appear in the technical appendix to this chapter at www.worldbank.org/eaptrade.

37. One important MEA is the Convention on Biodiversity, whose commitments on the exploitation of genetic resources are at odds with rights established under the intellectual property agreement in the WTO. The Convention on Biodiversity does not itself implicate trade policy directly, but a recently added provision, the Protocol on Bio-safety, essentially permits countries to exclude imports on the basis of the precautionary principle. By permitting unilateral import restraints that could be more rigorous than those in the WTO's Agreement on the Application of Sanitary and Phytosanitary Measures, this policy could negatively affect exports of genetically modified foodstuffs from developing countries. For the East Asian countries, such exports are not significant, so this issue may be of limited importance unless the principle is extended to other forms of production processes.

38. One example is the shrimp-turtle case, in which the United States threatened to limit imports of shrimp from certain Southeast Asian countries failing to use turtle-excluder devices in their fishing fleets.

References

The word *processed* describes informally reproduced works that may not be commonly available through libraries.

Aggarwal, Mita. 1995. "International Trade, Labor Standards, and Labor Market Conditions: An Evaluation of the Linkages." Working Paper 95-06-C. U.S. International Trade Commission, Washington, D.C.

Anderson, Kym. 1996. "The Intrusion of Environmental and Labor Standards into Trade Policy." In Will Martin and L. Alan Winters, eds., *The Uruguay Round and the Developing Countries*. Cambridge: Cambridge University Press.

Antweiler, Werner, Brian R. Copeland, and M. Scott Taylor. 2001. "Is Free Trade Good for the Environment?" *American Economic Review* 91: 877–908.

APEC (Asia Pacific Economic Cooperation). 1999. *Study of Non-Tariff Measures in the Forest Products Sector.* Committee on Trade and Investment. Singapore: APEC.

———. 2001. *Survey of Environmental Markets in APEC.* Committee on Trade and Investment. Singapore: APEC.

Arunanondchai, May. 2001. "Trade Policy and the Welfare of Southeast Asian Timber Exporters: Some Implications for Forest Resources." Research Report. Economy and Environment Program for Southeast Asia.

Barrett, Scott, and Kathryn Graddy. 2000. "Freedom, Growth, and the Environment." *Environment and Development Economics* 5: 433–56.

Beghin, John C., Bradley J. Bowland, Sebastien Dessus, David Roland-Holst, and Dominique van der Mensbrugghe. 2000. "Trade Integration, Environmental Degradation, and Public Health in Chile: Assessing the Linkages." *Environment and Development Economics* 7: 241–67.

Betcherman, Gordon, and Rizwanul Islam, eds. 2001. *East Asian Labor Markets and the Economic Crisis.* Washington, D.C.: World Bank.

Copeland, Brian R., and M. Scott Taylor. 2001. "International Trade and the Environment: A Framework for Analysis." NBER Working Paper 8540. National Bureau of Economic Research, Cambridge, Mass.

Dean, Judith M. 2002. "Does Trade Liberalization Harm the Environment? A New Test." *Canadian Journal of Economics* 35 (4): 819–42.

Dollar, David, and Paul Collier. 2001. *Globalization, Growth, and Poverty: Building an Inclusive World Economy.* Oxford: Oxford University Press.

Dollar, David, and Art Kraay. 2002. "Growth Is Good for the Poor." *Journal of Economic Growth* 7 (3): 195–225.

Drezner, Daniel W. 2001. "Fears of a 'Race to the Bottom' on Wages and Labor Standards: Why Aren't They Justified?" University of Chicago. Processed.

Edmonds, Eric, and Nina Pavcnik. 2002. "Does Globalization Increase Child Labor? Evidence from Vietnam." NBER Working Paper 8760. National Bureau of Economic Research, Cambridge, Mass.

Elliott, Kimberly A. 2001. "Finding Our Way on Trade and Labor Standards?" International Economic Policy Briefs no. 01-5. Institute for International Economics, Washington, D.C.

Eskeland, Gunnar S., and Ann E. Harrison. 1997. "Moving to Greener Pastures? Multinationals and the Pollution Haven Hypothesis." World Bank, Washington, D.C. Processed.

Esty, Daniel C., and Peter K. Cornelius. 2002. *Environmental Performance Measurement: The Global Report 2001–2002.* Oxford: Oxford University Press.

Fields, Gary S. 1995. *Trade and Labor Standards: A Review of the Issues.* Paris: Organisation for Economic Co-operation and Development.

Freeman, Richard B. 1994. "A Hard-Headed Look at Labor Standards." In W. Sengenberger and D. Campbell, eds., *International Labor Standards and Economic Interdependence.* Geneva: International Labour Organization.

Grootaert, Christian, and Ravi Kanbur. 1995. "Child Labor: An Economic Perspective." *International Labour Review* 134: 187–203.

Grossman, Gene M., and Alan B. Krueger. 1993. "Environmental Impacts of a North American Free Trade Agreement." In Peter Garber, ed., *The U.S.-Mexico Free Trade Agreement.* Cambridge, Mass.: MIT Press.

Hasan, Rana, and M. G. Quibria. 2002. "Poverty and Patterns of Growth." ERD Working Paper No. 18. Asian Development Bank, Manila.

ILO (International Labour Organisation). 2002. *Every Child Counts: New Global Estimates of Child Labor.* Geneva.

Jacobson, Mark. 1999. "The Philippines: The Case of Economic Zones." In *Alleviating Poverty through Foreign Direct Investment: Country Case Studies.* Washington, D.C.: World Bank.

Jaffe, A., S. Peterson, P. Portney, and R. Stavins. 1995. "Environmental Regulation and the Competitiveness of U.S. Manufacturing. What Does the Evidence Tell Us?" *Journal of Economic Literature* 33: 132–63.

Keller, Wolfgang, and Arik Levinson. 2002. "Environmental Regulations and FDI to U.S. States." *Review of Economics and Statistics* 84, no. 4.

Kucera, David. 2001. "The Effects of Core Workers' Rights on Labor Costs and Foreign Direct Investment: Evaluating the 'Conventional Wisdom.'" ILO Discussion Paper DP/130/2001. International Labour Organisation, Geneva.

Levinson, Arik. 1996. "Environmental Regulation and Manufacturers' Location Choices: Evidence from the Census of Manufactures." *Journal of Public Economics* 62: 5–29.

Levinson, Arik, and M. Scott Taylor. 2001. "Trade and the Environment: Unmasking the Pollution Haven Effect." Georgetown University, Washington, D.C. Processed.

Lim, Joseph Y. 2000. "The East Asian Crisis and Child Labor in the Philippines." ILO/IPEC Working Paper 2000. Available at http://www.ilo.org/public/english/standards/ipec/publ/policy/papers/philippines/.

List, John A., and Catherine Y. Co. 1999. "The Effects of Environmental Regulations on Foreign Direct Investment." *Journal of Environmental Economics and Management* 40: 1–20.

Low, Patrick, and Alexander Yeats. 1992. "Do Dirty Industries Migrate?" In Patrick Low, ed. "International Trade and the Environment." World Bank Discussion Paper 159. Washington, D.C.

Lucas, R. E. B., D. Wheeler, and H. Hettige. 1990. "Economic Development, Environmental Regulation, and the International Migration of Toxic Industrial Pollution." Paper presented at Symposium on International Trade and the Environment, Washington, D.C.

Madani, Dorsati. 1999. "A Review of the Role and Impact of Export Processing Zones." Policy Research Working Paper 2238. World Bank, Washington, D.C.

Mah, Jai S. 1997. "Core Labor Standards and Export Performance in Developing Countries." *World Economy* 20: 773–85.

Mani, M., S. Pargal, and M. Huq. 1997. "Does Environmental Regulation Matter? Determinants of the Location of New Manufacturing Plants in India." Policy Research Working Paper 1718. World Bank, Washington, D.C.

Marinova, Nadja. 1999. "Indonesia's Fiery Crises." *Journal of Environment and Development* 8: 70–81.

Martin, William J., and Keith E. Maskus. 2001. "The Economics of Core Labor Standards: Implications for International Trade Policy." *Review of International Economics* 9: 317–28.

Maskus, Keith E. 1997. "Should Core Labor Standards Be Imposed through Trade Policy?" Policy Research Working Paper 1817. World Bank, Washington, D.C.

McCulloch, Neil, L. Alan Winters, and Xavier Cirera. 2001. *Trade Liberalization and Poverty: A Handbook.* London: Centre for Economic Policy Research.

Moran, Theodore H. 2002. *Beyond Sweatshops: Foreign Direct Investment and Globalization in Developing Countries.* Washington, D.C.: Brookings Institution.

OECD (Organisation for Economic Co-operation and Development). 1996. *Trade, Employment, and Labor Standards: A Study of Core Workers' Rights and International Trade.* Paris.

———. 2000. *International Trade and Core Labor Standards.* Paris.

Rodrik, Dani. 1996. "Labor Standards in International Trade: Do They Matter and What Do We Do about Them?" Overseas Development Council, Washington, D.C.

Romero, Ana Teresa. 1995. "Labor Standards and Export Processing Zones: Situation and Pressures for Change." *Development Policy Review* 13: 247–76.

Smarzynska, Beata, and Shang-Jin Wei. 2001. "Pollution Havens and Foreign Direct Investment: Dirty Secret or Popular Myth?" CEPR Discussion Paper 2966. Centre for Economic Policy Research, London.

Suryahadi, Asep, Wenefrida Widyant, Daniel Perwira, and Sudarno Sumarto. 2003. "Minimum Wage Policy and Its Impact on Employment in the Urban Formal Sector." *Bulletin of Indonesian Economic Studies* 39 (1): 29–50.

Sykes, Allan. 1995. *Product Standards in a Globalizing World.* Washington, D.C.: Brookings Institution.

Tobey, J. A. 1990. "The Effects of Domestic Environmental Policies on Patterns of World Trade: An Empirical Test." *Kyklos* 43: 191–209.

UNICEF (United Nations Children's Fund). 1999. *The State of the World's Children, 1999: Education.* Geneva.

U.S. Department of Labor. 1994. *By the Sweat and Toil of Children.* Vol. 1, *The Use of Child Labor in U.S. Manufactured and Mined Imports.* Washington, D.C.

Van Beers, Cees. 1998. "Labor Standards and Trade Flows of OECD Countries." *World Economy* 21: 57–73.

Verite. 2002. "Report to California Public Employees' Retirement System (CalPERS): Emerging Markets Research Project." Available at verite@verite.org.

Wang, Hua, and David Wheeler. 1999. "Endogenous Enforcement and Effectiveness of China's Pollution Levy System." Development Research Group. World Bank, Washington, D.C.

Wheeler, David S. 2001. "Racing to the Bottom? Foreign Investment and Air Pollution in Developing Countries." *Journal of Environment and Development* 10: 225–45.

Wilson, John S., Tsunehiro Otsuki, and Mirvat Sewadeh. 2002. "Dirty Exports and Environmental Regulation: Do Standards Matter to Trade?" Development Research Group. World Bank, Washington, D.C.

World Bank. 1999. "*Environmental Implications of the Economic Crisis and Adjustment in East Asia.*" East Asia Environment and Social Development Unit, Discussion Paper 01. Washington, D.C.

———. 2000. *Korea: The Environmental Dimension of the Crisis: A Step Back of a New Way Forward?* Washington, D.C.

———. 2001a. *East Asia Regional Overview Special Focus: Environment.* Washington D.C.

———. 2001b. *Indonesia: Environment and Natural Resource Management in a Time of Transition.* Washington, D.C.

———. 2001c. *World Development Indicators 2001.* Washington, D.C.: World Bank.

World Resources Institute. 2002. *Reefs at Risk in Southeast Asia.* Available at: www.wri.org/wri/reefsatrisk/reefriskseasia.html.

Xu, X. 1999. *International Trade and Environmental Regulation: A Dynamic Perspective.* Huntington, N.Y.: Nova Science Publishers.

PART III

REINFORCING SOCIAL STABILITY THROUGH BROAD SHARING OF BENEFITS

8

HOUSEHOLD WELFARE IMPACTS OF CHINA'S ACCESSION TO THE WTO

Shaohua Chen
Martin Ravallion

China's recent accession to the World Trade Organization (WTO) brings with it sharp reductions in import tariffs, quantitative restrictions, and export subsidies, with implications for the domestic structure of prices and wages and thus for the welfare of Chinese households. Even if the trade reforms have little effect on poverty and income distribution in the aggregate, the impacts may vary across household types and regions, with implications for the design of compensatory policy responses.

In China, the economic geography of poverty, and its interaction with the geographic diversity in the impact of policy reforms, is high on the domestic policy agenda. A policy analysis that simply averages such differences would miss a great deal of what matters to the policy debate. In this chapter, data from national household surveys for rural and urban areas are used to measure and explain the welfare impacts on households of changes in goods and factor prices stemming from the accession. The approach respects the richness of detail that is available from a modern integrated household survey, allowing us to go well beyond the highly aggregative types of analysis one often finds. Our analysis measures the expected impacts across the distribution of initial levels of living, but it also examines the way in which the impacts vary by other household characteristics, including location and demographic characteristics. A reasonably detailed "map" of the predicted welfare impacts by location and socioeconomic characteristics therefore emerges.

The first section of this chapter briefly reviews the approaches that typically have been used in analyzing the welfare impacts of trade reform. It is followed by a summary of the approach taken in this chapter. The penultimate section describes the results of our analysis, and our conclusions follow.

The authors are grateful to Tamar Manuelyan-Atinc and Will Martin for their encouragement to undertake this task, to Elena Ianchovichina and Will Martin for the estimates of the price impacts of China's trade reform that are crucial to this study, and to Pingping Wang, Yan Fang, Liqun Peng, Honge Gong, and Min Yuan for their help in matching variables from China rural/urban household surveys to the categories of the general equilibrium model. The comments of François Bourguignon, John Cockburn, Neil McCulloch, Sangui Wang, Shujiro Urata and participants in the Fourth Asian Development Forum in Seoul, the seminar at the Tokyo office of the World Bank, and the National Bureau of Statistics in Beijing are gratefully acknowledged.

Measuring the Welfare Impacts of Trade Reform

The literature contains much debate about the welfare impacts of greater openness to trade. Some authors argue that external trade liberalization benefits the poor in developing countries, while others assert that the benefits are captured more by the nonpoor. Assessments have focused particularly on the expected impacts on relative wages (notably between skilled and unskilled labor) and relative prices (such as between food staples and luxury imports).

What does the evidence suggest? One might hope to provide a conclusive answer by comparing changes over time in measures of inequality or poverty between countries that are open to external trade and countries that are not. Thus several studies have combined levels of measured inequality, or changes over time in measured inequality or poverty, with data on trade openness and other control variables, using aggregate cross-country data sets (for example, see Bourguignon and Morisson 1990; Edwards 1997; Li, Squire, and Zou 1998; Lundberg and Squire 1999; Barro 2000; Dollar and Kraay 2002; and Milanovic 2002).

There are reasons, however, to be cautious in drawing policy inferences from such studies. First, concerns have emerged about data and econometric specification. Differences in survey design and processing between countries, and over time within countries, can distort the measured levels and the apparent differences in inequality. Second, the extent to which cross-country data sets can detect any underlying effects of greater openness or other covariates is unclear. Another issue is whether the volume of trade should be treated as exogenous in these cross-country regressions. It is clearly not a policy variable as such, and it may well be highly correlated with other (latent) attributes of country performance independently of trade policy. Attribution of inequality impacts to trade policy reforms per se is clearly problematic.

Furthermore, starting conditions vary widely among reforming countries, and averaging across this diversity can readily hide systematic effects of relevance to policy. For example, countries differ in their initial levels of economic development. It has been argued that greater openness to external trade

will have very different effects on inequality depending on the level of economic development—raising inequality in rich countries and reducing it in poor ones.[1] But the opposite outcome is possible when economic reforms, including trade liberalization, increase the demand for relatively skilled labor, which may well be less equally distributed in poor countries than in rich ones. Regressions for inequality across countries show some evidence of a *negative* interaction effect between openness to trade and initial gross domestic product (GDP) per capita (Barro 2000; Ravallion 2001; Milanovic 2002).

In principle, these problems can be dealt with by introducing suitable nonlinearities (including interaction effects) into the regressions based on compilations of country aggregates. However, the concerns go deeper. For example, although aggregate inequality or poverty may not change with trade reform, there may be both gainers and losers at all levels of living. Indeed, when surveys have tracked the same families over time, it is quite common to find that many people have escaped from poverty, while others have fallen into poverty, even though the overall poverty rate may have moved rather little.[2] As another example, geographic disparities in access to human and physical infrastructure, between and within developing countries, affect the prospects for participating in the growth generated by reform, and these disparities tend to be correlated with incomes.[3] A reform may well entail sizable redistributions between the poor and the rich, but in opposite directions in different regions within countries. One should not be surprised to find no correlation between growth and changes in inequality, or that, on average, a policy reform has virtually no impact on inequality. Yet nonrandom distributional changes could well be going on beneath the surface of the average impact statistics. A policy analysis that simply averages over such differences would miss a great deal of what matters to the debate on policy.

This chapter follows a different approach for which the attribution to trade policy changes is unambiguous and the diversity of welfare impacts is not lost. It studies welfare impacts at the household level of changes in commodity and factor prices attributed to a specific trade policy reform—China's accession to the WTO.

Our Approach in This Chapter

Past approaches to studying the welfare impacts of specific trade reforms have tended to be either *partial equilibrium analyses*, in which the welfare impacts of the direct price changes resulting from tariff changes are measured at the household level, or *general equilibrium analyses*, in which second-round responses are captured in a theoretically consistent way, but with considerable aggregation across household types.[4] Although partial equilibrium analysis requires little or no aggregation of the primary household data, it misses potentially important indirect effects on prices and wages. General equilibrium analysis has the power to capture these effects by simulating the economy-wide impacts on markets. Standard computable general equilibrium (CGE) models, however, entail consideration aggregation across household types, with rarely more than six or so "representative households." Such models are crude tools for welfare distributional analysis.

The challenge for applied work is to find an approach that respects the richness of detail available from a modern integrated household survey, while assuring that the price changes attributed to reform are internally consistent with economy-wide equilibrium conditions. Anyone addressing this challenge can in principle build the CGE model onto the household survey, such that the number of households in the model is the number sampled in the survey.[5] In our analysis, this degree of integration would require a CGE model of extraordinarily high dimensions, with 85,000 households (the total sample size of the surveys we use). This route is not a feasible one at present.

Instead, we follow an intermediate approach in which the reform-induced commodity and factor price changes simulated from a general equilibrium model are carried to the level of all the sampled households in the survey.[6] In measuring the welfare impacts, we use standard tools of analysis familiar from past work on the welfare effects of price changes associated with tax and trade policy reform. Our approach imposes minimal aggregation conditions on the survey data, within unavoidable data limitations. In addition to calculating the overall effects of a trade reform on poverty and inequality, we are able to provide a detailed socioe-

conomic "map" of impact, showing how it varies with other "non-income" characteristics, such as location. In this way, we are better able to answer the questions policymakers are asking about who gains and who loses from reform.

In our analysis, we use past estimates of the direct and indirect impacts of China's WTO accession on prices for both commodities and factors of production, as reported in Ianchovichina and Martin (2002), and apply standard methods of first-order welfare analysis to measure the gains and losses at the household level.[7]

The price changes induced by the trade policy change are simulated from the CGE model used by Ianchovichina and Martin (2002). This competitive market-clearing model originated in the Global Trade Analysis Project (GTAP).[8] In this model, the revenue implications of the trade policy change are reflected in changes in indirect tax rates.

The CGE model is applied to the data from large national sample surveys of households in urban and rural areas of China carried out by the National Bureau of Statistics (NBS). The general equilibrium analysis generates a set of price and wage changes. These changes embody both the direct price effects of the trade policy change and the "second-round" indirect effects on the prices of nontraded goods and on factor returns, including effects that make themselves felt through the government's budget constraint. Because the price changes are based on an explicit model, their attribution to the trade policy reform is unambiguous, thereby avoiding the identification problems common to past attempts to estimate the distributional effects of trade policy reform using cross-country comparisons.

The welfare impacts are derived from a household model that incorporates own-production activities. The CGE and household-level analyses are not integrated—with 85,000 households in the survey; doing so would require an extraordinarily large CGE model. The microsimulations are built on economic assumptions that are consistent with the CGE model—notably, that households take prices as given and that those prices clear all markets—but no attempt was made to ensure full consistency between the microanalysis and the predictions of the CGE model. Chen and Ravallion (2004) describe our methods of measuring the welfare impacts in detail.

The survey data were taken from the 1999 Rural Household Survey (RHS) and the 1999 Urban Household Survey (UHS), both carried out by China's National Bureau of Statistics. The RHS sample covers 67,900 households, and the UHS covers 16,900.[9] NBS kindly provided the microdata for three provinces (Liaoning, Guangdong, and Sichuan), called here the "test provinces." The computer program to implement the estimation method was written for these data, after which NBS staff ran the program on the entire national data set.

Before China's accession to the WTO in 2001, its economy had already begun to adapt to the expected change. Chinese trade reform can thus be considered as having two stages: a lead-up period, in which tariffs started to fall in anticipation of WTO accession, and the period from 2001 onward. Ianchovichina and Martin (2002) argue that 1995 is a plausible beginning of the lead-up period, and we use their estimates of the price changes induced by WTO accession for the periods 1995–2001 and 2001–07. The discussion that follows focuses mainly on the latter period, although estimates of the welfare impacts for the lead-up period are also provided.

We calculated the welfare impacts to the survey data for 1999. This year was chosen in part for data reasons; it was the most recent year for which access to the microdata could be obtained. Also, we believe that choosing a year near the middle of the lead-up period rather than at the beginning or end might diminish possible biases caused by any nonlinearity in the welfare impacts of price and wage changes.

Results

Summarized here are the results described in Chen and Ravallion (2004). Appendix Table 8.1 and Appendix Table 8.2[10] show the predicted changes in relative prices and wages in China during 1995–2001 and 2001–07, respectively, as obtained from the China GTAP model of Ianchovichina and Martin (2002). The tables also show the mean net revenue per capita for urban and rural areas, based on the 1999 rural and urban household surveys.

Measured Welfare Impacts of WTO Accession

Based on the relative price changes from the China GTAP model and production/consumption shares from the 1999 rural/urban household survey data,

the net gain (or loss) for each household can be computed.[11] Table 8.1 summarizes the results. Section 1 of the table gives the mean gains for the periods 1995–2001 and 2001–07, split by urban and rural areas.

Section 2 of Table 8.1 shows the impacts on income inequality, both actual (for the baseline year, 1999) and simulated for the two stages of the trade reform. The simulated income distribution is obtained, for the first stage, by subtracting the estimated gains over 1995–2001 from the 1999 incomes at household level and, for the second stage, by adding the household-specific gains from 2001–07 to the 1999 incomes. Thus the first simulation gives the distributional impact of the price changes during the first stage of the reform—that is, what the baseline distribution would have looked like without the reforms—and the second shows the impact of the post-2001 price changes—that is, how those changes are expected to affect the baseline distribution, looking forward.

Section 3 of Table 8.1 gives the headcount index of poverty as measured by various poverty lines. The "official poverty line" gives estimates based on the poverty lines used by the National Bureau of Statistics, while the "$1/day" and "$2/day" lines are those from Chen and Ravallion (2001).

The overall gain in mean income is about 1.5 percent, all in the period leading up to WTO accession. There is almost no impact on inequality, either in the period leading up to WTO accession or predicting forward. The aggregate Gini index increases slightly, from 39.3 percent without WTO accession to 39.5 percent post-WTO.

In 1999 the incidence of poverty would have been slightly higher had there been no trade policy changes over the lead-up period to WTO accession, but that from 2001 to 2007 will increase very slightly as a result of the price changes expected to be induced by the remaining tariff changes.

The impacts of WTO accession on poverty as measured by a wide range of poverty lines are revealed in Figures 8.1 and 8.2, which give the cumulative distributions of income for both the baseline and the two simulated distributions, for the poorest 60 percent in rural areas and the poorest 40 percent in urban areas.

In the aggregate, then, WTO accession has virtually no predicted impact on poverty and inequality. Disaggregating the results, predicting forward from

TABLE 8.1   Predicted Aggregate Impacts on Welfare of Rural and Urban Households

	Rural	Urban	National
1. Mean gains (yuan per capita)			
1995–2001	34.47	94.94	55.49 (1.54%)[a]
2001–07	–18.07	29.45	–1.54 (–0.04%)[a]
2. Inequality impacts (Gini index as %)			
Baseline (1999)	33.95	29.72	39.31
Simulated: less gains 1995–2001	33.90	29.68	39.27
Simulated: plus gains 2001–07	34.06	29.65	39.53
3. Poverty impacts (headcount index, %)			
Official poverty line			
Baseline (1999)	4.38	0.08	2.92
Simulated: less gains 1995–2001	4.56	0.08	3.04
Simulated: plus gains 2001–07	4.57	0.07	3.04
$1/day (1993 PPP)			
Baseline (1999)	10.51	0.29	7.04
Simulated: less gains 1995–2001	10.88	0.28	7.28
Simulated: plus gains 2001–07	10.81	0.28	7.23
$2/day (1993 PPP)			
Baseline (1999)	45.18	4.07	31.20
Simulated: less gains 1995–2001	46.10	4.27	31.88
Simulated: plus gains 2001–07	45.83	3.97	31.60

Note: PPP = purchasing power parity.
a. Percentage of mean income.
Source: The authors.

FIGURE 8.1   Poverty Incidence Curves: Rural

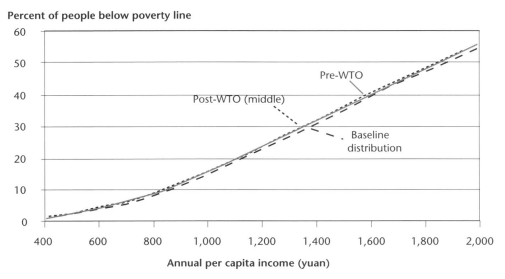

Source: The authors.

FIGURE 8.2   Poverty Incidence Curves: Urban

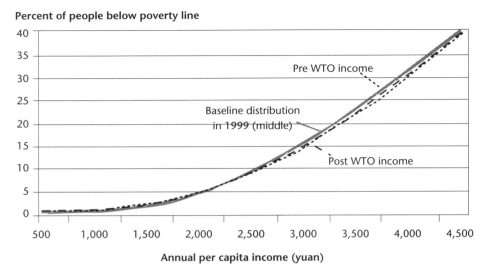

Source: The authors.

WTO accession, we focused on three indicators of impact at the household level: the absolute gain or loss in yuan, the percentage gain or loss, and whether the change is a gain or a loss. Our interest in the first two measures is obvious enough. We included the third to help determine where there might be high concentrations of losses—whether in specific geographic areas or socioeconomic groups.

About three-fourths of rural households and one-tenth of urban residents are predicted to lose real income in the period 2001–07. Farm income is predicted to drop by 18 yuan per person, while urban per capita income rises by 29 yuan (Appendix Table 5.3 and Appendix Table 5.4). The drop in rural income is caused by the drop in the wholesale prices of most farm products, plus higher prices for education and health care (Appendix Table 5.2). Yet farmers will benefit from the drop in some consumer prices and from the increase in nonfarm labor wages. Urban residents will enjoy lower prices for most farm products and higher wages, but they also will be hit by higher fees for education and health care.

Impacts differ widely across regions, as evident in Figures 8.3, 8.4, and 8.5, which plot the results by provinces ranked by mean income per person.[12] The mean absolute gains tend to be highest in the richest provinces in both urban and rural areas (Figure 8.3), although there is no correlation

between proportionate gains and the mean income of the province (Figure 8.4).

One spatially contiguous region stands out as losing the most from trade reform—the northeast provinces of Heilongjiang, Inner Mongolia, Jilin, and Liaoning (Appendix Table 5.3). Both the absolute and proportionate impacts are highest in this region; indeed, more than 90 percent of farmers in Heilongjiang and Jilin are expected to experience a net loss in income.

When households are ranked by initial income, there is a notable difference between urban and rural households. Figures 8.6, 8.7, and 8.8 plot the results given earlier against percentiles of the income distribution. For example, the mean impact in yuan per capita at the median income level is revealed by looking at the 50th percentile in Figure 8.6. (Figure 8.6 gives the horizontal differences in Figures 8.1 and 8.2 plotted against the point on the vertical axis.)

The absolute gains tend to be higher for higher-income households in urban areas and lower for low-income households in rural areas. Nationally (combining urban and rural areas using the weights described in the technical appendix to this chapter), there is a hint of a U-shaped relationship, though still with the highest absolute gains for the rich.

This pattern flips when one looks at the proportionate gains (Figure 8.7). In urban areas, the proportionate gains tend to fall as income rises, but in

FIGURE 8.3   Mean Gains by Provinces: Absolute Gains in Yuan Per Capita

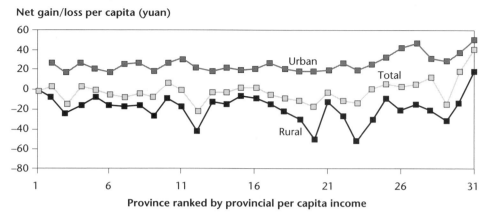

Source: The authors.

FIGURE 8.4   Mean Gains by Provinces: Proportionate Gains in Percent

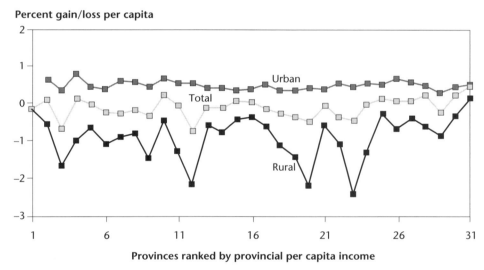

Source: The authors.

rural areas and nationally they rise with income. In the aggregate, a higher proportion of gainers is evident as one moves up the income ladder, which is driven by the rise in the number of gainers as income increases within rural areas (Figure 8.8).

Incidence of Gains and Losses

Which types of households gain and which lose? The technical appendix to this chapter describes in formal terms the model for explaining the incidence of gains and losses as a function of household characteristics. We estimated the model for the three test provinces—Liaoning, Guangdong, and Sichuan—for which complete microdata were available. The key characteristics considered included the age of household head, education and demographic characteristics, and land (interpreted as a fixed factor of production because it is allocated largely by administrative means in rural China). We considered rural and urban areas separately; there are some differences in the explanatory variables between them.

FIGURE 8.5   Mean Gains by Provinces: Percentage of Gainers

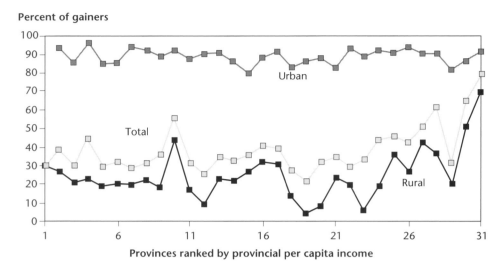

Source: The authors.

FIGURE 8.6   Mean Gains in Yuan, by Income Percentile

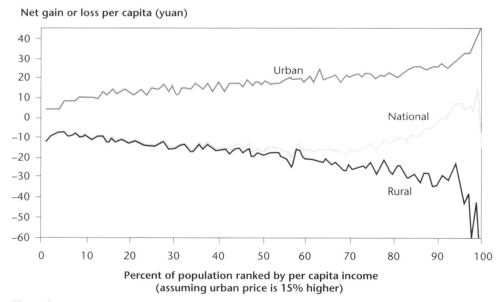

Source: The authors.

The results are given in Appendix Tables 8.6 and 8.7 for rural areas and Appendix Tables 8.8 and 8.9 for urban areas. Because these results are averages across the impacts of these characteristics on the consumption and production choices that determine the welfare impact of given price and wage changes, they are difficult to interpret. We view them as mainly of descriptive interest, to help iso-late covariates of potential relevance in thinking about compensatory policy responses.

Looking first at rural areas, in all three provinces the predicted gain from trade reform tends to be larger for larger households. There is also a U-shaped relationship with the age of the household head, such that the gains reach a minimum at about 50 years of age (47 in Liaoning, 52 in Guangdong,

FIGURE 8.7   Mean Percentage Gain, by Income Percentile

Percent net gain or loss per capita

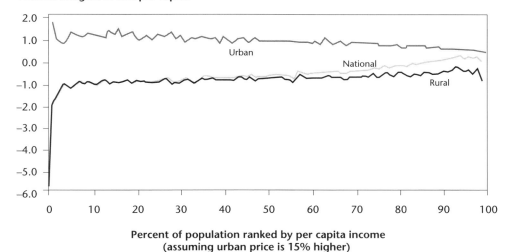

Percent of population ranked by per capita income
(assuming urban price is 15% higher)

Source: The authors.

FIGURE 8.8   Percentage of Gainers, by Income Percentile

Percent of gainers

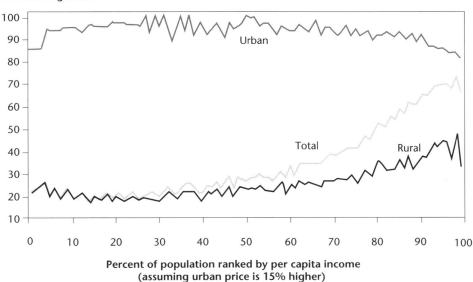

Percent of population ranked by per capita income
(assuming urban price is 15% higher)

Source: The authors.

and 55 in Sichuan). The gains are smaller for agricultural households. They are larger for households with more employees, more workers in township and village enterprises, more migrant workers, and less cultivated land (although the last finding is significant only in Liaoning). The only strong demographic effect is that younger households (those with a higher proportion of children under six) tend to be gainers in Liaoning.

For agricultural households, predicted losses are significantly higher than average in six counties in Liaoning (losses of from 3 to 5.6 percent versus the provincial average of 1.3 percent), seven counties in Guangdong (from 2.5 to 5.3 percent versus the provincial average of 0.8 percent), and six counties in Sichuan (from 2.8 to 5.7 percent versus the provincial average of 0.7 percent)—see Appendix Table 8.10.

In urban areas, the gains tend to be larger for smaller households (except in Guangdong). As in rural areas, there is a U-shaped pattern (except in Liaoning), with the smallest gains for households whose heads were 66 years of age in Guangdong and 51 years in Sichuan. By contrast with rural areas, where we find no relationship between education levels and welfare gains, in urban areas the gains tend to be larger for less well-educated households.[13] There are signs of some sectoral effects, although only significantly so in Liaoning, with higher gains for those in government jobs. Signs of larger gains are evident among those whose employer is the government. Retirees tend to gain less than others.

Conclusions

In the aggregate, the finding is that China's accession to the WTO has only a small impact on mean household income, inequality, and incidence of poverty. There is, however, a sizable, and at least partly explicable, variance in impacts across households of different characteristics. Rural families tend to lose; urban households tend to gain. Impacts are larger in some provinces than others, and largest in the geographically contiguous northeast region of Heilongjiang, Inner Mongolia, Jilin, and Liaoning. In this region rural households depend more on feed grain production (for which falling prices are expected from WTO accession) than those elsewhere in China. Such impact "mapping" can be used to guide targeted safety net programs.

Within rural or urban areas of a given province, the gains from WTO accession vary with observable household characteristics. The most vulnerable households tend to be rural, to be dependent on agriculture, to have relatively few workers, and to have weak economic links to the outside economy through migration. There are also some strong geographic concentrations of adverse impacts. For example, agricultural households in certain counties of Guangdong, Liaoning, and Sichuan incur predicted welfare losses of 3–5 percent of their incomes.

This incidence analysis suggests that encouraging labor flexibility is central to protecting households adversely affected by reforms. But workers need skills to be flexible, and they must be allowed to move occupationally and geographically, suggesting that labor market reforms must be carried out in parallel with trade reforms. In China, even though its degree of labor mobility is considerable (as evidenced by the large migrant population), restrictions and impediments remain. With increased labor flexibility, more rural households can potentially benefit from WTO accession. However, to assess properly the impact of changes in internal labor mobility policy on household welfare, we would require a richer data set and additional behavioral assumptions, which suggests a future research agenda.

Naturally, this approach has other limitations. A case in point: some dynamic gains from trade liberalization may not be captured by the model used to generate the relative price impacts. For example, trade may well facilitate learning about new technologies and innovation that brings longer-term gains in productivity. These effects may be better revealed by studying time-series evidence, combined with cross-country comparisons.

The geographic differences identified in welfare impacts arise entirely from differences in household consumption and production behavior. In reality, trade reform is likely to have differential impacts on local prices as a result of transport or other impediments to internal trade. Our approach does not incorporate such differences, and doing so would pose data and analytical problems. This direction might, however, be a fruitful one for future work in settings in which the necessary data on prices and wage levels by geographic area are available.

Another limitation of the approach is that, as explained in the technical appendix, we had to make linear approximations in the neighborhood of an initial optimum for each household. In other applications using this method, doing so may be deceptive if the price or wage changes are large, or if a household is initially out of equilibrium, perhaps because of rationing (including involuntary unemployment). In principle, there are ways to deal with these problems by estimating complete demand and supply systems, allowing for rationing. This avenue may prove to be a fruitful one for future research, but it should be noted that such methods generate their own problems, such as those arising from incomplete data on price and wage levels at the household level.

While acknowledging these limitations, we believe that the type of approach offered here can still illuminate the likely short-term distributional impacts of economy-wide reforms, with minimum aggregation. By avoiding unnecessary aggregation of the primary household-level data, the relatively simple tools described here can also offer insights into the kinds of policy responses that might be needed to compensate losers from reform.

Endnotes

1. Wood (1994) makes a qualified argument along these lines.
2. Jalan and Ravallion (1998) report evidence of such churning using panel data for rural China. Baulch and Hoddinott (2000) review evidence for a number of countries.
3. In the context of China's lagging poor areas, see Jalan and Ravallion (2002).
4. For an overview of alternative approaches to assessing the welfare impacts of trade policies and examples, see McCulloch, Winters, and Cirera (2001).
5. The only example of this full integration known to us is that by Cockburn (2002), who built a classic, trade-focused CGE model onto the Nepal Living Standards Survey covering about 3,000 households.
6. In an antecedent to our approach, Bourguignon, Robilliard, and Robinson (2003) also take price changes generated by a CGE model to survey data (for Indonesia). Methodologically, the main difference is that we derive first-order welfare impacts analytically from a standard competitive farm-household model, and Bourguignon and his colleagues generate income impacts at the household level from a microeconometric model of income determination.
7. Details of the methodology and data treatment are given in the technical appendix to this chapter at www.world bank.org/eaptrade. The appendix includes a discussion of the main assumptions underlying the CGE framework. See also Chen and Ravallion (2004).
8. Papers describing the standard GTAP with applications can be found in Hertel (1997). A full discussion of the assumptions of the general equilibrium model and the results of its application to China's accession to the WTO can be found in Ianchovichina and Martin (2002).
9. The full sample of the UHS in 1999 was about 40,000 households. Since 2002 the central office has kept the data on all 40,000 households.

   Over the past 15 years, the NBS has made a great effort to improve both the RHS and UHS, focusing on sample coverage, questionnaire design, survey methodology, and data processing. The number of variables in the surveys has increased dramatically, with additional details on income, expenditure, savings, housing, and productivity, among other things. However, some problems remain in the 1999 RHS and UHS. For its sample frame, the RHS relies on its sampled counties from 1985. The UHS excludes rural migrants, because the base of the UHS sample frame is the

legal registration system (*Hukou*). As in other countries, the RHS gives data on the remittances of migrant workers, but does not provide information about the migrant workers themselves, who (unlike in other countries) are not sampled in the urban survey either. It is therefore difficult to measure impacts through labor mobility and rural-urban transfers in the present study. Comparisons between the RHS and UHS also pose problems. For example, income in the RHS includes income in-kind (such as from own-farm production and other household enterprises), but income in the UHS ignores some in-kind components, notably subsidies received from the government. For further discussion in the context of the RHS, see Chen and Ravallion (1996).

10. All the appendix tables cited in this section appear in the technical appendix to this chapter at www.world bank.org/eaptrade. See also Chen and Ravallion (2004).
11. Using equation 3, as explained in the technical appendix.
12. For the province rankings, see Appendix Table 8.5 at www.worldbank.org/eaptrade.
13. This finding may be biased by the fact that, as explained in the technical appendix at www.worldbank.org/eaptrade, we had to use education levels to identify skilled labor (noting that wages of unskilled nonfarm workers are predicted to increase relative to those of skilled labor, as shown in Appendix Tables 8.6–8.8).

References

Barro, Robert. 2000. "Inequality and Growth in a Panel of Countries." *Journal of Economic Growth* 5: 5–32.

Baulch, Bob, and John Hoddinott. 2000. "Economic Mobility and Poverty Dynamics in Developing Countries." *Journal of Development Studies* 36 (6): 1–24.

Bourguignon, François, and C. Morisson. 1990. "Income Distribution, Development and Foreign Trade." *European Economic Review* 34: 1113–32.

Bourguignon, François, Anne-Sophie Robilliard, and Sherman Robinson. 2003. "Representative versus Real Households in the Macro-Economic Modeling of Inequality." Working Paper 2003-05. DELTA, Paris.

Chen, Shaohua, and Martin Ravallion. 1996. "Data in Transition: Assessing Rural Living Standards in Southern China." *China Economic Review* 7: 23–56.

———. 2001. "How Did the World's Poor Fare in the 1990s?" *Review of Income and Wealth* 47 (3): 283–300.

———. 2004. "Welfare Impacts of China's Accession to the WTO." *World Bank Economic Review*, forthcoming.

Cockburn, John. 2002. "Trade Liberalization and Poverty in Nepal: A Computable General Equilibrium Micro Simulation Analysis." University of Laval, Quebec. Processed.

Dollar, David, and Art Kraay. 2002. "Growth Is Good for the Poor." *Journal of Economic Growth* 7 (3): 195–225.

Edwards, S. 1997. "Trade Policy, Growth, and Income Distribution." *American Economic Review, Papers and Proceedings* 87 (2): 205–10.

Hertel, T. W., ed. 1997. *Global Trade Analysis: Modeling and Applications.* Cambridge: Cambridge University Press.

Ianchovichina, Elena, and William Martin. 2002. "Economic Impacts of China's Accession to the WTO." Paper presented at Seminar on WTO Accession, Policy Reform and Poverty Reduction in China, World Bank, Beijing, June 28–29.

Jalan, Jyotsna, and Martin Ravallion. 1998. "Transient Poverty in Post-reform Rural China." *Journal of Comparative Economics* 26: 338–57.

Li, Hongyi, Lyn Squire, and Heng-fu Zou. 1998. "Explaining International and Intertemporal Variations in Income Inequality." *Economic Journal* 108: 26–43.

Lundberg, Mattias, and Lyn Squire. 1999. "Growth and Inequality: Extracting the Lessons for Policymakers." World Bank, Washington, D.C. Processed.

McCulloch, Neil, L. Alan Winters, and Xavier Cirera. 2001. *Trade Liberalization and Poverty: A Handbook.* London: Centre for Economic Policy Research.

Milanovic, Branko. 2002. "Can We Discern the Effect of Globalization on Income Distribution?" Policy Research Working Paper 2876. World Bank, Washington, D.C.

Ravallion, Martin. 2001. "Growth, Inequality and Poverty: Looking Beyond Averages." *World Development* 29 (11): 1803–15.

Wood, Adrian. 1994. *North-South Trade, Employment and Inequality. Changing Fortunes in a Skill-Driven World.* Oxford: Clarendon Press.

9

TRADE IN SECTORS IMPORTANT TO THE POOR: RICE IN CAMBODIA AND VIETNAM AND CASHMERE IN MONGOLIA

Jehan Arulpragasam
Francesco Goletti
Tamar Manuelyan Atinc
Vera Songwe

Trade liberalization has profoundly changed the determinants of national economic growth and social development. World trade is now growing much faster than the world gross domestic product (GDP), so that growth opportunities are typically greater for exports than they are for domestic sales. But the extent to which poor people, especially poor producers, benefit from expanded trade opportunities often depends on complementary measures designed to tackle behind-the-border constraints to efficient production and exports. These measures include ones to foster the development of competitive markets and public action to provide information, reduce transaction costs that are often high as a result of corruption, deliver public services, and address market and collective action failures. Poor producers are not only economically disadvantaged but also often politically powerless, and when their interests are pitted against those of more powerful actors, they frequently lose. Understanding the institutional and political economy underpinnings of the organizational structure of a particular commodity or sector is crucial for designing a set of measures that enables the poor to take fuller advantage of greater access to markets.

The studies underpinning this chapter illustrate the kind of analysis—using a supply chain approach—that is needed to inform policymakers and the directions that need to be taken to ensure that trade opportunities reach the poor. The illustrative case studies focus on two sectors—rice in Cambodia and Vietnam and cashmere in Mongolia. Why rice and cashmere? For one important reason: in the countries considered, the two commodities provide a livelihood for the majority of poor people, and therefore any gains in productivity or in the share of producers in the value chain will lead to improvements in poor people's welfare. The value chain is the steps of the production system (from raw producer to consumer) as well as the linkages among the networks of producers, exporters, importers, and retailers along the way.

The authors gratefully acknowledge helpful comments from Florian Alburo and participants in seminars held at the Institute for Southeast Asian Studies of the National University of Singapore and at the World Bank office in Ulaanbaatar.

149

In Cambodia and Vietnam, as in much of Asia, most of the poor earn a living by growing rice, and the rice culture permeates the farming traditions of the region. In Mongolia, livestock herding, a tradition that is centuries old, provides a livelihood for most of the rural population. These are traditional economic activities of the poor, determined by history and country context, and higher productivity and returns to producers in these subsectors would have a vital impact on the livelihoods of the poor.

Why value chain analysis? The main remaining constraints to improvements in the welfare of poor producers engaging in rice and cashmere production are related to sectoral policy. Domestic trade policies, by and large, no longer represent important impediments, which means that exporters receive the undistorted prices signals from international markets. At the other end of the export chain, producers have incentives to respond to price signals, because they now have full property rights over their assets or the returns to those assets, thanks to the increased security of land tenure in Vietnam and the privatization of livestock in Mongolia. But between the two ends of the supply chain is a host of institutional and policy constraints that tend to interfere in the transmission of the price signals and reduce the ability of poor producers to benefit from expanding opportunities.

For transition economies such as Vietnam, Cambodia, and Mongolia, institutional constraints are particularly prevalent.[1] Indeed, transition economies making the complex move from a command economy regime to a more market-oriented one are subject to particular challenges and constraints that value chain analysis is well placed to identify and assess.

First, the removal of the administratively dictated value chains found under a command economy (e.g., where a certain set of economic agents is commanded to sell to another set of economic agents, perhaps with the prohibition of entry of other agents) is expected to (indeed, intended to) result in a structural transformation. State-owned enterprises that may have had a monopoly or a monopsony under such an arrangement will become subject to competition. Low levels of efficiency that may have been protected might prompt closures or a general restructuring of the value chain, raising serious political economy issues and resistance to full and effective implementation of reforms (Braguinsky and Yavlinsky 2000).

Second, at the same time, new entrants do not always readily appear to fill in market opportunities created by the removal of administrative constraints to entry. In addition to noncompetitive behavior by incumbent economic actors, often abetted by state agencies, low capacity, limited access to working capital, and low population density are factors that commonly constrain the development of the private sector in many transition economies (Sachs, Zinnes, and Eilat 2000; Smallbone and Welter 2003).

Third, a common market failure in early transition economies is imperfect information—about the changes in structural policies that affect the sector and about relevant prices.

Fourth, information services are just one of the many ancillary services and institutions on which a fully developed market economy relies for efficiency. Indeed, value chains in transition economies are often hindered by a lack of the relevant institutions, technology, and infrastructure that may have developed in step with market development, in response to market demands, in other more fully developed market economies (Havrylyshyn and van Rooden 2003). Institutional failure or missing markets in areas such as transport services, insurance, credit, and research and extension are just some examples of lacunae in linked markets that challenge the development of efficient value chains.

Fifth, the freeing up of prices is expected to lead to more competitive and efficient behavior. But behavioral changes are not instantaneous and are themselves closely linked with institutional change and the development of markets. For example, there may be a role for collective action or public action to raise the capacity of nascent private sector entrepreneurs to figure out how collective behavior might improve their efficiency, or how quality enhancements might improve their returns (e.g., through the establishment of grading systems). Moreover, in many transition economies, although the move to efficient markets calls for the development of market-related institutions and behavior, it also calls for dismantling the institutions of petty corruption and nuisance bribes that can add significantly to transaction costs (North 1991; World Bank 1996; Boeva 2002).

Value chain analysis (see Box 9.1) is a useful tool for understanding these constraints and proposing a set of measures to relieve them. Valuable in the context of any economy, it is particularly useful in diagnosing the constraints produced by market failures, institutional and capacity failures, as well as policy and actual policy implementation failures in transition economies. Value chain analysis evaluates the behavior of each major participant (producers, processors, traders, exporters) in the system that links production to final consumption and provides a detailed account of the constraints participants face at different stages of the chain.

The value chain analysis approach considers international trade relations as part of a series of networks of producers, exporters, importers, and retailers whereby knowledge and relationships are developed to gain access to markets and suppliers. In the shorter term, the relations among different participants in a sector, in turn, determine the means by which benefits are distributed within the chain and influence the way different actors try to improve their positions within the chain. From the constraints identified, it is possible to derive policy recommendations to raise the returns of poorer households within the sector. These recommendations can then be validated and assigned priority by means of quantitative methods. Over the longer term, measures to eliminate constraints need not be conflictual in nature, as would be the case in a zero-sum game. Policy, institutional, and governance changes can indeed eliminate constraints, improve efficiency and competitiveness within the chain, and permit incremental value to be "added" to the chain (e.g., by improving the quality of the final product or better placing it in the global marketplace).

Developing a value chain is tantamount to transforming the production function. The added value can result in important gains from trade for all participants: a positive-sum game. In fact, the focus on the links among various actors in the value chain can be a powerful means of building consensus around reform. The common objective of all participants—to enhance the value of their product in the global marketplace—could form an important constituency for, if not motivator of, reform at various levels of the economy (e.g., producers, traders, processors, exporters, etc.) with knock-on benefits for other sectors of the economy.

The analysis in the rest of the chapter describes the considerable impediments to both upgrading the value of rice and cashmere production and increasing the share of poor producers in the value chains. In all three countries, powerful constituents appropriate rents through explicit preferences (credit for state-owned enterprises in Vietnam, export tax in Mongolia), industrial structure (near monopsony for a few millers in Cambodia), and the toleration of corrupt practices (illegal fees). Meanwhile, poor producers remain trapped in low-productivity states in the absence of improvements in the delivery of public services such as the poor road network and inadequate research and extension. Our analysis shows that the poor can benefit from the expanded opportunities presented by global integration, provided that these institutional constraints are addressed. Giving voice to poor producers' interests by placing these issues on the policy agenda is crucial for fostering reforms that unleash the productivity potential of poor people and increase their bargaining power.

The first section of this chapter analyzes the value chain in rice in Cambodia and Vietnam and makes policy recommendations to address the constraints that face different groups of participants. It then validates these recommendations using quantitative methods and weighs their effectiveness in reducing poverty. The next section analyzes the cashmere value chain in Mongolia and makes policy recommendations. A concluding section follows.

Rice and the Poor in Cambodia and Vietnam

Rice is a central feature of life in Cambodia and Vietnam. More than 80 percent of the population of both countries is rural, and most of the rural population produce rice (Table 9.1). Rice covers much of the cultivated area (64 percent in Vietnam and 84 percent in Cambodia) and makes major contributions to agricultural GDP (35 percent in Vietnam and 22 percent in Cambodia) and to agricultural exports. It is the main staple food, representing 60–70 percent of the calories in the diet of the average rural household and absorbing about 30 percent of household expenditures. Food security in both countries is closely identified with rice, as supported by recent history.[2]

BOX 9.1   Value Added from Value Chains

Kaplinsky defines the value chain as "the full range of activities . . . required to bring a product or service from conception through the intermediary phases of production, delivery to final consumers, and final disposal after use" (Kaplinsky 1999: 121). The value chain methodology derives from two strains of literature: the business literature on strategy and organization (Porter 1990) and the literature on global commodity chains promoted by Gereffi and developed in numerous studies in the late 1990s (UNCTAD 2000).

Value chain analysis focuses on the interaction of actors along each step of the production system (from the producer of the raw material to consumer) as well as the linkages within each set of actors. Such an approach thus considers international trade relations as part of a series of networks of producers, exporters, importers, and retailers, whereby knowledge and relationships are developed to gain access to markets and suppliers. By mapping the range of activities in the chain, value chain analysis allows for a decomposition of earnings and rewards among different parties in the chain. As a diagnostic methodology, it allows identification of where rents are being captured, as well as the nature and extent of barriers to entry along the chain.

Value chain interventions can both affect the relative gains of the economic agents that participate in the chain and enhance the total value that accrues to the chain, enabling all participants to gain. Value chain analysis can contribute to an understanding of the governance structures within a value chain and to an understanding of where relative gains are likely to accrue. Also important, it can lead to strategies that improve the relative gains of certain actors (such as poor smallholder producers at the bottom of the chain) and to strategies in which all actors can benefit from the gains to trade.

Strategies to improve *relative positions* may involve cooperative solutions through vertical or horizontal integration within the chain. For example, farmer associations may help to improve the bargaining power of producers vis-à-vis traders, or direct contractual relations between smallholders and retailers might enhance the predictability and quality of supply

for the retailer while increasing producers' share in the value chain by cutting out the middlemen.

Strategies devised to improve the *overall value* in the chain could focus on upgrading upstream actors, which may take the form of either developing new, higher-value market niches or expanding the range of activities—for example, a manufacturer might expand into distribution or research and development. The growing role of supermarket procurement systems in developing countries is a key development in this regard (Reardon and others 2003; Weatherspoon and Reardon 2003). For example, exporters able to place packaged carrots in UK supermarkets can earn a premium 7–15 times that for exporting ordinary bulk carrots (Dolan and others 1998). Yet at the same time, such systems are leading to consolidation and a shift toward nontraditional wholesalers, as well as the introduction of stringent private standards, posing compliance challenges for small farmers.

The role of governance structures is important in how such upgrading by suppliers occurs, as is the support of government and other institutions (UNCTAD 2000). Indeed, there may be a regulatory or supportive role for the public sector in this regard. In addition, the overall value of the chain often benefits from improvements in the quality of raw material at the early stages of the value chain, pointing to the benefits of cooperative solutions among, for example, smallholder producers, traders, and processors. Presumably, there would be a common interest in ensuring that smallholder suppliers reduce the risks of plant disease and enhance the quality of their supply.

As market integration moves to sourcing of high-quality products for niche markets, action is also warranted to ensure that the average smallholder does not get marginalized (Dolan and others 1998; Reardon and others 2003). Also important to improving the overall value in the chain are measures taken to reduce marketing margins and transaction costs arising from infrastructure and transport constraints. There is substantial evidence, for example, that lowering transport margins through better rural roads benefits not only farmers but also other economic agents along the value chain (Hayami and Kawagoe 1993).

TABLE 9.1   Rice in Cambodia and Vietnam

Indicator	Unit	Vietnam	Cambodia
Agriculture as share of GDP[a]	percent	24	39
Agricultural labor as share of total labor[b]	percent	69	85
Rice as share of total cultivated area[c]	percent	64	84
Rice as share of GDP in agriculture[d]	percent	35	22
Share of rural households growing rice[e]	percent	80	78
Share of rural households selling rice[f]	percent	47	na
Rice exports[g]	thousand metric tons	3,600	310
Rice exports[h]	US$ million	644	55
Rice exports as share of agricultural exports[i]	percent	27	51
Agricultural exports as share of total exports[i]	percent	16	12
Total production of rice[j]	thousand metric tons	20,150	2,600
Total rice production per capita[j]	kilograms per capita per year	252	217
Share of rice in total calorie consumption[k]	percent	64	70
Budget share of rice in rural household food budget[k]	percent	36	29
Budget share of food in total rural household expenditures[l]	percent	51	69

a. Data for Vietnam refer to 1999 and for Cambodia to 2001.
b. Data for both Vietnam and Cambodia refer to 1998.
c. Data for Vietnam refer to 1999 and for Cambodia to 2000.
d. Data for Vietnam refer to 2000 and for Cambodia to 2001.
e. Data for Vietnam refer to 1998 and for Cambodia to 2002.
f. Data for Vietnam refer to 1998.
g. Data for Vietnam refer to 2001 and for Cambodia to 2001 and include rice equivalent of 400,000 metric tons of paddy.
h. Assume average price for Vietnam of US$179 per metric ton and for Cambodian paddy of US$90 per metric ton and rice of US$350 per metric ton.
i. Data for Vietnam refer to 2000 and for Cambodia to 2001.
j. Data for Vietnam and Cambodia refer to 2001.
k Data for Vietnam refer to 1998 and for Cambodia to 1998.
l. Data for Vietnam refer to 1998 and for Cambodia to 1999.
Sources: Royal Government of Cambodia (1999, 2001); Socialist Republic of Vietnam, *Statistical Yearbook* (various issues); Socialist Republic of Vietnam (1998); World Bank Study Team, 2002.

Poor households contribute 15–25 percent of total rice production, cultivating very small holdings. The average poor household has a rice landholding of less than a hectare in Cambodia and less than half a hectare in Vietnam (Table 9.2). In Vietnam, most farmers outside of the productive Mekong and Red River Deltas grow rice on small plots for subsistence reasons.

Income per hectare of rice ranges between US$100 and $250.[3] For the poor, rice provides a smaller share of total income than for the average rice farmer (Table 9.3).

Most of the poor in both countries grow traditional rice varieties, which, unlike modern high-yielding varieties (HYVs), can thrive on poor land with few modern inputs. These varieties usually fetch higher prices than HYV rice, because they are higher-quality and local consumers prefer them. The scope for increasing rice yields in the Mekong and Red River Deltas is limited, but the scope in the more remote and mountainous areas of Vietnam, and in all provinces of Cambodia, is considerable.

Rice Exports

In both countries, liberalization policies have pushed up rice supplies considerably over the past decade, at average rates of 4–5 percent a year, mostly as the result of increases in yield and cropping intensity (ANZDEC 2000; OPCV 2002). The pro-

TABLE 9.2 Land Size and Rice Profit, Cambodia and Vietnam

Indicator	Cambodia	Vietnam
Average landholding size (hectares)	1.71	1.08
Average size of cultivated rice land (hectares/household)	0.99	0.87
Average household size	5.3	4.9
Size of cultivated rice land by the poor (hectares/household)	< 1	< 0.5
Rice production gross margin on labor (US$/hectare)	49	96
Rice production gross margin, including labor (US$/hectare)	147	216

Sources: Cambodia: Goletti, Bhatta, and Srey (2002) and ACI (2002a); Vietnam: ACI (2002b).

TABLE 9.3 Rice and Income of the Poor, Cambodia and Vietnam (percent)

Indicator	Cambodia	Vietnam
Rice as share of total farmers' income	50.4	42.5
Rice as share of income of the rural poor	40.4	47.5

Sources: Cambodia: Goletti, Bhatta, and Srey (2002); Vietnam: Minot and Goletti (1998).

duction increases have allowed both countries to achieve self-sufficiency and to export rice. Vietnam has become a major player in international markets. Indeed, with exports of 3.5–4.5 million metric tons, it is now the world's second largest exporter after Thailand (see Appendix Table 9.3).[4] Cambodia has begun to export rice (milled) to international markets (316,000 metric tons currently) and paddy (threshed, unmilled rice) to Vietnam.

The values of rice exports are significant for both countries. For Vietnam, they range from $600 million to $1 billion a year and represent 30–50 percent of agricultural trade. For Cambodia, rice plus paddy exports provide about $40 million a year and represent about 40 percent of agricultural exports, surpassing rubber and forest products.

Cambodia and Vietnam have a comparative and competitive advantage in rice relative to other regional and international rice producers.[5] According to the computed domestic resource costs for different rice varieties and production patterns, both Vietnam (with domestic resource cost ratios for rice ranging from 0.42 to 0.66) and Cambodia (with the same ratios ranging from 0.87 to 0.77) have a comparative advantage in rice and would gain significantly from using more efficient farming practices.[6]

Exports are likely to be the main driver of further production expansion in rice in the medium term, given that the domestic demand for rice is unlikely to grow much faster than the population (at 2 percent a year). The world rice market is thin and growing only slowly, but it presents good opportunities for export gains by countries such as Vietnam and Cambodia that have a comparative advantage in rice, especially if global trade liberalization continues in the direction indicated by Uruguay Round trade negotiations. Vietnam and Cambodia are in competition with only a few other main suppliers, and the customers are many, with diverse preferences.

Currently, Cambodia and Vietnam have a 2 percent and a 16 percent share of world rice exports, respectively. If they want to maintain or increase their shares, they will need to maintain or increase their productivity relative to that of their competitors. Their success will also depend on establishing links with value chains that go beyond their national boundaries.

Some opportunities for export gains may lie in diversifying into higher-quality rice. Rice comes in many varieties, grades, standards, and qualities. Thailand, as a highly successful rice exporter, has been able to accommodate the diverse requirements of foreign markets—high quality, low quality, fragrant, nonfragrant, long grain, short grain, parboiled, normally milled, and so forth. If a producer like Vietnam continues to focus on delivering on contracts for low-quality rice, it will lose the opportunity to export to other markets, to diversify its clientele, and possibly to increase its overall market share.

In neither Vietnam nor Cambodia does trade policy per se offer significant further promise for expanding rice exports. Most of the traditional instruments of trade policy have already been used.[7] Some difficulties in import and export still exist as a result of irregularities, mostly corruption and weak institutions (inspection, customs, shipping, accounting, banking), but barriers to interprovincial trade have been lifted in both countries. Further progress in trade liberalization is certainly possible, but the most effective way to promote rice exports in both countries seems to be sector policy rather than trade policy.

Even if rice exports expand successfully, both Vietnam and Cambodia will face challenges in ensuring that the expansion benefits the poor. What can value chain analysis reveal about the specific constraints and challenges for Vietnam and Cambodia in expanding rice exports as an element of a strategy for poverty reduction?

Value Chain Analysis: Constraints on Production and Trade, and Policy Options

Numerous actors take part in the value chain that links rice producers to final consumers: farmers, collectors, millers, wholesalers, retailers, state-owned enterprises, and exporters. Other participants include transporters, seed companies, agrochemical companies, agricultural equipment companies, irrigation companies, shipping companies, port authorities, banks, inspection agencies, commerce and tax departments, agricultural departments, farm organizations, miller organizations, research organizations, extension organization, policymakers, and consumer organizations (Figure 9.1).

The market and power structures evident in the rice markets in Vietnam and Cambodia highlight the particular challenges facing transition economies that are struggling to overcome the legacies of their previous command economy structures in which the state and state-owned enterprises played a particularly important role, and that are seeing private sector activity (and even ownership) still in the process of being fully institutionalized. Value chain analysis is especially useful in identifying the links in the value chain where market failures or idiosyncrasies are hindering achievement of competitive behavior, diminished margins, or enhanced value.

In fact, this kind of analysis reveals that producers are not the dominant actors in the chain in either Cambodia or Vietnam; nor are there powerful retailers or multinationals. In Vietnam, a good deal of power rests with a state-owned enterprise engaged in rice trade, particularly through govern-

FIGURE 9.1   Profit Shares for Rice Value Chain, Cambodia and Vietnam

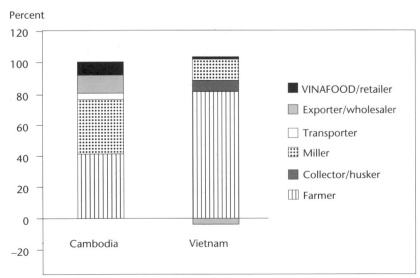

Source: ACI (2002a, 2002b).

ment-to-government contracts involving large amounts of low-quality rice. Financial sector markets have yet to develop that can serve the credit needs of Vietnamese farmers, and ancillary service delivery functions, such as in the delivery of appropriate irrigation and seed varieties, have yet not been developed. In Cambodia, power lies with a few large millers oriented toward high-quality rice exports, a new Rice Millers' Federation, and traders who ship paddy to Vietnam. Meanwhile, retailers in Cambodia suffer high transaction costs related to poor infrastructure and unofficial fees and other transaction costs, including poor infrastructure.

The sections that follow briefly analyze the characteristics, constraints, and behavior of each of the main groups of participants, and draw policy recommendations for improving efficiencies and distribution in each country.[8]

Cambodia. Cambodian rice *farmers* face serious constraints on increasing productivity and output quality. These include a lack of breeding-seed stock, many farmers' lack of title to the land they farm (which discourages them from investing in improvements), and a lack of access to commercial credit, in part because credit application procedures are cumbersome and not tailored to small loans. Water use systems, where irrigation is available, are highly politicized, with pervasive free riding, and many farmers struggle to subsist on rice production from plots that are just not suited to rice production.

Increased public investment is needed to maintain the breeder stock of seed, particularly for the traditional rice varieties grown by the poor. Such investment should be complemented with an appropriate institutional framework to ensure that research centers focus on basic research and varietal development, while private companies focus on the multiplication and sale of certified seed. The government also needs to redouble its efforts to implement the land law and raise public awareness of land rights. And improvements in the functioning of water user groups would go a long way toward raising productivity and returns. Those farmers who cannot profitably produce rice because of poor natural resource endowments should be encouraged to diversify into other products, with the aid of agricultural extension and advisory services.

Rice *processing*, too, faces some important constraints. The few millers that do operate have monopsony power, allowing them to capture higher margins than if the milling link were more competitive (Figure 9.1). Their reliance on obsolete milling equipment results in high levels of broken rice, reducing the value of the crop. Poor paddy quality, in the form of mixed varieties of seeds and inadequate postharvest handling, also increases the percentage of broken rice and lowers the price earned by most farmers. Lack of working capital and the high cost of credit limit millers' ability to buy paddy from farmers and update their machinery. In the end, such conditions encourage the unofficial export of paddy to Vietnam and Thailand and prevent the country from capturing the value added from rice milling. Because they are unable to produce consistent amounts of standardized varieties of milled rice and because they lack of information about foreign market conditions, rice millers have limited access to foreign markets.

Milling is the key bottleneck in the rice value chain in Cambodia. Millers and farmers have important unexploited opportunities for collaboration to encourage more productive cultivation of paddy as well as better sorting and postharvest handling. In Angkor Kasekam, farmer associations have linked up with millers and processors, providing a model that could well be replicated elsewhere. More important still is increased competition in milling to help reduce milling margins in Cambodia that are substantially higher than those in Vietnam and to increase prices to poor producers. Efforts to build capacity (both private and public) in marketing information services would be useful to improve knowledge among participants in the rice marketing chain.

As for the *distribution* of both retail products and exports, poor roads dampen production incentives and reduce market access. Unofficial checkpoints and port fees raise the costs of rice for Cambodian consumers and lower the competitiveness of all Cambodian rice products, including those bound for export. Nearly half of transport fees are unofficial costs. In addition, exporters are constrained by their inability to obtain consistent amounts of a standardized quality of milled rice.

Increased investment to improve roads, railways, and ports and to strengthen the market information system would reduce transaction costs and raise the profits for actors along the chain. So too would efforts to put into place transparent rules for export clearance and to build capacity in legal institutions to facilitate export transactions. Reducing transaction costs and marketing margins can go a long way toward improving returns.

Vietnam. Vietnamese *farmers* seeking credit face complicated borrowing procedures and unsuitable repayment schedules. They have difficulty obtaining high-quality seed in the absence of standardized seed specifications. And they are charged the same irrigation fees regardless of how much water they use and despite the poor quality of service.

As in Cambodia, Vietnam's research institutes and universities should focus on seed research and varietal development, while commercial seed companies focus on seed multiplication and sale of certified seed. Irrigation fees should be set on the basis of metered water use rather than area irrigated (at least at the level of farmer groups), and they should be set at levels high enough to cover capital costs and operations and maintenance. Also as in Cambodia, research is needed on alternative land use options and possibilities for diversification, especially for farmers who do not have suitable land or other endowments for productive rice farming.

Rice *processing* faces constraints as well. Vietnam's milling sector is in transition, from a bimodal structure—with a large number of small and medium-size mills catering to the domestic market and a few large mills catering to the export market—to a more modern industry with fewer, larger mills. Technology in the domestic milling sector is often outdated, resulting in high levels of broken rice, and, as in Cambodia, millers are fundamentally constrained by a lack of working capital. Small millers are also constrained by their limited storage space, as well as, for some, shortages of electricity. In the large milling sector, the preferential credit arrangements for state-owned mills hamper the ability of the private sector to compete effectively. The awarding of government-to-government contracts to state-owned mills also prevents expansion of the export base to private mills.

Interventions are needed to improve postharvest storage facilities and build the financial management capacity of millers. Leveling the playing field between state-owned and private mills would also foster enhanced private sector involvement in the milling sector. And, as in Cambodia, there is much to be gained by encouraging collaboration between farmers and millers, with millers providing seed and other inputs and enhancing farmers' incentives to supply higher-quality, less breakable paddy that would realize higher prices.

Rice *distribution* in Vietnam is hampered by inadequate infrastructure, particularly in areas outside the Mekong River Delta, and a multilayered distribution system makes it difficult for millers and exporters to obtain high-quality inputs from producers. State-owned enterprises benefit from preferences and are able to borrow the entire value of a contracted shipment of rice, while private firms can borrow only up to 70 percent. Rice exports from Vietnam are vulnerable because they are of relatively poor quality and go to only a limited number of markets. Most exports go through a small number of distributors, and most sales are made through government-to-government contracts.

Improving physical infrastructure, particularly in remote and mountainous regions, would lower transaction costs. Rationalizing state-owned enterprises, permitting their equitization, and leveling the playing field by removing their preferential access to credit arrangements would foster greater private sector participation and efficiencies in this link of the chain. The diversification of export outlets might be encouraged through simple steps such as the development of overseas trade promotion activities and strategy. Increased efficiency, lower transaction costs, and better placement of a final, higher-quality product would raise prices, lower costs, and benefit the various actors along the value chain.

Overview of Recommendations

To the extent that the poor are able to benefit from increased production, they will also benefit from trade. Most poor households in Vietnam and Cambodia are farm households, and because 80 percent of farmers grow rice, the poor are likely to benefit from any improvement in rice productivity or value added. They will probably benefit most from improvements in productivity and the technology associated with traditional varieties. Therefore, short-term strategies to reduce the number of people in poverty and the severity of poverty should focus on how to increase returns from these varieties. Steps should be taken to improve production technologies for traditional varieties, moderate postharvest losses,[9] introduce increased competition and more modern technology into milling, strengthen infrastructure, and lower transaction costs (including illegal fees). Particularly significant will be efforts to establish farm organizations. New institutions and markets that increase information about prices and permit the agents in a value chain to form strategic alliances can play an important role in increasing returns to players such as poor smallholder farmers.

The role of the public sector in direct investments to increase productivity should be limited to providing irrigation, where irrigation is economically viable. Elsewhere, the public sector should play an enabling role, both through legislation and through provision of services—especially improved infrastructure and public policies to reduce the transaction costs of providing credit.

For convenience, the recommendations that emerged from the value chain analysis are grouped as strategic options related to improvements in productivity, postharvest technology, and infrastructure and chain management (Table 9.4).[10] This section uses quantitative methods, applied to household data, to evaluate these options and explore their effects on different participants within the value chain.

Aggregate Effects. A multimarket model was built to explore the probable effects of the various policy options on aggregates, including production,

exports, and agricultural incomes. The results reported in Table 9.5 show that a combination of different approaches is needed to improve the income generated by the value chain. Improvements in productivity, postharvest technology, and marketing and institutions can go a long way toward increasing exports and agricultural income.

Clearly, policy design would require a more explicit idea of the costs involved and the time frame required to implement different options. Even so, some useful insights can be obtained from a qualitative analysis such as that reported in Table 9.6.

Effects on Farmers and the Poor. What are the marketing margins and profits for the different participants in the value chain? Tables 9.7 and 9.8 report these at each level of the chain for rice in Cambodia and Vietnam.[11] Farmers and millers have the largest marketing margins and profit margins[12] in both countries, but the distribution of profits differs; Cambodian millers capture a much higher share of profits than their Vietnamese counterparts.

In absolute terms, Cambodia's rice value chain realizes a higher profit than Vietnam's (Figure 9.2), in part because Cambodia exports higher-quality paddy than does Vietnam. Meanwhile, Cambodia's farmers realize lower unit profits than their Vietnamese counterparts. On average, their rice land is only half as productive as that in Vietnam, but the average Cambodian rice farmer has more than twice as much land as his Vietnamese counterpart. These features suggest that efforts to reduce poverty

TABLE 9.4   Strategic Options for Rice, Cambodia and Vietnam

	Option	Adoption of option
Productivity	Adopting green revolution package Improving traditional varieties	Dry season, Cambodia Wet season, Cambodia Upland areas in Vietnam
Postharvest technology	Reducing postharvest losses Improving milling	Cambodia, Vietnam Cambodia, Vietnam
Marketing and chain management	Improving road and port infrastructure Reducing transaction costs Establishing niche market (specialty rice) Establishing level playing field	Cambodia, Vietnam Cambodia, Vietnam Cambodia, Vietnam Private sector and state-owned enterprises, Vietnam

Source: ACI (2002a, 2002b).

TABLE 9.5   Effects of Various Policy Options on Rice Production, Income, and Exports: Cambodia and Vietnam

Cambodia	Option	Percent change in		
		Rice production	Agricultural income	Rice exports
Improved productivity	Green revolution technologies	4	1.5	31
	Traditional varieties	15	7	228
Improved postharvest handling	Milling technology	3.1	1.3	24
	Postharvest losses	4.6	2	37
Marketing and chain management	Marketing costs farm to port	1.6	5	25

Vietnam	Option	Percent change in		
		Rice production	Total income	Rice exports
Improved productivity	Yield improvement	18.2	1.2	39
Improved postharvest handling	Milling technology	0.5	0.37	12
	Postharvest losses	1.31	0.1	1

Source: Authors' simulation of multimarket model; see ACI (2002a).

TABLE 9.6   Qualitative Analysis of Strategic Options, Cambodia

Cambodia	Option	Benefit in agricultural income	Cost	Benefit/ cost ratio	Time frame
Improved productivity	Green revolution technologies	2	4	0.5	3–10 years
	Traditional varieties	5	3	1.7	3–10 years
Improved postharvest handling	Milling technology	1	1	1.0	3–5 years
	Postharvest losses	3	2	1.5	3–5 years
Marketing and chain management	Marketing costs farm to port	4	5	0.8	5–10 years

Note: Scoring method: 1 = lowest, 2 = low, 3 = average, 4 = high, 5 = highest.
Source: ACI (2002a).

by raising productivity might be more effective in Cambodia than in Vietnam. Because rice production represents between 30 and 50 percent of the incomes of the poor in the two countries, even small improvements in productivity can lead to important direct income gains for the poor. In addition, the combined effects of higher productivity for mil-

lions of small rice farmers could be dramatic increases in rural nonfarm activities.

Assessing the overall direct impact on the poor of the proposed improvements in the rice subsector would require a more in-depth model based on household data (e.g., those available from living standards surveys). Such a model could trace the

TABLE 9.7   Marketing Costs and Margins for Rice in Cambodia, 2002

	Inputs	Farmer	Collector	Miller	Trans-porter	Whole-saler	Retailer	Total
Transport cost			15		26	10		
Operating cost				34		6		
Input cost		355	453	469	526	561	605	
Total costs		355	468	503	553	577	605	
Price received	355	453	469	526	561	605	625	
Value of byproduct				65				
Total revenue	355	453	469	592	561	605	625	
Profit (%)	355	98 (21.7)	1 (0.3)	88 (14.9)	8 (1.5)	27 (4.5)	20 (3.2)	244
Percent of total profit		40	1	36	3	11	8	100
Marketing margins (%)	56.8	15.7	2.6	9.1	5.6	6.9	3.2	27.5
Markup over farm gate price (%)		0	3.6	31	24	33	38	

Notes: Costs are shown in riels per kilogram of paddy rice; yield is calculated at 2 metric tons per hectare; transport is from Battambang to Phnom Penh; and milling recovery is 0.64.
Sources: Derived from data collected by World Bank Study Team, July 2002; ACI (2002a).

TABLE 9.8   Marketing Costs and Margins for Export Rice in Vietnam, 2002

	Inputs	Farmer	Collector/husker	Large miller	Trans-porter	Exporter	VINA-FOOD	Total
Transport cost			32	4	2			
Operating cost			37	47	14	13		
Input cost		1,000	1,600	1,717	1,716	1,742	1,727	
Total costs		1,000	1,669	1,769	1,732	1,755	1,727	
Price received	1,000	1,600	1,717	1,716	1,742	1,727	1,736	
Value of byproduct				144.10				
Total revenue	1,000	1,600	1,717	1,860	1,742	1,727	1,736	
Profit (%)	1,000	600 (37.5)	48 (2.8)	90 (4.9)	9 (0.5)	–27 (–1..6)	9 (0.5)	729
Percent of total profit		82	6	12	1	–4	1	100
Marketing margins (%)	57.5	34.5	6.7	–0.06	1.5	–0.8	0.5	7.8
Markup over farm gate price (%)		0	7.3	16	9	8	9	

Notes: Costs are shown in dong per kilogram paddy equivalent. Milling recovery is: brown rice, 0.77; white rice from brown rice, 0.85; white rice from paddy, 0.66. Export price is: (assuming 15 percent broken rice) US$172 per metric ton = 2,632 dong per kilogram.
Sources: Derived from data collected by World Bank Study Team, July 2002; ACI (2002b).

microeconomic behavior of poor households. Higher consumer prices for rice will undoubtedly hurt households that are net consumers of rice, including the urban poor. Also, it is clear that net sellers of rice in rural areas would benefit from higher prices or increased trade volumes. An in-depth study might look usefully at the distribution of poor households in rural areas, seek to understand who is going to be a net buyer or net seller,

and consider the effect of changes on each category in detail. To the extent that the farm gate prices of paddy increase more than the retail prices for rice, not only net sellers of rice but also some of the net buyers will benefit from increased exports, and a reduction in overall poverty might result (Minot and Goletti 1998).

Rice farmers in both countries have limited capacity to capture a larger share of the profit or

FIGURE 9.2   Profit Structure of Rice Value Chain, Cambodia and Vietnam (US$/ton)

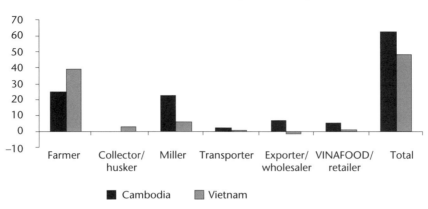

Profits of each actor (US$ per 1,000 kilograms)

■ Cambodia   ■ Vietnam

Source: ACI (2002a, 2002b).

marketing margins produced along the value chain. Comparisons of four countries at increasing levels of development suggest that the marketing margins of farmers are smaller in the less developed economies than in the more developed economies (Table 9.9). As national income per capita increases, farmers get a progressively bigger size of the total price (higher margins) and higher profits. The reasons farmers get less in Cambodia and Vietnam than in the other countries shown are related partly to infrastructure and partly to political economy. In the United States, where the farm lobby has garnered substantial subsidies, leading to farm gate prices higher than FOB prices, farmers are better positioned to influence decisions than are farmers in Cambodia, who have very small and dispersed holdings, are less effective in influencing policy, and

TABLE 9.9   Marketing Margins of Farmers in Cambodia, Vietnam, Thailand, and United States

Country	Farm price/FOB price (%)
Cambodia	72
Vietnam	80
Thailand	90
USA	111

Sources: Cambodia and Vietnam: fieldwork of World Bank Study Team, July 2002; ACI (2002a, 2002b). Thailand: personal communication, Tom Slayton, October 2002. United States: USDA-ERS (2002).

face relatively much higher costs for transport, processing, marketing, credit search, and information.

Policies that promote infrastructure, information systems, and farm organizations will help to transfer some of the benefits to farmers. Better infrastructure will lower the cost of transport from farm gate to port and the marketing costs of traders. For farmers, such reductions will likely result in higher prices and a greater share of the value added. Better information systems will help farmers to adopt better technology and orient marketing agents toward the higher-quality rice that is demanded by international markets. The result will be higher production and higher prices for the raw material, and both suggest that farmers will capture a larger share of the value added. The promotion of farm organizations will raise the bargaining power of farmers vis-à-vis millers, traders, and exporters. The development and strengthening of farm organizations, and their alliance with milling firms and other agencies in the value chain, can lead to substantial improvements in efficiencies and quality.

Cashmere and the Poor in Mongolia

Mongolia produces one-fourth of the world's supply of raw cashmere and is the world's second largest producer after neighboring China. Over the last decade annual production has more than doubled. All cashmere production is traded, and almost all is exported. Cashmere exports of $70 million accounted for 13 percent of Mongolia's official exports in 2001 and generally have been even higher (Table 9.10).[13]

The cashmere subsector provides more than a third of the country's 2.4 million people with incomes. It is the single largest employer—providing jobs for more than 16 percent of the work force and accounting for more than 6 percent of GDP in 1993–2001 (see World Bank 2003)—and it is a principal source of livelihood for Mongolia's poor. Average household income from cashmere for herding households is estimated at $220 for 2001. The variation around this average, however, is substantial, with 44 percent of livestock herding households earning less than $100 a year, another 44 percent earning between $100 and $500 a year, and the remaining 12 percent earning more than $500 a year.[14]

When COMECON (Council for Mutual Economic Assistance) collapsed in 1991, Mongolia privatized collective farms and livestock and removed price controls, fueling a boom in the livestock sector and ushering in substantial increases in the livestock population. The number of cashmere goats doubled, to 10.3 million by the end of 2000, and the per capita incomes of herders rose from about $30 to $55 between 1991 and 1996. The characteristics

TABLE 9.10   Cashmere in Mongolia

Indicator	Unit	1998	1999	2000	2001
Agriculture as share of GDP	percent	39.9	40.3	34.2	28.4
Livestock sector as share of GDP	percent	36.1	36.8	30.8	24.8
Agricultural labor as share of total labor	percent	49.7	49.5	48.6	48.3
Goat herd as share of total livestock	percent	33.6	32.9	34.0	36.8
Cashmere production as share of GDP	percent	3.5	6.7	11.7	5.7
Cashmere exports[a]	metric tons	1,812.1	3,499.6	2,770.6	2,369.1
Cashmere exports[b]	US$ million	38.7	70.3	90.1	67.8
Cashmere exports as share of total exports	percent	8.4	15.5	16.8	13.0
Cashmere exports as share of agricultural exports[c]	percent	41.6	53.7	53.8	50.0
Agricultural exports as share of total exports	percent	17.3	24.7	26.5	24.5
Total production of cashmere	metric tons	3,126.7	3,194.8	3,084.5	2,930.0
Total cashmere production per capita	kilograms per capita per year	1.3	1.3	1.3	1.2
Cashmere revenue per capita	US$	15.2	26.5	49.1	25.0
Share of cashmere revenue per capita in GDP per capita	percent	3.8	6.9	12.2	6.0
Total cashmere production/household with livestock	kilograms per capita per year	11.4	11.8	11.5	11.4
Cashmere revenue/household with livestock	US$	124.4	223.4	423.4	229.0
Share of cashmere revenue/household with livestock in GDP per capita	percent	31.1	55.9	105.9	57.3
Livestock per capita	head	13.6	14.1	12.6	10.7
Livestock/household with livestock	head	119.6	124.4	112.5	101.6
Goats per capita	head	4.58	4.64	4.26	3.98
Goats/household with livestock	head	40.2	40.9	38.2	37.4

a. Data for semiprocessed and finished cashmere products converted to raw cashmere.
b. Official exports; value of smuggled cashmere is not included.
c. Here the finished cashmere products (tops and garments) are excluded from total cashmere exports and agricultural exports.
Sources: National Statistical Office of Mongolia, 2001, and World Bank staff estimates.

of the herder population changed as well. The number of herding households more than doubled during the 1990s, to 185,500 (one-third of households nationwide) in 2001, reflecting an influx of nontraditional herders.

Mongolia now has three groups of herders, distinguished by herd size, income levels, and grazing techniques. The first group is made up of households that were in poverty after the collapse of COMECON and moved into cashmere production for lack of alternative income opportunities (World Bank 2001).[15] Unlike traditional herders, most of these families own small herds of up to 100 goats that they graze on common areas, and more than 30 percent of them—with fewer than 30 goats on average—live in urban areas. The average annual income of these families from cashmere sales in 2000 was less than $55 per capita. Their intensive and stationary herd management is a major source of serious land degradation. As their livestock numbers have increased, land degradation has become more acute, imposing costs on both the poor and the state. Overgrazing increases the incidence of respiratory diseases from dust, and it lowers productivity because herders have to travel further to tend their stock. It also exacerbates the impact of harsh winters on animals and on the households that depend on them. These households have been able to operate at the margin thanks only to the implicit subsidies—free public land and water—and explicit subsidies—free restocking of goats after the devastation of livestock in the successive harsh winters of 2000 and 2001. Taking into account the cost of inputs and land degradation, the social returns from the livestock practices of these households may be negative.

The second group of herders, who own herds of from 101 to 500 head, account for the bulk of cashmere production. They own 38 percent of the national herd and produce more than 65 percent of Mongolia's cashmere. Most live in rural areas, previously worked in state-owned livestock cooperatives, have herding experience, and bought livestock using vouchers when collective enterprises were privatized. They depend almost entirely on livestock herding for income. Not all of these herders are poor, but all are vulnerable to bad weather and changes in demand.

The third group makes up 2 percent of all herder families and produces about 3 percent of Mongo-

lian cashmere. These households are considered rich and are generally not at risk.

Both the second and third groups of herders are nomadic and can afford to move to three or more different camps a year. They have access to winter shelters by tradition or kinship, and they have longer experience in selecting and occupying rangeland in distant areas (World Bank 2001).

Potential Gains for the Poor from Trade in Cashmere

Because a high share of its production is exported, the cashmere subsector in Mongolia is much more directly influenced by trends in the international market, including quality standards, than is the rice sector in Cambodia and Vietnam. Looking ahead, there are many reasons for optimism about the international market. Demand for luxury goods is growing worldwide and is well balanced globally. Demand for finished cashmere articles is highly income-elastic, and trade in cashmere and cashmere products is likely to continue growing.[16]

Quality is an important consideration in assessing Mongolia's prospects for expanding export earnings and incomes. Mongolia has historically supplied some of the world's best cashmere, but quality has declined significantly over the last 15 years as the country's production has increased. Quality cashmere commands a 30–40 percent price premium in international markets, and quality discounts cost Mongolian herders about $18 million in 2001—23 percent of the income of the average household with livestock.

Higher export earnings from cashmere would help to boost the incomes of a large number of Mongolians. Although information about the relative position of herder households in the income distribution is not available, it is clear that many of these households represent the poorest segments of Mongolian society. However, the sustainability of cashmere production as a livelihood for households in the first group just described is open to question.

Value Chain Analysis: Constraints on Production and Trade, and Policy Options

Many different actors—herders, traders, processors, retailers, and exporters—take part in the value chain linking producers to final consumers. Others are veterinary service providers, local and central government officials, herder organizations, graders, and external partners, including donors and nongovernmental organizations. Most of the power within the value chain resides with the state-owned processing firm and retailer, Gobi; herders are the largest group of actors but perhaps the least powerful.

This section looks at the policy and institutional constraints faced by each of the main actors and suggests possible policy responses. Like the situation for rice in Cambodia and Vietnam, many of the constraints in the sector represent shortcomings of sectoral policies and institutions rather than of trade policy. Once again, value chain analysis proves particularly useful in pointing out the particular challenges to developing efficient and high-value products, with returns that benefit the poor, in the context of transition economies.

The difficulties faced by transition economies are particularly evident in Mongolia where, with traditional practices under stress and state institutions being dismantled, efficient market development is facing the challenge of developing new institutions and overcoming the legacy of passing ones. For example, in overcoming the history of collectivization in Mongolia, economic agents must spend some time allaying suspicions and work to develop new and efficient institutions through collective action with a view toward benefiting from economies of scale. The development of new herder cooperatives and responsive private sector veterinary services to replace defunct communal and public service institutions has been a slow process.

Two requirements—understanding the need for quality control and grading systems and developing an effective demand for such systems through appropriate price signals—have yet to be met. The breakdown of traditional pastureland and risk management practices is resulting in overgrazing and severe losses of herds after a particularly harsh winter (*dzud*), and an inability to maintain wells and bores. Likewise, missing markets, weak institutions, and an absence of ancillary markets in services—such as a lack of physical marketplaces, traders, and insurance markets—are challenging the development of value chains in Mongolia. Indeed, this situation plagues many transition economies.

Herders. Herders face several serious impediments in improving the quality and expanding the supply of cashmere without undue environmental damage. The combination of easy entry into cashmere production and failing institutions for key inputs has led to deterioration of the water supply, collapse of the fodder industry, and an absence of pasture management. These factors have therefore put pressure on environmentally fragile land and increased both the private and social costs of production.

Mongolia's existing legal and administrative mechanisms for controlling grazing are unlikely to be able to resolve the problems of land degradation. The primary input for cashmere—grazing and pastureland—continues to be a public good, and privatization is not a realistic option.[17] Strengthening social controls would require introducing provisions into the land laws to allow groups of herders, organized as legal entities, to exclude others from well-defined areas of pastureland. Other options would include land user fees, whose feasibility would have to be assessed, or modifications of the head tax on livestock to ensure that it reflects the social costs associated with land degradation.[18] Improvements in land use laws or a revision of the livestock tax would provide incentives for herders to rationalize their stocks, pool resources, and employ more efficient grazing techniques. Imposing fees on land use would also spur the development of a sustainable fodder market. Rehabilitating water bores is crucial to increased livestock productivity and supply and could generate rural employment. Bores and wells are constitutionally the responsibility of local government administrators, but the Gobi Initiative, funded by the U.S. Agency for International Development (USAID), has shown that herders are willing to pay for water facilities if exclusive use is guaranteed. Support from government and donor agencies is needed in scaling up this successful public-private partnership nationwide.

Mongolia is vulnerable to severe winters.[19] Better herding practices can help to mitigate the impact of severe weather, but herders will remain highly vulnerable without insurance. Only about 0.3 percent of Mongolia's livestock was insured in 2001, when Mongolia had a particularly harsh winter.[20] It is estimated that the government spent that year about 2 billion tugriks (about 1.1 percent of GDP) on providing subsidized fodder and other disaster relief services.

A well-developed insurance market for livestock could reduce these costs substantially for the government and help to stabilize herders' incomes. The development of insurance options faces important challenges, including herders' nomadic lifestyle, the difficulties of gathering adequate information on herd management techniques, and a lack of sufficient skills and information to determine appropriate insurance premiums. But recent pilot projects aimed at providing index-based livestock insurance provide a good start to the introduction of market-based techniques for addressing risks.[21] The persistence of an implicit government guarantee of livestock assets will discourage the development of an insurance market and delay the needed exit of marginal producers. Donors and the government need to desist from restocking herds free of charge and at levels too high for long-term sustainability.

Finally, restoring quality is critical to increasing the value of Mongolian cashmere and the incomes of herders. Reasons for the drop in quality over the last decade include herders' lack of information on grades and prices, and on veterinary and other herd improvement topics, together with a lack of grading and testing facilities. When herders lack market information, they are vulnerable to exploitation by processors and traders, and without price differentials between high-quality cashmere and other grades, herders lack incentives to invest in improving their herds.

The way to restore the quality of Mongolian cashmere is through herd selection, superior genetics, and price incentives that reward quality improvement. Improvements in the legal and regulatory framework could encourage the establishment of innovative joint venture agreements and partnerships in research and development. New technological developments in rearing cashmere goats could improve the supply and quality of Mongolian cashmere without damaging the environment. The provision of services for testing and grading should be encouraged, and the Mongolian herders' association should use internationally accepted grading standards. Grading will allow for product differentiation and will allow herders and processors to determine the best mix of quality and price for production and sale.

Traders and Marketing and Distribution Channels. Mongolia's one major cashmere market—the Tsaiz market in Ulaanbataar—is 600–1,000 kilometers from most regional production centers. Almost all herders must sell their cashmere either to traders at the farm gate or at informal provincial marketplaces, at discounts of 10–45 percent from capital city prices. Generally, they sell as individuals, often on a barter basis, with little knowledge of market demand and little ability to influence market outcomes. They incur additional expenses for transporting goods to the market day locations with no certainty of concluding sales.

Steps to stimulate growth in Mongolia's cashmere industry, and in poor herders' incomes in particular, will require strategies to improve marketing channels, so that herders are able to get their products to processors at least cost and so that they are remunerated fairly for superior quality. Development of regional market centers, such as those in the Gobi Initiative funded by USAID, and improvements in infrastructure could significantly increase the incomes of rural herders. Other promising initiatives are the development of herder cooperatives and attempts by government to improve herders' access to markets by creating wholesale networks. Mongolia has a good law on cooperatives, but assistance is needed to improve governance and financial management in cooperatives.

Vertical integration between herders and processors could in principle lead to a sharing of transport costs between agents, improve herders' income security, and reduce the uncertainty of supply for processors. But developing such strategic alliances would be challenging; with their nomadic lifestyle, herders would find it difficult to enter into formal marketing agreements. Moreover, such formal relationships require a lot of trust and strong social cohesion, which has been eroding in Mongolia. Credible mechanisms to enforce contractual obligations would have to be in place and so would a system that rewards herders for cooperation and organization.

Processors. Since Mongolia's transition from a command economy to a more market-oriented economy, the number of cashmere processing and dehairing companies has risen to more than 30, and herders can trade directly with international buyers, middlemen, or trading agents. Although the state abandoned cashmere producers in the wake of the transition, it retained a heavy influence in cashmere processing through the ownership of Gobi, the largest processing company, and other joint venture partnerships in Mongol-Amical and Mon-Forte.[22] Processing capacity exceeds domestic supply even in the best of years, and in 2000 the four large factories that account for about two-thirds of processing capacity were running at only one-fifth of their capacity.

Policies to reform this segment of the value chain need to level the playing field among processors; Gobi benefits from continued government support in raw cashmere procurement. The industry's excess processing capacity also should be rationalized, which adds to production costs.

Cashmere Trade Policies. In 1994 the government banned exports of raw and washed cashmere on the grounds of the need to "protect domestic industry from external competition and increase domestic value added." In 1997 the export ban was replaced by an export tax on raw cashmere of 4,000 tugriks per kilogram, equivalent to 13 percent in 2001 prices.

Although these policies were meant to protect domestic processing firms by providing them with larger volumes of cashmere at cheaper prices, and to increase the value added by the cashmere subsector to the economy, these goals have not been met. Rather, these policies have stimulated activities that circumvent the ban and the export tax, in fact low-

ering the supply of raw cashmere to the domestic processing industry and exacerbating the problems associated with low-capacity utilization. Smuggling has grown rampant, given the length and porosity of the border with China, and Mongolia's final goods exports have remained quite limited (Figure 9.3).

Proceeds from the export tax in 2001 amounted to less than 0.01 percent of total government revenues. The decline in recorded raw cashmere exports cost Mongolia about $100 million in official export earnings between 1996 and 2001. In addition, by pitting the interests of processors against those of herders, the export tax may have damaged the prospects for forming strategic alliances within the domestic supply chain.

The case for retaining the export tax is unconvincing. The tax has shown itself to be unenforceable, but if it were to have its intended effects, the result would be a transfer of resources in the value chain away from the poorest members to the more powerful ones. Abolishing the tax is likely to have beneficial consequences both for herder incomes and for the overall development of the cashmere subsector.

Overview of Recommendations

As a matter of priority, measures are needed to stop the degradation of grazing land and ensure more secure supplies of water and fodder.

FIGURE 9.3   Share of Cashmere Products in Mongolia's Total Cashmere Exports, 1993–2001

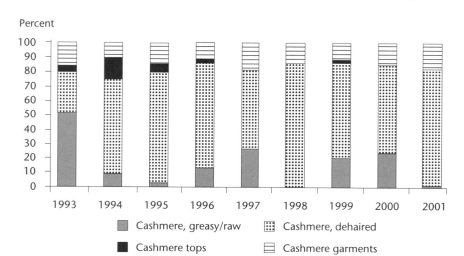

Source: Government of Mongolia.

For herders, the scope is significant for expanding incomes and reducing poverty by upgrading the quality of cashmere produced. Simple simulations suggest that closing half the quality gap between Mongolian and Chinese cashmere would have increased average annual incomes for herder households from $220 to $263, or by 20 percent, in 2001. This increase is a feasible target over the next 6–10 years.

Reducing poverty will require a combination of measures to increase both the value of output—through upgrading quality—and herders' share of that value. A host of measures would help to increase herders' share of profits in the value chain: increasing their security of access to pastureland; enabling the development of input and insurance markets; providing livestock support services and reliable information about quality standards and prices that are differentiated by quality; developing markets in regional centers, reducing transport costs, and increasing the bargaining power of herders; and fostering cooperative solutions to help households attain economies of scale or strategic alliances to increase the security and quality of supply.

Government has a necessary role in improving the policies and institutions to support the cashmere value chain. For the most part, it must play an enabling role, but some instances of market failure require nonmarket solutions. These solutions include pastureland management, veterinary services, standard setting, and dealing with information asymmetry in insurance markets. In addition, there is a case for revising Mongolia's trade policies for cashmere: although the government should pursue relaxation of the ban on breeder stock imports from China, in the context of discussions on China's accession to the World Trade Organization the tax on exports of raw cashmere appears counterproductive.

Detailed household survey data are not yet available for Mongolia, and without them it is difficult to estimate the net impact of the recommended changes on the welfare of various participants in the cashmere supply chain.[23] It seems clear, however, that upgrading cashmere quality is likely to increase value, and that reducing transaction costs (by developing regional market centers) and reducing volatility (through insurance) would yield unambiguous welfare gains. Some of the recommendations, particularly elimination of the cashmere export tax, would transfer gains from one set of participants to

another, and others would increase private costs to reflect more accurately the economic costs of input provision and of externalities, notably environmental degradation from overgrazing.

Without subsidies, the marginal segments of the herder population might no longer find cashmere production a sustainable activity. This possibility raises difficult questions about the role of livestock herding in Mongolia, which has acted as a safety net for many households adversely affected by the transition from a planned to a market economy. For such families, a transition out of herding would have to be phased over time and accompanied by measures to stimulate alternative employment—for example, in storage, maintenance and repair of wells, and fodder production.

Conclusions

An analysis of value chains provides a good understanding of the behavior and constraints of different actors involved in the addition of value as a product moves from producers to consumers, and at the same time allows the analyst to identify the major constraints in the sector as a whole. Such analysis reveals that the poor can benefit from the expanded opportunities presented by global integration, provided that these institutional constraints are addressed. Giving voice to poor producers' interests by placing these issues on the policy agenda is crucial for fostering reforms that unleash the productivity potential of poor people and increase their bargaining power.

Growth in trade can be achieved through improvements in productivity, combined with improvements in postproduction technologies and marketing and institutions. This finding is true for rice in Vietnam and Cambodia, where a small proportion of total production is actually traded and an even smaller proportion is exported. It is also true for cashmere in Mongolia, where all output is traded and almost all is exported in some form.

Both rice and cashmere are commodities central to the livelihood of a large proportion of poor households in the countries studied, but between the countries there are differences in the prospects for income gains from improvements in the supply chain. These different prospects stem largely from differences in the nature of the commodities—which affect the prospects for growth in the international market, for gains from upgrading quality, and for gains in the relative share of producers, who are the poorest participants in the value chain. Although cashmere is a luxury good for which demand is highly income-elastic, most rice is a basic good where growth in the overall market is sluggish and tied to population growth rather than income trends. Moreover, few poor households engaged in rice production are likely to be able to raise their incomes from producing high-quality rice; the niche market for high-quality rice is small, and Cambodia and Vietnam have limited potential for supplying it. By contrast, for cashmere producers the prospects for income gains from quality improvements are sizable and would have widespread impacts among all herder households.

Within the value chains for both rice and cashmere, power rests not with producers but with processing firms, especially state-owned Gobi in Mongolia, millers in Cambodia, and the state-owned trading company in Vietnam. The share that producers capture of the final value of the products differs among countries—and so, therefore, do the prospects for raising their incomes through gains in efficiency and strategic alliances in the form of either greater horizontal or vertical integration. In Vietnam, where farm gate prices are 80 percent of the border price for rice and farmers capture as much as 82 percent of the profits from the value chain, there is less scope for gains from either improving efficiency or restructuring the value chain. In Cambodia, where farm gate prices are somewhat lower, at 72 percent of the border price, and the farmers' share of total profits is substantially less, at 40 percent, there is considerable scope for productivity and efficiency gains along the value chain and for improvements in farmers' bargaining position. In Mongolia, it is difficult to decompose the value chain, but it is clear that herders capture only a very small portion of profits and that they have significant potential for raising their incomes. Finally, all three countries are highly vulnerable to external shocks, and coping with risk is a major concern for households engaged in both rice and cashmere production.

Endnotes

1. Early on, Fischer and Gelb (1991) flagged the role of institutional reforms in the transition.

2. For a brief history of rice cultivation in the two countries, see the technical appendix to this chapter at www.world bank.org/eaptrade.

3. All dollar amounts are current U.S. dollars.

4. All appendix tables cited in this chapter can be found at www.worldbank.org/eaptrade.

5. As shown in the technical appendix to this chapter at www.worldbank.org/eaptrade.

6. Domestic resource cost (DRC) is an indicator of comparative advantage. It measures the ratio of value added from domestic, nontraded activities to the foreign exchange earned or saved from domestic production. A DRC of less than 1.00 suggests comparative advantage and efficiency in production.

7. Quotas have been lifted, export taxes are zero, import tariffs are low in Cambodia (7 percent) and, even though tariffs are relatively high in Vietnam (at 30 percent), they are not binding.

8. The background papers for this chapter contain a detailed analysis of the constraints for each actor along the chain (see ACI 2000a, 2000b). Based on these papers, a more extensive analysis of the specific constraints and policy recommendations related to each link of the value chain is detailed in Appendix Tables 5–12 at www.world bank.org/eaptrade.

9. These losses, which occur at different stages after harvest, and are the result of moisture, pests, rodents, outdated milling technology, and pilferage. Losses at the village level can be substantial, from 5 to 20 percent of production.

10. Details of these options are described in the technical appendix to this chapter at www.worldbank.org/eaptrade

11. This breakdown may not be an appropriate metric for cross-country comparisons of the efficiencies of agents (such as farmers), because farmers in some countries may take on more functions (e.g., postharvest storage) than they do in other countries. In Vietnam and Cambodia, however, the comparison would appear to be appropriate.

12. In Cambodia, these two groups together get about 80 percent of the profits, whereas in Vietnam they get about 90 percent of the profit (see Figure 9.1).

13. These figures considerably understate the importance of the industry to the Mongolian economy. It is estimated that about 45 percent of the raw cashmere produced in 2000—worth about $50 million—was smuggled to China. This estimate is derived from deducting official exports and sales to domestic processors from total known production.

14. 2001 Household Income and Expenditure Survey, Mongolian National Statistics Office.

15. The collapse of the Soviet Union ushered in a difficult period of transition for Mongolia. The Mongolian economy imploded, and real GDP declined by 20 percent between 1989 and 1993. The one bright spot was the expansion in agriculture and herding, fueled by wholesale privatization of the livestock sector in 1991. The privatization of livestock using the voucher system was largely equitable and successfully put assets in the hands of poor households. Every Mongolian citizen received vouchers worth 10,000 tugriks (roughly $10) for the purchase of state assets, particularly livestock and small businesses, but only members of state-owned cooperatives (about 40 percent of the population) could use vouchers to purchase livestock. The voucher distribution system was not economically optimal, because it created incentives for production but encouraged suboptimal herd sizes. Over time,

concentration was aimed at yielding an economically sustainable herd size, but this process was interrupted in 1999 by external shocks.

16. Trends in the global cashmere market are outlined in the technical appendix to this chapter at www.world bank.org/eaptrade.

17. Private ownership is prohibited under Mongolia's constitution and its 2002 land laws. Traditionally, private herds have used public lands, with herders having rights to certain areas at certain times of the year. Mobility and knowledge are essential if the pastures are not to suffer from overgrazing.

18. Mongolia already has a specific tax on livestock, but the level of the tax would have to be reassessed to determine whether it is sufficient to capture the social costs associated with land degradation. Local administrators already have detailed records of stock ownership by herder that enable the tax to be administered efficiently.

19. The winters of 2000 and 2001 were particularly harsh, and drove down the stock of goats by more than 700,000 animals. Rising prices cushioned the impact of declining production and export volumes, but more than 19,000 herders—about 8 percent of the households with livestock—lost all of their animals.

20. They were insured by Mongol Daatgal, a state-owned insurance company.

21. For example, the livestock insurance program under the Sustainable Livelihoods Project supported by the World Bank is a public-private initiative aimed at developing a risk index that private insurance companies would use in offering insurance to livestock owners to cover risks arising from drought or other weather-related events. Details of this scheme are in the technical appendix to this chapter at www.worldbank.org/eaptrade.

22. Gobi remains in state hands, despite having been slated for privatization for some time.

23. A new household survey, including a special module on cashmere production, is currently under way and will yield useful information to enable a more quantitative estimation of both net impacts and distributional changes.

References

ACI (Agrifood Consulting International). 2002a. "Rice Value Chain Study: Cambodia." Report Prepared for the World Bank. Phnom Penh, September.

————-. 2002b. "Rice Value Chain Study: Vietnam." Report Prepared for the World Bank. Ha Noi, September.

ANZDEC. 2000. "Agricultural Sector Program, Inception Report." ADB TA 3223-VIE. March.

Boeva, Bistra. 2002. "Governance in the Transition Economies: Current Issues in Bulgaria." Center for International Private Enterprise, Washington, D.C.

Braguinsky, Serguey, and Grigory Yavlinsky. 2000. *Incentives and Institutions: The Transition to a Market Economy in Russia.* Princeton, N.J.: Princeton University Press.

Dolan, C., and others. 1998. "Horticulture Commodity Chains: The Impact of the UK Market on the African Fresh Vegetable Industry." IDS Working Paper 96. Institute for Development Studies, University of Sussex.

Fischer, Stanley, and Alan Gelb. 1991. "The Process of Socialist Economic Transformation." *Journal of Economic Perspectives* 5 (4): 91–106.

Goletti, F., A. Bhatta, and C. Srey. 2002. "Farmer Survey: Tabulation of Results." Discussion Paper No. 5. Agricultural Sector Development Program, ADB TA 3695-CAM. Phnom Penh, October.

Havrylyshyn, Oleh, and Ron van Rooden. 2003. "Institutions Matter in Transition, But So Do Policies." *Comparative Economic Studies* 45 (1): 2–24.

Hayami, Yujiro, and Toshihiko Kawagoe. 1993. *The Agrarian Origins of Commerce and Industry.* New York: St. Martin's Press.

Kaplinsky, R. 1999. "Globalisation and Unequalization: What Can Be Learned from Value Chain Analysis." *Journal of Development Studies* 30 (2): 117–46.

Minot, N., and F. Goletti. 1998. "Export Liberalization and Household Welfare: The Case of Rice in Vietnam." *American Journal of Agricultural Economics* 80 (4): 738–49.

North, Douglass C. 1991. "Institutions." *Journal of Economic Perspective* 5 (1): 97–112.

OPCV (Overseas Projects Corporation of Victoria). 2002. "Agricultural Sector Performance Review." Final Report submitted to Asian Development Bank. TA 3695-CAM. Manila.

Porter, M. E. 1990. *The Competitive Advantage of Nations.* New York: Free Press.

Reardon, Thomas, C. Peter Timmer, Christopher B. Barrett, and Julio Berdegue. 2003. "The Rise of Supermarkets in Africa, Asia and Latin America." *American Journal of Agricultural Economics* (December).

Royal Government of Cambodia. 1999. *Cambodia Socioeconomic Survey 1999.* National Institute of Statistics, Ministry of Planning.

————. 2001. *Statistical Yearbook 2001.* National Institute of Statistics, Ministry of Planning.

Sachs, Jeffrey, Clifford Zinnes, and Yair Eilat. 2000. "The Gains from Privatization in Transition Economies: Is 'Change of Ownership' Enough?" CAER Project II, Harvard Institute for International Development.

Smallbone, David, and Friederike Welter. 2003. "Institutional Development and Entrepreneurship in Transition Economies." Paper presented at ICSB 48th World Conference—Advancing Entrepreneurship and Small Business, Belfast, June 15–18.

Socialist Republic of Vietnam. 1998. *Vietnam Living Standard Survey 1998.* Government Statistics Office.

UNCTAD (UN Conference on Trade and Development). 2000. "Strategies for Diversification and Adding Value to Food Exports: A Value Chain Perspective." UNCTAD/DITC/COM/TM/1. Geneva.

USDA-ERS (United States Department of Agriculture, Economic Research Service). 2002. "Rice Outlook." Report RCS-0802. Washington, D.C.

Weatherspoon, Dave D., and Thomas Reardon. 2003. "The Rise of Supermarkets in Africa: Implications for Agrifood Systems and the Rural Poor." *Development Policy Review* 21 (5): 333–55.

World Bank. *World Development Report 1996: From Plan to Market.* New York: Oxford University Press, 1996.

————. 2001. "Mongolia Participatory Living Standards Assessment." Washington, D.C.

————. 2003. "From Goats to Coats: Institutional Reforms in the Mongolian Cashmere Sector." Washington, D.C.

10

TRADE AND LABOR MARKET VULNERABILITY IN INDONESIA, REPUBLIC OF KOREA, AND THAILAND

François Bourguignon
Chor-ching Goh

The links between openness to international trade and economic growth have been the subject of many research papers. Although somewhat controversial, evidence suggests that openness to international trade tends to raise national income (Frankel and Romer 1999; Irvin and Tervio 2002).[1] More controversial are debates about the distribution of the benefits from higher economic growth—both across countries and within countries. Proponents of integration posit that for a small, labor-abundant economy, opening up to trade leads to rising wages and greater stability. They point to the substantial increases in average real wages in open developing countries over the last several decades as evidence that international trade does indeed increase demand for the abundant factor—labor in most developing countries—much like trade theory predicts. They also argue that trade benefits the poor at least as much as the average household, and that opening a small economy permits access to more stable international markets and thus greater opportunities for hedging and insurance.

Opponents of integration, by contrast, see growing inequality between and within nations where proponents see average gains in welfare. They speak about the uneven distribution of gains from openness to trade and the increased uncertainty and vulnerability associated with being more exposed to the vagaries of international markets and more susceptible to shocks that can be transmitted rapidly across countries and regions as evidenced during the 1997–98 East Asian financial crisis.

Recent empirical work analyzing the determinants of distributional changes over time shows that indeed some evidence (from Latin America as well as some Asian countries) suggests that greater integration may be generating higher returns to skills, which, when coupled with unequal access to education, is leading to growing wage inequality in some liberalizing economies. Other papers also lend support to the hypothesis that macroeconomic shocks have become more frequent in today's more integrated international markets, even though their severity and duration may be less

We would like to thank the following people for their contributions to this chapter: Tamar M. Atinc, Mun S. Ho, Caroline Hoxby, Lawrence Katz, William Maloney, and Martin Rama for valuable suggestions and ideas when we embarked on this work; Vivi Alatas (Indonesia) and Dae Il Kim (Korea) for excellent analysis; and Anant Chiarawongse and Binh Nguyen for data assistance. We are also grateful for comments from participants in the seminars held at the World Bank's Tokyo Resident Mission; the Institute of Southeast Asia Studies in Singapore; the Thailand Development Research Institute; the Fourth Asian Development Forum in Seoul; and the World Bank's Jakarta office. All errors remain ours.

because governments are better equipped to respond to them than in the past. But little empirical work has been done to test whether a greater propensity to experience shocks at the macro level translates into more vulnerability at the level of individual workers.

It is indeed possible that many of the concerns expressed by the opponents of integration reflect anxiety about the future prospects for employment and wages even if the evidence points to an increase in average returns to labor. For East Asian countries that are closely integrated into world markets, and becoming more so, an examination of whether this concern indeed rests on solid ground should have crucial implications in three policy areas: trade, labor markets, and social safety nets.

Within the large literature on wage inequality and wage differentials in relation to trade liberalization, only a handful of studies—mostly on Latin American economies, perhaps because macroeconomic volatility appears to be structurally higher there—examine trade, volatility, and insecurity in the labor market, most of them taking changes in employment as the indicator of vulnerability. The literature suggests that trade liberalization has only a small impact on aggregate employment. Papageorgiou, Choksi, and Michaely (1990) found that, by and large, trade liberalization did not significantly raise unemployment in the 19 countries they examined. Revenga (1994) discovered that Mexico's trade reform of 1985–88 reduced employment modestly, but did not reduce wages. Cox and Edwards (1996) found that Chile's trade liberalization of the 1970s affected workers' duration of unemployment, but that its effect was small relative to those of other variables, and declined over time. Currie and Harrison (1997) discovered that during trade liberalization between 1984 and 1990 in Morocco, changes in import tariffs and quota coverage had no impact on aggregate employment. Using rotating panel household surveys, Arango and Maloney (2002) saw some evidence of a higher incidence of involuntary separation, mostly among skilled workers, in sectors that are opening to trade in Mexico and Argentina, but the impact is transitory.

One concern has been that trade liberalization may make the demand for labor more elastic. Issues of worker insecurity and economic openness in Latin America are summarized in De Ferranti and others (2000), who found that wage volatility is affected more by inflation than by openness, and that in Argentina, Bolivia, Brazil, Chile, and Peru wages became more stable in the 1990s. Although job turnover rates increased and informal sector employment rose, unemployment was stable over the period 1970–90, and there was no evidence of a higher probability of unemployment or of longer unemployment spells. Fajnzylber and Maloney (2000) found no evidence in Chile, Colombia, and Mexico that trade liberalization has increased workers' insecurity.

This chapter is a first attempt to investigate the topic in an East Asian context. The analysis was applied to three East Asian countries: Indonesia, Republic of Korea, and Thailand. We sought to determine whether workers' earnings and working hours have fluctuated more as countries have liberalized their trade regimes. Because no data were available for testing that hypothesis directly, a twofold approach was followed. First, we asked whether output and average wages become more volatile as the economies become more open. Second, we looked for signs that workers in sectors and industries highly exposed to world markets are more vulnerable to falling into poverty than those in sectors less exposed.

We begin here by describing the evolution of growth and volatility of output and wages as the economies became more open. Then, in the first stage of the analysis, we examine the dynamics of earnings and employment across sectors and industries with different degrees of exposure to trade and thus external shocks over time. Entering the second stage of the analysis, we explore more formally the relationship between trade intensity and workers' vulnerability to falling into poverty. Because our findings for all three countries yielded similar conclusions, for the sake of brevity we present only selected examples in this chapter.[2]

Overview of Trade Liberalization and Labor Market Volatility

This chapter examines the relationship between trade liberalization and vulnerability by comparing two time periods in each country under study: one in which the economy was more closed and one in which it was more open. The periods covered in the three countries differ, depending on data availability. For Indonesia and Thailand, we used labor force surveys, and for Korea, we used both the establishment surveys (known as occupation wage surveys) and labor force surveys. The labor force data cover 1991–2000 for Thailand, 1986–2001 for Indonesia, and 1976 and 1981–2000 for Korea.

We also compared workers' experiences according to the sectors and industry groups in which they work, because these sectors and groups have different degrees of exposure to world markets. For each country, sector definitions are governed by the source data. Agriculture, fishery, and forestry were excluded from the tradable sector because of data constraints.[3]

Korea has three broad sectors—manufacturing; construction and social services; and "others," which include public utilities, wholesale and retail trades, transport, communications, and financial services.[4] In Indonesia, industry classification is restricted to a few categories, and so it has only two sectors: manufacturing and nontradables. Nontradables include all nonmanufacturing and non-primary industries.[5] Within the manufacturing sectors of Thailand and Korea, we define groups of industries that have differing degrees of exposure to trade, determined by the share of trading volume (exports and imports) in their output.[6]

The main question explored in this section is whether changes in trade regimes in the three economies under study were accompanied by changes in the volatility of various aggregate output and labor market indicators. But, first, were the three economies indeed more open in the 1990s than in the 1980s, as commonly believed? To answer this question, we begin by determining whether the usual structural measures such as tariff rates, nontariff barriers, and tariff revenue conform to this view.

Measures of Trade Liberalization

All the economies examined in this study were already open in the early 1970s (see, for example, Sachs and Warner 1995), but they have become more open since then. Table 10.1 shows the average import tariffs in manufacturing during the 1980s and 1990s and their rates of reduction from one decade to the next. In manufacturing, the average tariff dropped by 26 percent in Indonesia, by 42 percent in Korea, and by 8 percent in Thailand. In the category of duty called the most-favored-nation status rate, the reductions were even bigger.

As for the import tariffs faced by specific industry groups, Figure 10.1 shows the average import tariff rates in 11 industry groups within manufacturing. In all three countries, tariffs decreased noticeably in all these industries, with a few exceptions, from the 1980s to the 1990s.

Core nontariff barrier measures followed the same evolution (Table 10.2). They fell between 1989–94 and 1995–98 in all three countries, more or less at the same rate as tariffs. Changes in individual measures such as licensing, variable levies, and minimum pricing also generally suggest that these economies have become more open in practically all dimensions.

That the preceding measures have been effective is confirmed by the evolution of import tax revenue. In all three countries in the 1980s and the

TABLE 10.1 Average Import Tariffs (Applied Duty Rates) and Percentage Change in Tariffs of Indonesia, Republic of Korea, and Thailand between 1980s and 1990s

Manufacturing	Indonesia	Korea	Thailand
Average tariff (applied duty rate) during 1980s	24.23	18.74	39.04
Average tariff (applied duty rate) during 1990s	17.97	10.96	36.06
Percentage reduction (applied duty rate)	25.84	41.50	7.64
Percentage reduction (most-favored-nation status rate)	45.65	46.31	22.46

Source: Simple averages from United Nations Conference on Trade and Development (UNCTAD).

FIGURE 10.1   Decade Averages of Import Tariffs for Manufacturing Industries: Indonesia, Republic of Korea, and Thailand, 1980s and 1990s

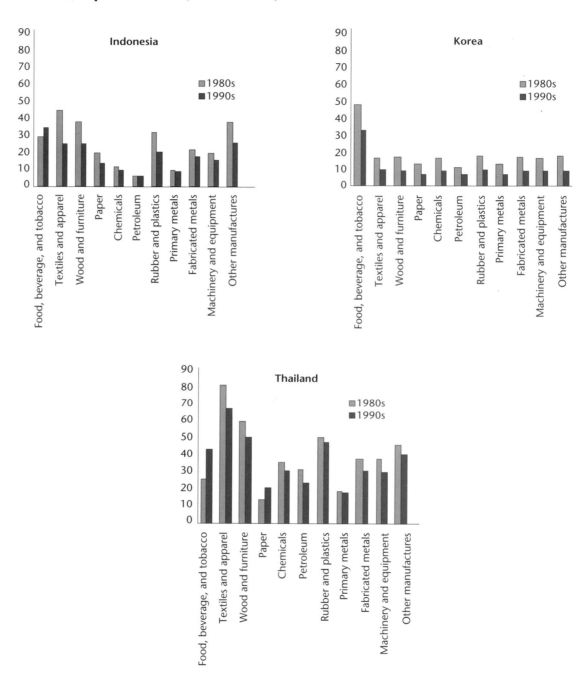

Source: United Nations Conference on Trade and Development (UNCTAD).

1990s, these revenues fell as a proportion of total trading value as well as of total government revenue (Table 10.3), suggesting that these economies became effectively less protected. Korea's import tax revenue fell from about 16 percent of total rev-

enue to about 8 percent. In Thailand, import revenue also fell substantially in terms of both total revenue and total import value. This downward trend is much less pronounced for Indonesia, but that country's trade liberalization also proceeded

TABLE 10.2   Core Nontariff Barrier Measures: Indonesia, Republic of Korea, and Thailand, 1989–99

Country	Core nontariff barrier measures		
	1989–94	1995–99	
Indonesia	53.6	31.3	
Korea	50.5	25.0	
Thailand	36.5	17.5	

Note: Table shows the percentage of items with various types of nontariff barrier measures among all Standard International Trade Classification (SITC) or harmonized system (HS) two-digit products. Core nontariff barrier measures are licensing, prohibition, quotas, and administered pricing. Nonauto licensing includes various forms of administrative approvals.
Source: Michalopoulos (1999).

TABLE 10.3   Decade Average Shares of Import Tax Revenue in Total Government Revenue and Total Trading: Indonesia, Republic of Korea, and Thailand, 1980–2000

Country	Decade	Import duties as percentage of total import value	Import duties as percentage of government revenue
Indonesia	1980s	4.6	4.7
	1990s	3.7	4.5
Korea	1980s	8.3	16.3
	1990s	5.1	8.3
Thailand	1980s	12.2	21.1
	1990s	7.6	16.4

Source: Trade Analysis and Information System of United Nations Conference on Trade and Development (UNCTAD).

on the export side, with export duties as a proportion of total tax revenue falling by more than half.

Volatility of Some Aggregate Indicators

Did this increased openness make these economies more vulnerable to international shocks, with greater fluctuations in the growth of output and wages? The evolution of the observed volatility in the growth of the gross domestic product (GDP), manufacturing value added, and wages gives a first rough answer. Table 10.4 shows the volatility of GDP growth rates by decade, as measured by the coefficient of variation.[7] According to the table, the 1990s—the decade of greatest openness (up to and excluding the financial crisis of 1997–98)—was not only less volatile than the 1980s, but in fact the least volatile of the last three decades. The same conclusion holds when considering only the manufacturing sector, which appears to be generally more volatile than the overall economy.

If there are short-term adverse shocks, they are likely to be transmitted into fluctuations of earnings and employment. Unemployment rates have been stable and uniformly low in all these economies as they have become more open, and for Korea and Thailand, where sectoral unemployment rates are available, there are no significant differences among industries of varied intensity in trade.

Less unemployment volatility could have been achieved at the expense of more variability in wages. However, in general, the year-to-year fluctuation of wages was much less in the more open 1990s than it was in the previous decade. Moreover, we found no evidence that volatility of wages was greater in more trade-intensive industries. In Korea, for example, wages were significantly less volatile in the later, supposedly more open period than in the earlier period, whereas industries with high trade exposure experienced less volatility in the later period and roughly the same volatility as other sectors in the first period (Table 10.5).

TABLE 10.4   Volatility of Annual Growth Rates in GDP and Value Added in Manufacturing, Measured by Coefficient of Variation: Indonesia, Republic of Korea, and Thailand, 1970–96

	Coefficient of variation of annual growth rates in		
	GDP	Manufacturing (value added)	
Indonesia			
1970–1979	0.16	0.34	
1980–1989	0.40	0.55	
1990–1996	0.10	0.10	
Korea			
1970–1979	0.26	0.31	
1980–1989	0.52	0.64	
1990–1996	0.22	0.30	
Thailand			
1970–1979	0.39	0.35	
1980–1989	0.43	0.75	
1990–1996	0.19	0.26	

Sources: Bank of Thailand, Bank of Korea, and Bank of Indonesia.

TABLE 10.5   Level and Fluctuation of Wage Growth Rates (Males) by Trade Exposure Groups: Republic of Korea, 1976–1997

		Low exposure	Medium exposure	High exposure
Annual growth rate	1976–1987	0.022	0.020	0.018
	1988–1997	0.064	0.066	0.076
Standard deviation of growth rates	1976–1987	0.077	0.071	0.068
	1988–1997	0.038	0.054	0.038

Note: Low trade exposure industries: food and beverage, paper, petroleum, and rubber and plastics. Medium trade exposure industries: wood, chemical, and iron and steel. High trade exposure industries: textile and apparel, fabricated metal, machinery, and others not elsewhere classified.
Source: Wage Structure Survey (formerly the Occupational Wage Survey).

But the preceding aggregate evidence must be interpreted with caution. First, because volatility is evaluated for only a small number of years in each subperiod, the results may be strongly influenced by single observations. In particular, the economic shocks of the 1980s may be responsible for the higher volatility observed during that period, which therefore may not be fully comparable to the 1990s, when the crisis that occurred late in that decade is ignored. Second, although volatility is practically constant at the aggregate or even at the industry level, it may have increased at the individual level. The stability of aggregate employment

levels or average wage rates may actually hide an increased turnover rate among employees and higher variance in their earnings over time.

Any study of workers' vulnerability to shocks requires panel data that follow individual workers over time. Unfortunately, the only panel data available were for Korea, and for too short a period to be really useful.[8] For the first stage of our approach, we used synthetic panels, which were created by following cohorts of randomly selected individual workers over time in successive cross-sectional surveys. Cohort cells in this synthetic panel were defined by workers' year of birth, gender, and educational attainment. Because the resulting samples are small for some countries, it was sometimes necessary to use a more aggregate definition of cohorts.[9]

For the second stage of the analysis, we recovered information on the dynamics of individual earnings from the observation of the time patterns of the mean and the variance of earnings in cohort cells. We then used that information to simulate the likely vulnerability of workers to poverty under a set of simplifying assumptions.

Trends in Earnings and Employment in Synthetic Panels

In Korea and Indonesia, where longer time-series data are available, average real wages have been rising steadily since the early 1980s, except for a modest drop in Korea and a sharper decline in Indonesia associated with the 1997–98 financial crisis. In Thailand, average real wages stayed quite constant between 1991 and 2001.

Figure 10.2 shows that for Korea (1976–2000) this evolution is the same for a specific cohort and that trends do not differ between broad sectors or across industries of varying trade intensity. The same consistency is observed for other cohorts and for Thailand (1991–2001) in Figure 10.3 and Indonesia (1986–1999) in Figure 10.4.

This similarity suggests that labor markets in the three countries are quite integrated, with no evidence of segmentation between tradable and nontradable sectors or among industries with different degrees of exposure to trade. In a flexible labor market where workers are mobile, a shock that originates in the tradable sector will be transmitted to other sectors. For Korea, where the time series are longer, there is no noticeable change in trend when the economy experiences greater openness in trade. There is also no sign of greater variability in growth rates.

It is quite possible that the steady and parallel trends in a cohort's mean wage hide a variability in individual earnings that increases over time or is very different across sectors. A simple way to check this possibility is to examine whether the variance of individual earnings changes very much over time or differs markedly across sectors. If so, such a change or difference could correspond to some increase in the variance of transitory earnings, thereby reflecting increased instability at the individual level.[10]

The variance of (log) wages within cohort cells in the three countries does not show any rising trend, and patterns are similar across the tradable and nontradable sectors as well as across the industry groups with varying degrees of trade exposure. An example is given in Figure 10.5, which shows for Korea the evolution of the variance of (log) earnings in a male cohort (born in 1950, attained a secondary education) between 1976 and 2000.

This result in Figure 10.5 appears to contradict the finding in the pioneering work by Deaton and Paxson (1994). In an analogous cohort analysis in the United States, the United Kingdom, and Taiwan

FIGURE 10.2   Average Log of Real Wages of Males by Broad Sectors (Manufacturing, Services and Construction, and Others) and by Trade Exposure (Low, Medium, and High): Republic of Korea, 1976–2000

Males, 38 years old in 1990, primary education

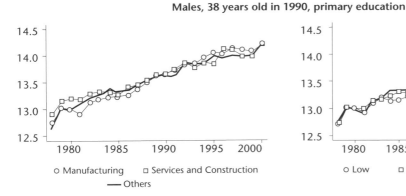
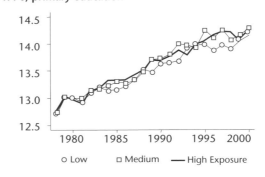

Source: Wage Structure Survey (formerly the Occupational Wage Survey).

FIGURE 10.3   Average Log of Real Wages of Males by Broad Sectors (Manufacturing and Services) and by Trade Exposure (Low, Medium, and High): Thailand, 1991–2000

Males, 35–39 years old in 1991, primary education

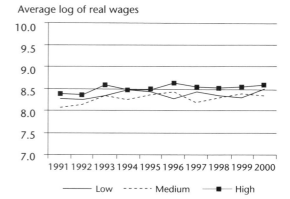

Source: Thailand Labor Force Surveys.

FIGURE 10.4   Average Log of Real Wages of Males by Broad Sectors (Manufacturing and Services): Indonesia, 1986–1999

Males, 35–39 years old in 1986, primary or less education

Source: Indonesia Labor Force Surveys (SAKERNAS).

(China), these authors found that the variance of the log of household consumption, income, and earnings tended to increase with the age of the household head.

The discrepancy between the present result for Korea and their results for Taiwan, two very similar economies, might be more apparent than real, however. First, Deaton and Paxson also found that the variance of (log) earnings was extremely stable in Taiwan between ages 20 and 50 (and then doubled between ages 50 and 65)—which is in full conformity with our results. Second, our results for Korea refer to active wage workers, whereas Deaton and Paxson's data for Taiwan include changes in participation and in wage work status. Finally, it is also possible that a slightly increasing trend in

FIGURE 10.5   Standard Deviation of Log of Real Wages of a Male Cohort in Low, Medium, and High Trade Exposure Industries: Republic of Korea, 1976–2000

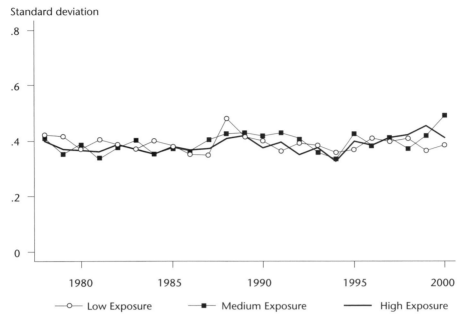

Males, 40 years old in 1990, secondary education

—○— Low Exposure   —■— Medium Exposure   —— High Exposure

Source: Wage Structure Survey (formerly, Occupational Wage Survey).

inequality might be observed in the Korean data if cohorts with different educational levels were taken together, as in Deaton and Paxson.

Changes in labor market conditions possibly associated with more openness might have affected employment or working hours rather than earning rates. But Figures 10.6 and 10.7 suggest this is not the case. In general, the distribution of employment status and of sector of employment within cohort cell shows no noticeable change in trend in the 1990s in comparison with the 1980s, except, of course, during the 1997–98 financial crisis in East Asia.

For example, for a cohort of Korean males born from 1950 to 1954 who attained a primary education or less, the rising trend in the share of the nontradable sector showed no discontinuity until 1998, and the same was true of the declining trend in agriculture and manufacturing (Figure 10.6). These trends may therefore reflect the long-run process of change in the economic structure rather than the effect of a change in the trade regime. Likewise, the unemployment rate remained remarkably constant until the 1997–98 crisis. The inactivity rate increased somewhat a few years before the crisis,

and this increase might be taken as hiding a slight increase in disguised unemployment, possibly imputable to the rising openness of the economy. However, the change in the inactivity rate seems too modest to be of real concern.

The evolution of average working hours within cohorts leads to the same conclusion: the absence of an openness effect. Because of data limitations, it was not possible to compare the 1980s and the 1990s in Thailand. For a cohort of educated men, no significant trend appears to be present in the 1990s until the 1997–98 financial shock (Figure 10.7). The evolution was similar in other cohorts. In most of them, it is true that working hours tend to be longer in trade-exposed manufacturing than in trade-protected services. But this variation seems to be true in many countries, and it is more suggestive of differences in the conditions of production than of differences in trade exposure. Within manufacturing, by contrast, work hours do not differ according to the trade intensity of industries.

In summary, looking at the evolution of labor market indicators for synthetic cohorts, we found no evidence of a systematic difference associated

FIGURE 10.6 Distribution of Employment Status and Employment Sectors of a Male Cohort: Republic of Korea, 1985–2000

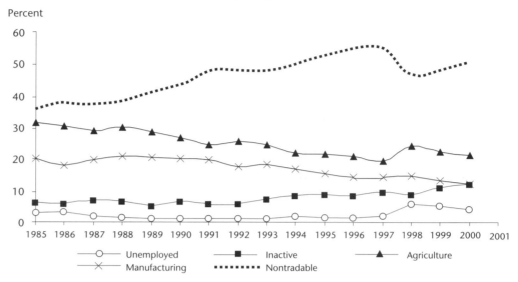

Males, born in 1950–54, primary education or less

Source: Surveys of the Economically Active Population, Korea.

FIGURE 10.7 Average Monthly Hours Worked of a Male Cohort in Manufacturing and Services: Thailand, 1991–2000

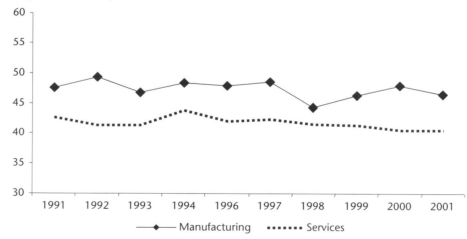

Males, born in 1951–55, secondary education or more

Source: Thailand Labor Force Surveys.

with the degree of exposure to trade in any of the three countries studied. No systematic difference in workers' earnings or employment was found between the tradable and nontradable sectors, or among manufacturing industry groups according to trade exposure. And there was no evidence that trends in earnings or employment changed, or that working hours became more unstable as economies liberalized their trade policies during the 1990s.

Indirect Estimation of Changes in Workers' Vulnerability to Poverty from Cross-Sectional Data

A steady aggregate evolution of earnings and employment levels for the whole population or for cohorts of individuals may hide changes in the variability of conditions for individual workers. The share of employment in manufacturing or services may change steadily over time, but, meanwhile, an increasing proportion of people may be switching among sectors or switching between employment and inactivity within a cohort. Likewise, average earnings may go up at a steady pace while individual variability in earnings is increasing.[11]

Any attempt to determine whether there are changes in the variability of individual conditions in a labor market, and therefore in personal vulnerability to poverty, would ideally require panel data that would allow a sample of people to be followed over time. Unfortunately, such data are seldom available in developing countries, and Thailand and Indonesia are no exception.[12]

To estimate the individual variability of earnings and the vulnerability of workers to having their earnings fall below a poverty threshold, we used an indirect method based on comparing successive cross sections. The idea is as follows: if it can be assumed that all individuals within a cohort face a stochastic earning process that has common characteristics, then these characteristics can be recovered at the aggregate level without observing actual earning paths. Observing the evolution of the mean and the variance of earnings within a cohort is sufficient for estimating the common characteristics of individual earning processes. On this basis, simple estimates of the probability of a worker observed in year t falling into poverty in year $t + 1$ can be obtained.

Now returning to the issue of trade exposure, the problem is one of knowing whether the insecurity and uncertainty evaluated with the preceding technique changed between less liberal and more liberal time periods, as well as between industries of varying exposure to trade. This comparative estimation of vulnerability to poverty was made for each of the three countries. For all countries, a poverty threshold of 60 percent of the national median wage was used. Findings for the three countries were very similar, so only a typical selection is presented here.

A Simple Model

The earnings, w_{it}, at time t of individual i belonging to cohort group j may be represented by

$$(10.1) \qquad \ln w_{it}^j = X_{it}^j \beta_t^j + \xi_{it}^j$$

where X_{it} is a set of characteristics that are not used in the definition of cohort group j—that is, they are not from age, gender, and education. In addition, it is assumed that the unobserved residual term ξ_{it}^j follows a first-order autoregressive process AR(1)—that is

$$(10.2) \qquad \xi_{it}^j = \rho^j \xi_{it-1}^j + \varepsilon_{it}^j.$$

This is the simplest time dependency assumption that can be made.[13]

In the absence of panel data, the dynamic equation cannot be estimated directly on individual-level data. However, some indirect estimation is possible by considering successive observations of individuals in the same cohort, even though those individuals are not the same from one period to the next. Indeed, (10.2) implies that

$$(10.3) \qquad \sigma_{\xi jt}^2 = \rho^{j2} \sigma_{\xi jt-1}^2 + \sigma_{\varepsilon jt}^2$$

where $\sigma_{\xi jt}^2$ is the variance of the residual term of the earning equation at time t, and $\sigma_{\varepsilon j}^2$ is the variance of the innovation term during the same period in the dynamic equation (10.2). Both variances are evaluated for the whole cohort j of individuals observed at time t. The sequence of $\sigma_{\xi jt}^2$ is a time series. Estimating a standard autoregressive model on this series yields estimates of ρ^j and $\sigma_{\varepsilon jt}^2$. Of course, a crucial identifying assumption here is that the regression coefficient ρ^j is constant over time.

If the model is well specified and the time series is long enough, then the estimated $\hat{\rho}^j$ and $\hat{\sigma}_{\varepsilon jt}^2$ should have the expected signs and orders of magnitude. In particular, it should be the case that $0 < \hat{\rho}^j < 1$ and $\hat{\sigma}_{\varepsilon jt}^2 > 0$. However, if well-behaved estimates of $\hat{\rho}^j$ and $\hat{\sigma}_{\varepsilon jt}^2$ (for every t) are not forthcoming, then it may be necessary to use alternative estimates of ρ^j lying in the confidence interval obtained in the original estimation.[14] However, this step seldom proved necessary.

With estimates of ρ^j and $\sigma_{\varepsilon jt}^2$, it is now possible to simulate the dynamics of individual earnings, according to equations 10.1 and 10.2. One begins by drawing a value $\hat{\varepsilon}_{it+1}^{j}$ in the normal distribution with mean 0 and variance $\sigma_{\varepsilon it+1}^{2}$. Substituting the draw, $\hat{\varepsilon}_{it+1}^{j}$, into equation 10.2, and combining it with estimated $\hat{\rho}^{j}$ from equation 10.3 and predicted $\hat{\xi}_{it}^{j}$ from ordinary least-squares in equation 10.1, yields an estimate $\hat{\xi}_{it+1}^{j}$. Substituting this value in (10.1) at time $t + 1$ then gives the (log) earnings for an individual in cohort j at time $t + 1$, conditional on the earnings at time t and assuming exogenous changes in characteristics.

Using the preceding reasoning, one can see that the probability for individual i, observed at time t, of receiving e earnings below a survival threshold w at time $t + 1$, conditional on characteristics and earnings in period t, is given by

(10.4)

$$\hat{v}_{it+1}^{j} = \Pr(w_{it+1}^{j} < \underline{w} \mid X_{it}^{j}, X_{it+1}^{j}, w_{it+1}^{j})$$

$$= \Phi\left(\frac{\log(\underline{w}) - X_{it+1}^{j}\hat{\beta}_{t+1}^{j} - \hat{\rho}^{j}\left[\log(w_{it}^{j}) - X_{it}^{j}\hat{\beta}_{t}^{j}\right]}{\sigma_{\varepsilon jt+1}^{2}} \right)$$

where $\Phi(.)$ denotes the cumulative density of the standard normal. But this expression requires determining the characteristics of individual i at time $t + 1$. Indeed, X_{it}^{j} is observed, but X_{it+1}^{j} is not. Without a special reason to do otherwise, the simplest approach is to assume the same characteristics in time t and $t + 1$ except, of course, for age. Such an assumption should be satisfactory if the characteristics in X are truly exogenous.

According to equation 10.4, vulnerability—that is, the probability of being below the earning poverty threshold in year $t + 1$, conditional on earnings in year t—depends on the following parameters: initial earnings, individual characteristics, changes in the returns to these characteristics, the persistence of earning shocks from one period to the next, and, finally, the variance of these shocks. As noted earlier, differences in trade regimes did not seem to be associated with differences in overall earning inequality. This finding suggests either that some of the previous parameters, or their distribution within cohorts, remained more or less constant over time, or that compensating variations have taken place. In what follows, no attempt is made to isolate the effect of each set of parameters on the evolution of vulnerability. Yet

the comparison of the evolution of the mean and the variance of earnings within the typical cohort with vulnerability as proxied by the preceding technique should be informative.

The definition and estimation of vulnerability given here do not take into account employment mobility. Vulnerability is estimated for those individuals in a cohort who are employed in each period, and thus ignores the part of vulnerability that is associated with losing one's job. As revealed earlier, net flows into unemployment did not seem to have increased because of the change in trade regime in the three countries under analysis. But gross flows may have become bigger. Not enough information is available to verify this point.

Also, in comparing the vulnerability of workers in sectors with different degrees of exposure to trade, it is tempting to apply the preceding technique in equation 10.4 to cohorts of individuals employed in the same sector. But then the same proviso applies. The resulting proxy for vulnerability is valid insofar as intersectoral movements did not change substantially during the period under study. Again, the analysis just described suggests that they did not, in net terms, but this finding is not necessarily inconsistent with increased vulnerability to poverty through forced mobility. Under these conditions, our findings must be interpreted cautiously.

Findings

Reasonable estimates of the parameters of the model were obtained for all three countries. In particular, estimated persistence coefficients, ρ, in equation 10.2 range from zero to one, and generally significantly so, suggesting that earning shocks in the current period are actually transmitted to consecutive periods, but that the effect of the shocks will eventually fade out.[15] For example, Table 10.6 presents the estimates of ρ^{2} for Indonesia (note that cohorts are pooled to estimate ρ^{2}). The estimated ρ^{2} ranges from 0.06 to 0.45. All of these ρ^{2} are statistically significantly greater than zero—the smallest t-statistic being 3.5—and less than one. An exception is female workers with secondary education working in the nontradable sector for whom ρ^{2} is not significantly different from zero because of the limited number of observations within these cohorts. Figure 10.8 presents the estimated ρ for every birth cohort of workers in Korea. The estimates of ρ^{j}

TABLE 10.6 Estimated ρ^2 Correlation of Variance of Residual Earnings by Education, Gender, and Sector: Indonesia

Education	Manufacturing		Nontradable		
	Male	Female	Male	Female	
Primary or less	0.3548	0.3746	0.4583	0.4098	
Secondary	0.3547	0.3549	0.1841	0.0617	
Tertiary	0.4124	—	0.2165	—	

Notes: For female workers, tertiary education falls within secondary education because there are not enough observations for those with tertiary education to treat them separately.
Source: Alatas (2002).

FIGURE 10.8 Estimated ρ by Birth Year Cohort: Republic of Korea, 1929–69

Source: Wage Structure Survey (formerly the Occupational Wage Survey).

range from 0.3 to 0.9 in most cohorts and the average is 0.74 for men and 0.59 for women.[16]

In Korea, a worker's risk of falling into poverty differed rather little among the three sectors, and these differences narrowed over time. Differences among manufacturing industries with different degrees of trade exposure narrowed, too, as vulnerability decreased. Remarkably, the drop in vulnerability was the most pronounced for the manufacturing sector, which has the highest exposure to trade (Figure 10.9). In the Korean manufacturing sector, vulnerability to relative poverty decreased until 1998 and increased again somewhat afterward. Vulnerability may have increased slightly in services and construction a little before the 1997–98 financial crisis, but it remained stable in the other sectors. It must be stressed, however, that

the extent of vulnerability was extremely limited—with an overall average of 3 percent—reflecting the very low inequality of individual earnings in Korea.

Overall growth in Korea and in the other two countries between the early 1980s and 1998 was such that the strongly decreasing trend in absolute poverty hides any variation that might be the result of more trade exposure.

In all three countries, not surprisingly, vulnerability tended to differ widely according to gender and educational attainment. As reflected in Figure 10.10 for Thailand and Table 10.7 for Indonesia, the expected earnings of women and people with little education were much below national averages. The vulnerability of less educated workers to poverty may be considerable, reaching 20 percent for male workers in Indonesia.

FIGURE 10.9   Vulnerability by Sectors and Trade Exposure Groups: Republic of Korea, 1976–2000

Conditional likelihood of earning less than poverty threshold

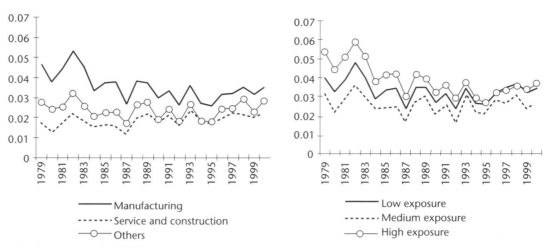

Manufacturing
Service and construction
Others

Low exposure
Medium exposure
High exposure

Note: The figure shows the evolution of Korean workers' vulnerability as defined in year *t* by their conditional likelihood of earning less than the poverty threshold in year *t* + 1 by sector of employment and, within manufacturing, by industries with different degrees of exposure to trade. The evolution is shown for the 21-year period 1979–2000 and for the average across all cohorts in each year of observation.
Source: Wage Structure Survey (formerly the Occupational Wage Survey).

TABLE 10.7   Vulnerability by Education, Gender, and Sector: Indonesia, 2001 (Conditional likelihood of earnings falling beneath poverty level)

Education	Male		Female	
	Manufacturing	Nontradable	Manufacturing	Nontradable
Primary or less	0.1971	0.2147	0.3098	0.4076
Secondary	0.0890	0.1047	0.1552	0.1777
Tertiary	0.0050	0.0261	—	—

Note: For female workers, tertiary education falls within secondary education because there are not enough observations for those with tertiary education to treat them separately.
Source: Alatas (2002).

In summary, we found no firm evidence to support a correlation between workers' vulnerability to sinking into poverty and periods of greater economic openness, or between their vulnerability and their sectors of employment. This conclusion is, however, conditional on the limitations of the indirect method used in this analysis to evaluate vulnerability. The analysis could have been strengthened had we been able to take into account gross flows in and out of employment or across sectors of employment. Yet evidence on net flows does not suggest significant differences across industries with different degrees of trade exposure. In any

case, the differences in earnings security and vulnerability associated at any point in time with education or gender seem much larger than what could be imputed to trade openness. To reduce the overall vulnerability of workers to poverty, it might be more efficient to tackle these disparities first.

Conclusions

Determining whether trade liberalization is associated with greater earnings volatility or increased vulnerability of workers requires comprehensive panel data on individual employment status and

FIGURE 10.10   Vulnerability by Gender and Educational Attainment: Thailand, 1991–2000

Males by educational attainment

Females by educational attainment

Conditional likelihood of earning less than poverty threshold

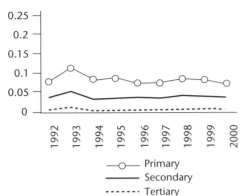

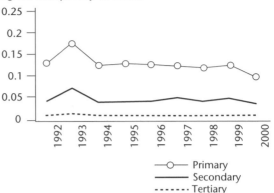

Source: Thailand Labor Force Surveys.

earnings. In the absence of such data, only indirect evidence or indirect proxies for individual earning volatility and vulnerability may be used. This chapter has reviewed such evidence for three East and Southeast Asian countries where trade barriers were lowered significantly during the 1990s.

Indirect evidence revealed no significant change in year-to-year fluctuations in workers' earnings and employment after trade was further liberalized in the 1990s or in sectors that were more exposed to foreign competition. The mean and variance of earnings, and net flows in employment, proved to be very similar in tradable and nontradable sectors. We did not find any systematic differences in employment or earnings volatility. Nor did workers' vulnerability, as approximated using an original methodology developed in this chapter, seem to differ significantly across manufacturing industries with different degrees of exposure to trade. Our results, in fact, show that vulnerability to relative poverty—defined as 60 percent of the national median wage—seems to have declined over the last 10–20 years in the three countries and that differences across sectors seem to have narrowed considerably.

These conclusions may be criticized because they rely on indirect evidence. In particular, it may be that the stability of net employment flows and the steady evolution of the mean and the variance of earnings behind the proxy used for vulnerability actually hide an increased instability for individual workers in the labor market. Again, to reach a definite conclusion would require panel data.

Now it is time to make a point that will reinforce the general findings in this chapter and at the same time suggest another, more subtle way through which openness to trade may actually affect earnings volatility. The apparent stability of net employment flows and the evolution of earnings and their variance in the decade or so preceding the 1997–98 East Asian financial crisis are meaningful precisely because the crisis corresponded to quite significant changes in practically all existing trends. Thus the crisis shows that there *may be* some variability in all the indicators used in this chapter. The remarkable result is therefore that no systematic variation showed up at the time the three economies were becoming more open, or in the comparison across sectors with distinct exposures to trade. This finding seems indeed to confirm that opening up to trade in the late 1980s and early 1990s did not have strong negative effects on poverty and vulnerability, whereas the 1997–98 crisis did have such effects. In turn, one may wonder whether it was openness that made that crisis much more serious than the various shocks that hit the three economies in the 1980s. If this were true, then it could be asserted that openness actually contributed to more individual vulnerability in East and Southeast Asia through increased macroeconomic volatility, rather than through the interplay of modified microeconomic mechanisms. The question is open.

Although it is not unreasonable to suggest that short-term idiosyncratic shocks in the global market may affect the more exposed sectors disproportionately, the fact that we did not find such evidence suggests that a possible reason is that, in the absence of systemic shocks like the one in 1997–98, an open economy is subject to many uncorrelated shocks that tend to cancel one another out thanks to a well-functioning labor market—certainly a characteristic of the three economies under study. Another possibility is that liberalization in small economies may facilitate access to the international market, which provides hedging and self-insuring opportunities. In addition, these Asian economies were already relatively open by the 1970s, and have been exposed to world markets and their fluctuations since then. Thus the tariff reductions of the 1980s and 1990s may have had only negligible effects on domestic industries. As is well known, a country's tariff regime is a complex combination of step function, multiple tiers, and various types of percentage-quantity barriers. Under these conditions, it is extremely difficult to quantify the magnitude of additional exposure that actually follows from an observed reduction in the average tariff rates.

Although we find no obvious link between trade and vulnerability, the analysis in this chapter confirms that some workers are more vulnerable than others. Women workers are more vulnerable to falling into poverty, as are workers who have less schooling. This result reflects the dominant evidence in the literature that gender and skill have a strong discriminatory power in determining a person's earnings. An important conclusion is that remedies to vulnerability to poverty must be sought more in education than in trade openness. A more open trade regime is unlikely to justify by itself the creation of effective safety nets. Such insurance systems may be justified independently, either because of the presence of a substantial proportion of unskilled workers with limited capacity to face adverse shocks or possibly because of an increased likelihood of a major macroeconomic or systemic crisis.

Endnotes

1. For a critical view, see Rodriguez and Rodrik (1999).
2. Detailed and comprehensive findings for Indonesia, Korea, and Thailand are available from the authors upon request.
3. The sample of wage workers in the primary sector in the labor force surveys of Thailand and Indonesia is small, and it is not possible to isolate precisely agriculture from other activities in the income of rural self-employed. In Korea, we worked primarily with the establishment surveys, because the labor force surveys do not contain wage information and the establishment surveys do not include the primary sector.
4. For Korea, we were able to break up services into the strictly nontradable construction, social, and communal services, and nontradable industries that may depend on trade activity and are categorized as "others."
5. Services, retail and wholesale, transport, and communications.
6. We also examined the ranking by trade per worker, which gives very similar groupings. In Korea, the industries in the group of highest trade exposure are textile and apparel, fabricated metal, machinery, and others not elsewhere classified; those in the group of medium exposure are wood, chemical, and iron and steel; and those in the group of low exposure are food and beverage, paper, petroleum, and rubber and plastic. In Thailand, the highest trade exposure group consists of the chemical, primary metal, machinery, and other industries not elsewhere classified; the medium exposure group consists of the food and beverage, tobacco, textile, apparel, footwear, wood product, furniture, and fabricated metals industries; and the low exposure group is made up of the paper product, petroleum, and rubber and plastics industries.

    The Indonesian data do not permit a comparable breakdown. Before 1988, SAKERNAS, the Indonesian labor force surveys from which our data are taken, provided only a rough five-way classification of the sectors in which workers were employed: agriculture, manufacturing, trade, services, and other industries. Between 1989 and 2000 the sectoral classification was expanded from 5 categories to 18, but within manufacturing it provided for only four industry groups: food, beverages, and tobacco; apparel and textiles; wood products; and others.
7. Standard deviation of growth divided by the decade-average growth.
8. Daewoo Economic Research Institute carried out the Korea Household Panel Survey from 1994 to 1998. The survey collected information on income, assets, expenditures, the labor market, and other household and individual characteristics. There were no replacements of households, but the data covered split-off households stemming from marriage or other reasons. The survey was conducted through stratified random sampling by street blocks, and it covered all Korean prefectures except Jeju-do. In 1994 there were about 3,500 households and in 1998 about 2,200 households.
9. The synthetic panels could be assembled for only a limited time period (except for Korea where establishment surveys are available for as early as 1976, and labor force surveys for as early as 1985). Because of this limitation, it was not possible to compare systematically the 1980s and the 1990s—that is, moderate versus pronounced openness to trade—for all three countries. The comparison performed on sectors with high and low exposure to trade did not present this difficulty.
10. It is also known that the inequality of earnings tends to increase with age because the stochastic process behind individual earnings is close to a random walk, a substantial proportion of shocks being persistent.
11. Such an evolution is even consistent with a constant variance of relative earnings. It is sufficient that individuals within a cohort switch rank more and more frequently.

12. In Korea, there is the household panel survey conducted by Daewoo Economic Research Institute, but the five-year period covered was too short for our analysis.

13. A more general specification would also include a persistent component in the innovation term xjt. Some implications of this specification are considered in Deaton and Paxson (1994).

14. Let us rewrite equation 10.3 as $\sigma^2_{\xi jt} = a_j \sigma^2_{\xi jt-1} + b_j + u^j_t$, where $\sigma^2_{\xi jt} = B_j + u^j_t$. Let the ordinary least-squares (OLS) estimates of the two coefficients a_j and b_j be A and B. Two bad cases are possible. Scenario 1: suppose that A is positive but some $B_j + u^j_t$ are negative. We can then try to find a value $\rho^2 < A$ in the confidence interval of A, such that all $B_j + u^j_t$ are positive. Scenario 2: suppose that OLS gives a negative A or a value that exceeds one. In the first case, it is best to start with small positive values of ρ^2 in the confidence interval of A and proceed as in scenario 1. In the second case, we would start with values below but close to $\rho^2 = 1$ and proceed as in Scenario 1. Practically, A was never found significantly smaller than zero or greater than one with standard tests—in theory, nonstationarity tests of the Dickey-Fuller type should be applied to test $A = 1$.

15. This finding is in apparent contradiction with the finding by Deaton and Paxson (1994), who applied a similar methodology to Taiwan (China). They found that shocks on household consumption expenditures—and implicitly income—tend to be persistent. Thus there is an increasing trend in the variance of log expenditures. The reason for the difference with the findings reported in this chapter might be that we focus on individual earnings and wage earners rather than household consumption per capita. We therefore ignore shocks linked to the demographic composition of the household and labor supply.

16. Note that ρ is highest among the youngest cohorts for both men and women, because earning changes persistently take place early in a worker's career.

References

The word *processed* describes informally reproduced works that may not be commonly available through libraries.

Alatas, Vivi. 2002. "Labor Market Vulnerability in Indonesia: A Synthetic Cohort Panel Simulation Exercise." World Bank, Washington, D.C. Processed.

Arango, Carlos, and William Maloney. 2002. "Unemployment Dynamics in Latin America: Estimates of Continuous Time Markov Models for Mexico and Argentina." World Bank, Washington, D.C. Processed.

Cox, Edwards A., and Sebastian Edwards. 1996. "Trade Liberalization and Unemployment: Policy Issues and Evidence from Chile." *Cuadernos de Economia* 33 (99): 227–50.

Currie, Janet, and Ann E. Harrison. 1997. "Sharing the Costs: The Impact of Trade Reform on Capital and Labor in Morocco." *Journal of Labor Economics* 15 (13) (part 2, July): S44–S71.

Deaton, Angus, and Christina Paxson. 1994. "Intertemporal Choice and Inequality." *Journal of Political Economy* 102: 437–67.

De Ferranti, David, Guillermo E. Perry, Indermit S. Gill, and Luis Servén Region. 2000. *Securing Our Future in a Global Economy.* Washington, D.C.: World Bank.

Fajnzylber, Pablo, and W. F. Maloney. 2000. "Labor Demand and Trade Liberalization in Latin America." Latin America and Caribbean Sector Management Unit for Poverty Reduction and Economic Management. World Bank, Washington, D.C.

Frankel, Jeffrey, and David Romer. 1999. "Does Trade Cause Growth?" *American Economic Review* 89 (3): 1–16.

Irvin, D., and M. Tervio. 2002. "Does Trade Raise Income? Evidence from the Twentieth Century." *Journal of International Economics* 58: 1–18.

Michalopoulos, Constantine. 1999. *Trade Policy and Market Access Issues for Developing Countries.* Policy Research Working Paper 2214. World Bank, Washington, D.C., October.

Papageorgiou, Demetrios, Armeane M. Choksi, and Michael Michaely. 1990. *Liberalizing Foreign Trade in Developing Countries: The Lessons of Experience.* Washington, D.C.: World Bank.

Revenga, Ana. 1994. "Employment and Wage Effects of Trade Liberalization: The Case of Mexican Manufacturing." Policy Research Working Paper 1524. World Bank, Washington, D.C.

Rodriguez, Francisco, and Dani Rodrik. 1999. "Trade Policy and Economic Growth: A Skeptic's Guide to the Cross-National Evidence." NBER Working Paper No. 7081. National Bureau of Economic Research, Cambridge, Mass.

Sachs, Jeffrey, and Andrew Warner. 1995. "Economic Reform and the Process of Global Integration." Brookings Papers on Economic Activity No. 1. Brookings Institution, Washington, D.C.

AUTHORS AND THEIR AFFILIATIONS

Kathie Krumm
The World Bank

Homi Kharas
The World Bank

William J. Martin
The World Bank

Deepak Bhattasali
The World Bank

Shantong Li
Development Research Centre of the State Council,
China

Mari Pangestu
Center for Strategic and International Studies,
Indonesia

Sudarshan Gooptu
The World Bank

Bijit Bora
World Trade Organization

Robin Carruthers
The World Bank

Jitendra N. Bajpai
The World Bank

David Hummels
Purdue University, United States

Manjula Luthria
The World Bank

Keith E. Maskus
University of Colorado at Boulder,
United States

Shaohua Chen
The World Bank

Martin Ravallion
The World Bank

Jehan Arulpragasam
The World Bank

Francesco Goletti
Agrifood Consulting, United States

Tamar Manuelyan Atinc
The World Bank

Vera Songwe
The World Bank

François Bourguignon
DELTA, France

Chor-ching Goh
The World Bank

INDEX